English A: Language and Literature

for the IB Diploma

COURSEBOOK

Brad Philpot

Teachers play an important part in shaping futures. Our Dedicated Teacher Awards recognise the hard work that teachers put in every day.

ıank you to everyone who nominated this year, we have been inspired and moved ı all of your stories. Well done to all of our nominees for your dedication to learning and for inspiring the next generation of thinkers, leaders and innovators.

Congratulations to our incredible winner and finalists

ıed Saya
School for A-Level, Pakistan

Sharon Kong Foong
Sunway College, Malaysia

Anthony Chelliah
Gateway College, Sri Lanka

Candice Green
St Augustine's College, Australia

Jimrey Buntas Dapin
University of San Jose-Recoletos, Philippines

For more information about our dedicated teachers and their stories, go to

dedicatedteacher.cambridge.org

Brighter Thinking
Better Learning

CAMBRIDGE
UNIVERSITY PRESS

University Printing House, Cambridge CB2 8BS, United Kingdom

One Liberty Plaza, 20th Floor, New York, NY 10006, USA

477 Williamstown Road, Port Melbourne, VIC 3207, Australia

314-321, 3rd Floor, Plot 3, Splendor Forum, Jasola District Centre, New Delhi – 10025, India

79 Anson Road, #06–04/06, Singapore 079906

Cambridge University Press is part of the University of Cambridge.

It furthers the University's mission by disseminating knowledge in the pursuit of education, learning and research at the highest international levels of excellence.

www.cambridge.org
Information on this title: www.cambridge.org/9781108704939

© Cambridge University Press 2019

This publication is in copyright. Subject to statutory exception and to the provisions of relevant collective licensing agreements, no reproduction of any part may take place without the written permission of Cambridge University Press.

First published 2019

20 19 18 17 16 15 14 13 12 11 10 9 8 7 6 5 4 3 2 1

Printed in Spain by GraphyCems

A catalogue record for this publication is available from the British Library

ISBN 978-1-108-70493-9 Paperback

Cambridge University Press has no responsibility for the persistence or accuracy of URLs for external or third-party internet websites referred to in this publication, and does not guarantee that any content on such websites is, or will remain, accurate or appropriate.

This work has been developed independently from, and is not endorsed by, the International Baccalaureate (IB).

Contents

How to use this book vi

Introduction to the English A: Language and Literature course xiv

Section 1: Text types

Chapter 1: Exploring text types

Unit 1.1 Images and magazine covers 2

Unit 1.2 Advertisements 9

Unit 1.3 Film and commercials 14

Unit 1.4 Political cartoons 19

Unit 1.5 Comics and graphic novels 24

Unit 1.6 Street art 30

Unit 1.7 Speeches 34

Unit 1.8 News articles 43

Unit 1.9 Blogs 52

Unit 1.10 Short stories and novels 58

Unit 1.11 Playscripts 67

Unit 1.12 Poems 77

Section 2: Global issues for the learner portfolio

Chapter 2: Beliefs and values

Unit 2.1 Femininity 91

Unit 2.2 Masculinity 108

Unit 2.3 Beauty 126

Chapter 3: Identity, culture and community

Unit 3.1 Racism 144

Unit 3.2 Colonialism 163

Unit 3.3 Immigration 185

Chapter 4: Politics, power and justice

Unit 4.1 War 206

Unit 4.2 Protest 221

Unit 4.3 Politics 240

Section 3: Assessment

Chapter 5: Paper 1: Guided textual analysis (SL/HL) 257

Chapter 6: Paper 2: Comparative essay (SL/HL) 278

Chapter 7: HL essay 300

Chapter 8: Individual oral (SL/HL) 320

Glossary 338

Index 346

Acknowledgements 350

How to use this book

The introduction gives you confidence in the course guide and assessment, including transparent assessment criteria.

Section 1 deconstructs a range of text types including graphic novels and advertisements.

Section 2 is structured around nine global issues. Each unit progressively explores the three areas of exploration.

Contents

How to use this book vi

Introduction to the English A: Language and Literature course xiv

Section 1: Text types

Chapter 1: Exploring text types

Unit 1.1 Images and magazine covers 2
Unit 1.2 Advertisements 9
Unit 1.3 Film and commercials 14
Unit 1.4 Political cartoons 19
Unit 1.5 Comics and graphic novels 24
Unit 1.6 Street art 30
Unit 1.7 Speeches 34
Unit 1.8 News articles 43
Unit 1.9 Blogs 52
Unit 1.10 Short stories and novels 58
Unit 1.11 Playscripts 67
Unit 1.12 Poems 77

Section 2: Global issues for the learner portfolio

Chapter 2: Beliefs and values

Unit 2.1 Femininity 91
Unit 2.2 Masculinity 108
Unit 2.3 Beauty 126

Chapter 3: Identity, culture and community

Unit 3.1 Racism 144
Unit 3.2 Colonialism 163
Unit 3.3 Immigration 185

Chapter 4: Politics, power and justice

Unit 4.1 War 206
Unit 4.2 Protest 221
Unit 4.3 Politics 240

Section 3: Assessment

Chapter 5: Paper 1: Guided textual analysis (SL/HL) 257

Chapter 6: Paper 2: Comparative essay (SL/HL) 278

Chapter 7: HL essay 300

Chapter 8: Individual oral (SL/HL) 320

Glossary 338

Acknowledgements 346

v

Section 3 takes an activity-driven approach to develop skills in all four assessments.

Word banks provide key terms (Criterion D in assessment). These are compiled in the glossary.

Clear Learning objectives ensure you know where you are going.

Getting started features activate existing knowledge and help you engage with the topic.

Unit 1.7 Speeches

Word bank

rhetorical device
paralanguage
anaphora
diacope
antithesis
chiasmus
anadiplosis
amplification
metaphor
alliteration
tricolon
appeal
ethos
pathos
logos
argument
parallelism
hypophora
repetition
figurative speech
polysyndeton
allusion
target audience
persona

Learning objectives

- learn to identify several commonly used rhetorical devices and discuss how they construct meaning
- develop the skills to analyse how context helps shape the language and meaning of speeches.

Throughout this course, you will study speeches and the contexts in which they were spoken. You will be asked to consider: what makes a speech engaging for its audience? Great speeches are full of interesting **rhetorical devices**, several of which will be explored in this unit. But most important, in your study of speeches, is to explore the potential *effects* of these devices on their audiences. This unit will give you the tools to deconstruct and analyse speeches by introducing you to several rhetorical devices and getting you to look closely at two great speeches.

TIP

For any speech that you explore in class, you may want to do an online search to see or hear the speech being delivered. Hearing a speech and watching the speaker will allow you to appreciate their use of **paralanguage**. Paralanguage refers to the non-lexical component of communication, such as facial expressions, pitch, intonation, speed of speaking and gestures.

Getting started

7.1 How much do you already know about rhetorical devices? Nine rhetorical devices are introduced here in a matching exercise. Match the quotations in the left column with their rhetorical devices and counter examples on the right.

1 'Ask not what your country can do for you, but what you can do for your country.' – John F. Kennedy	a **Anaphora**: the repetition of word or phrase at the beginning of a sentence, such as 'I have a dream' (Martin Luther King).
2 'We will have no truce or parley with you, or the grisly gang who work your wicked will.' – Winston Churchill	b **Diacope**: the repetition of a phrase, after an intervening word or phrase such as 'Free at last, free at last; thank God almighty, free at last!' (Martin Luther King).
3 'We shall fight on the beaches, we shall fight on the landing grounds, we shall fight in the fields and in the streets, we shall fight in the hills.' – Winston Churchill	c **Antithesis**: contrasting two opposing ideas in consecutive sentences, such as 'many are called, but few are chosen' (Jesus Christ).

34

Model texts are analysed to help you understand the key features of the text type.

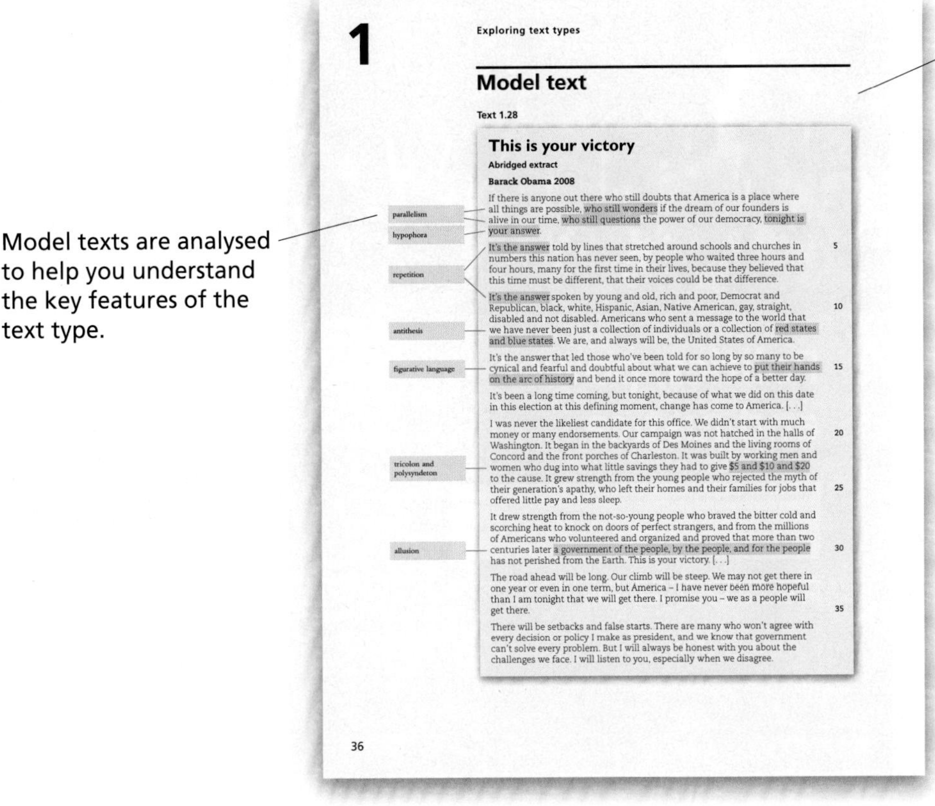

1

Exploring text types

Model text

Text 1.28

This is your victory

Abridged extract

Barack Obama 2008

If there is anyone out there who still doubts that America is a place where all things are possible, who still wonders if the dream of our founders is alive in our time, who still questions the power of our democracy, tonight is your answer.

It's the answer told by lines that stretched around schools and churches in numbers this nation has never seen, by people who waited three hours and four hours, many for the first time in their lives, because they believed that this time must be different, that their voices could be that difference.

It's the answer spoken by young and old, rich and poor, Democrat and Republican, black, white, Hispanic, Asian, Native American, gay, straight, disabled and not disabled. Americans who sent a message to the world that we have never been just a collection of individuals or a collection of red states and blue states. We are, and always will be, the United States of America.

It's the answer that led those who've been told for so long by so many to be cynical and fearful and doubtful about what we can achieve to put their hands on the arc of history and bend it once more toward the hope of a better day.

It's been a long time coming, but tonight, because of what we did on this date in this election at this defining moment, change has come to America. [. . .]

I was never the likeliest candidate for this office. We didn't start with much money or many endorsements. Our campaign was not hatched in the halls of Washington. It began in the backyards of Des Moines and the living rooms of Concord and the front porches of Charleston. It was built by working men and women who dug into what little savings they had to give $5 and $10 and $20 to the cause. It grew strength from the young people who rejected the myth of their generation's apathy, who left their homes and their families for jobs that offered little pay and less sleep.

It drew strength from the not-so-young people who braved the bitter cold and scorching heat to knock on doors of perfect strangers, and from the millions of Americans who volunteered and organized and proved that more than two centuries later a government of the people, by the people, and for the people has not perished from the Earth. This is your victory. [. . .]

The road ahead will be long. Our climb will be steep. We may not get there in one year or even in one term, but America – I have never been more hopeful than I am tonight that we will get there. I promise you – we as a people will get there.

There will be setbacks and false starts. There are many who won't agree with every decision or policy I make as president, and we know that government can't solve every problem. But I will always be honest with you about the challenges we face. I will listen to you, especially when we disagree.

36

This 2nd edition has been completely revised and contains many more texts.

Unit 1.7 Speeches

Over to you

There are ideas for integrating video.

7.5 Do an online search for a video called 'Chocolate Biscuits' by TeachingHeads. It is a speech about chocolate biscuits, which has little meaning but a lot of formal elements of good speech writing. After watching this video, discuss your answers to these questions:

a What is the purpose of this speech, entitled 'Chocolate Biscuits'?

b In which ways is it effective in achieving its purpose?

c What is the effect of the speech on you?

d Look up definitions of the words 'satire', 'parody', 'pastiche' and 'spoof'. Which word or words best describe the 'Chocolate Biscuits' speech? Give examples to support your answers.

Step-by-step writing sequences provide differentiated support where required.

7.6 Try writing your own speech for 5 to 8 minutes about any topic. Take these steps to make this activity a meaningful experience for you and your classmates:

a Find a news article or other text about a topic that matters to you. Identify an argument that can be made in response to this text.

b Write down your argument in the form of a thesis statement. This should be an opinion, claim or statement about the way you see the world or how the world should be.

c Imagine a group of people or **target audience** who would be interested in your opinion. Write down a description of a context in which you could deliver a speech to these people. If you need to alter your argument or claim, you may. You may consider adopting a **persona**, meaning that you pretend to be someone you are not.

d Create a mind map or outline which includes evidence that supports your argument. It can include a few key words. Evidence may be taken from any source texts that you can find or from real-life experiences.

e Show your teacher your argument, description of context and outline. You can call this a proposal. Discuss your proposal and the nature of your speech with your teacher. If your teacher wants to assess you on this activity, discuss the criteria on which you will be assessed. You may want to discuss expectations for appropriate language and conventions of the text type (speech), including choice of register.

f Before you write your speech, review some of the rhetorical devices that you have studied in this unit. Can you see an opportunity to include similar devices in your speech?

g Write your speech and show your teacher a complete draft of it. Ask them for feedback which is informed by any assessment criteria that you have agreed upon.

h Submit your final speech. This may be a piece of formative assessment. As a school group, you may decide to hold a 'speech night' in which you deliver your speeches to your classmates, friends and family. Explain and introduce the context of your speech to your audience before you deliver your speech.

TIP

Activity 7.6 refers to 'formative assessment', which is assessment *for* learning and not assessment *of* learning (summative assessment). As you write and deliver your own speech, think about the skills you are developing. How are these skills useful for your Paper 1, Paper 2, HL essay or individual oral?

Tips prepare you for assessment.

41

Chapter 4

Politics, power and justice

How do politicians and poets write about war?
How do people use language to protest social inequality?
How is language used in election campaigns, public speeches and signs to promote political ideas?

In this chapter you will:

- analyse how language is used for various purposes, such as campaigning for political office, warmongering or protesting in the streets
- discuss the representation and misrepresentation of politicians and political ideas through various media
- analyse the use of rhetorical devices and argumentation fallacies by politicians.

Each chapter has questions to activate prior knowledge.

Each chapter has clear objectives to help you navigate the book.

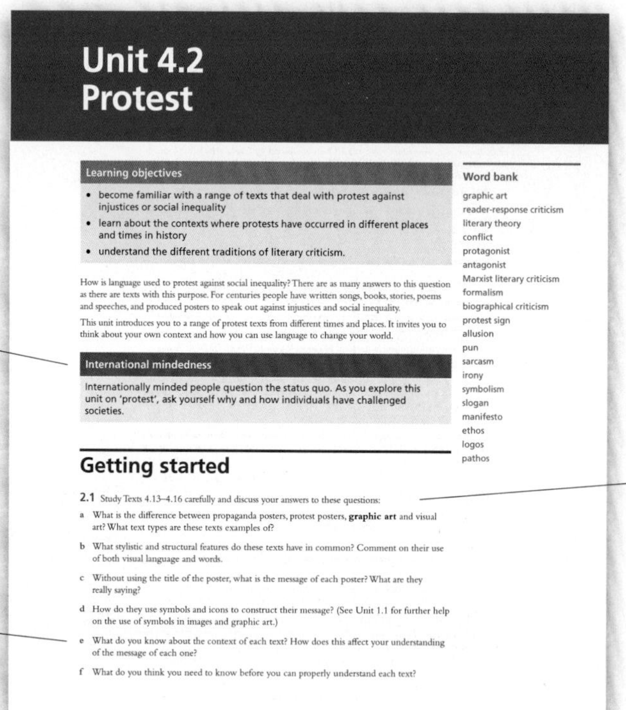

Unit 4.2 Protest

Learning objectives

- become familiar with a range of texts that deal with protest against injustices or social inequality
- learn about the contexts where protests have occurred in different places and times in history
- understand the different traditions of literary criticism.

How is language used to protest against social inequality? There are as many answers to this question as there are texts with this purpose. For centuries people have written songs, books, stories, poems and speeches, and produced posters to speak out against injustices and social inequality.

This unit introduces you to a range of protest texts from different times and places. It invites you to think about your own context and how you can use language to change your world.

International mindedness

Internationally minded people question the status quo. As you explore this unit on 'protest', ask yourself why and how individuals have challenged societies.

Word bank

graphic art
reader-response criticism
literary theory
conflict
protagonist
antagonist
Marxist literary criticism
formalism
biographical criticism
protest sign
allusion
pun
sarcasm
irony
symbolism
slogan
manifesto
ethos
logos
pathos

Getting started

2.1 Study Texts 4.13–4.16 carefully and discuss your answers to these questions:

a What is the difference between propaganda posters, protest posters, **graphic art** and visual art? What text types are these texts examples of?

b What stylistic and structural features do these texts have in common? Comment on their use of both visual language and words.

c Without using the title of the poster, what is the message of each poster? What are they really saying?

d How do they use symbols and icons to construct their message? (See Unit 1.1 for further help on the use of symbols in images and graphic art.)

e What do you know about the context of each text? How does this affect your understanding of the message of each one?

f What do you think you need to know before you can properly understand each text?

221

International mindedness features foster open-mindedness and global perspectives.

Tasks are designed to promote collaboration.

The context of texts is explored.

4 Politics, power and justice

Text 4.13

LABOUR CLEARS THE WAY

Text 4.15

FREE SOUTH AFRICA

Text 4.14

MAKE LOVE NOT WAR

Text 4.16

POWER & EQUALITY

This edition includes all new images including many more visual texts.

AOE question

How can the 'meaning' of a text be constructed, negotiated, expressed and interpreted by readers and writers?

Discuss your class's answers to this question in response to Texts 4.13–4.16. What can you learn about Keith Haring, Angela Davis, the Labour Party and the hippie movement by studying these images on their own? What can you learn without researching any contextual information and analysing them?

AOE questions reference the areas of exploration.

222

Unit 4.2 Protest

2.2 Texts 4.13-4.16 may seem outdated in today's world. Do people still create protest posters? What issues are people protesting about today, and what media or text types do they use to do this? Can you find an example of a modern-day text whose purpose is to protest against something? Bring it into class and discuss how it uses language to serve its purpose.

2.3 Create a piece of graphic art to protest about a current problem in the world. You do not have to be a skilled artist to do this. You can draw stick figures or copy images from the web. Share your creation with your classmates and explain the choices you made when designing your protest poster.

CONCEPT

Creativity

Activity 2.3 asks you to create your own protest poster. *Creativity*, it can be said, is a higher-order thinking skill. In order to create it, you have to consider how your poster will be received and how you will construct your message using language, symbols, colour and layout. As a result, you will be more analytical when viewing other posters.

CAS

How can you make the world a better place? Use this question for guidance when developing a CAS project. While CAS is an opportunity to work on self-fulfilment, you can make positive contributions to your community at the same time. Think about the 'protest' theme in this unit and how you could make a difference.

The seven key concepts are integrated throughout. These activities help develop 21st-century skills through doing.

CAS and TOK features provide additional activities, while Extended essay features provide sample research questions.

Readers, writers and texts

2.4 Text 4.17 is a short story which can be seen as a kind of a riddle. For this activity, let's turn the roles around. Rather than answer discussion questions from this coursebook, think of five questions that you would ask your classmates about this text. These questions should require close reading and textual analysis.

Write each question on a sticky note and display them on a wall. Read everyone's questions and take down five questions *that you did not write*. Write a short answer on the back of each sticky note in response to each question. Take turns reading aloud the answers to the questions that you selected. How many of you had similar questions and answers?

The areas of exploration provide the backbone to each unit.

Text 4.17

Sitting

H.E. Francis 1983

In the morning the man and woman were sitting on his front steps. They sat all day. They would not move. With metronomic regularity he peered at them through the pane in the front door. They did not leave at dark. He wondered when they ate or slept or did their duties. At dawn they were still there. They sat through sun and rain.

At first only the immediate neighbours called: Who are they? What are they doing there? He did not know. Then neighbours from farther down the street called. People who passed and saw the couple called. He never heard the man or woman talk. When he started getting calls from all over the city, from strangers and city fathers, professionals and clerks, garbage and utilities men, and the postman, who had to walk around them to deliver letters, he had to do something. He asked them to leave. They said nothing. They sat. They sat. They stared, indifferent. He said he would call the police. The police gave

The course takes an activity-driven approach, rather than using explanatory narrative.

223

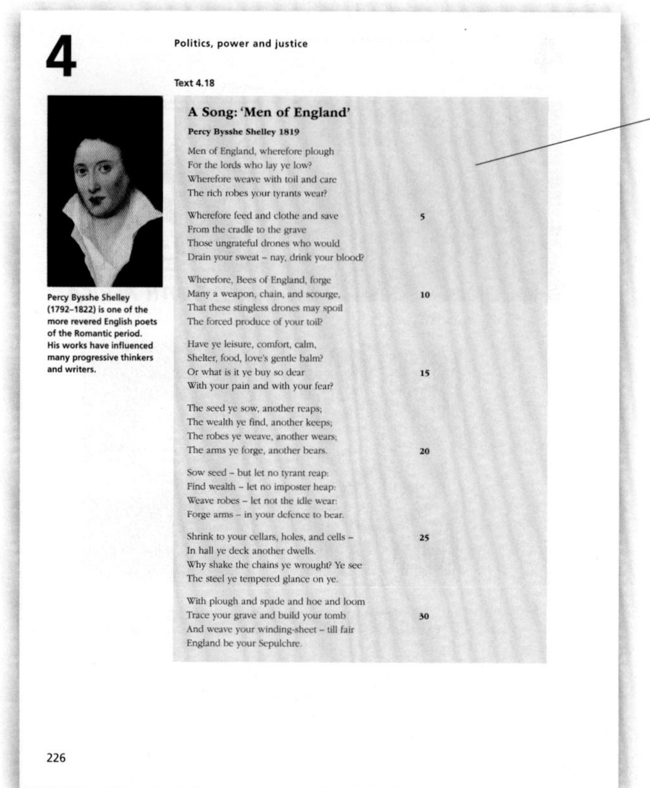

4

Politics, power and justice

Text 4.18

A Song: 'Men of England'

Percy Bysshe Shelley 1819

Men of England, wherefore plough
For the lords who lay ye low?
Wherefore weave with toil and care
The rich robes your tyrants wear?

Wherefore feed and clothe and save
From the cradle to the grave
Those ungrateful drones who would
Drain your sweat – nay, drink your blood?

Wherefore, Bees of England, forge
Many a weapon, chain, and scourge,
That these stingless drones may spoil
The forced produce of your toil?

Have ye leisure, comfort, calm,
Shelter, food, love's gentle balm?
Or what is it ye buy so dear
With your pain and with your fear?

The seed ye sow, another reaps;
The wealth ye find, another keeps;
The robes ye weave, another wears;
The arms ye forge, another bears.

Sow seed – but let no tyrant reap:
Find wealth – let no imposter heap:
Weave robes – let not the idle wear:
Forge arms – in your defence to bear.

Shrink to your cellars, holes, and cells –
In hall ye deck another dwells.
Why shake the chains ye wrought? Ye see
The steel ye tempered glance on ye.

With plough and spade and hoe and loom
Trace your grave and build your tomb
And weave your winding-sheet – till fair
England be your Sepulchre.

Percy Bysshe Shelley (1792–1822) is one of the more revered English poets of the Romantic period. His works have influenced many progressive thinkers and writers.

226

Literature and poetry (and song lyrics found online) are integrated throughout.

Unit 4.2 Protest

Time and space

2.9 Another approach to analysing literary texts is **biographical criticism**. This approach suggests that it is difficult to understand and appreciate a text without knowledge of the author's life and times.

Try to find answers to these questions. How do their answers inform your understanding of Text 4.18? Which sources did you find most useful in your research? Why?

- **a** Who was Percy Bysshe Shelley?
- **b** What kinds of political ideas did Shelley propagate?
- **c** What kind of life did he lead?
- **d** What else did he write?
- **e** How were influential leaders such as Karl Marx and Mahatma Gandhi influenced by Shelley?

2.10 Place a copy of Shelley's poem (Text 4.18) in your learner portfolio and add your own annotations to it. Include any other clippings that you came across in your research for Activities 2.8 and 2.9. How can you connect this poem to 'protest' as a global issue? How could you use this text in preparation for an individual oral?

2.11 Text 4.19 is a famous speech by Mahatma Gandhi from 1942. The annotations ask questions about the context of the speech. In pairs, research the answers to these questions and then discuss as a class:

- **a** Could you understand the speech without knowing the answers to the questions in the annotations ? Why, or why not?
- **b** How was your understanding of Gandhi's speech affected by what you already knew about him and his cause, before you started researching answers to the questions?
- **c** What were your answers to the questions in the annotations?
- **d** What sources did you find valuable in helping you answer the annotation questions?
- **e** Why do you think this speech is often cited as one of the most important speeches of the 20th century?

AOE question

How do readers approach texts from different times and different cultures from their own?

Text 4.19 might seem like an artefact from a different time and place. By asking questions about the text, as has been done in the annotations, we have a starting point for researching its context. Apply this method to other texts that you may not understand.

LEARNER PROFILE

Inquirer

An IB learner is an *inquirer*. To become a better inquirer, get into the habit of asking questions of texts by annotating them, as has been done with Text 4.19.

ATL

Research

Effective research starts by asking appropriate questions. The annotations to Text 4.19 show you how to ask questions of primary sources. These types of questions should guide you on your search for secondary sources, when analysing texts.

227

The areas of exploration are addressed progressively.

Suggestions for building a learner portfolio appear throughout.

You can be confident that the ten attributes of the IB learner profile are being developed.

The five approaches to learning develop metacognitive skills to make you a better learner. The work to integrate these approaches has been done for you.

This coursebook provides you with a range of contemporary 'language' texts, because you told us that was what you found most time-consuming to source.

International texts are from five continents.

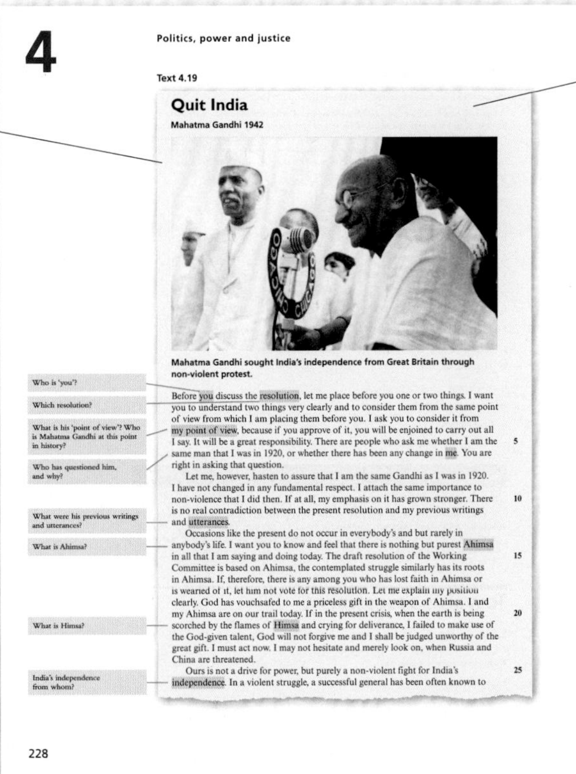

4

Politics, power and justice

Text 4.19

Quit India

Mahatma Gandhi 1942

Mahatma Gandhi sought India's independence from Great Britain through non-violent protest.

Who is 'you'?

Which resolution?

What is his 'point of view'? Who is Mahatma Gandhi at this point in history?

Who has questioned him, and why?

What were his previous writings and utterances?

What is Ahimsa?

What is Himsa?

India's independence from whom?

Before you discuss the resolution, let me place before you one or two things. I want you to understand two things very clearly and to consider them from the same point of view from which I am placing them before you. I ask you to consider it from my point of view, because if you approve of it, you will be enjoined to carry out all I say. It will be a great responsibility. There are people who ask me whether I am the same man that I was in 1920, or whether there has been any change in me. You are right in asking that question.

Let me, however, hasten to assure that I am the same Gandhi as I was in 1920. I have not changed in any fundamental respect. I attach the same importance to non-violence that I did then. If at all, my emphasis on it has grown stronger. There is no real contradiction between the present resolution and my previous writings and utterances.

Occasions like the present do not occur in everybody's and but rarely in anybody's life. I want you to know and feel that there is nothing but purest Ahimsa in all that I am saying and doing today. The draft resolution of the Working Committee is based on Ahimsa, the contemplated struggle similarly has its roots in Ahimsa. If, therefore, there is any among you who has lost faith in Ahimsa or is wearied of it, let him not vote for this resolution. Let me explain my position clearly. God has vouchsafed to me a priceless gift in the weapon of Ahimsa. I and my Ahimsa are on our trail today. If in the present crisis, when the earth is being scorched by the flames of Himsa and crying for deliverance, I failed to make use of the God-given talent, God will not forgive me and I shall be judged unworthy of the great gift. I must act now. I may not hesitate and merely look on, when Russia and China are threatened.

Ours is not a drive for power, but purely a non-violent fight for India's independence. In a violent struggle, a successful general has been often known to

228

4

Politics, power and justice

Intertextuality: connecting texts

2.12 An interesting type of text for analysis is the **protest sign**. These are often homemade products of cardboard, pens, glue and tape. Their use of language must be concise and punchy in order to be effective. Furthermore, they often express criticism through the use of:

- **allusion**, which is a reference to another text
- **pun**, a kind of play on words
- other linguistic devices, such as **sarcasm**, **irony** or **symbolism**.

Text 4.20 is a photograph taken during an anti-Trump rally in the UK in July 2018. This protest sign borrows elements from another text that you have already studied, the Second World War 'We Can Do It!' poster (Text 2.4 from Unit 2.1). Study these two images and discuss your answers to these questions:

a How does the 'We Can Do It!' poster (Text 2.4) add meaning to the anti-Trump protest sign (Text 4.20)?

b Besides alluding to the 'We Can Do It!' poster, how else is meaning constructed? What are the effects of colour, punctuation, font and layout on her audience?

c The raised fist is a common symbol of protest. What can you find out about this symbol? Where does it come from? How has it been used before? Why do you think the protester has used it here?

d How do other symbols construct meaning in this protest sign?

e The woman's T-shirt also protests against Brexit. What does Brexit (the UK's 'exit' from the European Union) have to do with an anti-Trump rally? Research the parallels between these two issues.

f When you think of the word 'protester', is this woman the kind of person who comes to mind? What makes you say that? Has she changed your associations with the word 'protester'?

Text 4.20

230

Opportunities are presented for differentiated research.

Unit 4.2 Protest

2.13 As well as using images, protest signs often include words. Here are several phrases that have been used on signs to protest about the presidency of Donald Trump in the USA. You may find them confusing without much contextual knowledge.

Assign each person in your class a different phrase. Do an online search to learn more about the contexts in which your phrase was used. Try to find how your text is connected to another text or texts of some kind. The phrases allude to statements that President Trump has used, other famous protest signs or **slogans** from other campaigns. Explain how the meaning of your protest sign's text is dependent on another text and context. Present your findings to your classmates.

a We shall overcome.

b Keep your tiny hands off my rights.

c No you can't.

d Pussies grab back.

e Nope.

f I wish this were fake news.

g 40% approval. Sad!

h Resist bigly.

i Trump: bad hombre for the whole world.

j Are we winning yet? I was told there would be winning.

k Make love not walls.

l You're fired.

m Nasty women vote.

n Lock him up.

o Make Russia Great Again.

AOE question

How can comparing and interpreting texts transform readers?

As you research the language of the signs that protest against Donald Trump (Activity 2.13) you may learn something about US politics, presidential campaigns and the 45th President of the United States. What have you learnt from your research?

Towards assessment

2.14 In small groups, select a protest movement from these options or think of another one that you would like to research:

- women's suffrage movement
- protest against the war in Vietnam
- UK coal miners' strike in 1984–85

231

This section addresses Paper 1, Paper 2 and/or the individual oral. Sample questions and responses engage you to actively develop skills to approach these assessments.

Unit 4.3 Politics

It starts with a vote – your vote. And so, I'm calling on you – on May 2nd – to mark your ballot for change. Together, we can do this. We can show that: Here, our priority is job creation, the environment and world peace. Here, we dare to use words like "change," "hope," and "progress." Here, we dare to look beyond old politics and have the audacity to ask for something better. Here, we dare to look cynicism directly in the eye, and have faith that the best has yet to come. And especially because there is so much to do.

The time has come for someone to take on those responsibilities. We are ready to take on this challenge! It can't be done without you. Let's work together. Let's roll up our sleeves and start the work right now. Thank you!

3.14 In this activity you will use your analysis of Text 4.33 that you wrote for Activity 3.13.

a Compare your analysis of Text 4.33 with the sample analysis that has been provided here. How similar was your analysis to the approach taken by this student? How different were the aspects of the text that you focused on?

b Assess this sample analysis using the assessment criteria for Paper 1 at the beginning of this book. As a class, discuss your marks.

c Read the annotations to the sample Paper 1 script carefully. How could you improve your analysis by taking these points into consideration?

d After writing a Paper 1 analysis on Text 4.33 and comparing it to the sample analysis, save your work in your learner portfolio and reflect on your Paper 1 writing skills. What did you learn from this activity? What do you still need to work on? How are you going to develop these skills?

Paper 1 – Sample 1

Guiding question

In what ways does the speaker, Jack Layton, use language that is typical of the text type, in order to achieve his purpose?

Analysis

In 2011 Jack Layton delivered a speech to his fellow New Democrats in Québec, encouraging them to vote for him as the new Prime Minister of Canada. His use of language, especially his use of anaphora, tricolon and pronouns, is typical of speech writing and helps him achieve his purpose of getting people to vote for his New Democrats party.

Political speeches are often full of anaphora, and Jack Layton's speech is no different. Anaphora is the repetition of a word or phrase at the beginning of a sentence. He uses anaphora to give his speech a sense of direction and pace, so that listeners are captured and eager to learn more about his campaign promises. Already in his introduction, Mr Layton speaks of a 'wind of change' (line 3). Then he elaborates on this change by starting three sentences with the word 'wind': 'A wind that blows along the St Lawrence River' (line 3), 'A wind of renewal coming from as far as James Bay' (line 5), and 'Wind from every corner of Québec'

Notice the thesis statement uses words from the guiding question. This is good practice.

Notice how the thesis statement answers the guiding question.

After you refer to a stylistic device, be sure to explain it.

251

Annotated sample learner responses help you understand what is expected.

Unit 4.2 Protest

Higher level extension

2.18 Here are several quotations about democracy. From these quotations, select:

- the one that you *agree* with most
- the one that you *disagree* with most
- one that you find confusing
- one that you find funny.

For each quote that you have chosen, explain to your classmates why you agree or disagree with it or find it confusing or funny. Then find out more about the person who said *one* of these things and explain to your classmate why you think he or she may have said this:

a 'Democracy is the art and science of running the circus from the monkey cage.' – H.L. Mencken

b 'Democracy is good. I say this because other systems are worse.' – Jawaharlal Nehru

c 'There cannot be true democracy unless women's voices are heard.' – Hillary Clinton

d 'The best argument against democracy is a five-minute conversation with the average voter.' – Winston Churchill

e 'Democracy cannot succeed unless those who express their choice are prepared to choose wisely. The real safeguard of democracy, therefore, is education.' – Franklin D. Roosevelt

f 'Democracy must be something more than two wolves and a sheep voting on what to have for dinner.' – James Bovard

g 'Democracy is the road to socialism.' – Karl Marx

h 'Democracy is a device that insures we shall be governed no better than we deserve.' – George Bernard Shaw

i 'A mature society understands that at the heart of democracy is argument.' – Salman Rushdie

j 'Without God, democracy will not and cannot long endure.' – Ronald Reagan

k 'Republics decline into democracies and democracies degenerate into despotisms.' - Aristotle

l 'If you have a sense of purpose and a sense of direction, I believe people will follow you. Democracy isn't just about deducing what the people want. Democracy is leading the people as well.' – Margaret Thatcher

AOE question

How can different texts offer different perspectives on a topic or theme?

Activity 2.18 offers several different perspectives on a single topic: democracy. For any other topic that you are studying, find a range of interesting quotations, discuss them and write about them in your learner portfolio.

2.19 If you and your classmates could 'take over' the United Nations for a day, and be able to voice your opinions on how to make the world a better place, what would you say? As a class, make a list of key global issues for the UN to address to ensure that the world becomes a safer, more prosperous place for everyone.

235

Unit 4.2 Protest

c If you could interview Malala Yousafzai, what would you ask her? Why would you ask her this?

d In what ways is her speech similar to, or different from, Mahatma Gandhi's speech (Text 4.19)? Make a list of similarities and differences.

2.22 In Activity 2.19 you were asked to make a list of global issues that you found particularly important. Choose *one* of these issues and write a speech about it, which you might deliver at a Youth Takeover of the United Nations. You may adopt a persona (pretending to be someone you are not). Or you may write from your own perspective. Refer to real-life situations, current events and statistics. Your speech should be between 800 and 1000 words. As a school, you may wish to organise an event where speeches are read aloud for friends and parents. Or you may simply read your speech to your classmates in class. Look to Unit 1.7 and other speeches in this coursebook, such as Text 4.22, for inspiration.

Further reading includes suggested texts in translation and audiovisual recommendations.

Further reading

- *Kiss of the Spider Woman* is a highly acclaimed novel by Manuel Puig, originally in Spanish, about two cellmates in an Argentinean prison.
- *Nineteen Eighty-Four* by George Orwell is a classic novel – and for good reasons. It details all aspects of an imaginary oppressive regime through the eyes of Winston Smith, who is tasked with rewriting history for the Ministry of Truth.
- Martin Luther King's speeches and letters may also be studied as 'prose other than fiction' as a literary text for your English language and literature course. These texts will give you an excellent insight into the mind of a revolutionary.
- *Letters from Robben Island* by Achmed Kathrada is an excellent account of the African National Congress's struggle against apartheid in South Africa in the 1960s.
- There are many songwriters on the Prescribed Reading List (PRL) who have sung songs of protest. Joni Mitchell, John Lennon and Bob Dylan are a few that you can choose from. Lyrics from a protest song are appropriate for the individual oral, in which you analyse both a literary text and a non-literary text in relation to a global issue.

REFLECT

Do an online search for a video called 'The Power of Words', by Andrea Gardner for Purple Feather, which features a woman helping a blind man. What do you think of this video?

Look back at the texts you have read in this unit from Mahatma Gandhi to Percy Bysshe Shelley, from Keith Haring to Malala Yousafzai. To what extent have these people been successful in changing the world through their words? Give a short answer to this question with regard to at least *one* of the texts studied in this unit. As a class, discuss how you can change the world using words.

Reflect features enable you to look back on the unit, develop learning skills and document ideas in your learner portfolio.

239

Introduction to the English A: Language and Literature course

Congratulations! You have signed up for English A: Language and Literature for the IB Diploma Programme. This course will take you on a journey into the worlds of textual analysis, communication studies and language arts.

At the heart of this course is the question: 'How is meaning constructed through language and for what purpose?' By 'language' we mean the methods that writers use to construct meaning, including the use of images, colour, lighting, camera angle, headings and, of course, words. By 'texts' we mean anything that conveys meaning, such as poems, speeches, song lyrics, films, posters, websites, magazine covers, images, tweets or blog entries, to name just a few! With such a broad landscape to explore, it helps to have AOE questions and definitions of text types. This introduction provides you with an overview of the course curriculum and the assessment components. It also explains how this coursebook has been organised and the support it provides for your course.

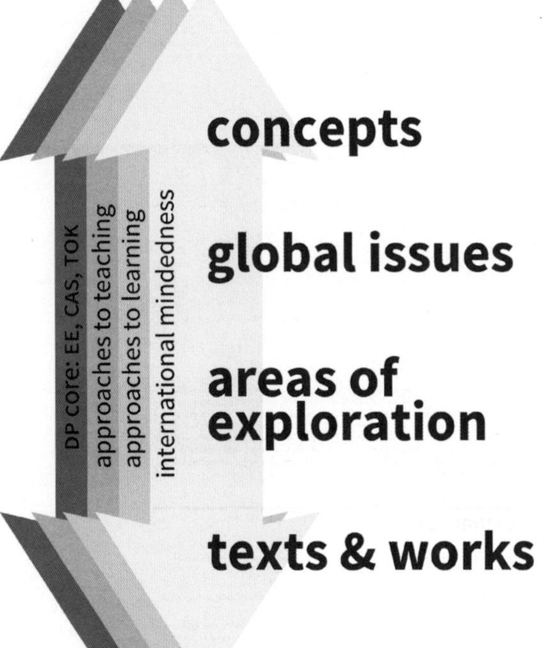

creativity, culture, community, identity, perspective, transformation, representation

femininity, masculinity, beauty
racism, colonialism, immigration
war, protest, politics, etc.

readers, writers and texts
time and space
intertextuality: connecting texts

novels, plays, poems, graphic novels, lyrics, advertisements, cartoons, photographs, letters, websites, etc.

Non-literary texts

What will you study in this course? The simple answer is 'texts'. At higher and standard level you will read a range of non-literary texts from advertisements to brochures. Technically, you must explore at least six different types of non-literary text. In practice, you will explore many more, considering that the definition of 'text' is quite broad. You may also find that the difference between a 'literary' and a 'non-literary' text is not always clear. This, however, is an ambiguity worth embracing and discussing as a class. Furthermore, the non-literary texts that you explore in class should have a 'sense of authorship'. This is to say, for example, that each photograph should be explored in relation to other photographs by the same photographer, advertisements should be analysed in relation to other advertisements from the same campaign, speeches should be understood in relation to other speeches by the same author and so on. Here are a few suggested text types for you to study. While it is neither a prescriptive nor an exhaustive list, you should be familiar with these text types in preparation for Paper 1: Guided textual analysis. Some of these text types are explored in Chapter 1 of this coursebook.

advertisement (Unit 1.2)
appeal
biography
blog (Unit 1.9)
brochure/leaflet
cartoon (Unit 1.4)
commercial
comic/graphic novel (Unit 1.5)
diary
email
encyclopaedia entry
essay (Chapters 5–7)
film (Unit 1.3)
guide book
infographic
interview
instructions
letter (formal or informal)
magazine cover (Unit 1.1)
manifesto
memoir
news article (Unit 1.8)
playscript (Unit 1.11)
photograph (Unit 1.1)
radio broadcast
speech (Unit 1.7)
street art (Unit 1.6)
TV show
travel writing
webpage
parody
pastiche

Literary works

At *higher level* you will read *six* literary works:

- two works from the prescribed reading list (PRL) for English
- two works from the PRLs of other IB-approved languages, translated into English
- two works that are freely chosen, either by you or by your teacher. These may also be works in translation.

For each of the areas of exploration, you should have read at least two works. Across these six literary works, at least three literary forms, three time periods and three places should be represented. Although it is not a requirement, you are encouraged to read an equal number of works written by men and women.

At *standard level* you will read *four* literary works:

- one work from the prescribed reading list (PRL) for English
- one work from the PRLs of other IB-approved languages, translated into English
- two works that are freely chosen, either by you or by your teacher. These may also be works in translation.

For each of the areas of exploration, you should have read at least one literary work. Across these four literary works, at least two literary forms, two time periods and two places should be represented. Although it is not a requirement, you are encouraged to read an equal number of works written by men and women.

A literary work is defined as:

- one novel, play, autobiography or biography
- two or more novellas
- five to ten short stories
- five to eight essays
- ten to 15 letters by the same author
- one very long poem or a 600-line selection from this poem
- 15 to 20 poems (Unit 1.12).

Note: Where more than one text is read as a 'work' (such as poetry, short stories, letters or essays), these texts should have been written by the same author.

Chapter 1 includes units on short stories and novels (Unit 1.10), playscripts (Unit 1.11) and poems (Unit 1.12), giving you a toolkit to deconstruct any of these literary works that you are exploring in class.

Areas of exploration

How will you study these texts? The Language and Literature course consists of three *areas of exploration*, each of which asks *six* AOE questions.

Readers, writers and texts

- How and why do people study language and literature?
- What are the different ways in which people are affected by texts?
- How can the 'meaning' of a text be constructed, negotiated, expressed and interpreted by readers and writers?
- How does the use of language vary among different types of text?
- How do the style and structure of a text affect its meaning?
- How can texts present challenges and offer insights?

Time and space

- How can cultural contexts influence how texts are written and received?
- How do readers approach texts from different times and different cultures from their own?
- How can texts offer insights into other cultures?
- How can the meaning of a text and its impact change over time?
- How do texts engage with local and global issues?
- How can language represent social differences and identities?

Intertextuality: connecting texts

- How do texts follow or move away from the conventions associated with different types of text?
- How do the conventions of different types of text develop over time?
- What can diverse texts have in common?

- How useful is it to describe a work as 'classic'?
- How can different texts offer different perspectives on a topic or theme?
- How can comparing and interpreting texts transform readers?

(Adapted from the IBDP Guide on Language A: Language and Literature)

It helps to think of these 'areas' as 'lenses' or 'approaches' to reading. For each text that you explore in class, whether literary or non-literary, you may find that multiple questions from multiple areas are relevant. For this reason, your teacher may mix questions from different areas of exploration into each lesson.

Chapters 2–4 of this coursebook take an integrated approach. Each of the three units in these chapters focuses on a particular global issue. These units give you the opportunity to explore a range of literary and non-literary texts, and to ask questions from all three areas of exploration, starting with 'Readers, writers and texts' and ending with 'Intertextuality: connecting texts'. Each unit concludes with a 'Higher-level extension' for broader and deeper understanding of the global issue being studied (see 'Learner portfolio' for a definition of 'global issue').

Concepts

The questions from the areas of exploration aim to help you gain a conceptual understanding of texts. What is meant by 'conceptual understanding'? 'Concepts', as the educational consultant Lynn Erickson has outlined in her research, are mental constructs that are timeless, universal, broad and abstract. This is to say that texts are not just about the people, places or topics in them; they are about bigger ideas that are shared with and explored through other texts. Gaining an understanding of these bigger ideas or 'concepts' will help you understand and attach meaning to the world around you as you explore texts. While there are hundreds of meaningful concepts in the Language and Literature course, the IB has selected *seven* concepts which you will explore explicitly:

- identity
- culture
- creativity
- communication
- perspective
- transformation
- representation.

This coursebook integrates these key concepts into the exploration of texts and global issues. Regular Concept features appear throughout the coursebook to help you think about how these concepts relate to what you are studying.

Assessment

Your understanding of the coursework and the skills that you have acquired are assessed through *three* assessment components at standard level and *four* components at higher level. The assessment components can correspond to any or all areas of exploration.

		SL%	Standard level	Higher level	HL%
External assessment	Paper 1	35	1 hour 15 minutes One commentary on one of two non-literary texts	2 hours 15 minutes Two commentaries on each of two non-literary texts	35
	Paper 2	35	1 hour 45 minutes A comparative essay on two literary texts that haven't been used for the IO or the HL essay, based on one of four unseen questions		25
	HL essay			A 1200– 1500-word essay (coursework) on a literary or non-literary text and 'line of inquiry'	20
Internal assessment	Individual oral (IO)	30	A 10-minute oral and a 5-minute discussion on two prepared passages chosen by the student: one literary passage and one non-literary passage, connected by a 'global issue' of choice		20

Paper 1: Guided textual analysis

Standard and higher level students receive the same Paper 1 exam, which includes *two* unseen passages. Each passage will be roughly one page or 30 lines long, accompanied by a question and taken from a broad range of non-literary text types, including websites, advertisements, comic strips and letters.

The only difference between standard and higher level is that SL students write only *one* analysis on *one* of the passages of their choice. HL students write *two* analyses, one on each of the passages. For this reason, HL students have 2 hours and 15 minutes, whereas SL students have 1 hour and 15 minutes to complete the task. At both standard and higher level, Paper 1 counts for 35% of your final grade. The assessment criteria for Paper 1 are the same for standard and higher level. The assessment criteria are applied twice at higher level, once for each of the analyses. They can be found at the end of this introduction. See Chapter 5 on Paper 1 for further guidance on this component, sample student responses and examiner comments.

Paper 2: Comparative essay

Standard and higher level students of English A: Language and Literature and English A: Literature receive the same Paper 2 exam. It includes *four* unseen essay questions, of which you will answer *one* by comparing *two* of your literary texts. These must be literary texts that you have not used for your individual oral or higher level essay.

The essay questions will encourage you to explore theme, context, purpose, style and structure. Both SL and HL students have 1 hour and 45 minutes to write this essay. At standard level, Paper 2 counts for 35% of your final grade. At higher level, Paper 2 counts for 25% of your final grade. The assessment criteria for Paper 2 are the same for standard and higher level. They can be found at the end of this introduction. See Chapter 6 on Paper 2 for further guidance on this component, sample student responses and examiner comments.

HL essay

Higher level students write an essay of 1200–1500 words on *one* literary or non-literary text. It must be a text that you have not already used for your individual oral and do not plan to use for your Paper 2 exam. The essay should explore a 'line of inquiry' of your own choice. A line of inquiry is a kind of research question. You are advised to draw from the seven concepts and the 18 AOE questions for inspiration when designing your line of inquiry. It helps to think of this piece of coursework as a shorter extended essay, with a research question, thesis statement and primary source. Although they are not required, you may want to include secondary sources, citations and a bibliography. The HL essay counts for 20% of your final grade at higher level. The assessment criteria for the HL essay can be found at the end of this introduction. See Chapter 7 on the HL essay for further guidance on this component, sample student essays and examiner comments.

Individual oral

The individual oral is the only component of assessment that is assessed internally. Like all internal assessment, it is marked by your teacher using the assessment criteria and moderated by an IB moderator. You will select and prepare *two* extracts for your oral – one literary and one non-literary - which are connected by a common 'global issue' of your choice. Your teacher should be made aware of your global issue and the extracts that you have selected at least one week before your individual oral is conducted. Both extracts should be taken from a 'body of work' that has been explored in class. In other words, an extract is a scene from a play, a poem from a poet's collection, a passage from a novel, a page from a graphic novel, an advertisement from a campaign, a still from a movie, a section from a series of speeches by the same author or one of several blog entries – each text should have a sense of authorship. You may prepare a one-page outline of no more than ten bullet-pointed notes to take with you to the oral. The oral must address this prompt:

> 'Examine the ways in which the global issue of your choice is presented through the content and form of one of the works and one of the texts that you have studied.' (IBDP Guide on Language A: Language and Literature)

In the first 10 minutes of your individual oral, you will relate the extracts to the bodies of work from which they were taken, analyse them and connect them each to the common global issue of your choice. After this time, you will engage in a 5-minute discussion with your teacher in which you develop and explore further your ideas on the texts from which the extracts are derived and your chosen global issue. This component of assessment counts for 30% of your final grade at standard level and 20% of your final grade at higher level. The assessment criteria for the individual oral are the same at standard and higher level. They can be found at the end of this introduction. Chapter 8 provides further guidance on this component, sample student performances, their outlines and teacher comments.

Learner portfolio

Throughout your studies you will explore a range of texts, both literary and non-literary, on a range of global issues. A 'global issue' is a social, global or artistic theme, topic or area of study, such as feminism, racism or war. Your teacher will ask you to answer questions, write tasks, find texts, reflect on activities, take quizzes, write practice papers and give presentations.

It is important, especially in preparation for the individual oral, that you collect your work in a portfolio and connect each entry to a global issue. You may do this in an online or offline format, such as a journal or blog. You might find it helpful to create a kind of 'tagging' system early in your course so that you can find additional materials later, before the final assessment.

Chapters 2–4 introduce you to nine global issues, each of which invites you to engage with between eight and 15 texts, both literary and non-literary, by doing activities with your teacher and classmates. You can record your activity participation in your portfolio.

Connecting to the core

The Language and Literature course is part of the Diploma Programme, meaning that the IB core should be integrated into your everyday learning. This coursebook shows you where and how to make connections to the IB core. Even if you are not doing the entire Diploma at your school, you are encouraged to make these connections:

- **Theory of knowledge** (TOK) asks 'How do you know what you know?' Language is considered a way of knowing and the arts are considered an area of knowledge. Textual analysis, the study of how meaning is constructed, relates to TOK, as you explore weasel words, argumentation fallacies, bias, connotation and many other concepts.
- The **extended essay** (EE) is a 4000-word research paper that allows you to explore a topic of your choice. Many students choose to write their EE on one of the three 'categories' for Studies in Language and Literature (Group 1 of the DP). Example research questions are suggested in each unit, where relevant to the unit content. You can use these suggestions as a springboard for your own research if you choose to write your EE on English A.
- **Creativity, activity, service** (CAS) encourages you to learn by reflecting on experiences that you have had outside class. You may want to integrate these reflections into your language and literature studies. You may have intercultural experiences that prove valuable for class discussion. Furthermore, you may find the skills that you learn in this course useful for your CAS activities and projects.
- The **learner profile** is a set of ten character traits that you are encouraged to explore throughout your IB learning career. This coursebook aims to develop learners who are: inquirers, knowledgeable, thinkers, communicators, principled, open-minded, caring, risk takers, balanced and reflective.
- The **approaches to teaching and learning** (ATL) are a set of guidelines given to IB teachers about the pedagogy and methods of delivery that are inherent to the IB classroom. This coursebook aims to develop five approaches to learning: thinking skills, communication skills, social skills, self-management skills and research skills.
- **International mindedness** is at the heart of studying the IB Diploma. It encourages you to look beyond the borders of one country in order to understand globalisation, intercultural awareness, and that 'others, with their differences, can be right' (IB mission statement).

Over to you

This coursebook cannot teach you English A: Language and Literature. It offers a starting point for understanding both the course and the texts that you see every day around you. You live in a world that is full of texts, from billboards and commercials to songs and speeches. To understand how people construct meaning through language is to understand how the world works.

This course and this coursebook aim to help you develop an appreciation of language and literature. But you are the one on this exploration. So be active, notice more and – above all – have fun!

Paper 1: Guided textual analysis

Criterion A: Understanding and interpretation

What is assessed?

Understanding of what is revealed and inferred in the text, using supporting references.

Marks	Description of level
0	The response does not meet the standards described by the following descriptors.
1	There is little understanding of the literal meaning. The response seldom supports claims with evidence, or supporting evidence is seldom appropriate.
2	There is some understanding of the literal meaning. The response supports claims with evidence that is sometimes appropriate.
3	There is an understanding of the literal meaning and some inferential understanding. The response supports claims with evidence that is mainly relevant.
4	There is a detailed understanding of the literal meaning and a convincing inferential understanding. The response supports claims with relevant evidence.
5	There is a detailed and insightful understanding of literal meaning, and a convincing and nuanced inferential understanding. The response supports claims with well-selected evidence.

Criterion B: Analysis and evaluation

What is assessed?

Understanding of language, style, and structure, and the ability to critically evaluate how the writer's choices construct meaning.

Marks	Description of level
0	The response does not meet the standards described by the following descriptors.
1	There is little analysis of how language and style are used. The commentary is descriptive.
2	There is some analysis of how language and style are used. The commentary is mainly descriptive.
3	The analysis of the ways language and style are used is mainly appropriate.
4	There is an appropriate analysis of language and style. Some of the analysis is insightful. There is some evaluation of how meaning is shaped by the writer's choices.
5	There is an insightful and convincing analysis of the ways language and style are used. There is very good evaluation of how meaning is shaped by the writer's choices.

Criterion C: Focus and organisation

What is assessed?

The ability to organise ideas in a coherent and focused way.

Marks	Description of level
0	The response does not meet the standards described by the following descriptors.
1	There is little organisation of ideas and no clear focus in the analysis.
2	There is some organisation of ideas and a degree of focus in the analysis.
3	There is adequate organisation and coherence of ideas, and some focus in the analysis.
4	There is good organisation and coherence of idea, and adequate focus in the analysis.
5	There is effective organisation and coherence of ideas, and a good focus in the analysis.

Criterion D: Language

What is assessed?

The ability to write using language which is clear, accurate and varied, in an appropriate academic style and register, and using relevant terminology where appropriate.

Marks	Description of level
0	The response does not meet the standards described by the following descriptors.
1	There is little clarity, accuracy, or sense of register, and the language is rarely appropriate.
2	There is some clarity and accuracy, and some sense of an appropriate register, although There are errors.
3	There is adequate clarity and accuracy, and the register is generally appropriate, with occasional errors.
4	There is good clarity and accuracy, and the register is consistently appropriate.
5	There is very good clarity and accuracy, and careful use of language. The register is appropriate and effective.

Paper 2: Comparative essay

Criterion A: Knowledge, understanding and interpretation

What is assessed?

Knowledge and understanding of the literary works, and how well this is used in response to the question to show similarities and differences.

Marks	Description of level
0	The response does not meet the standards described by the following descriptors.
1–2	There is little knowledge and understanding of the works, and little comparison or contrast of the works in response to the question.
3–4	There is limited knowledge and understanding of the works, and limited comparison of the works in response to the question.
5–6	There is satisfactory knowledge and understanding of the works, and satisfactory comparison of the works in response to the question.
7–8	There is good knowledge and understanding of the works, and relevant comparison of the works in response to the question. The discussion is sustained and convincing.
9–10	There is very good knowledge and understanding of the works, and insightful comparison of the works in response to the question. The discussion is perceptive and persuasive.

Criterion B: Analysis and evaluation

What is assessed?

The analysis and evaluation of how the writers' choice of language, technique, and style are used to create meaning and effect. How well analysis and evaluation are used to show similarities and differences between the works in response to the question.

Marks	Description of level
0	The response does not meet the standards described by the following descriptors.
1–2	The response is descriptive, offering little relevant analysis.
3–4	The response offers some analysis, but is mainly descriptive. There is limited comparison of the writers' choices.
5–6	The response offers relevant analysis, and some understanding of the ways in which language, technique, and style establish meaning and effect. There is some adequate comparison of the writers' choices.
7–8	The response is analytical and evaluative, offering understanding of the ways in which language, technique, and style establish meaning and effect. There is a good comparison of the writers' choices.
9–10	The response is analytical and evaluative, offering a perceptive and persuasive understanding of the ways in which language, technique, and style establish meaning and effect. There is very good comparison of the writers' choices.

Criterion C: Focus and organisation

What is assessed?

Structure, focus, and balance in expressing ideas.

Marks	Description of level
0	The response does not meet the standards described by the following descriptors.
1	There is limited focus on the question, and the ideas are mainly unconnected.
2	There is some focus on the question and some ideas are connected, but not always clearly. The discussion of works may lack balance.
3	There is mainly a good focus on the question, although this is sometimes lost. There is reasonable balance and general sense of cohesion in the development of ideas.
4	There is a good focus on the question that is generally maintained. There is a good balance; ideas are well connected and develop logically.
5	There is a clear focus on the question throughout. There is very good balance; ideas are connected persuasively and develop in a logical and compelling way.

Criterion D: Language

What is assessed?

The ability to write using language which is clear, accurate and varied, in an appropriate academic style and register, and using relevant terminology where appropriate.

Marks	Description of level
0	The response does not meet the standards described by the following descriptors.
1	There is little clarity, accuracy, or sense of register, and the language is rarely appropriate.
2	There is some clarity and accuracy, and some sense of an appropriate register, although There are errors.
3	There is adequate clarity and accuracy, and the register is generally appropriate. There are some errors.
4	There is good clarity and accuracy, and the register is consistently appropriate.
5	There is very good clarity and accuracy, and careful use of language. The register is appropriate and effective.

Individual oral

Criterion A: Knowledge, understanding, and interpretation

What is assessed?

Knowledge and understanding of the extracts, and the wider works and texts from which they are taken. The application of this knowledge to the global issue chosen, drawing conclusions with reference to the works and texts.

Marks	Description of level
0	The response does not meet the standards described by the following descriptors.
1–2	Little knowledge and understanding of extracts, texts, and works in the context of the global issue chosen. Supporting evidence is limited or inappropriate.
3–4	Limited knowledge and understanding of extracts, texts, and works in the context of the global issue chosen. Supporting evidence is sometimes appropriate.
5–6	Satisfactory knowledge and understanding of extracts, texts, and works, offering an interpretation in the context of the global issue chosen. Evidence is mainly appropriate and supports the development of ideas.
7–8	Good knowledge and understanding of extracts, texts, and works, offering interpretation throughout in the context of the global issue chosen. Evidence is appropriate and supports the development of ideas.
9–10	There is excellent knowledge and understanding of extracts, texts, and works, offering a compelling interpretation in the context of the global issue chosen. Evidence is appropriate, carefully selected, and supports the development of ideas well.

Criterion B: Analysis and evaluation

What is assessed?

Knowledge and understanding of the extracts, and the wider works and texts from which they are taken; how this is used to analyse and evaluate how writers' choices of language, structure, and style create a perspective on the global issue chosen.

Marks	Description of level
0	The response does not meet the standards described by the following descriptors.
1–2	The oral is descriptive, or analysis is irrelevant. There is little discussion of language, structure, and style and how they relate to the global issue chosen.
3–4	Some relevant analysis, but this is largely descriptive. Aspects of language, structure and style are highlighted, but with little understanding of how they relate to the context of the global issue chosen.
5–6	There is analysis, with appropriate and evaluative commentary. There is reasonable understanding of language, structure, and style in the context of the global issue chosen.
7–8	There is analysis, with appropriate and evaluative commentary that is at times perceptive. There is good understanding of language, structure, and style in the context of the global issue chosen.
9–10	There is analysis, revealing appropriate and evaluative commentary that is perceptive. There is excellent and nuanced understanding of language, structure, and style in the context of the global issue chosen.

Criterion C: Focus and organisation

What is assessed?

Structure, focus, and balance. The ability to connect ideas coherently.

Marks	Description of level
0	The response does not meet the standards described by the descriptors below.
1–2	There is little focus on the question, and ideas are rarely connected.
3–4	There is some focus on the question, but there may be a lack of balance in how works and texts are discussed. Connections are established between ideas, but not always coherently.
5–6	There is focus on the question, but this may occasionally lapse. Works and texts are discussed in a generally balanced way. Ideas are developed in a logical way, and are clearly connected.
7–8	The oral is generally clear and sustained. Works and texts are discussed in a balanced way. Ideas develop consistently and coherently. The presentation of ideas is convincing.
9–10	The oral is clear and sustained. There is good balance in how works and texts are discussed. The presentation of ideas is logical and convincing, with ideas connected insightfully.

Criterion D: Language

What is assessed?

Clarity, accuracy and effective use of language.

Marks	Description of level
0	The response does not meet the standards described by the following descriptors.
1–2	There is a general lack of clarity and precision. Frequent errors affect communication. Aspects of style are inappropriate.
3–4	There is general clarity. Errors may affect communication. Aspects of style are often inappropriate.
5–6	There is clarity. Errors do not affect communication. Vocabulary and sentence structure are appropriate, but lack variation and sophistication. Aspects of style are appropriate.
7–8	There is clarity and accuracy. There may be small errors, but these do not affect communication. Vocabulary and sentence structure are appropriate and varied. Aspects of style are appropriate and may enhance the oral.
9–10	There is clarity, accuracy, and variation. There may be small errors, but these do not affect communication. Vocabulary and sentence structure are appropriate, varied, and enhance the presentation of ideas. Aspects of style are appropriate and enhance the oral.

Higher level (HL) essay

Criterion A: Knowledge, understanding and interpretation

What is assessed?

Knowledge and understanding of literary works or texts, using appropriate supporting references to make inferences and draw conclusions relevant to the chosen question.

Marks	Description of level
0	The response does not meet the standards described by the following descriptors.
1	There is little knowledge and understanding of the works or texts relevant to the chosen question. There are few references to the work or text, or references are mainly inappropriate.
2	There is some knowledge and understanding of the works or texts relevant to the chosen question. There are some references to the work or text, and these are sometimes appropriate.
3	There is a satisfactory knowledge and understanding of the works or texts relevant to the chosen question. References to the work or text are generally relevant, and generally support claims and arguments.
4	There is a good knowledge and understanding of the works or texts relevant to the chosen question. Claims and arguments are sustained, and supported by references.
5	There is excellent knowledge and understanding of the works or texts relevant to the chosen question. Claims and arguments are persuasive, and supported effectively by well-chosen references.

Criterion B: Analysis and evaluation

What is assessed?

Analysis and evaluation of language, technique and style to establish meaning and effect relevant to the chosen question.

Marks	Description of level
0	The response does not meet the standards described by the following descriptors.
1	The response is descriptive, offering little appropriate analysis relevant to the chosen topic.
2	The response offers some analysis relevant to the chosen topic, but this is mainly descriptive.
3	The response is generally analytical, offering some understanding of the ways in which language, technique, and style establish meaning and effect relevant to the chosen topic.
4	The response is analytical and evaluative, offering understanding of the ways in which language, technique, and style establish meaning and effect relevant to the chosen topic.
5	The response is analytical and evaluative, offering a perceptive and persuasive understanding of the ways in which language, technique, and style establish meaning and effect relevant to the chosen topic.

Criterion C: Focus, organisation and development

What is assessed?

Structure, focus, development of ideas and the integration of examples.

Marks	Description of level
0	The response does not meet the standards described by the following descriptors.
1	There is little attempt at organisation, and no clear development of ideas. Supporting examples are not embedded into the essay.
2	There is some attempt at organisation, although ideas lack development. Supporting examples are rarely embedded into the essay.
3	There is adequate organisation and generally coherent. Ideas are developed. Supporting examples are sometimes embedded into the essay.
4	There is good organisation and the essay is mostly coherent. Ideas are generally well developed. Supporting examples are generally well embedded into the essay.
5	There is effective organisation and the essay is coherent. Ideas are well developed. Supporting examples are well embedded into the essay.

Criterion D: Language

What is assessed?

The ability to write using language which is clear, accurate and varied, in an appropriate academic style and register, and the use of relevant terminology where appropriate.

Marks	Description of level
0	The response does not meet the standards described by the following descriptors.
1	There is little clarity, accuracy, or sense of register, and the language is rarely appropriate.
2	There is some clarity and accuracy, and some sense of an appropriate register, although There are errors.
3	There is adequate clarity and accuracy, and the register is generally appropriate, with occasional errors.
4	There is good clarity and accuracy, and the register is consistently appropriate.
5	There is very good clarity and accuracy, and careful use of language. The register is appropriate and effective.

Exploring text types

Chapter 1

How do the style and structure of a text affect its meaning?
What should you look out for when analysing different types of text?
How do texts adhere to, or break, the conventions of a particular text type?
Why is it important to identify particular features as typical or atypical of a particular text type?

In this chapter you will:

- explore 12 different text types, including magazine covers, advertisements, commercials, cartoons, graphic novels, street art, speeches, newspapers, blogs, prose fiction, plays and poems
- identify and analyse their defining features
- apply your own knowledge to different text types by writing various texts.

Unit 1.1 Images and magazine covers

Word bank

signifier
symbol
icon
logo
composition
negative space
rule of thirds
visual narrative
anchoring
caption
illustration
ears
teasers
headlines
body language
gaze

Learning objectives

- learn how to read visual texts, exploring the relationship between words and images
- develop skills to analyse how meaning is constructed in magazine covers.

In your English A: Language and Literature course you will often be asked to *deconstruct* images. For example, there could be a cartoon on your Paper 1 exam. In class, your teacher may ask you to analyse graphic novels and advertisements. This unit will help you to develop useful skills for deconstructing the images that you can find in a range of texts. Furthermore, you can apply these tools to the type of text that is featured in this unit: the magazine cover.

Getting started

1.1 'An image says a thousand words', as the saying goes. Most likely, you see hundreds of images, photographs and advertisements every day, whether you are conscious of it or not. But how do images communicate ideas? Images communicate ideas through **signifiers**. The message they communicate is what is signified. Texts 1.1–1.3 each depict an apple, the same signifier. What is signified in each image, however, is different. On a copy of the table, indicate what is signified in Texts 1.1–1.3.

Text 1.1

Text 1.2

Text 1.3

Signifier		Signified
Text 1.1 – apple	means	
Text 1.2 – apple	means	
Text 1.3 – apple	means	

1.2 When analysing images, you will need to describe the relationship between *signifiers* and the things they *signify*. An image may be a **symbol**, meaning that it stands for something abstract. A heart, for example is often a symbol of love. An image may be an **icon**, meaning it resembles the thing it represents. In this case, a heart may direct you to the cardiology department of a hospital. A **logo** is a design used to represent an organisation so that the company or organisation becomes associated with the design. On a copy of the table, indicate what is *signified* in Texts 1.4–1.7. Are these images symbols or icons?

Text 1.4

Text 1.5

Text 1.6

Text 1.7

Signifier	What is signified?	Symbol or icon?
Text 1.4 – hammer and sickle		
Text 1.5 – dove		
Text 1.6 – envelope		
Text 1.7 – emoji		

CONCEPT

Communication

People use symbols and icons for *communication* on a daily basis. Think, for example, of emoticons, which are a mix of icons and symbols. Some emoji faces resemble the emotions that they represent, meaning they are icons. Some hand signs, such as a 'thumbs up', are cultural and arbitrary, meaning there is nothing inherent in how they construct meaning. Do you use emojis to communicate? In which context do you use them?

TOK

How do you know what you know? This is the guiding question for theory of knowledge. How do you know that a hammer and sickle are visual symbols for 'communism'? Were you taught this? Did you discover this? Have you only just learnt this by doing Activity 1.2? Think of other symbols which are not inherently obvious in their meaning. Bring an image of a symbol to class and ask your classmates if they know its meaning and how they know this.

1.3 Before you can deconstruct images, it helps to think about how images are constructed. When analysing symbols and their placement in an image, you need to consider an image's **composition**, a term taken from visual arts, which refers to the author's arrangement of objects in relation to each other, the use of colour and contrast, the amount of **negative space**, and the use of light and depth. Study Text 1.8 and answer these questions:

a Why has the creator of this image chosen a white dress?

b What else can you say about the use of colour?

c What is the effect of the dark space behind Gabriela Sabatini?

d As a symbol, what does the milk moustache stand for?

1.4 Photographers do not always place their subject in the centre of their photos. If you were to draw lines over Text 1.8, cutting up the image into three even columns and three even rows, Sabatini's milk moustache appears at the intersection of the top row and the right column. The **rule of thirds**, often applied by artists and photographers, tells us that viewers often look to the places where these three columns and three rows intersect. Study Text 1.9 and divide the image into nine equal-sized boxes, using the rule of thirds. What appears near the intersections of the imaginary columns and lines?

Text 1.8

You thought I'd be endorsing an after-sports drink. And I am. Milk. 2%. Not only is it a better source of potassium than the leading sports drink, but it also has more vitamins and minerals per ounce. And besides tasting great, it happens to go really well with all my outfits.
MILK
What a surprise!™

Text 1.9

1.5 The Russian playwright Anton Chekhov once said: 'Never place a loaded rifle on the stage if it isn't going to go off.' Although Chekhov was speaking about theatre, the same holds true for images. If there is a causal relationship between the signifier and the signified, then there is a **visual narrative**. What does this mean? It means that an image can tell a story. Smoke suggests fire. A bruised eye suggests a fistfight. Comment on the visual narratives of Texts 1.8 and 1.9 by answering these questions:

a What is *signified* in each image?

b What *signifiers* have constructed these meanings?

c What story is being told in these images? What happened *before* each image? What will happen *after* each image?

d How do these stories achieve their respective purpose?

1.6 Imagine Texts 1.8 and 1.9 without any words. It may seem rather funny to see a tennis star with a milk moustache and a giant gorilla with a hurt foot with no explanation. The images' meanings are anchored in the words. **Anchoring** is the process of making an image meaningful by adding words, such as a **caption**. It is also the process of making words meaningful by adding images, such as an **illustration**.

a How does the meaning of the image in Text 1.10, an HSBC advertisement, change when it is anchored in three different captions: 'decor', 'souvenir' and 'place of prayer'?

b How does the meaning of the word 'accomplishment' change when anchored in three different illustrations in Text 1.11?

LEARNER PROFILE

Open-minded

How do Texts 1.10 and 1.11 promote open-mindedness?

Text 1.10

Text 1.11

AOE question

In what ways is meaning discovered, constructed and expressed?

As you can see from Texts 1.10 and 1.11, you can discover meaning by exploring the relationship between images and words. Many mass media texts such as advertisements construct meaning by combining words with images in illustrations and captions.

International mindedness

The HSBC advertisements used for Activity 1.6 (Texts 1.10 and 1.11) are perfect for discussing international mindedness. How can people see the same thing differently? Part of becoming internationally minded is accepting that people may interpret what you see differently and also be right. The last line of the IB mission statement states that 'others, with their differences, can be right'. What does this mean for you?

CONCEPT

Perspective

Notice how Texts 1.10 and 1.11 encourage you to see things from a different *perspective*. As a fun activity, find an interesting advertisement, remove or hide the slogan and ask a classmate to guess the slogan to give the image meaning. How do words give you a perspective on an image or vice versa?

Model text

1.7 Study Text 1.12, a magazine cover depicting US Republican politician Sarah Palin. Read the accompanying box defining the features of a magazine. Have a discussion on how *Newsweek* has depicted Sarah Palin as a strong or weak political figure.

Text 1.12

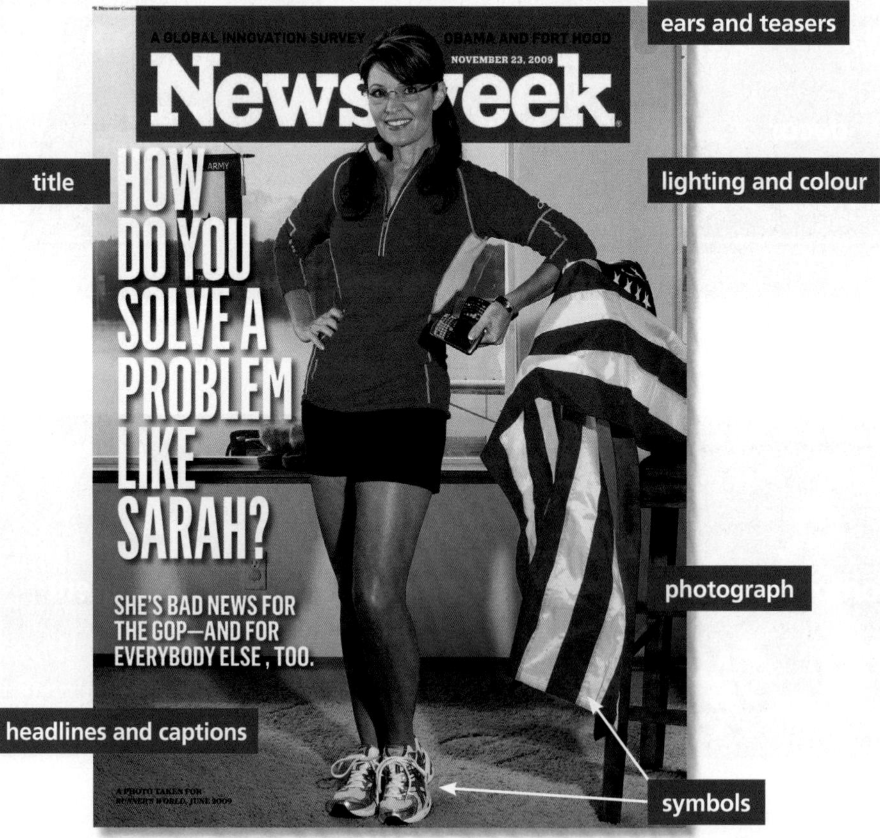

Key features explained

Key features	Examples from Text 1.12
Title: The type of font and its use of colour comment on the nature of the magazine and the context of its readership. Consider how some magazines place their title in front of the subject on the cover, while others place it behind their subject.	Bold, serif and high contrast suggest strength and are often used for opinion magazines such as *Newsweek*.
Ears and **teasers**: The upper left and right corners are known as the 'ears' of the cover. Headlines in the ears are also called 'teasers', as they invite the reader to look inside the newspaper or magazine.	'A Global Innovation Survey' and 'Obama and Fort Hood' appear in the ears and act as teasers.
Headlines and captions: These are statements, questions or phrases which capture the reader's attention and lead the articles. Which lines stand out most?	'How do you solve a problem like Sarah?' captures the reader's attention. The caption 'She's bad news for the GOP – and for everybody else, too' smacks of bias, which is appropriate for opinion magazines.
Photograph: Most magazine covers include photographs of people or people's heads (known as 'headshots'). Consider the camera angle in relation to the subject. Looking down on a subject may make her appear weak. Looking up at a subject may make her appear strong.	The camera is slightly below Sarah Palin's eye level, making her appear relatively strong. However, this full body shot makes her look rather insecure.
Symbols: What goes into the composition? Objects tend to symbolise abstract ideas.	The American flag, the mobile phones (plural!) and Palin's trainers are not arbitrarily placed into the frame. They symbolise something. Can you guess what?
Lighting and colour: Is the lighting crisp or warm? Is there high or low contrast? What associations do you have with the colours? Brighter images generally exude warmth and friendliness.	Notice the use of red, which grabs the reader's attention. Red is in the US flag, the title and Palin's running shirt. It is also the colour of the Republican Party. Her legs reflect and 'shine'.

1.8 In order to analyse photographs of people thoroughly, such as the one of Sarah Palin on the cover of *Newsweek* (Text 1.12), you may need to know more about **body language**. Body language may be considered as a kind of stylistic device or structural feature of a visual text. Study these five aspects of body language and discuss how they relate to Text 1.12. How do they add to or take away from the 'power' that Sarah Palin seems to have?

- *Smiles and teeth*: The mouth can express emotions quite clearly. Smiles, especially those showing teeth, make one look friendly, jovial and affable.
- ***Gaze***: Is the subject looking at the camera, to the side of the camera, or to a faraway place? The subject's gaze has an effect on the reader. Looking away from the camera can make the subject appear aloof, distant or unapproachable. Looking into the camera, however, makes the subject appear engaged with the reader.
- *Position of hands*: Hands matter. Crossed arms tend to make the subject look strong. Fidgeting hands are a sign of weakness.

- *Skin*: Skin means exposure. This may be interpreted as vulnerability, sexual availability or athletic ability, depending on the context.
- *Torso*: If the subject leans forward, they appear eager to engage with the reader or listener. If they lean backward, they seem disengaged.

ATL

Research

Each unit in Chapter 1 explores a different text type. Each unit presents a different 'model text' and 'key features explained'. While definitions from this coursebook may be useful, you should research more examples of each text type and discuss any features that you find typical of the text type. Try to curate a range of text types in your learner portfolio as you study this language and literature course.

Over to you

1.9 Study Text 1.13, a magazine cover featuring Julia Gillard, Australia's first female Prime Minister. Analyse Text 1.13 using the 'Key features' of a magazine cover (Activity 1.7) and the tips for understanding body language (Activity 1.8). Do this as a class by drawing a large table like this one on a whiteboard. Individually write a sticky note for each row of the table, including your ideas about each aspect of the text and body language. Then place your sticky note on the board and read everyone's notes. How similar or different are your ideas from your classmates' ideas? Discuss your answers as a class.

Key feature	Your sticky notes	Body language	Your sticky notes
Title		Smiles and teeth	
Ears and teasers		Gaze	
Headlines		Position of hands	
Photograph		Skin	
Symbols		Torso	
Lighting and colour			

CONCEPT

Representation

Imagine that Text 1.13 depicted a male politician, instead of a female politician. How would the effect of this image be different, if he were to appear in the same position with the same clothing and facial expression? This raises a greater question: 'How are male and female politicians represented differently by the media and for what reasons?' Discuss your answers as a class.

Text 1.13

Further reading

- *This Means This, This Means That: A User's Guide to Semiotics* by Sean Hall is a good starting point for those who are interested in learning more about how meaning is constructed by text and image.
- *Picturing Texts* by Lester Faigley, Diana George, Anna Palchik and Cynthia Selfe offers a well-illustrated introduction to visual literacy and semiotics.

Unit 1.2 Advertisements

Learning objectives

- become familiar with a range of different types of advertisements
- be able to define the key features of print advertisements
- understand the effects of various advertising techniques.

We see advertisements on a daily basis in many different forms. Think of pop-ups in web browsers, billboards on the roadside, commercials on TV or print advertisements in magazines and newspapers. Advertisers will try all kinds of tricks and techniques to grab your interest, even if it is just for a few seconds. This unit introduces you to the conventions of print advertising, and helps you to identify their defining characteristics and features when analysing these texts in class. You may find that seemingly simple advertisements lend themselves well to in-depth textual analysis.

Getting started

2.1 Look at Texts 1.14–1.17: which of them are advertisements? How can you identify them? List the features that these texts have in common.

Text 1.14

Text 1.15

Word bank

banner
sponsored link
marketing
ambient advertising
billboard
guerrilla advertising
product placement
spoof ad
celebrity endorsement
advertorial
commercial
public service announcement
subvertising
visual narrative
copy
tagline
signature
logo
slogan
advertising techniques
problem and benefit
bandwagon effect
testimonial
association

CONCEPT

Creativity

Notice how Texts 1.14–1.17 all relate to a common topic of preserving the environment. How does each text, in its own way, use *creativity* to engage its audience with this topic?

Text 1.17

Text 1.16

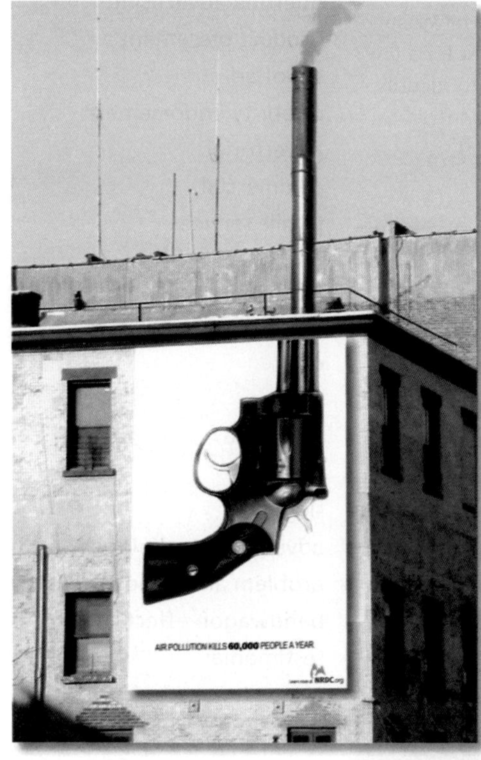

2.2 In fact, Texts 1.14–1.17 are all various forms of modern advertising.

- Text 1.14 is a **banner** or **sponsored link**, a kind of advertisement which is automatically embedded on third-party websites.
- Text 1.15 is a shopping bag, which may be considered **marketing** material for a brand.
- Text 1.16 is a kind of advertisement known as **ambient advertising**, as it utilises physical surroundings to construct meaning.
- Text 1.17, which may not promote a commercial product or company, can still be considered an advertisement, in the form of a **billboard**.

There are many different forms of advertising in the world.

- In small groups research the definition of *one* of the terms listed a–t.
- Each group should work on a different term.
- Research the definition of your term and find an example of it through an online search.
- Present your definition and text to your classmates.

Terms printed in bold are used throughout this coursebook.

a **guerrilla advertising**
b **product placement**
c **spoof ad**
d sponsored content
e interstitial
f publicity stunt
g **celebrity endorsement**
h co-branding
i **advertorial**
j TV **commercial**
k direct mail
l radio advertisement
m **public service announcement**
n branded goods
o social media campaign
p flash mob
q **subvertising**
r outdoor advertising
s transit advertising
t jingle

AOE question

How do texts follow or move away from the conventions associated with different types of text?

Activity 2.2 introduces a range of text types, most of which deviate from the standard conventions of print advertising. What does your text type have in common, if anything, with conventional print advertisements?

Model text

2.3 What are the key features of print advertising? Several structural features are shared by many traditional print advertisements. Study Text 1.18 and the table 'Key features explained'. What features does this text have in common with Texts 1.14–1.17, the less traditional advertisements in this unit?

Text 1.18

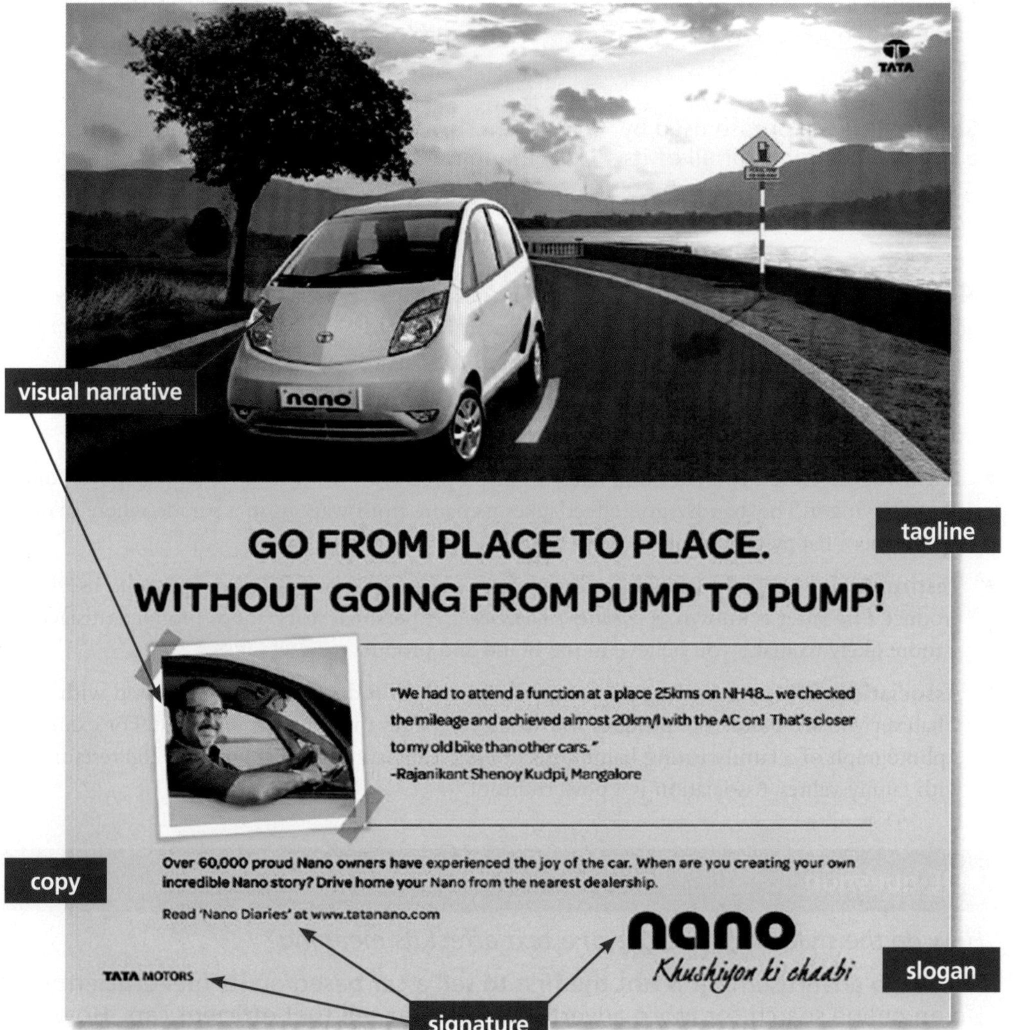

LEARNER PROFILE

Principled

An IB learner is *principled*. Can you list three principles that are important to you in life? What do you believe in? Can you find an advertisement that appeals to one or more of these principles or beliefs? Do some research online and bring an advertisement to class to discuss with your classmates. Add this advertisement to your portfolio and think about how it will connect to a global issue that you are exploring in class.

Key features explained

Key feature	Examples from Text 1.18
Visual narrative: Advertisements usually include a photograph or image which tells a story.	Where is this little yellow car going? Why is the driver smiling? The reader can find answers to these questions in the advertisement.
Copy: This is the term used to describe the text or words in the advertisement.	'Over 60,000 proud Nano owners have experienced the joy of the car.' This is one part of the copy. Mr Shenoy Kudpi's story is another part.
Tagline: This is the catchphrase that leads the advertisement. It should be memorable.	'Go from place to place. Without going from pump to pump!' The use of alliteration and repetition makes this tagline memorable.
Signature: The use of the product's name and **logo** acts as a kind of signature.	The Tata Motors logos appear in the upper right and lower left corners.
Slogan: This is a phrase used by a product or brand for all of its marketing purposes.	'Khushiyon ki chaabi' means 'the key to happiness', which is the Nano slogan in the lower right corner.

TOK

How do you know if a product is worth buying? How do you know if advertisers are telling the truth? Advertisements are great texts for exploring TOK, because they often use reason and language as a means to sell you something. Bring an advertisement to class and present it to your classmates, asking them these two questions. Discuss reason and language, as ways of knowing (WOKs), in relation to your advertisement.

2.4 There are a range of **advertising techniques** used by advertisers to persuade you to buy a product. Can you find evidence of these techniques in Text 1.18?

- **Problem and benefit**: Advertisements may try to blur the lines between what you want and what you need, convincing you of problems that you never knew existed. By creating a problem, they can then offer you a solution.
- **Bandwagon effect**: You are more likely to buy a product if it is the latest rage and everyone else is buying it. The 'bandwagon effect' takes its name from wagons in a parade where many people seem happy to join in.
- **Testimonial:** Many advertisements feature happy customers or famous people who use a product. The latter is known as *celebrity endorsement*. A personal story about product satisfaction is more likely to make you believe in the brand and product.
- **Association:** Where does the product appear, literally? Products become associated with whatever you see beside the product and whatever values those things represent. For example, a photograph of a family eating hamburgers might associate the hamburgers at the restaurant with family values. Association is a powerful tool.

AOE question

How do the style and structure of a text affect its meaning?

The Nano advertisement is not the first to sell a car based on its fuel efficiency. Do an online search for more advertisements that sell fuel-efficient cars. How do they use style and structure similarly or differently? Which advertisement is most convincing and for what reasons?

Over to you

2.5 Design your own advertisement for an imaginary product, such as 'toothpaste for children' or a 'robot vacuum'. Present it to your classmates and comment on your use of structural features and advertising techniques. Ask your classmates how likely they are to buy your product, based on your advertisement.

a Think of a product that may be unique or even slightly silly. You may want this product to be connected to a global issue that you are exploring in your learner portfolio.

b Try to find images online which could form the foundation of your advertisement. These images should tell a story (visual narrative).

c Think of a product name, slogan, tagline and copy to go with the image. Use text-editing software to add layers of text over the image(s) you have found. How do the words add meaning to the images?

d Show your advertisement to a classmate and discuss how typical your advertisement is of the text type.

CONCEPT

Representation

Are you struggling to think of a product to advertise for Activity 2.5? Ask yourself how a certain group of people are often represented in advertisements. Advertisements, after all, play a large role in constructing stereotypes. Can you create an advertisement that breaks these stereotypes by depicting a person or people in a different way from what is expected?

Extended essay

Are you interested in writing your extended essay about advertisements? This is possible under the requirements of the Category 3 extended essay. As you think about a research question for your essay, however, be sure to focus on several advertisements from a single campaign which you can analyse in detail in your essay. Make sure that there are sufficient secondary sources about how the advertisements from this campaign were received. Include (some of) the advertisements in an appendix to the essay.

Further reading

- *Ogilvy on Advertising* is a classic 'how to' book, written by one of the most prominent advertisers of the 20th century, David Ogilvy. His earlier book, *Confessions of an Advertising Man,* also has its place in history.
- *Buyology: Truth and Lies About Why We Buy* by Martin Lindstrom explores the biology behind brand loyalty, offering insights from brain scans of people who view advertisements.
- Rory Sutherland has an interesting TED Talk called 'Life lessons from an ad man', about how advertisements can add value to a product by changing people's perception of the product.
- You may find it interesting to watch an episode from *Mad Men,* a TV series about advertising agencies in the 1960s in the USA. An online search for 'Don Draper's Kodak Carousel as pitch' will reveal a video for discussion.

Unit 1.3
Film and commercials

Word bank

cinematography
public service announcement
still
dystopia
mise en scène
camera angle
camera shot
dolly
pan
zoom
diegetic sound
non-diegetic sound
voice-over
montage
allegory

Learning objectives

- gain a better understanding of how film as a medium can be used to construct meaning
- appreciate a range of different kinds of commercials.

Most likely you have been to the cinema, watched online videos or even made your own movie on a smartphone or other device. But have you ever thought about how the language of film constructs meaning? Remember that the words 'text' and 'language', as used in your language and literature course, are broad terms. A film could be considered a 'text' and **cinematography** may be considered part of the language of film. In this unit, you will study how meaning is constructed through the language of film, by exploring several commercials and **public service announcements**.

Getting started

3.1 Get into small groups and assign each group a different video from the bullet list provided. As a group, do an online search for your commercial or public service announcement, using the name of the commercial from the list. Watch your commercial a few times and prepare a presentation on it for your classmates. Present your group's commercial to your classmates by following these steps:

a Give your classmates a question to consider before playing the commercial. Then show them your commercial and ask them to answer your question.

b Show your classmates three important '**stills**' from your commercial. A still is a freeze-frame from the video. For each still, explain why you think it captures the spirit of the advertisement.

c Play your commercial again for your classmates, but this time without any sound. What is lost? What is preserved? Discuss your answers to these two questions with your classmates.

d After you have seen each presentation, explain in which ways your commercial was different from everyone else's commercial.

Suggested commercials to consider for Activity 3.1

- 'Proud to Be (Mascots)' by National Congress of American Indians
- 'Onslaught' by Dove
- 'Imported from Detroit' by Chrysler
- 'Listen' by No More
- 'The Force' by Volkswagen

Extended essay

It is recommended that you write your extended essay on one of the six subjects that you are taking (if you are taking the full IB Diploma). Keep in mind that film is an entire field of research and study. In fact, it is an IB subject in itself.

If you want to write your essay about a film or commercial, read the requirements for a Category 3 extended essay and see how you can meet them.

AOE question

How can comparing and interpreting texts transform readers?

After watching the 'Onslaught' commercial by Dove, try watching 'Onslaught(er)' by Greenpeace and compare the two. How does this comparison transform the way you think about Dove, Greenpeace and palm oil?

TOK

How do commercials appeal to the imagination of the viewer? In TOK you may have learnt that imagination is a way of knowing (WOK). As you explore various commercials in Activity 3.1, discuss the role of imagination in constructing meaning.

Model text

3.2 When analysing film, there is a lot to consider. Do an online search for '1984 Apple Super Bowl commercial'. Discuss your answers to these questions:

a Imagine that the year is 1984 and you have never heard of the Apple Macintosh computer. Based on your viewing of this commercial, what would you think of the product?

b What do you think of the commercial? What is your gut feeling or initial response? What makes you say this?

c What is the message of this commercial?

d How does the director, Ridley Scott, use film as a medium to convey a message to you, the viewer?

e Read the 'Key features explained' table. Did you already know some of these terms? To what degree do these terms help you articulate your answers from questions a–d here?

AOE question

How useful is it to describe a work as 'classic'?

The '1984' Apple Macintosh commercial has become something of a 'classic' in the advertising world. The novel to which it alludes is a classic in the world of English literature. Why do you think people are drawn to **dystopian** stories, like the one depicted in Ridley Scott's commercial?

TEXT AND CONTEXT

You can learn more about Ridley Scott's famous commercial '1984' by doing an online search for 'The making of Apple's "1984" commercial – with Ridley Scott' or 'The real story behind Apple's famous "1984"Super Bowl ad'.

Key features explained

Key feature	Examples from 1984 Apple Super Bowl commercial
Mise en scène: This refers to what goes into the frame, including the subjects, backdrop and props. It also refers to the positioning of everything or the composition of the shot, including the lighting.	The large room, where men with shaved heads sit staring at Big Brother on the screen, is featured in many scenes. The gas masks, the boots, the grey clothing and tunnel all contribute to the dystopian atmosphere. The use of colour in the hammer thrower's clothing is sharply contrasted with the blues and greys in the scene, suggesting she brings hope and change.
Camera angle. What is the angle of the camera in relation to its subject? Is it a bird's-eye view, high angle, eye-level angle, low angle or worm's-eye view?	The scene opens with a bird's-eye view of a transparent tunnel, where we see the heads of prisoners marching. There is a worm's-eye view of the boots, and eye-level shots of the prisoners.
Camera shot: The distance between the camera and the subject is important to consider. You may see an extreme-close shot (XCS), a close shot (CS), medium shot (MS), long shot (LS) or extreme long shot (XLS) (see the diagram on perspective). Does the camera move or stay still in relation to its subject? Sometimes the camera is put on a **dolly**. Sometimes it rotates on its access, creating a **pan**. Cameras can also **zoom** in and out, often in combination with camera movement for special effects. Finally, consider the length or duration of the shot, which will help determine the pace of the film.	The camera is on a dolly as it pans along the rows of prisoners. Close-up shots of the prisoners' faces, as they march or sit, give the impression that they are brainwashed like zombies. The running woman with her hammer approaches the camera, which switches between her getting closer, the guards chasing her and Big Brother speaking. Each shot zooms in on its subject more and more, intensifying the experience for the viewer.
Diegetic and **non-diegetic sound**: Sounds which are created by the characters, objects or events on the screen, such as dialogue, are known as diegetic sounds. Sounds with an unknown source, added after filming, such as music, are known as non-diegetic sound.	The sound of Big Brother speaking is at first non-diegetic and then later diegetic, which creates suspense. The hammer thrower's scream, as she throws her hammer at the screen, seems to cut through all of the background robotic noises. The prisoners make a strange singing noise in response to the exploding screen, as the **voice-over** tells us about Apple's new computer.
Montage: How are all of the shots and music put together? The skill of editing and joining shots to get a particular effect is called 'montage'.	The shots switch between the woman with the hammer and the prisoners with increasing frequency. This creates tension and suspense, as the reader sees the inevitable conflict between her and the guards and Big Brother. The final text about the launch of the new Apple Macintosh frames the whole scene as an allusion to the novel *Nineteen Eighty-Four*.

TOK

The 1984 Super Bowl commercial for the Apple Macintosh is an allusion to the novel *Nineteen Eighty-Four* by George Orwell. But it also resembles Greek philosopher Plato's *Allegory of the Cave*, which suggests that humans might be like prisoners trapped in a cave making observations that are not real. Find out more about Plato's **allegory**, and discuss the parallels between his ideas and Ridley Scott's commercial.

CONCEPT

Perspective

When we analyse a director's use of camera angle or shot duration, we are really talking about *perspective*. Film directors carefully choose how they film their stories in order to give their audiences a different perspective on a topic or theme. Remember to use the word 'perspective' frequently when analysing film.

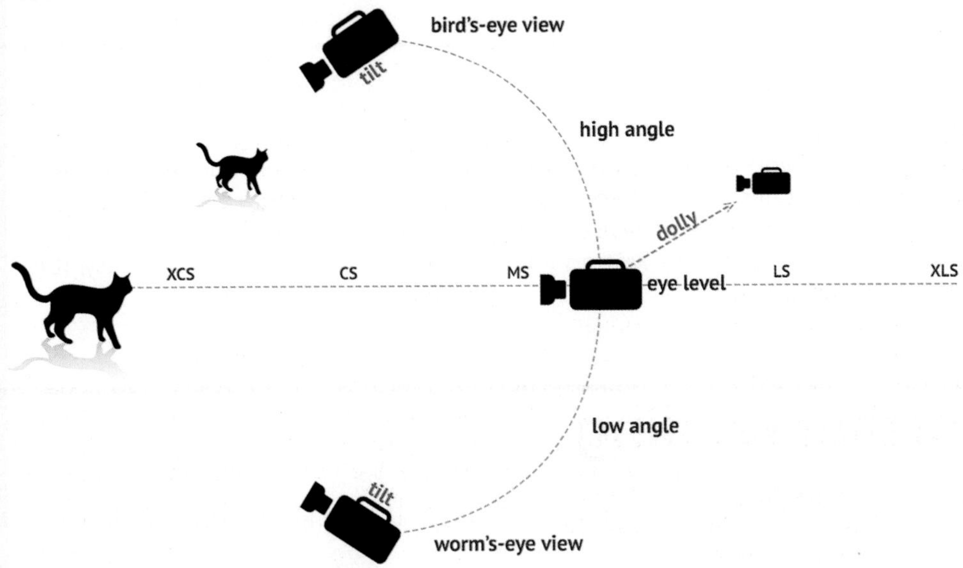

Cinematography is a term used to refer to camera work, including use of light, mise en scène, camera angle, shot distance, shot movement, shot duration, sound and montage.

3.3 After reading the 'Key features explained', return to the commercials that you explored in your presentations for Activity 3.1. Watch them again and prepare another brief presentation on one of them. In this presentation, use the terminology that you have learnt and apply it to your group's commercial. Explain how the 'key features' helped you understand these commercials better. Discuss as a class.

International mindedness

Have you ever seen a commercial in a language that you cannot understand? It is an interesting cultural experience. If possible, show your classmates a commercial in a language that you understand but they do not. Ask them what cultural differences they see. Ask them what they think the commercial is about. Then explain it to them. Alternatively, you can watch a foreign commercial without subtitles before watching it with subtitles. How do commercials differ from culture to culture?

Over to you

3.4 Shoot your own 60-second commercial. Create an imaginary product and think of a way to sell it, using film as a medium. Consider all of the points mentioned in the 'Key features explained' section. You may want to work in groups or individually. You could use either a smartphone or a video camera. Your commercial does not have to sound or look professional in order for it to be effective. Present your commercial to the class and explain the choices that you had to make in creating it.

CAS

How are you recording your CAS experiences? Are you creating a video journal? You may want to consider this medium for documenting and reflecting on the activities that you undertake, so that others can appreciate what you have done. If you film your experiences, consider what you have learnt from this unit on film as a medium.

ATL

Communication

Activity 3.4 asks you to make your own short commercial. As you develop your communication skills in the diploma programme, try making a few videos. So many people rely on video these days, as a means of persuading, entertaining or informing audiences. Try writing your own script. Although it is not easy, it is certainly a useful skill.

Further reading

- *The Filmmaker's Eye* by Gustavo Mercado is an excellent book for understanding the nuts and bolts of cinematography.
- *101 Things I Learned in Film School* by Neil Landau is a highly simplistic but effective list of tips on how to construct meaning, using a (video) camera. These short paragraphs and drawings will make you think more about the art of story-telling in general.

Unit 1.4
Political cartoons

Learning objectives

- understand the way meaning is constructed in political cartoons
- learn the skills to analyse some political cartoons, including several from the Cold War.

Word bank

public opinion
bias
caricature
symbolism
labelling
caption
irony
situational irony
topical

Public opinion is often reflected in cartoons or comic strips in newspapers or on websites. Political cartoons, specifically, aim to comment on politics and public figures. They often combine drawings and words into a single frame to succinctly criticise policies or people in a humorous way. This unit introduces you to several political cartoons and the methods they use to construct meaning.

Getting started

4.1 Texts 1.19 and 1.21 give you two perspectives on the Soviet Union and USA during the Cold War. Text 1.20 comments on more recent relations between Russia and Ukraine. The Soviet-era cartoons have been translated. Study these three texts and discuss your answers to these questions:

a How does each cartoon show an opinion on a political matter? Where do you see evidence of **bias**?

b Comment on the style of all three cartoonists. How do they use drawings to express their opinions?

c How dated are these cartoons? How meaningful are they in the current political context?

Text 1.19

Text 1.20

Text 1.21

The title translates as 'Phases and . . . bases'. The words from the broadcaster in the back pocket are 'Peace', 'Defence', 'Disarmament'.

AOE question

How can cultural contexts influence how texts are written and received?

As you explore Texts 1.19 and 1.21, consider what you know already about US–Soviet relations during the Cold War. How do these cartoons give you a better understanding of this and how each country viewed the other?

International mindedness

In order to develop international mindedness, you will need to develop a sense of history and a willingness to look at other people's perspectives on past events. While English is the target language of this course, it is important to look at texts in translation, including political cartoons from other cultures and times than your own. As in Activity 4.1, try to find political cartoons that express both sides of a political conflict.

Model text

4.2 Do an online search for a political cartoon that depicts Russian President Vladimir Putin. In a short presentation, compare your cartoon to Text 1.22. Use the 'Key features explained' section to prepare your comparative analysis. Complete a copy of this table.

	Text 1.22	Another Putin cartoon
Caricature		
Symbolism		
Labelling and captions		
Irony		
Topical		

Text 1.22

caricature
topical
symbolism
BORIS YELTSIN FREED RUSSIA FROM ITS AUTHORITARIAN PAST
NOW I CAN BUILD A BETTER FUTURE
THE NEW AND IMPROVED! AUTHORITARIAN RUSSIA
BY V. PUTIN
KAL 2007 The Economist
labelling and captions
irony

LEARNER PROFILE

Knowledgeable

An IB learner is knowledgeable. You may find political cartoons a fun way of keeping up with news and world politics. While good political cartoons are topical, they are also biased. Take this into consideration as you study them.

ATL

Research

The IB asks you to develop your research skills. Activity 4.2 asks you to find a political cartoon that depicts Vladimir Putin. How are you going to do this? Will you simply type 'Vladimir Putin political cartoon' into a search engine? This could lead to very simplistic results. Instead you may want to start with other terms, such as 'political cartoon' in combination with 'research guide' or 'database' to find out where to begin.

Key features explained

Key feature	Examples from Text 1.22
Caricature: Cartoonists often exaggerate the facial features of political figures as a comment on the person's character. This is a process known as caricature.	The caricature of Vladimir Putin depicts his lack of emotion. He seems detached, cold and determined.
Topical: What makes a political cartoon political is that it is topical. It comments critically on a current affair, a much discussed political figure or a recent event. Political cartoons tend to comment on the news.	Vladimir Putin was in the news in 2007 as he was running for President of Russia for a second term.
Symbolism: Political cartoons must succinctly communicate abstract ideas through concrete objects. Icons and symbols do this effectively.	The bear is a common symbol for Russia. The star on the bear's hat is a common symbol for the Soviet Union. By taking the statue of the bear down, the cartoon suggests there will be a change from Soviet times.
Labelling and **captions**: Cartoons often use labels and captions in order to make their message and any use of symbolism clear.	The pedestal reads: 'The new and improved authoritarian Russia', which adds meaning to the image of Putin dismantling the old iconic bear.
Irony: Many political cartoons highlight the irony of a particular situation. Irony is when one means the opposite of what one says. **Situational irony** occurs when one's actions have the opposite of the intended effect.	The cartoonist suggests that Boris Yeltsin freed Russia from its authoritarian past so that it could elect a dictator. This is rather ironic.

4.3 Think of an issue or person currently in the news, in your own country or region, or in the global news. Do an online search for political cartoons about this person, issue or event.

a Place the cartoon in the middle of a digital document or piece of paper. In the margins, label the features of your cartoon and write comments about how these features construct meaning and express an opinion.

b Share your document digitally or display your page for others in your class to see and read.

c Have a classroom discussion about your chosen issue or person, and share opinions about these current affairs.

Over to you

4.4 Do an online search for '*New Yorker* Cartoon Caption Contest'. Every week, this magazine presents a cartoon without a caption. You can submit a suggested caption, vote for nominated captions or view previous winners. Try writing a caption for the cartoon of the week, adding meaning to the cartoon. Share your caption with your classmates and discuss which ones you think are the best.

CONCEPT

Creativity

Activity 4.4 asks you to invent a caption in response to an existing cartoon. *Creativity* is one of the key concepts of this course. You can have a lot of fun creating captions for cartoons or taglines for advertisements. Often, when you are in a position to create, you have to be analytical as well. Even though creativity is not assessed in this course, you are encouraged to write your own texts, draw your own cartoons or make up your own advertisements.

Extended essay

The featured cartoon by Kevin Kallaugher (Text 1.22) is one of many that you may want to explore. His website provides a very broad range of his political cartoons about the USA and world politics. A good Category 3 research question might read: 'To what degree have Kevin Kallaugher's cartoons shown equal criticism of US Presidents over the past 40 years?'

Further reading

- *The Complete Cartoons of the New Yorker* edited by Robert Mankoff is a nearly inexhaustible book of fun.
- *The Art of Controversy: Political Cartoons and Their Enduring Power* by Victor S. Navasky offers insightful analysis into history's more controversial cartoons.

Unit 1.5
Comics and graphic novels

Word bank

comic
graphic novel
caricature
symmetry
memoir
cartoon
satire
negative space
speech bubble
thought bubble
voice-over
panel
gutter
symbol
emanata
camera angle
punchline
cartoonification

Learning objectives

- learn how meaning is constructed in comics and graphic novels
- become familiar with terminology for analysing comics and graphic novels.

The art of the **comic** book or comic strip has been around for a long time. Arguably, the humorous drawings of monks in medieval manuscripts were not too dissimilar from some modern-day comics. Comics are often associated with childhood and growing up, as if they are perceived as 'easier' texts to read than novels or poetry. This is not to say, however, that comic books cannot be literary. Comics can explore serious topics effectively and they can have a high artistic quality. Comics of this type are often referred to as **graphic novels**.

This unit introduces you to comics and graphic novels by showing you an example of each. You are given several helpful tools for deconstructing comics, which you may want to use if you should decide to read a graphic novel in class.

Getting started

5.1 Study Text 1.23 – the opening page from *Persepolis*, a graphic novel by Marjane Satrapi about growing up in Iran in the 1980s. Discuss your answers to these questions:

a What is the first thing you notice when you look at this page? Write down one or two words on a sticky note and place them on a wall for your classmates to see and discuss.

b Which features of this text make it a 'graphic novel'? As a class, make a list of what you think are the key features of graphic novels (without looking ahead to the next section).

c Why do you think the artist chose this medium and style in order to write her memoir about growing up in Iran in the 1980s?

d What do you predict will happen next in this graphic novel?

LEARNER PROFILE

Inquirer

Activity 5.1 asks you to predict what will happen in the graphic novel *Persepolis* after studying its first page. Making predictions about texts is a good way to engage with them and make your reading experience more meaningful. Making predictions and testing hypotheses are ways of being an inquirer. You can never ask too many questions or be too curious when analysing texts.

TOK

Can comic books be considered 'art'? In TOK you are asked to consider whether there are universal definitions of art. Art critics often look to technique or mastery of skill when defining art. Do Texts 1.23 and 1.24 seem skilfully created? Is this a prerequisite of art?

Text 1.23

AOE question

How do the style and structure of a text affect its meaning?

Consider this question in relation to Text 1.23. The artist, Marjane Satrapi, has made many choices in depicting her life this way. Why has she chosen to use only black and white? Why does she open with two frames of herself in nearly the same position? Continue to ask questions like this as you do Activity 5.2.

Extended essay

If you like *Persepolis*, you may want to write an extended essay about it. It is a very accessible and fascinating work. You may want to read the sample HL essay in Chapter 7 about it for inspiration as well. If you should write about this work, keep in mind that it was originally written in French. So you will have to compare it to another work to meet the Category 2 extended essay requirement. A good research question might read: 'In what ways and for what reasons do Joe Sacco and Marjane Satrapi depict marginalised people in *Palestine* and *Persepolis*?' This question will allow you to compare and contrast style and technique in a meaningful way. See Unit 4.1 for an extract from *Palestine*.

5.2 Either working on your own or in a small group, choose a word from this list. Look up the definition of your word if you are not already familiar with it. Explain to your classmates how the term is relevant to the extract from Text 1.23.

caricature	symbolism	heading	**symmetry**	dialogue	voice-over
memoir	**cartoon**	**satire**	uniformity	point of view	juxtaposition

Model text

5.3 After you have discussed the terms from Activity 5.2, try to find evidence of these same terms in Text 1.24, a comic strip called *Calvin and Hobbes*.

Text 1.24

International mindedness

How does this comic strip comment on the importance of international mindedness? How does it comment on the nature of war and make a case for diplomacy?

Key features explained

Key feature	Examples from Text 1.23
Negative space: Any time you analyse a piece of visual art, it is important to comment both on what is included and what is left out. Negative space or blank space has a purpose.	The negative space in the opening panel allows readers to get into the story quickly. It creates room for Hobbes's philosophical question as well.
Speech bubble: In comics, readers read characters' dialogue through their speech bubbles. **Thought bubbles**, often depicted with cloud-like bubbles, can let the reader know what a character is thinking. **Voice-over**, a term often used in film, can also be used in comics, with a narrator's words appearing above or below the panel. Keep in mind that the writer does not have much space for long prose in comics.	The dialogue of this story uses speech bubbles, meaning the reader is a distant observer eavesdropping on Calvin and his imaginary friend Hobbes.
Panel: At first glance you will notice that comics are divided into multiple frames or panels. These panels help build a sense of time and space. Some panels do not even have a frame.	This comic strip strikes a balance between square and rectangular frames. Bill Watterson uses distinct lines to give the reader a window into Calvin's world.
Gutter: What happens between the panels? In comics, the reader actively has to 'fill in the gap', and make assumptions about what happens between frames or panels. This space between panels is known as the 'gutter'. If we follow the design principle of 'what is left out is as important as what is included', then the gutter plays a key role in constructing meaning.	What happens between the sixth and seventh panel? It seems that after Calvin and Hobbes's violent episode (panel 6), they are not sure who hit whom first with their dart guns (panel 7). It remains a mystery for the reader as well, because we do not know what happened in between. This may be Bill Watterson's way of saying that war is a mystery with no clear winners.
Symbols: Like political cartoons, comics have to convey a message succinctly. Symbols are useful in communicating abstract ideas effectively.	Calvin's helmet and dart gun symbolise a young child's fascination with war. It is through these symbols and the dialogue that the artist, Bill Watterson, comments critically on the purpose of war.
Emanata: This curious term refers to the dots, lines, exclamation marks, tear drops or any other drawings that can depict emotion, motion or sound.	In this comic strip, little lines appear near the muzzle of Calvin and Hobbes's dart guns, suggesting a firing noise. This is an example of emanata.
Camera angle: It may seem strange to think of camera angle when analysing a drawing, but cartoonists use angles all the time to give their readers a perspective on their characters.	In this comic strip, Bill Watterson depicts Calvin looking up. It is as if the reader looks down on Calvin as an adult might look. Hobbes is often at eye level. This is especially the case in panel 7.
Punchline: This feature is typical of comic strips, as they tend to build up to a single phrase or word which makes one want to laugh.	'Kind of a stupid game, isn't it?' says Calvin in the last panel. This captures the message of the comic strip as it comments critically on war itself, not just the game called 'war'.

> **TIP**
>
> A comic strip may appear on your Paper 1 exam. Using correct terminology in relation to this text type, such as 'emanate' and 'gutter', may help you on Criterion D: Language. Do not forget to define any stylistic feature and explain how its use affects the reader. This will help you on Criterion B: Analysis and evaluation.

5.4 Can you apply the terminology from the 'Key features explained' section to Text 1.23, the first page from *Persepolis*? Discuss the relevance of each term, with the exception of 'punchline', which will not be relevant here. How do these terms help you understand the structural features of Satrapi's memoir? Had you already discussed their relevance in Activity 5.2 without using these terms?

5.5 Besides being able to define the key features of graphic novels and cartoons, it is useful to be able to analyse the style of a cartoonist. Scott McCloud, in his book *Understanding Comics*, explains that there are five scales on which viewers can analyse the artist's level of **cartoonification**. Study Images A–D. The most cartoonified drawings on the left are simple, iconic, subjective, universal and abstract. The least cartoonified images on the right are complex, realistic, objective, specific and concrete. Where would you place Marjane Satrapi's *Persepolis* (Text 1.23) on these scales? Discuss her style in relation to these terms.

Image A	Image B	Image C	Image D
Simple	⟵	⟶	Complex
Iconic	⟵	⟶	Realistic
Subjective	⟵	⟶	Objective
Universal	⟵	⟶	Specific
Abstract	⟵	⟶	Concrete

Image A

Hobbes, the soft toy: in the comic strip *Calvin and Hobbes*, Hobbes (the tiger) appears this way to everyone but Calvin. It could be said that this is the simplest, most subjective yet universal, iconic and abstract tiger of Images A–D.

Image B

This is how Hobbes is most often depicted in the comic strip, as Calvin sees his imaginary friend. Notice that he is slightly more detailed, more human and complex than the soft toy in Image A.

Image C

This is a piece of fan art, which is artwork created by a fan, as a homage to the original artist. It is much more detailed, realistic and complex than Watterson's original versions of Hobbes in Images A and B.

Image D

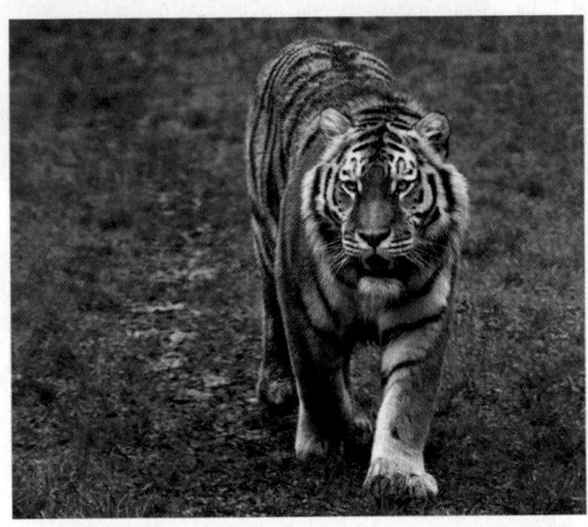

Photographs are at the far end of the continuum of cartoonification, as they are as close to being concrete, specific, realistic, objective and complex as possible.

CONCEPT

Representation

'Cartoonification' may seem like a silly word. Think of this term as a form of *representation*, a key concept in this course. Why would an artist want to turn any subject into a cartoon? What are the advantages of representing something or someone as a cartoon?

Over to you

5.6 Are there any comic strips that you like to read? Search for a comic strip or page from a graphic novel and bring this into class for a 'show and tell' session. Show your classmates what you brought and tell them why you like it. Make a collage of your class's favourite comics and graphic novels. On the edges of this collage place some of the key terms from this unit, along with your own definitions of them. You may find this activity a good preparation for the study of a graphic novel in class.

TIP

You may find a comic strip on a topic that you would like to explore in your individual oral, by comparing it to a passage from a literary text or poem. You may also come across a comic strip in your Paper 1 exam. You can prepare for this by writing a mock Paper 1 commentary on Text 1.24 or anything your classmates or teacher brought to class for Activity 5.6. For further ideas, see Chapter 5 for a student's Paper 1 commentary on a comic strip.

Further reading

- *Understanding Comics* is a seminal work in its field. Even if you are not interested in comics, it is worth reading Scott McCloud's explanation of this genre. He has used the comic book medium effectively as a way of exploring all facets of the medium.
- *99 Ways to Tell a Story: Exercises in Style* by Matt Madden tells the most banal story in 99 interesting ways. Each retelling of the story explores a different genre of the comic strip.
- *Persepolis*, *Palestine* and *Maus*, all of which are memoirs, are popular graphic novels for the English language and literature classroom.

Unit 1.6 Street art

Word bank

graffiti
ephemeral
street art
social commentary
guerrilla art
situational irony
icon
symbol
stencil
trompe l'oeil
mural

Learning objectives

- develop your analytical skills by deconstructing street art as a text type
- appreciate how the context of street art helps shape its meaning.

Have you ever thought of **graffiti** as 'art' or as a 'text'? There are, of course, many types of graffiti, such as tags, posters and stickers, all of which aim to convey meaning. But when can they be considered artistic? If the creators are guilty of defacing public property, can they be considered artists? If their identities are anonymous, can they be considered artists? If their work is **ephemeral**, meaning it is temporary, can it be considered art? If a person removes the artist's work from a public space and sells it to a private gallery, is it then art or copyright infringement?

Aside from such philosophical questions, this unit explores **street art** as a type of text with structural and stylistic conventions. Because most street art is unconventional, this unit will focus on the conventions of one artist and his work. While his real name is unknown, he is commonly referred to as Banksy.

Getting started

6.1 Study Text 1.25 and discuss your answers to these questions:

a Why do you think Banksy created this piece?

b Why has Banksy depicted a child in bare feet?

c Why has Banksy included a streamer of Union Jack flags, the flag of the UK?

d Why is a sewing machine depicted?

e How do you think Banksy made this piece? Literally, what kinds of materials and methods were used? How do you think this choice of materials affected the message of the image?

f Do you consider this as 'art'?

Text 1.25

6.2 Study Text 1.26, which was made in Cheltenham, UK in 2014. Cheltenham is where the United Kingdom Government Communication Headquarters is located. Compare it to Text 1.25. What do they have in common? Do you see similarities in style, structure or message?

Text 1.26

LEARNER PROFILE

Risk taker

Graffiti artists or street artists are certainly risk takers. Defacing public property is a crime in many countries, and artists risk punishment for getting caught. Are artists such as Banksy justified in breaking the law? Can you think of a scenario in which making street art is a risk that needs to be taken?

Model text

Text 1.27

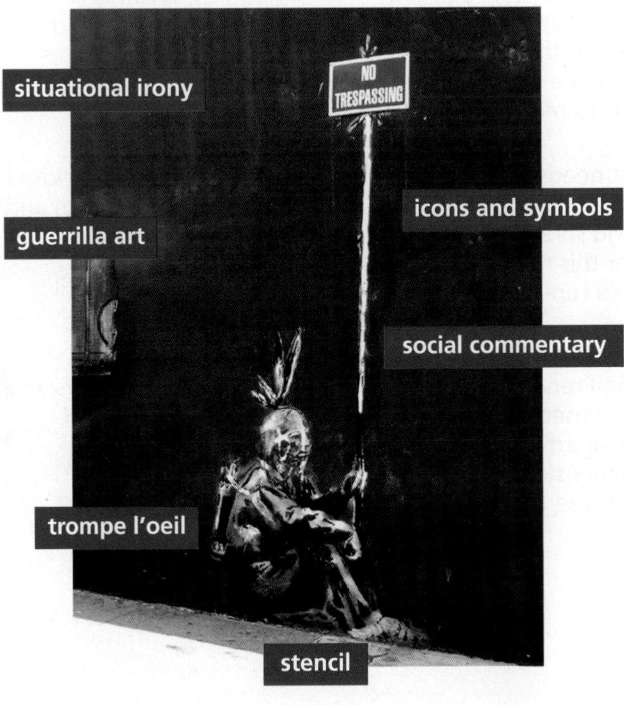

TOK

How do we know when something qualifies as 'art'? Generally speaking, people use three criteria to define 'art':

a mastery of technique or skill

b audience reception

c the creator's intention.

You may find these three criteria useful for analysing any text, visual or written. Do an online search for graffiti 'tags' (a kind of signature) and discuss why these examples may or may not be considered art. Can you think of other criteria for defining 'art'?

CONCEPT

Communication

Street art is a form of *communication*, like any other text. After studying Texts 1.25–1.27, think about what Banksy is aiming to communicate. What is the underlying message of each of these pieces?

Key features explained

Key feature	Examples from Text 1.27
Social commentary: Many graffiti artists aim to make a political statement with their work.	Banksy's work comments on the USA's treatment of Native Americans and questions ownership rights to land.
Guerrilla art: Artists often integrate pre-existing physical objects and public space into their work to help create meaning. Guerrilla art blurs the external boundaries of the artwork.	Banksy has integrated the 'No trespassing' sign into his artwork featuring the Native American, in order to make a political statement.
Situational irony: Like political cartoons, street art often uses irony. By integrating physical space into art, graffiti artists can create situational irony as well.	It is ironic that Banksy defaced a piece of property on which he is not allowed to trespass. It is ironic that a Native American, whose land was taken, should hold up a 'No trespassing' sign.
Icons and **symbols:** Street art communicates succinctly through the use of icons and symbols. Icons are images that look like the concepts they represent. Symbols are like signs that we have been taught to read.	The Native American, as depicted here by Banksy, is rather iconic. The character's headdress, arrows and clothing are almost stereotypical.
Stencil: Street art needs to be made quickly, to avoid being caught by the police. Stencils and spray paint are effective tools for this reason. It also allows the artist to replicate the work easily.	Banksy's Native American is a combination of stencil and free painting with spray paint.
Trompe l'oeil: This French phrase for 'deceive the eye' is used with reference to two-dimensional art that gives the viewer a three-dimensional impression. Many street artists use trompe l'oeil.	Banksy's Native American appears to be sitting on the ground.

6.3 You have now looked at three works by Banksy. Imagine that you could interview Banksy for a magazine or website:

a What kinds of question would you ask him? Write a list of questions that would elicit interesting responses and allow him to comment on his art. Consider the key features of street art as explored in the previous section.

b Do some online research on Banksy to learn more about the kinds of works he has done. If you have time, watch the documentary *Exit through the Gift Shop*. See if you can find answers to your questions.

c Think of an appropriate magazine or website for your interview with Banksy. Read an article from that magazine in which an artist is interviewed. Consider the author's style and the conventions of this text type.

d Write your article as if you had interviewed Banksy. How do you think he would have answered your questions? Use your imagination to make the article interesting for your target audience.

e Share your article with your teacher and classmates. Discuss the merits of your work and reflect on this activity.

Over to you

6.4 Research the work of another popular street artist from this list of well-known artists or anyone else you know.

a Bring an image of a piece of street art by your chosen artist into class and analyse its use of the 'key features' and any other prominent stylistic and structural devices.

b Comment on your chosen piece of street art in a brief presentation. Refer to any contextual information that you can find on the artist and his or her works.

- Shepard Fairey
- Vhils
- Invader
- Blu
- Swoon
- Anthony Lister
- OSGEMEOS
- Keith Haring
- Blek le Rat.
- ROA
- Mr. Brainwash

AOE question

How can texts offer insights into other cultures?

Activity 6.4 lists street artists from around the world. If you consider that art is often a response to something, then what are these artists responding to? Consider these questions when preparing your presentation on one of their works.

Further reading

- *Exit through the Gift Shop* is a documentary by Banksy about a street artist, Thierry Guetta (or Mr. Brainwash), making a documentary about street art. It raises questions about the value of street art and authenticity.
- *Banksy: Wall and Piece* is a book by Banksy in which he comments on his own art and how he utilises physical space and context to construct meaning.

Extended essay

After watching your classmates present and critique street art, you may find inspiration for an extended essay. You can explore street art as a Category 3 extended essay, because visual texts are part of the 'language' course. If you do this, be sure to find a suitable selection of primary sources by one or two artists, and relevant secondary sources that comment on how the works have been received. A good research question might read: 'In what ways did the work of Keith Haring raise awareness, challenge stereotypes and break taboos about AIDS in the late 1980s?'

CAS

Have you ever thought about the power of **murals**? You can greatly improve a neighbourhood by creating a beautiful and meaningful mural. What is the difference between murals and graffiti? Murals require permission and often serve a community purpose. Making one as a CAS project is very appropriate, as you will be engaging in creative, service-based learning.

Unit 1.7 Speeches

Word bank

rhetorical device
paralanguage
anaphora
diacope
antithesis
chiasmus
anadiplosis
amplification
metaphor
alliteration
tricolon
appeal
ethos
pathos
logos
argument
parallelism
hypophora
repetition
figurative speech
polysyndeton
allusion
target audience
persona

Learning objectives

- learn to identify several commonly used rhetorical devices and discuss how they construct meaning
- develop the skills to analyse how context helps shape the language and meaning of speeches.

Throughout this course, you will study speeches and the contexts in which they were spoken. You will be asked to consider: what makes a speech engaging for its audience? Great speeches are full of interesting **rhetorical devices**, several of which will be explored in this unit. But most important, in your study of speeches, is to explore the potential *effects* of these devices on their audiences. This unit will give you the tools to deconstruct and analyse speeches by introducing you to several rhetorical devices and getting you to look closely at two great speeches.

TIP

For any speech that you explore in class, you may want to do an online search to see or hear the speech being delivered. Hearing a speech and watching the speaker will allow you to appreciate their use of **paralanguage**. Paralanguage refers to the non-lexical component of communication, such as facial expressions, pitch, intonation, speed of speaking and gestures.

Getting started

7.1 How much do you already know about rhetorical devices? Nine rhetorical devices are introduced here in a matching exercise. Match the quotations in the left column with their rhetorical devices and counter examples on the right.

1 'Ask not what your country can do for you, but what you can do for your country.' – John F. Kennedy	**a** **Anaphora**: the repetition of word or phrase at the beginning of a sentence, such as 'I have a dream' (Martin Luther King).
2 'We will have no truce or parley with you, or the grisly gang who work your wicked will.' – Winston Churchill	**b** **Diacope**: the repetition of a phrase, after an intervening word or phrase such as 'Free at last, free at last; thank God almighty, free at last!' (Martin Luther King).
3 'We shall fight on the beaches, we shall fight on the landing grounds, we shall fight in the fields and in the streets, we shall fight in the hills.' – Winston Churchill	**c** **Antithesis**: contrasting two opposing ideas in consecutive sentences, such as 'many are called, but few are chosen' (Jesus Christ).

4 'I know I have but the body of a weak and feeble woman; but I have the heart of a king, and of a king of England, too.' – Queen Elizabeth I	**d** **Chiasmus**: the inversion of parts of sentences in sequence, such as 'Fair is foul, and foul is fair' (Shakespeare).
5 'The people everywhere, not just here in Britain, everywhere – they kept faith with Princess Diana.' – Tony Blair	**e** **Anadiplosis**: the repetition of the last word of a sentence as the first word of the next sentence, such as 'They call for you: the general who became a slave; the slave *who became a* gladiator; the gladiator *who defied an Emperor'* (*Gladiator*).
6 'That's one small step for a man, one giant leap for mankind.' – Neil Armstrong	**f** **Amplification**: the repetition of a word or phrase with the addition of more detail, in order to emphasise something. For example: 'America has given the Negro people a bad check, a check which has come back marked "insufficient funds"' (Martin Luther King).
7 'This nation, under God, shall have a new birth of freedom – and that government of the people, by the people, for the people, shall not perish from the earth.' – Abraham Lincoln	**g** **Metaphor**: the comparison of two things by speaking of one in terms of the other, such as 'The mother of all battles' (Saddam Hussein).
8 'All the world's a stage, and all the men and women merely players.' – William Shakespeare	**h** **Alliteration**: the repetition of the same sound or letter at the beginning of several words in a sequence, such as 'Let us go forth to lead the land we love' (John F. Kennedy).
9 'Fear is the path to the dark side. Fear leads to anger. Anger leads to hate. Hate leads to suffering.' – Yoda in *The Phantom Menace*	**i** **Tricolon**: a list of three, or a sentence with three parts or clauses, such as 'veni, vidi, vici' or 'I came, I saw, I conquered' (Julius Caesar).

You can find definitions for key terms at the back of this coursebook. Rather than just memorising lists of words, create contexts for yourself in which you can apply them and show your understanding of them.

7.2 Rhetorical devices are like the nuts and bolts of any speech. But what is the fuel that powers a speech? **Appeal** is a key term for understanding the effectiveness of speeches. The ancient Greeks, who also studied the art of rhetoric, spoke of three kinds of appeal:

- **Ethos** is an appeal to the audience's sense of ethics. To what moral principles does the speaker refer or appeal?
- **Pathos** is an appeal to the audience's emotions. How does the speech evoke an emotional response?
- **Logos** is an appeal to logic. How does the speaker present a convincing, logical **argument**? How does the speaker reason with their audience?

Read Text 1.28, Barack Obama's victory speech from 2008. Where do you see evidence of ethos, pathos and logos? Discuss your findings as a class.

ATL

Self-management

Throughout your language and literature course you will learn many interesting terms, such as *tricolon* and *anadiplosis*. How are you going to keep a record of these? As you manage a learner portfolio, you may want to include key terms and concepts. You may want to make games for yourself, such as the matching exercise in Activity 7.1.

Model text

Text 1.28

This is your victory

Abridged extract

Barack Obama 2008

parallelism · *hypophora*

If there is anyone out there who still doubts that America is a place where all things are possible, who still wonders if the dream of our founders is alive in our time, who still questions the power of our democracy, tonight is your answer.

repetition

It's the answer told by lines that stretched around schools and churches in numbers this nation has never seen, by people who waited three hours and four hours, many for the first time in their lives, because they believed that this time must be different, that their voices could be that difference.

antithesis

It's the answer spoken by young and old, rich and poor, Democrat and Republican, black, white, Hispanic, Asian, Native American, gay, straight, disabled and not disabled. Americans who sent a message to the world that we have never been just a collection of individuals or a collection of red states and blue states. We are, and always will be, the United States of America.

figurative language

It's the answer that led those who've been told for so long by so many to be cynical and fearful and doubtful about what we can achieve to put their hands on the arc of history and bend it once more toward the hope of a better day.

It's been a long time coming, but tonight, because of what we did on this date in this election at this defining moment, change has come to America. [. . .]

tricolon and polysyndeton

I was never the likeliest candidate for this office. We didn't start with much money or many endorsements. Our campaign was not hatched in the halls of Washington. It began in the backyards of Des Moines and the living rooms of Concord and the front porches of Charleston. It was built by working men and women who dug into what little savings they had to give $5 and $10 and $20 to the cause. It grew strength from the young people who rejected the myth of their generation's apathy, who left their homes and their families for jobs that offered little pay and less sleep.

allusion

It drew strength from the not-so-young people who braved the bitter cold and scorching heat to knock on doors of perfect strangers, and from the millions of Americans who volunteered and organized and proved that more than two centuries later a government of the people, by the people, and for the people has not perished from the Earth. This is your victory. [. . .]

The road ahead will be long. Our climb will be steep. We may not get there in one year or even in one term, but America – I have never been more hopeful than I am tonight that we will get there. I promise you – we as a people will get there.

There will be setbacks and false starts. There are many who won't agree with every decision or policy I make as president, and we know that government can't solve every problem. But I will always be honest with you about the challenges we face. I will listen to you, especially when we disagree.

Key features explained

Key features	Text 1.28
Parallelisms: This device refers to the use of parallel sentence structures or phrases in consecutive order.	Obama uses three clauses, making the sentence very long, but the clauses are easy to follow because they all have the same structure: If there is anyone out there (1) who still doubts . . . (2) who still wonders . . . (3) who still questions . . . . Obama's speeches are famous for their use of parallelisms, and there is more than one example in this victory speech.
Hypophora: A common technique is to start a speech with hypophora, in which the speaker first asks a question and then answers it.	In Obama's speech, the word 'answer' is used regularly as an obvious signpost of the speaker's intention to give his audience answers. Note that here the questions were embedded in the first sentence and not asked as direct questions, as is customary with hypophora.
Repetition: This is a key ingredient to any speech. There are different forms of repetition, such as anaphora, which is the same phrase at the beginning of each sentence.	Notice that the opening words of the second, third and fourth paragraphs are the same: 'It's the answer.' This gives the audience a sense of direction and the speech a sense of structure.
Antithesis: This is the contrasting of two ideas in a sequence. The word 'but' is sometimes used to highlight the opposite nature of these ideas.	Obama states: 'We have never been just a collection of individuals or a collection of red states and blue states. We are, and always will be, the United States of America.'
Figurative speech: Figurative speech refers to any form of language that is not meant literally. This can include many devices from rhetorical questions to imagery.	Obama refers to 'the arc of history' which can be bent, 'once more toward the hope of a better day'. Furthermore, he sketches images in the minds of his audience by referring to 'backyards of Des Moines' and 'the living rooms of Concord', suggesting he is the candidate of the average American.
Tricolon and **polysyndeton**: Speeches often include lists of three, as this appeals to audiences' ears. Polysyndeton is a way of listing items to include 'and' instead of commas, in order to stress the importance of something.	Obama uses the word 'and' twice in the line 'It was built by working men and women who dug into what little savings they had to give $5 and $10 and $20 to the cause,' in order to emphasise the value of small amounts.
Allusion: Allusion is the reference to another speech or famous phrase. By using allusion, speakers not only associate themselves with the ideas of the original text but also create a bond with the audience by evoking shared knowledge.	Obama's 'arc of history' phrase comes from Martin Luther King's famous speech, 'I have a dream'. The words 'government of the people, by the people, and for the people' are taken from Abraham Lincoln's Gettysburg Address.
Varied sentence length: cadence and rhythm are in important in speech writing, as speeches are meant to be spoken and heard. One way to capture an audience is by varying the length of sentences.	Obama is famous for his long, eloquent sentences which are followed by short, punchy ones. For example the long line that starts with 'It drew strength from the not-so-young' is juxtaposed with 'This is your victory'.

7.3 Rhetorical devices are the tools of communicators. The devices listed here under 'key features' are only a few of the tools that speechwriters use to convey a message.

Through an online search, you will be able to find some of the most influential speeches in the history of the English language. Select one from your search or from the list provided here:

a Can you find evidence of the 'key features' in your chosen speech?

b Can you find other rhetorical devices which are not mentioned in the 'key features' section?

c Present your speech to your classmates, highlighting any key features and rhetorical devices that are used.

Famous speeches in the English language

- 'Against the Spanish Armada', Queen Elizabeth I
- 'Give me liberty or give me death', Patrick Henry
- 'Gettysburg address', Abraham Lincoln
- 'Abolition speech', William Wilberforce
- 'The meaning of July Fourth for the Negro', Frederick Douglas
- 'Surrender speech', Chief Joseph
- 'Women's rights to the suffrage', Susan B. Anthony
- 'Quit India', Mahatma Gandhi
- '1961 inaugural address', John F. Kennedy
- 'I have a dream', Martin Luther King
- 'A cause for which I am prepared to die', Nelson Mandela
- 'We shall fight on the beaches', Winston Churchill
- 'Give me blood and I will give you freedom', Subhas Chandra Bose
- 'Yes we can', Barack Obama.

7.4 Get into pairs and sit across from each other. Each pair should pick a different rhetorical device from the key terms at the beginning of this unit.

a Read Text 1.29 and look for evidence of your rhetorical device. Do an online search for this speech and watch a video recording of it.

b Do you see evidence of your rhetorical device?

c What is the effect of this device on Robert Kennedy's audience?

d After having a 2-minute discussion with your partner about your rhetorical device as featured in this speech, split up. Conduct a 'speed dating' game in your classroom, where half of the class remains seated. The other half rotates around to each desk, so that everyone has the chance to discuss their rhetorical device with everyone else for 2 or 3 minutes.

e After you have completed this 'speed dating' activity, come together and discuss the speech as a class. Consider the points from the 'AOE question' about cultural context.

CONCEPT

Transformation

Political speeches can be transformative. Voters may be persuaded to vote a certain way after hearing a campaign speech. Leaders can transform a nation through their words. Read Obama's speech again (Text 1.28), imagining that you were someone who did not vote for him in 2008. How might his words appeal to you, even if your political views differed from his?

Text 1.29

Statement on the assassination of Martin Luther King

Robert F. Kennedy 1968

I have bad news for you, for all of our fellow citizens, and people who love peace all over the world, and that is that Martin Luther King was shot and killed tonight.

Martin Luther King dedicated his life to love and to justice for his fellow human beings, and he died because of that effort.

In this difficult day, in this difficult time for the United States, it is perhaps well to ask what kind of a nation we are and what direction we want to move in. For those of you who are black – considering the evidence there evidently is that there were white people who were responsible – you can be filled with bitterness, with hatred, and a desire for revenge. We can move in that direction as a country, in great polarization – black people amongst black, white people amongst white, filled with hatred toward one another.

Or we can make an effort, as Martin Luther King did, to understand and to comprehend, and to replace that violence, that stain of bloodshed that has spread across our land, with an effort to understand with compassion and love.

For those of you who are black and are tempted to be filled with hatred and distrust at the injustice of such an act, against all white people, I can only say that I feel in my own heart the same kind of feeling. I had a member of my family killed, but he was killed by a white man. But we have to make an effort in the United States, we have to make an effort to understand, to go beyond these rather difficult times.

My favorite poet was Aeschylus. He wrote: 'In our sleep, pain which cannot forget falls drop by drop upon the heart until, in our own despair, against our will, comes wisdom through the awful grace of God.'

What we need in the United States is not division; what we need in the United States is not hatred; what we need in the United States is not violence or lawlessness; but love and wisdom, and compassion toward one another, and a feeling of justice toward those who still suffer within our country, whether they be white or they be black.

So I shall ask you tonight to return home, to say a prayer for the family of Martin Luther King, that's true, but more importantly to say a prayer for our own country, which all of us love – a prayer for understanding and that compassion of which I spoke.

We can do well in this country. We will have difficult times; we've had difficult times in the past; we will have difficult times in the future. It is not the end of violence; it is not the end of lawlessness; it is not the end of disorder.

But the vast majority of white people and the vast majority of black people in this country want to live together, want to improve the quality of our life, and want justice for all human beings who abide in our land.

Let us dedicate ourselves to what the Greeks wrote so many years ago: to tame the savageness of man and make gentle the life of this world.

Let us dedicate ourselves to that, and say a prayer for our country and for our people.

AOE question

How can cultural contexts influence how texts are written and received?

As you analyse Text 1.29 in Activity 7.4, consider the context. How does this list of points change your understanding of Robert F. Kennedy's speech?

- Robert Kennedy was scheduled to speak for his presidential campaign on that evening in 1968, when he received news of Martin Luther King's death. He did not have time to prepare his speech.
- There were riots in most American cities on that evening, except in Indianapolis, where Robert Kennedy spoke.
- His own brother, John Kennedy, had been assassinated five years earlier.
- The summer of 1968 was fraught with demonstrations and riots around the USA, as people protested the war in Vietnam, which both King and Robert Kennedy opposed.
- Racial tensions were high. Poverty levels in the USA were very high. While the Kennedys were members of the wealthy, political elite, Robert Kennedy was known, as a Senator, for defending civil rights and fighting poverty.
- Only months after delivering this speech, he was presidential candidate favourite. On the night of winning the primaries in California, he too was assassinated.

International mindedness

How does Robert F. Kennedy's speech (Text 1.29) show the importance for international mindedness?

AOE question

How can different texts offer different perspectives on a topic or theme?

This question is taken from the intertextuality part of the course. Compare the Robert F. Kennedy speech (Text 1.29) to Barack Obama's victory speech (Text 1.28). Focus on the themes of race and unity. How do they approach these themes from different perspectives?

LEARNER PROFILE

What traits, from the IB learner profile, does Robert F. Kennedy represent and exemplify in his speech (Text 1.29)? Remember, the ten traits of the IB learner profile are: open-minded, balanced, caring, knowledgeable, principled, thinker, communicator, inquirer, reflective, risk taker.

Over to you

7.5 Do an online search for a video called 'Chocolate Biscuits' by TeachingHeads. It is a speech about chocolate biscuits, which has little meaning but a lot of formal elements of good speech writing. After watching this video, discuss your answers to these questions:

a What is the purpose of this speech, entitled 'Chocolate Biscuits'?

b In which ways is it effective in achieving its purpose?

c What is the effect of the speech on you?

d Look up definitions of the words 'satire', 'parody', 'pastiche' and 'spoof'. Which word or words best describe the 'Chocolate Biscuits' speech? Give examples to support your answers.

7.6 Try writing your own speech for 5 to 8 minutes about any topic. Take these steps to make this activity a meaningful experience for you and your classmates:

a Find a news article or other text about a topic that matters to you. Identify an argument that can be made in response to this text.

b Write down your argument in the form of a thesis statement. This should be an opinion, claim or statement about the way you see the world or how the world should be.

c Imagine a group of people or **target audience** who would be interested in your opinion. Write down a description of a context in which you could deliver a speech to these people. If you need to alter your argument or claim, you may. You may consider adopting a **persona**, meaning that you pretend to be someone you are not.

d Create a mind map or outline which includes evidence that supports your argument. It can include a few key words. Evidence may be taken from any source texts that you can find or from real-life experiences.

e Show your teacher your argument, description of context and outline. You can call this a proposal. Discuss your proposal and the nature of your speech with your teacher. If your teacher wants to assess you on this activity, discuss the criteria on which you will be assessed. You may want to discuss expectations for appropriate language and conventions of the text type (speech), including choice of register.

f Before you write your speech, review some of the rhetorical devices that you have studied in this unit. Can you see an opportunity to include similar devices in your speech?

g Write your speech and show your teacher a complete draft of it. Ask them for feedback which is informed by any assessment criteria that you have agreed upon.

h Submit your final speech. This may be a piece of formative assessment. As a school group, you may decide to hold a 'speech night' in which you deliver your speeches to your classmates, friends and family. Explain and introduce the context of your speech to your audience before you deliver your speech.

TIP

Activity 7.6 refers to 'formative assessment', which is assessment *for* learning and not assessment *of* learning (summative assessment). As you write and deliver your own speech, think about the skills you are developing. How are these skills useful for your Paper 1, Paper 2, HL essay or individual oral?

LEARNER PROFILE

Risk taker

Activity 7.6 suggests that you organise and deliver a speech in front of a live audience. Does this sound intimidating? Are you too shy for something like this? Does this count for a grade? What if you embarrass yourself?

While this coursebook cannot answer such questions, keep in mind that, as an IB Diploma student, you should develop your powers of expression. Speaking in front of a group of people is an incredibly educational experience. Of course you will make mistakes. Everyone makes mistakes in public speaking. Reflect on these mistakes and you will inevitably grow as a speaker and effective communicator. You cannot learn, though, if you do not take the risk. So go for it!

Further reading

- *When They Go Low, We Go High*, by Tony Blair's former speechwriter, Philip Collins, analyses many great speeches in the context of when, where and by whom they were spoken.
- *Speeches That Changed the World* by Simon Sebag Montefiore is a collection of 20 speeches from the 20th century, with biographies on each speaker and an accompanying DVD.
- *You Talkin' to Me?* is a fun and enlightening book by Sam Leith which explores the art of rhetoric from Aristotle to Obama.

Unit 1.8 News articles

Learning objectives

- understand how different newspapers target different audiences through their use of language
- develop skills for writing your own news article and applying the relevant conventions for this type of text.

While many people read their news on digital devices, printed newspapers are sold and read all over the world. With print newspapers come considerations for layout and design. The first page of a print newspaper, also known as the **front page**, is, in itself, an interesting text type to study. The front page often reflects the ideals of the newspaper's **readership**. While most newspapers aim to report the news, many express *opinion* as well. Some newspapers mix opinion and **reporting**, reflecting a **political bias**.

This unit explores front pages, political bias and the conventions of news writing in general. The newspaper article is a type of text that you will come across throughout your life. A *critical* reading of the news is an important and invaluable skill.

Word bank

front page
readership
reporting
political bias
weasel word
glittering generalities
euphemism
dysphemism
loaded word
headline
subheading
newsworthiness
source
quotation
facts
photograph
context
news satire
fake news
click bait
disinformation
passive voice
reported speech
feature article
human-interest story

LEARNER PROFILE

Inquirer

What are the qualities of a good journalist? As a class, create a list of character traits. Is *inquirer* on your list? What does it mean to be an *inquirer*? It means you are curious. It means you ask questions. It means that you want to figure out how the world works. In this sense, if you go through life like an investigative journalist, it will help you to become knowledgeable and wise.

Getting started

8.1 Texts 1.30–1.33 are all newspaper front pages published on 25 June 2016, the day after the UK held its referendum on remaining or leaving the European Union, also known as the 'Brexit' referendum (from 'Britain' and 'exit').

a In small groups, study the language of these four front pages. Place them on a spectrum, with 'anti-Brexit' bias on your left and 'pro-Brexit' bias on your right, with neutral reporting somewhere in between.

b Discuss your findings with your classmates. What features of these front pages communicated bias? To what degree can you comment on the readership of these newspapers based on your analyses of these front pages?

Text 1.30

SATURDAY 25 JUNE 2016 WWW.INDEPENDENT.CO.UK

The INDEPENDENT

INSIDE: THE BREXIT SURVIVAL GUIDE
FINANCIAL ADVICE YOU CAN'T AFFORD TO MISS

We've broken off with Europe, the PM has resigned, Nigel Farage is rampant, markets have crashed, Scotland wants another referendum, there are 52 trade deals to be renegotiated – and one man is favourite to be the next prime minister...

Welcome to Boris Island

Full reports & analysis from OLIVER WRIGHT / JOHN CURTICE / MATTHEW NORMAN / JOHN LICHFIELD / MARY DEJEVSKY / TOM PECK / JOHN RENTOUL / ANDREW GRICE / GRACE DENT / PATRICK COCKBURN / JANET STREET-PORTER / HAMISH MCRAE

Text 1.31

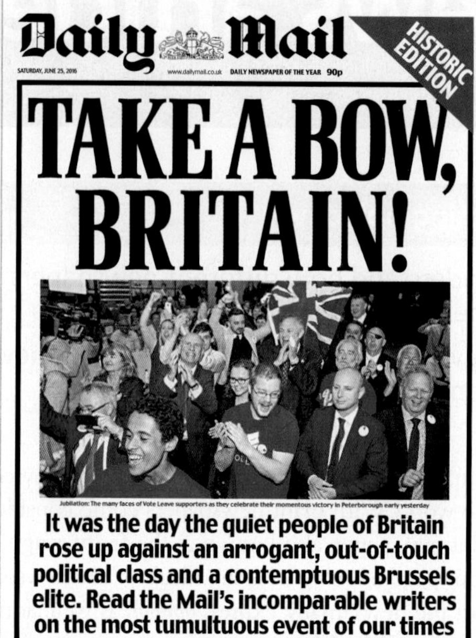
Daily Mail

SATURDAY, JUNE 25, 2016 www.dailymail.co.uk DAILY NEWSPAPER OF THE YEAR 90p

HISTORIC EDITION

TAKE A BOW, BRITAIN!

It was the day the quiet people of Britain rose up against an arrogant, out-of-touch political class and a contemptuous Brussels elite. Read the Mail's incomparable writers on the most tumultuous event of our times

Text 1.32

mirror.co.uk

DAILY Mirror NEWSPAPER OF THE YEAR Saturday, June 25, 2016 £1

DAY ONE OF BREXIT BRITAIN

Cameron resigns and Corbyn fights mutiny in 'worst crisis since WW2'

World leaders stunned as shares plummet by £1.2trillion & pound falls

Find out what leaving Europe actually means for you and your family

So what the hell happens now?

INSIDE: FULL COVERAGE AND ANALYSIS OF THE DAY THAT SHOOK THE WORLD

Text 1.33

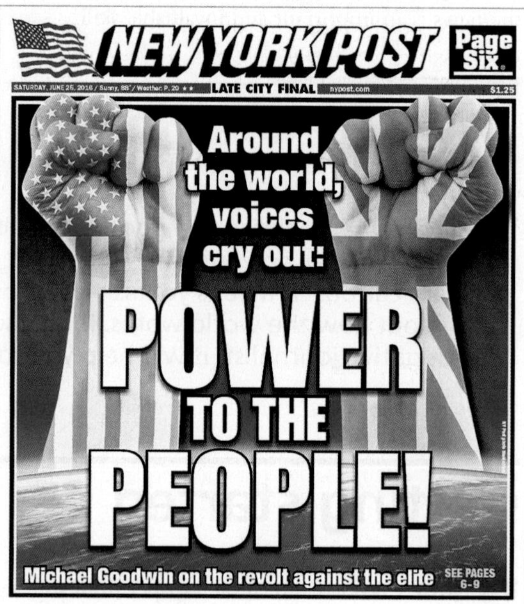
NEW YORK POST Page Six

LATE CITY FINAL nypost.com $1.25

Around the world, voices cry out:

POWER TO THE PEOPLE!

Michael Goodwin on the revolt against the elite SEE PAGES 6-9

CONCEPT

Perspective

How do Texts 1.30–1.33 offer multiple perspectives on Brexit? As in Activity 8.1, you may want to find several news stories from the same day on the same issue to explore their different uses of language to target different audiences. Discuss how one or more texts offer you a perspective with which you were not previously familiar.

TOK

In TOK you study language as a way of acquiring knowledge. When the language of an article is biased, you can question its value as a source of knowledge. How do you identify biased language? Here are a few tips. Can you find one or more of these in Texts 1.30–1.33?

- **Weasel words**: these words are intentionally ambiguous, vague or misleading, such as: 'milk *can* improve your strength'.
- **Glittering generalities**: these words appeal to the principles that few people could be against, such as 'freedom' and 'opportunity'.
- **Euphemism**: such words make things sound better than they are, such as 'pass away' instead of 'die'.
- **Dysphemism**: this is the opposite of euphemism, where a word is used to make something sound worse than it is, such as 'kick the bucket' instead of 'die'.
- **Loaded words**: these words are filled with emotion and their use is often unquestioned. 'Regime' and 'terrorist' are two examples.

International mindedness

As the late Stephen Covey, educator and author, once said, successful people 'seek first to understand, then to be understood'. By reading five articles on the same topic, all written from different viewpoints on a political spectrum, you are more likely to understand people better. Then, when formulating and expressing your own political opinions, you are more likely to be understood by a wider audience. Internationally minded people listen before speaking.

Model text

8.2 When reading news reports, you should look out for the 'five Ws and one H':

- *Who* is involved?
- *What* has happened?
- *When* did it happen?
- *Where* did it happen?
- *Why* did it happen?
- *How* did it happen?

As you analyse news reports, you may find it helpful to annotate them using the 'five Ws and one H', writing these words next to the relevant words or phrases in the text. Copy this table and read Text 1.34. Write key words and phrases in the relevant columns to help you gain a quick understanding of the article.

Who	What	When	Where	Why	How

Text 1.34

Birth of a new Britain

photograph

headlines and subheadings

- **Shock vote to leave Europe pushes Prime Minister to resign**
- **Boris reaches out to Remain supporters with plea for Unity**
- **Johnson and Gove prepare to head 'Brexit government'**

Boris Johnson and Michael Gove are preparing a "dream team" attempt to take control of the leadership of the Conservative Party in the wake of the most dramatic week in modern British political history.

newsworthiness

David Cameron announced his resignation as Prime Minister yesterday morning after Britain voted to leave the European Union, sparking a political, economic and constitutional crisis.

Within hours of the surprise result, Mr Cameron made his statement in Downing Street, the Bank of England intervened in the financial markets to prevent a crash and the Scottish government threatened to hold another referendum on splitting from the rest of the United Kingdom.

quotation

In a statesmanlike address from the Vote Leave headquarters, Mr Johnson positioned himself as a prime minister in waiting by urging unity across the nation and speaking of the bright future that now awaits an outward-looking Britain. "I want to speak to the millions of people who did not vote for this outcome, especially young people who may feel that this decision in some way involves pulling up the drawbridge of any kind of isolationism. I think the opposite is true.

"To those who may be anxious at home or abroad, this does not mean that the UK will be in any way less united, nor indeed does it mean that it will be any less European."

He added: "We cannot turn our backs on Europe. We are part of Europe. Our children and grandchildren will continue to have a wonderful future as Europeans, travelling to the continent, understanding the languages and cultures that make up our common European civilization."

sources

It is now expected that Mr Johnson will stand as leader, with Mr Gove, the Justice Secretary, becoming the Chancellor in a "Brexit Government", sources claimed.

George Osborne could work alongside the pair after it emerged that he made overtures towards Mr Johnson, sending an olive branch text message in the early hours yesterday following the shock victory by the Leave campaign.

It came on a day described as the most sensational in the recent history of British politics.

As the financial markets crashed to a 30-year low, Nicola Sturgeon, the Scottish First Minister, said a second independence referendum was "highly likely" and there were calls for a united Ireland after both Scotland and Northern Ireland voted to Remain against the prevailing national mood.

After a night of tension which saw the Brexit campaign score major victories across middle England and the north, it became clear shortly after dawn that Mr Cameron was going to resign.

At 8.15am he gave a speech in Downing Street, flanked by his wife Samantha, who appeared tearful as her husband said it was "in the national interest to have a period of stability and then the new leadership required".

Sources close to Mr Johnson say he was left "extremely upset" by Mr Cameron's resignation and "felt personally responsible" as he watched an emotional Mr Cameron tell the nation that he was no longer the right person to be "the captain that steers our country to its next destination".

While Mr Cameron called Mr Gove before making his resignation speech, he pointedly declined to make contact with Mr Johnson, only replying to a text message sent later in the morning by the former London mayor.

Within minutes of Mr Cameron saying that he wanted a new Tory leader in place by the beginning of October, there was speculation about his potential successor.

The *Daily Telegraph* 2016

facts

context

AOE question

How can language represent social differences and identities?

You have seen five texts on Brexit from five different newspapers. Who reads these newspapers? In the UK social distinctions between classes are often reflected in the newspapers that people read. Do an online search to find out more about the perceived social differences between the readers of these newspapers, and report to your classmates on your findings. How are these differences expressed through language?

Extended essay

You may be inspired by Texts 1.30–1.34 to write an extended essay about the language of newspapers and their effects on readers. If you want to focus on Brexit and news reporting as a Category 3 essay, you may want to concentrate on one aspect, such as the newspapers' coverage of topics such as health care, immigration or leadership in May and June of 2016, leading up to the referendum. A focused Category 3 research question may read: 'To what extent and for what reasons did the the *Daily Mail* and the *Sun* make Brexit about immigration in their opinion columns in the months leading up to the referendum?'

Key features explained

8.3 Here are the key features of news articles, explained in relation to Text 1.34.

a Return to the front pages from Activity 8.1 and find evidence of these features in *one* of the Texts 1.30-1.33.

b Get into small groups and assign each group a different text. Each group should do a short presentation to explain how their text uses some or all of the key features of news articles.

Key features	Examples from Text 1.34
Photograph: News articles, especially on front pages, are accompanied by photographs. Headshots are particularly common.	The photograph of Cameron and his wife captures their mood on the morning of his resignation. The camera angle and focus on her especially emphasise their sorrow and frustration.
Headlines and **subheadings**: Headlines capture the main sentiments of an article. Subheadings are often used to outline key aspects of longer articles.	'Birth of a new Britain' shows a pro-Brexit bias. 'Shock vote' may seem sensational, despite its rather accurate description of the situation on 25 June 2016.
Newsworthiness: Readers look for news stories that are either relevant to their lives, extraordinary, negative or any combination of these things.	The results of the Brexit referendum were featured in all British newspapers on this date, as the results were relevant. Further, it was not expected that David Cameron would resign.
Quotations: Direct quotations from the relevant people add to the stories' reliability as well.	The newspaper quotes several political leaders directly, though Boris Johnson is featured most prominently.
Source: Every news story needs a source for it to be deemed reliable.	While 'sources claimed' is not the most accurate reporting, the article gives several first-hand accounts of events.
Facts: Numbers, statistics, dates, and names all help news articles build a factual report of events.	The article includes several facts, such as the time of Cameron's speech and that the financial markets crashed to a '30-year low'.
Context: Most news stories go beyond facts and quotations to give more contextual information that accounts for events.	The referendum had consequences for Scotland and Northern Ireland, and Cameron did not call Johnson. These stories give the main story more context.

8.4 As you study news reports, you should ask yourself what makes a report or article 'newsworthy'. Newsworthiness refers to the value or interest that the story of the report may have for its audience. There are three main reasons why readers are interested in news stories:

- Negativity – many people are drawn to bad news. 'If it bleeds, it leads' is an expression in the media world, meaning that if the story is about something negative, it will come before (lead) all the other stories in the newspaper.
- Relevance – a story is newsworthy if it affects the daily lives of the audience. For example, if taxes increase, people will care, because it is relevant to their own lives.
- Extraordinary – if something unexpected or unique happens, it is often considered newsworthy. Even seemingly unimportant news will sometimes be published in national newspapers, for example if a little child catches a very big fish. Newspapers sometimes include such extraordinary 'feel good' stories to counterbalance the bad news.

Here are several news headlines. For each headline, explain which of the three aspects of newsworthiness are relevant. Make a copy of the table for this activity. An example has been done for you. As the source of each headline is unknown, you may think about their relevance to different audiences.

Heading	Negativity	Relevance	Extraordinary
'18-year-old student from Tamil Nadu designs world's lightest satellite weighing just 64 grams'	There is nothing negative about this story. In fact, it is rather positive!	The news that a young Indian invented this satellite is relevant to the readership of the *Times of India*.	A satellite that weighs only 64 grams is rather extraordinary. The fact that the inventor is so young and from a small town is also extraordinary.

a '18-year-old student from Tamil Nadu designs world's lightest satellite weighing just 64 grams' (see example)

b 'Dutch King secretly piloted passenger flights for 21 years with KLM'

c '84 confirmed dead after lorry crashes into crowd during Bastille Day celebration'

d 'FCC [Federal Communications Commission] ends net neutrality, critics cry "war on open internet"'

e 'Trump denies collusion with Russia, calls investigation a "witch hunt"'

f 'Global warming opens shipping routes over North Pole'

g 'FA [Football Association] includes women on governing council'

8.5 One way to understand the conventions of news writing is to study **news satire**. These texts expose the ridiculousness of human behaviour by writing seemingly serious articles about outrageous events and people. They aim to entertain. They are not to be confused with **fake news**, a growing concern on the World Wide Web, which often uses **click bait** or sensational headings to get readers to click through to websites that claim to report facts, when in fact they mislead readers. The aim of these sites is to confuse, persuade and lie. They spread **disinformation**.

a Do an online search to find an example of both news satire and fake news. You may want to go to *The Onion* or *The Spoof* for news satire. Do an online search for the latest fake news sites (as they tend to arrive and disappear quickly).

b Give your classmates copies of the articles and highlight where stylistics and structural features are similar and different. Comment on the different purposes and effects of the articles.

AOE question

How and why do people study language and literature?

Why study fake news, click bait or news satire? Reflect on the purpose of Activity 8.5 and relate it to the purpose of the IB Diploma Programme.

8.6 Text 1.35 is an example of 'pretend' news. It was written by a student to show his understanding of the novel *The Great Gatsby*. You do not have to have read the novel to appreciate the text. On a copy of the text:

a Highlight in one colour where you see evidence of the student's understanding of the novel.

b Highlight in another colour where you see evidence of the student's understanding of the *conventions* of the text type (newspaper article).

c How 'real' is this article? How is it different from the 'fake' news that you discussed in the previous activity? Discuss as a class.

ATL

Communication

Headlines are interesting text types. In order to engage with texts and read for understanding, try reading a news article without its headline. Then try writing your own headline for the article. Compare it to other classmates' headlines and to the actual headline from the article. How did it compare? How does this activity help you develop your own powers of communication?

Text 1.35

Mystery shrouds death of Jay Gatsby

Peter Parker 1922

Businessman and socialite gunned down in his own swimming pool.

NEW YORK – Police have confirmed the identity of the body found earlier today in the swimming pool of the Gatsby estate in West Egg to be that of entrepreneur and socialite Jay Gatsby. Authorities are operating on the theory that he was murdered by auto-mechanic George Wilson, whose body was found in the woods near the estate. Wilson is thought to have murdered Gatsby out of revenge before turning the same revolver on himself.

The murder-suicide comes after Myrtle Wilson, George Wilson's wife, was killed in a hit-and-run incident on the previous evening outside her husband's gas station near Flushing in the 'Valley of Ashes'. Witnesses claim that the perpetrator drove a yellow Rolls Royce.

During the investigation of the Gatsby murder, police discovered a yellow Rolls Royce with bloodstains and a broken headlight on the premises of the Gatsby estate. It is unclear, however, if Mr. Gatsby was personally involved in the hit-and-run incident, as witnesses claim to have seen a woman driving the automobile. The identity of the woman remains unknown, and the investigation is ongoing.

Jay Gatsby was last seen leaving the Plaza Hotel in Manhattan on 25 October around 7 p.m. He had rented a suite there for the afternoon. From his suite, a heated argument was heard by guests. Receptionists confirm that he left the suite with a woman in a fit of rage.

Persons with information on the murder of Mr. Gatsby and Mrs. Wilson are asked to come forward and provide local authorities with this information to assist investigations further.

Little is known about Jay Gatsby, despite the lavish parties that were hosted at his West Egg mansion. It is believed that his extravagant lifestyle was financed by a flourishing business in the illegal distribution of alcohol. One acquaintance of Gatsby's, who wishes to remain anonymous, claims to have seen Gatsby with New York crime kingpin Meyer Wolfsheim, though this cannot be confirmed.

To some, Jay Gatsby was known as an 'Oxford Man', though there is no record of him attending any college in Oxford, England. Sources within the US Army, however, confirm that he received a scholarship to attend schooling in Oxford after his valiant efforts in the Great War. Drafted into the Army, Gatsby quickly rose to the rank of Major. Rumours that Gatsby was a German spy appear to be ill-founded.

Gatsby's neighbour, Nick Carraway, had this to say about him: 'Gatsby was misunderstood by many, but he was a good man with a clear focus.' When asked what captured the focus of this aloof, though well-known man, Carraway answered vaguely: ' His focus was on the past, and regaining what he had lost years ago. But it was in vain. He was like a boat rowing against the tide. And the world of Old Money will never give an inch to people like Jay Gatsby, people with New Money. They have to row their own boat. And for Gatsby, he simply wasn't strong enough.'

It is thought that Jay Gatsby is survived by none. Any family members or relatives are asked to make themselves known to the County of Great Neck.

An estate-sale will be organized by Nick Carraway and friend Jordan Baker on the 1st of November. Proceeds from this sale will benefit the Golf for Youth Foundation, of which Ms. Baker is the founder.

An open funeral will be held at Great Neck Memorial on October 31st at 3 p.m.

8.7 Return to the language that you highlighted in Text 1.35 as typical of newspaper writing. Put these words into a list that you share with your classmates and add to your learner portfolio. This list should be called: 'typical language of newspapers'.

a Find another news article on a topic that interests you. You may want to find an article on a global issue that you are exploring in class.

b Highlight the language from this article which characterises it as a news article.

c Add this language to your list of 'typical language of newspapers'.

d Study your list of phrases, words and sentence structures. Beside each item, explain what makes it typical of newspaper language. Think about these linguistic devices. You may have to look up their definitions:

- use of pronouns
- verb tense
- quoted speech or **reported speech**
- active or **passive voice**
- adjectives and adverbs

CONCEPT

Creativity

Text 1.35 includes a level of student *creativity*. How can you use creativity to show understanding of the literary works that you have read for this course?

Over to you

8.8 Write a news article based on the events from one of the literary works that you are reading for class by taking these steps:

a Find a scene, passage or section from a play or novel that might lend itself to a news story. Think about the time and place in which the story takes place and the kinds of people who lived then and there. Discuss with your classmates why a news story on those events would be appropriate for that context.

b Reread Text 1.35 as a model for how to incorporate your knowledge and understanding of a literary work into a news article. Revisit your list of 'typical language of newspapers'.

c Write an outline for your news article.

d Find a good photograph to accompany the article. This may be a stock image that you find online.

e Write your article, based on your outline. Write the headline and subheading last. Let your writing be informed by your list of 'typical language of newspapers'.

f Exchange a copy of your news article with a fellow classmate. Check to see if your classmate has included examples from your 'typical language of newspapers' list'. Discuss your understanding of the literary works as well, including any representations of characters, setting or plot.

g Submit your article to your teacher for feedback and add it to your learner portfolio under a section on the literary work that you have explored.

CAS

For your CAS requirement, you may want to help a local club or organisation with the writing and editing of a newsletter. Find a group of people that you would like to support and help them communicate their ideas effectively.

Further reading

Writing Feature Stories by Matthew Ricketson is a user-friendly textbook on journalism. While this unit has focused on the 'news article' as a text type, your coursework should include an exploration of **features articles** as well. These longer, more in-depth, journalistic texts, which appear in newspapers, websites and magazines, rely on research and interviews. They are also called **human-interest stories**. This book gives you insight into feature story writing and helps you develop skills which you may find helpful for your extended essay.

Unit 1.9 Blogs

Word bank

blog post
opinion column
tautology
anecdote
topical
voice
signpost

Learning objectives

- learn the key features of blog writing
- develop skills for analysing a blog post
- develop the skills for writing your own blog post, in the style of another blogger.

Have you ever written a blog or a **blog post**? These days it is remarkably easy to start a blog and publish your ideas instantly on the World Wide Web. Perhaps 'blog' as a text type is so difficult to define because so many people write them for so many different reasons. What is a blog?

The term 'blog' comes from the words 'web' and 'log'. A log is an account of what happens, as it happens. A log is written for future reference. It allows you to keep a record, look back and reflect on something that has happened. You can search through their archives, using a tagging and dating system.

Content-wise, blogs can be about anything. In this unit you will explore the features of blog writing. You are encouraged to discover the world of blogs and to write a blog post of your own.

TOK

How much of your understanding of the world comes from online newspapers? Do you read or write blog posts? With the advent of the World Wide Web in the 1990s, many people expected information technology to broaden people's access to the truth, tackle corruption, spread democracy, expose injustices and protect human rights. As newspapers have moved online in the past decades, and as every person in the world with a device can now publish fact, fiction or opinion instantly, has the world become more knowledgeable, safer and fairer? Discuss these weighty questions as a class.

AOE question

How do texts follow or move away from the conventions associated with different types of text?

This question, from the part of the course on intertextuality, is interesting with regard to blogs. The word 'blog' may say more about a text's medium of publication than its content. Similarly, the word 'book' describes several bound pages without any description of what it contains. Do you think that blog posts have 'conventions' at all? How might the nature of the medium help shape the style and structure of writing? Consider these questions as you do the activities in this unit.

Getting started

9.1 Here is a list of text types that are similar to, but different from, blogs. Based on what you know, explain how blogs might be like each of these text types, and how they can be different:

a diary
b essay
c **opinion column**
d news report
e review
f journal
g website
h press release
i tweet
j Facebook post.

9.2 Does the cartoon (Text 1.36) show us the truth about blogging? Do you agree or disagree with this understanding of what blogging is? Why do people blog?

Text 1.36

9.3 Is there a blog that you like to read?

- Does it fit into one of the three categories from the 'Blog breakdown' cartoon (Text 1.36)?
- Why do you like to read this blog?
- How does the language of your favourite blog target a particular audience?

Bring an example into class to share with your classmates.

Model text

9.4 Read Text 1.37, a piece about transgender women by Hadley Freeman:

a Look for *one* sentence that captures the author's main message.

b Write this sentence on a piece of paper and give it to your teacher. Your teacher will read out the various sentences that were identified.

c Discuss, as a class, why you chose these sentences and try to decide which one is most accurate.

d Where does this sentence appear in the blog post? Is this a typical place to write the main message in a blog post? Discuss.

Text 1.37

Identity is the issue of our age: so why can't we talk more honestly about trans women?

Abridged

Hadley Freeman 2017

tip

anecdote

Should you be struggling with a gift idea for that special person in your life, here's a suggestion: how about a home DNA kit? These are all the rage in America, I recently read in the *New York Times*, with 3m sold by ancestry.com alone in the past five years. At last, Americans can find out how Irish they actually are. [. . .]

topical

Nowhere is the discussion about identity more passionately felt than within the transgender movement. If you feel you are a woman, you are a woman is the rule, although some women are querying this. Last week, the novelist Chimamanda Ngozi Adichie was asked by Channel 4's Cathy Newman whether trans women are "real women". "My feeling is trans women are trans women," Adichie replied, a response not so much tautological as almost palindromic. "I don't think it's a good thing to conflate everything into one." [. . .]

voice

This kumbaya approach is an increasingly popular one. Why can't we ladies all just get along? Hakuna matata! Yet no one is asking why more women than men are raising objections here. Perhaps people think this is just what women are like: uniquely catty. But there are real ethical issues here, and they overwhelmingly affect women.

examples

Sport is one obvious example. Male-born bodies have had different testosterone levels and muscle distribution from female ones. No one knows what the solution is but pretending there isn't a difference is ridiculous.

opinion

Just as the fringe elements of the political world have taken centre stage, so the more extreme end of the trans movement – which insists there are no differences between trans and cis women – has moved to the frontline. Some will call this progress; to me, it seems more a case of throwing out the commonsensical baby with the transphobic bath water. [. . .]

That trans people have long suffered from hideous prejudice and violence, and continue to do so, is without question. But as Adichie said, acknowledging differences and being supportive are not mutually exclusive. If anything, they go hand in hand, because they allow women, trans and non-trans, to talk honestly and see each other as people, instead of reducing themselves to manicures and menstruation.

Hadley Freeman

Chimamanda Ngozi Adichie

TEXT AND CONTEXT

- A **tautology** is a phrase which says the same thing twice.
- A palindrome is a word or phrase that reads the same forwards and backwards.
- Kumbaya is a word from a gospel song with spiritual associations.
- Hakuna matata is a Swahili phrase that translates roughly to 'no worries'.
- Transgender refers to a gender identity that is the opposite of one's birth gender.
- Cisgender is the gender you are assigned at birth.
- 'To throw out the baby with the bathwater' means to accidentally get rid of something good when cleaning up the bad.

LEARNER PROFILE

Open-minded

Text 1.37 raises an interesting question about transgender people. Should men who want to be treated as women be treated as women, or as men who want to be treated as women? The author suggests that the latter can be respectable. Do you agree? Part of being an IB learner is being *open-minded*, acknowledging and respecting people's differences.

CONCEPT

Identity

Identity is a key concept in this course. How does Hadley Freeman express her identity in Text 1.37 through her use of language? How does she feel about people's rights to express their own identity?

9.5 Discuss your answers to these questions:

a Do you agree with Hadley Freeman about how trans women should be treated? Which arguments do you find persuasive? Where do you disagree with her, and for which reasons?

b Do an online search for Hadley Freeman and her column for the *Guardian*, a UK newspaper. Whom does she target with her writing? What can you say about her target audience, and what makes you say this?

c How would you describe Freeman's writing style?

d If you could write to Hadley Freeman about anything, what would you ask her?

e Based on your understanding of her writing, is Hadley Freeman a 'blogger' or a 'columnist'? What is the difference? Could Text 1.37 be considered an opinion column? Give reasons for your answer.

Extended essay

Are you interested in reading more columns by Hadley Freeman? For your extended essay you may want to explore her columns or another author's posts as primary sources. Like any extended essay that you write, be sure to comment on how the blogger's message is constructed through language, shaped by purpose and received by audiences. A research question might read: 'To what extent does the writing of Hadley Freeman use diction, voice and tone to appeal to and express the ideas that matter most to Millennials?'

Key features explained

Key features	Examples from Text 1.37
Tip: Blogs often offer advice or help, especially 'how to' blogs. Use imperative verbs for this.	Hadley Freeman writes 'here's a suggestion', which clearly shows her purpose in writing.
Anecdote: Blogs can be like public diaries or journals in this sense. Anecdotes are common.	Hadley Freeman tells a story from her own life, as she begins with 'I recently read . . .'
Topical: Popular blogs are often topical, meaning they are about current affairs that people care about.	'Last week' and 'I recently read' are two phrases that make her opinions topical.
Voice: Popular bloggers have a style that followers recognise and like. It can be rather personal. Generally speaking, a good blog should be informal without sounding chatty, punchy but not terse, focused but relevant to a larger audience, and short but not thin on content.	Hadley Freeman has her own writing style. Rhetorical questions, such as 'Why can't we ladies just get along?' and allusions to pop culture, such as 'Hakuna matata!' make her writing fun and engaging.
Examples: For any opinions, blog readers will expect to learn about real-life examples as evidence to support the arguments.	Hadley Freeman explores transgender differences by referring to transgender athletes. She uses **signposts** for the reader with the words 'example' and 'then' in the sentence 'Sport is one obvious example'.
Opinion: Many blogs clearly state the writer's opinion.	'Some will call this progress; to me it seems like throwing out the commonsensical baby with the transphobic bathwater.'

9.6 Study the features of blog writing as outlined in the 'key features explained' table, which includes examples from Text 1.37. Then, as a group, find one blog post from one of the popular blogs in the box provided here or from another blog that you like. Can you find examples of these key features in your blog post? Share a copy of your blog post with your classmates and, in a short presentation, explain how these features are used to appeal to the audiences of these blogs.

HuffPost, TMZ, Business Insider, Mashable, Gizmodo, LifeHacker, The Verge, Tech Crunch, Perez Hilton, Engadget, Cheezburger, Deadspin, Kotaku

International mindedness

Besides studying one of the popular blogs listed here, you may want to explore and discuss the blog called internationalmindedness.org. What kinds of topics are explored in this blog? How do the authors use the conventions of the text type to spread international mindedness effectively? Whom does this blog target? Where do you see evidence to suggest this? Have you learnt something new or interesting through your exploration of this blog?

Over to you

9.7 In your exploration of blog posts from previous activities, return to a popular or favourite blogger that you have discovered. Try to find a blog entry from your favourite blogger about a topic that relates to a global issue you're exploring in your learner portfolio.

a Read multiple blog entries by this person to get a feeling for their style.

b Write a blog post in this person's style, about a topic they usually write about, and for an audience they usually write for. Consider the key features of blog writing as introduced in this unit.

c Give your blog post to your teacher, along with two other blog posts from the actual author. Be sure that the formatting of all three blog entries is uniform.

d Ask your teacher if they can identify which one out of the three blog entries was written by you. How could you change the structure and style of your blog to be more like that of the original blogger? Ask your teacher's advice about this if necessary.

e Send a copy of your blog post to the original blogger, if possible, to find out what they think of your topic and style.

f Add your blog entry to your learner portfolio, along with any comments your teacher has provided.

ATL

Research

As you conduct research for your extended essay or any form of IB assessment, you may come across blogs as secondary sources. It is important to carefully evaluate the value of blog posts as sources, by questioning their currency, reliability, relevance, academic authority and purpose. Evaluating secondary sources is a research skill that you can continue to develop into higher education as well.

Further reading

- Thomas Friedman writes excellent blogs for the *New York Times* which are freely available online.
- The *Times of India* or *The Straits Times* are good, non-Western sources to consider for opinion.
- There are a number of websites that offer tips on how to blog effectively, and there are many reasons why you might want to consider it. Do an online search on 'how to blog effectively' to find lots of tips on writing for the web and organising your ideas coherently.

Unit 1.10 Short stories and novels

Word bank

tension
diction
prose fiction
plot
plot twist
conflict
character
protagonist
antagonist
foil
characterisation
narrative technique
narrator
unreliable narrator
omniscient narrator
limited narrator
limited-omniscient narrator
reported speech
direct speech
setting
atmosphere
alienation
exposition
rising action
climax
falling action
denouement

TOK

What is the value of studying fiction? Pablo Picasso once said: 'Art is the lie that enables us to realise the truth.' What do you think he meant by this? Do you agree? To what degree is reading fiction about finding the 'truth'?

Learning objectives

- learn how to analyse prose fiction to identify the stylistic and structural techniques used to engage readers
- develop the writing skills required for the Paper 2 comparative essay.

Have you ever been completely consumed by a novel or short story? What makes a 'page-turner' so engaging and exciting for readers ? Is the **tension** of a story created through interesting characters, intriguing story lines or beautiful **diction**?

In your language and literature course you will study works of **prose fiction**, such as short stories and novels. This unit introduces you to the key features that engage readers of prose fiction, and to examples of short fiction. The two short stories used here will generate discussion and explore literary terms that are relevant to the works you are reading in class.

ATL

Self-management

As you explore the question 'why study fiction?' consider how your capacity to show empathy for other people might grow when reading fiction. Part of developing your self-management skills is affective learning, which is the ability to understand other people's problems, desires and contexts. How do the literary works that you are studying in this course help you learn about other people in the real world?

Getting started

10.1 What makes a story? Are there special ingredients? How do readers recognise fiction? There is a famous six-word story, often attributed to Ernest Hemingway (though there is no evidence for this), which reads: 'For sale: Baby shoes, never worn.'

Is this a short work of fiction? If so, what makes it so? Discuss.

CONCEPTS

Creativity and communication

Activities 10.1 and 10.2 raise an interesting question about *creativity* and *communication*. How does the length of a literary text affect its meaning? Are shorter works of fiction easier to write and therefore less literary? To answer these questions, research genres of extremely short fiction, such as:

- flash fiction
- twitterature
- drabble.

Find examples of these and, as a class, discuss their literary merit.

10.2 Based on your discussion from the previous activity, discuss whether these six-word stories (a–k) qualify as 'stories'. Based on your discussion of each example, create a set of criteria which can be used to determine whether or not a text qualifies as a 'story'.

a After falling, she would rise up.

b 'Could the spy raise his hand?'

c Again, she said 'Never, never again!'

d Please read this after I die.

e Technology works fine, until it doesn't.

f They cheered when the turtle won.

g They lived happily ever after, divorced.

h She wanted to be a man.

i The brother mourned. The sister didn't.

j Her kiss began a terrible pandemic.

k 'Roar!' [Gun shot.] 'You saved me!'

Text 1.38

10.3 Use the criteria from Activity 10.2 to discuss whether Text 1.38 qualifies as a short story.

10.4 You may not consider Text 1.38, 'Story Template' by Roz Chast, to be literary, but most likely it passed (some of) your 'story' criteria from the previous activities. You may have recognised some basic elements of **plot**. Plot refers to the main events in a work of fiction, as presented by the writer in an interrelated sequence.

Here are seven basic plot types, as outlined by Christopher Booker. Have you recently seen a film that fits into one of these types? Share a synopsis with your classmates. Do you think that all stories fit into one or more of these neatly defined types of plot? If you have already read a literary work in your language and literature class, describe how it fits or breaks one of the plot templates shown here.

- 'Overcoming the monster' is a plot structure that involves a threatening predator: a person or thing that is abnormal and/or dangerous.
- 'Rags to riches' is a plot structure that focuses on the improvement of a character from a lower or deprived state of being to a more enlightened and wealthy position in society.
- 'The quest' involves a call to a journey with a purpose, some thrilling ordeals and a triumphant end.
- 'The voyage and return' is different from 'the quest', as the main characters end up in a strange place and must find a way to get home.
- 'The comedy' is a classical term for works whose purpose is to make us laugh about the nature of life.
- 'The tragedy' is another classical term, to describe works that show how life can be sad and apparently unjust.
- 'Rebirth' is a kind of story where the main character goes through a change and discovers a truth by which to live a more fruitful life.

10.5 Read Text 1.39 and discuss your answers to these questions:

a Does this story meet your criteria for short fiction from Activity 10.2?

b Does it contain other elements of fiction that you would like to add to your criteria?

c Does the plot of this story relate to one of the seven plot types introduced in Activity 10.4?

d What is your initial response to this story?

e How does the author use language to elicit this response?

f What is this story's message? Can you articulate its main ideas or message? What makes you say this?

Text 1.39

The Story of an Hour

Kate Chopin 1894

Knowing that Mrs. Mallard was afflicted with a heart trouble, great care was taken to break to her as gently as possible the news of her husband's death.

It was her sister Josephine who told her, in broken sentences; veiled hints that revealed in half concealing. Her husband's friend Richards was there, too, near her. It was he who had been in the newspaper office when intelligence of the railroad disaster was received, with Brently Mallard's name leading the list of "killed." He had only taken the time to assure himself of its truth by a second telegram, and had hastened to forestall any less careful, less tender friend in bearing the sad message.

She did not hear the story as many women have heard the same, with a paralyzed inability to accept its significance. She wept at once, with sudden, wild abandonment, in her sister's arms. When the storm of grief had spent itself she went away to her room alone. She would have no one follow her.

There stood, facing the open window, a comfortable, roomy armchair. Into this she sank, pressed down by a physical exhaustion that haunted her body and seemed to reach into her soul.

She could see in the open square before her house the tops of trees that were all aquiver with the new spring life. The delicious breath of rain was in the air. In the street below a peddler was crying his wares. The notes of a distant song which some one was singing reached her faintly, and countless sparrows were twittering in the eaves.

There were patches of blue sky showing here and there through the clouds that had met and piled one above the other in the west facing her window.

She sat with her head thrown back upon the cushion of the chair, quite motionless, except when a sob came up into her throat and shook her, as a child who has cried itself to sleep continues to sob in its dreams.

She was young, with a fair, calm face, whose lines bespoke repression and even a certain strength. But now there was a dull stare in her eyes, whose gaze was fixed away off yonder on one of those patches of blue sky. It was not a glance of reflection, but rather indicated a suspension of intelligent thought.

There was something coming to her and she was waiting for it, fearfully. What was it? She did not know; it was too subtle and elusive to name. But she felt it, creeping out of the sky, reaching toward her through the sounds, the scents, the color that filled the air.

Now her bosom rose and fell tumultuously. She was beginning to recognize this thing that was approaching to possess her, and she was striving to beat it back with her will – as powerless as her two white slender hands would have been. When she abandoned herself a little whispered word escaped her slightly parted lips. She said it over and over under her breath: "free, free, free!" The vacant stare and the look of terror that had followed it went from her eyes. They stayed keen and bright. Her pulses beat fast, and the coursing blood warmed and relaxed every inch of her body.

She did not stop to ask if it were or were not a monstrous joy that held her. A clear and exalted perception enabled her to dismiss the suggestion as trivial. She knew that she would weep again when she saw the kind, tender hands folded in death; the face that had never looked save with love upon her, fixed and gray and dead. But she saw beyond that bitter moment a long procession of years to come that would belong to her absolutely. And she opened and spread her arms out to them in welcome.

There would be no one to live for during those coming years; she would live for herself. There would be no powerful will bending hers in that blind persistence with which men and women believe they have a right to impose a private will upon a fellow-creature. A kind intention or a cruel intention made the act seem no less a crime as she looked upon it in that brief moment of illumination.

And yet she had loved him – sometimes. Often she had not. What did it matter! What could love, the unsolved mystery, count for in the face of this possession of self-assertion which she suddenly recognized as the strongest impulse of her being!

"Free! Body and soul free!" she kept whispering.

Josephine was kneeling before the closed door with her lips to the keyhole, imploring for admission. "Louise, open the door! I beg; open the door – you will make yourself ill. What are you doing, Louise? For heaven's sake open the door."

"Go away. I am not making myself ill." No; she was drinking in a very elixir of life through that open window.

Her fancy was running riot along those days ahead of her. Spring days, and summer days, and all sorts of days that would be her own. She breathed a quick prayer that life might be long. It was only yesterday she had thought with a shudder that life might be long.

She arose at length and opened the door to her sister's importunities. There was a feverish triumph in her eyes, and she carried herself unwittingly like a goddess of Victory. She clasped her sister's waist, and together they descended the stairs. Richards stood waiting for them at the bottom.

Some one was opening the front door with a latchkey. It was Brently Mallard who entered, a little travel-stained, composedly carrying his grip-sack and umbrella. He had been far from the scene of the accident, and did not even know there had been one. He stood amazed at Josephine's piercing cry; at Richards' quick motion to screen him from the view of his wife.

When the doctors came they said she had died of heart disease – of the joy that kills.

AOE question

What are the different ways in which people are affected by texts?

As you read Texts 1.39 and 1.40, consider the fact that both texts include a **plot twist**, an unexpected turn of events that has an intended effect on the reader. How are you affected by these plot twists? As a class discuss your responses.

Model text

10.6 Read Text 1.40, 'The Flowers' by Alice Walker. After your reading of this short story, write a 100-word response which captures your initial reaction to the text. This can include anything that you have noticed in the text, for example:

- the ways in which the author uses language to engage you, the reader
- a description of the emotions you feel after reading this text.

Share your response with your classmates by reading aloud what you have written.

Text 1.40

The Flowers

Alice Walker 1988

character

conflict

narrative technique

setting

exposition

It seemed to Myop as she skipped lightly from hen house to pigpen to smokehouse that the days had never been as beautiful as these. The air held a keenness that made her nose twitch. The harvesting of the corn and cotton, peanuts and squash, made each day a golden surprise that caused excited little tremors to run up her jaws.

characterisation

Myop carried a short, knobby stick. She struck out at random at chickens she liked, and worked out the beat of a song on the fence around the pigpen. She felt light and good in the warm sun. She was ten, and nothing existed for her but her song, the stick clutched in her dark brown hand, and the tat-de-ta-ta-ta of accompaniment,

Turning her back on the rusty boards of her family's sharecropper cabin, Myop walked along the fence till it ran into the stream made by the spring. Around the spring, where the family got drinking water, silver ferns and wildflowers grew. Along the shallow banks pigs rooted. Myop watched the tiny white bubbles disrupt the thin black scale of soil and the water that silently rose and slid away down the stream.

She had explored the woods behind the house many times. Often, in late autumn, her mother took her to gather nuts among the fallen leaves. Today she made her own path, bouncing this way and that way, vaguely keeping an eye out for snakes. She found, in addition to various common but pretty ferns and leaves, an armful of strange blue flowers with velvety ridges and a sweet suds bush full of the brown, fragrant buds.

rising action

By twelve o'clock, her arms laden with sprigs of her findings, she was a mile or more from home. She had often been as far before, but the strangeness of the land made it not as pleasant as her usual haunts. It seemed gloomy in the little cove in which she found herself. The air was damp, the silence close and deep.

climax

Myop began to circle back to the house, back to the peacefulness of the morning. It was then she stepped smack into his eyes. Her heel became lodged in the broken ridge between brow and nose, and she reached down quickly, unafraid, to free herself. It was only when she saw his naked grin that she gave a little yelp of surprise.

He had been a tall man. From feet to neck covered a long space. His head lay beside him. When she pushed back the leaves and layers of earth and debris Myop saw that he'd had large white teeth, all of them cracked or broken, long fingers, and very big bones. All his clothes had rotted away except some threads of blue denim from his overalls. The buckles of the overall had turned green.

Myop gazed around the spot with interest. Very near where she'd stepped into the head was a wild pink rose. As she picked it to add to her bundle she noticed a raised mound, a ring, around the rose's root. It was the rotted remains of a noose, a bit of shredding plowline, now blending benignly into the soil. Around an overhanging limb of a great spreading oak clung another piece. Frayed, rotted, bleached, and frazzled – barely there – but spinning restlessly in the breeze. Myop laid down her flowers.

And the summer was over.

denouement

falling action

Key features explained

10.7 Read the key features and the examples from Text 1.40. Work in small groups and assign each group a different key feature from this table. Return to Text 1.39 and analyse Kate Chopin's use of your key feature in her short story, 'The Story of an Hour'. Present to your class and take notes on each other's presentations.

Key features	Examples from Text 1.40
Conflict: At the heart of any story is a conflict, and there are several types of conflict: individual versus society, individual versus another individual, individual versus circumstances and individual versus himself or herself.	The simple word 'seemed' in the opening line of 'The Flowers' suggests that there is a conflict looming in the background. The discovery of a dead black man ends her child-like innocence, and the conflict is exposed: the little, innocent girl finds herself in a big, scary, racist world where black people are lynched and hanged.
Character: Every story needs characters. The **protagonist** instigates the development of a story. The **antagonist** stands in the protagonist's way. And the **foil** is a character who is in stark contrast with the protagonist and highlights his or her defining character traits.	Myop is an apt name for the story's protagonist, as 'myopic' means 'to lack foresight'. In other words, she does not see the evils of her world before she comes face to face with them. The dead man is not the antagonist of this story. Rather he is the foil of the story, as his eyes are wide open. If Myop represents life, he represents death. If Myop represents innocence, he represents experience.
Setting: Where the story is set is important for reflecting the **atmosphere** of the story. In this sense the setting can act as a mirror of the characters' problems. It can also act as a mould in shaping the characters' personalities. Authors may also engage readers by depicting an escapist setting, which is fantastically different from the reader's own world. Finally, you may want to consider the degree to which characters are alienated by their surroundings. **Alienation** is a common conflict between character and setting.	The setting of 'The Flowers' reflects the problems of the US South. On the surface everything is beautiful with 'streams', 'silver ferns' and 'wildflowers'. But under the surface, metaphorically, there are 'snakes'. Myop's traumatic experience of finding this dead body has shaped her, meaning she'll never be so sweet and innocent again.

Exposition: This is the opening part of a story, where the characters, the setting and the conflict are introduced to the reader.	In the opening lines, Myop is introduced and the idyllic countryside is described. But the words 'black', 'snake', 'strange' and 'gloomy' suggest that trouble awaits.
Narrative technique: Who is the storyteller or **narrator**? To whom is the narrator speaking? Is it a reliable or **unreliable narrator**? Is it an all-knowing, **omniscient narrator**, a single point of view **limited narrator** or a combination of the two, a **limited-omniscient narrator**? How does the narrator tell the story? Which verb tense is used (past, present or future)? Which pronouns are used (first-, second- or third-person narration)? The narrator might retell the events in **reported speech**, or the narrator may act as a fly on the wall and use **direct speech**, relying heavily on dialogue and objective accounts of the action.	From the moment the narrator uses the word 'seemed' in the first line, the reader suspects that the narrator is omniscient and can hear the thoughts of Myop and see the events as they happen to her. 'The air held a keenness that made her nose twitch' uses personification to suggest that the narrator can even feel the interactions between Myop and the world around her. Furthermore, the narration is limited to the experiences of Myop, as the reader's first encounter with the dead man is Myop's first encounter with him. The story is told in the past tense, like a memory, in reported speech, 'she gave a little yelp of surprise', all of which makes the narrator reliable, as if she was there.
Characterisation: How does the writer use language to bring the characters to life, so that they live in the mind of the reader? Authors can show readers their characters' thoughts, actions and words, besides physical descriptions of the characters.	'[Myop] was ten, and nothing existed for her but her song, the stick clutched in her dark brown hand, and the tat-de-ta-ta-ta of accompaniment.' This line tells the reader that she is young, black and ignorant to the evils of her world.
Rising action: This is the part of the story where things become complicated. The action heightens and the characters become entwined in a conflict of some kind.	Myop finds herself in a dark, strange land, in a 'cove' where the air is 'damp' and the silence 'close and deep'. By this point, the reader realises that something is terribly wrong for the little girl.
Climax: This is the turning point of a story, where the events come to a head and tension has reached its highest point.	Myop accidentally steps on the dead man's face, 'between brow and nose'. At this point the reader is horrified by what it must be like for the ten-year-old girl to see such a gruesome sight.
Falling action: This comes after the climax, where the consequences of the action become clear.	Myop's response to this horrific moment is to 'lay down her flowers'. It suggests that she is both distraught by the sight and respectful of the man's death.
Denouement: This French word, which means 'unknotting', suggests that the conflict of the story is entirely unravelled. This is the final part of a story where lessons have been learnt and the reader feels some sense of closure.	The ending of the story is clearly marked with the line 'And the summer was over'. Seeing as summer technically ends on 21 September in the northern hemisphere, the reader can infer that Myop's summer has ended. More specifically, her innocence has come to an end.

AOE question

How can cultural contexts influence how texts are written and received?

While this unit takes a rather formative approach to analysing texts, you should not lose sight of the importance of context in shaping meaning. Before writing a comparative essay on Texts 1.39 and 1.40 (Activity 10.8), do some research on the authors of the texts, the themes found in their work and the contexts that have shaped their writings.

Over to you

10.8 You have studied two short stories in this unit, Texts 1.39 and 1.40, both related to death. What are the similarities and differences between these stories?

a Divide your class into two groups with one group focusing on the differences and the other focusing on the similarities. As a group, make a bullet-point list of the similarities or differences on a large sheet of paper or digital document. Refer to the key features as explained in the table. Share your group's list with everyone.

b Individually, write a comparative essay in the style of Paper 2. You can find out more about writing Paper 2 essays in Chapter 6. You might find it helpful to follow these steps. Your essay should aim to answer the question:

'In what ways and for what reasons is "death" explored in two literary works?'

- You may want to start by organising your ideas using a mind map.
- Write an outline for your essay.
- Write a good thesis statement, which makes a claim about the authors' purpose in writing these stories. Refer to the stylistic features that they used to construct their message.
- Find evidence from both texts to support the claims that you make in your thesis statement.
- Write paragraphs that follow the PEACE ACT structure, which is introduced in Chapter 6:

Point
Evidence from text 1
Analysis on text 1
Comparison of texts 1 and 2
Evidence from text 2
Analysis on text 2
Comparison of texts 1 and 2
Tie back to thesis statement

c Ask your teacher to assess your essay using the assessment criteria for Paper 2. How could your essay be improved? Rewrite your essay so that it would achieve higher marks on the criteria. Keep in mind that this is a practice essay, so your teacher may annotate your work.

d Share your essay with everyone in your class. Read through a selection of your classmates' essays. Collectively, as a class, make a list of 'useful phrases for comparing prose fiction' based on the strongest essays from your class.

TIP

Activity 10.8 asks you to write a comparative essay on two short stories as a practice exercise for Paper 2. When you write your actual Paper 2 essay, you can go into the exam room with two literary works in mind. These are works that you have not used for your individual oral or HL essay. You may have practised writing essays on these works already in class.

The only unknown factor is the four essay questions that appear on the exam paper. It helps to compare and contrast literary texts that are the same text type. This approach opens avenues for closer comparison and deeper exploration of your texts. Read Chapter 6 for further advice on Paper 2.

Extended essay

Are you considering writing a Category 1 essay on one or more literary works in English? Are you considering a Category 2 essay on a literary work in English and another in translation? Comparing and contrasting works, as you do in Activity 10.8, is a more difficult skill than analysing one work. However, comparison tends to increase the level of analysis, which is good for Criterion C (critical thinking). A good research question for an extended essay might read: 'To what degree do the authors of *The God of Small Things* and *The Passage to India* use narrative technique, characterisation and plot to depict the similar struggles of Indian society in the early and mid-20th century?'

10.9 This unit began with several six-word stories. Write your own six-word story on a sticky note, and display it on a wall for all of your classmates to see. Alternatively, share your story digitally with your classmates or create one online document of six-word stories as a class.

In a short 2-minute presentation, analyse one of your classmates' six-word stories. In your presentation, analyse how meaning is constructed through language. You can refer to the key terms from this unit or other relevant literary terms in your analysis. If you want to take this activity one step further, you can try turning a six-word story into a longer short story.

Further reading

- *How to Read Literature Like a Professor*, by Thomas C. Foster, is both a fun read and a helpful tool for language and literature students. The author explores several archetypal plots, common symbols and recurring themes in many great works of literature.
- *Exercises in Style* is a classic work by Raymond Queneau, originally in French but translated into English, which includes 99 retellings of the same story using different narrative techniques and plot structures.

Unit 1.11 Playscripts

Learning objectives

- become familiar with the key features of playscripts, and how playwrights use these features to construct meaning
- gain an understanding of playscripts by performing scenes and lines from them.

The word '**drama**' has two definitions: one referring to a play written for theatre, film or radio; the other referring to a highly emotional experience. Writers achieve drama, in both senses of the word, through **playscripts**. Playscripts are an interesting type of text because, like film scripts, they are written for the purpose of **performance**. While they are meant to be memorised, rehearsed and performed by actors on the **stage**, they are often analysed and explored by students in language and literature classrooms.

Throughout your exploration of playscripts in this unit, keep in mind that **playwrights** write with the expectation that actors and directors will understand how to bring their words to life. They did not write their plays just to be read. This unit invites you to analyse and perform some playscripts in an effort to better understand this text type.

TIP

HL students have to study at least *three* different literary forms. SL students have to study at least *two* different literary forms. Exploring one or more plays is a good way to meet this requirement. Studying a Shakespeare play will also help you meet the 'time' requirement (three different time periods at HL and two at SL).

TOK

Why visit the **theatre**? The Greek philosopher Aristotle suggested that people become better citizens by seeing a performance at a theatre. He believed that people could purge themselves of their emotions through the experiences offered by watching plays – a process known as **catharsis**. This idea suggests that, by becoming consumed in the drama of a story or a character's dilemma, audiences release emotions that they would otherwise repress. Think about the last time you visited the theatre or cinema. How did you feel afterward? Did you feel relieved or revitalised? Do you believe in the benefits of catharsis? Discuss your answers with classmates.

Word bank

drama
playscript
performance
stage
playwright
theatre
catharsis
lines
inflection
body language
character
characterisation
scene
freeze-frame
act
staging
props
set
lighting
costumes
entrance
exit
dialogue
monologue
soliloquy
dramatic aside
stage directions
speech directions
intonation
sound
music
offstage

Getting started

11.1 Stand in a circle so that you can see your classmates. You do not need chairs or tables. Here is a list of famous **lines** from famous plays and films. You do not need to know the play or film they were taken from or which characters spoke them.

Let everyone in your class read out the first line (a). Listen to how each person reads the line differently. Do this for each line (b–g). After going around the circle each time, have a brief discussion about which play or film you think the line is from and why you spoke it the way you did. How did the meaning change depending on the **inflection** of your voice and your use of **body language**?

a I have always depended on the kindness of strangers.

b Toto, I've got a feeling we're not in Kansas anymore.

c Misery acquaints a man with strange bedfellows.

d A martini. Shaken, not stirred.

e The truth is rarely pure and never simple.

f I'm going to make him an offer he can't refuse.

g Travelling through hyperspace ain't like dusting crops, farm boy!

LEARNER PROFILE

Communicator

An IB learner is a communicator. As you practise performing famous lines from famous films (Activity 11.1), you may discover that there are many different ways of saying the same thing. As you study language and literature, consider how people communicate through non-verbal uses of language.

11.2 Get into groups and assign each group one of the lines from Activity 11.1. As a group, do an online search for your quotation. Find out who said these words, in which play or film and what they possibly mean. Then report back to the class about the context in which the line was originally spoken.

a What does this line mean?

b What does it tell you about the **character** who spoke it? How does it contribute to the development of character? How does it contribute to **characterisation**?

c How is this line appropriate for the context in which it is spoken?

d With this information, how might you perform the line if you were the actor? Ask one member of your group to speak the line as you feel it should be spoken.

11.3 Read Text 1.41, the opening **scene** from *A Doll's House* by the Norwegian playwright Henrik Ibsen, and discuss your answers to these questions:

a Who are these characters? What kind of people are they? How are they similar or different? What is their relationship like?

b What makes you say this about the characters and their relationship? Can you find lines that they speak, actions they take or directions from the playwright that make you say these things about them?

c Search online for a video recording of a performance of this piece and watch it as a class. How does this recording change or confirm your impression of the characters and their relationship?

d Is your video recording of *A Doll's House* a recording of the play for the stage, performed before an audience? Or is it a film, for viewing on a screen? How does this affect your experience of this play?

e Based on your understanding of these opening lines, where is this play going? What predictions can you make about the play's characters and plot?

f Why, to the best of your understanding, did Henrik Ibsen write this play in 1879? Make an informed and educated guess, based on your analysis of these opening lines.

g Do an online search to find answers to the questions above. How accurate were your predictions? What could you find out about the author's purpose and message?

h Would you be interested in reading or watching the rest of *A Doll's House*? Why, or why not?

ATL

Thinking

Activity 11.3 asks you to make predictions on *A Doll's House* based on your reading of the opening lines. You can use similar strategies for engaging with the literary works that you are reading in your language and literature course. Making predictions is a good way to activate and encourage critical thinking, because you are mapping new ideas onto existing knowledge.

Text 1.41

A Doll's House

Henrik Ibsen 1879

ACT I

[SCENE.—A room furnished comfortably and tastefully, but not extravagantly. At the back, a door to the right leads to the entrance-hall, another to the left leads to Helmer's study. Between the doors stands a piano. In the middle of the left-hand wall is a door, and beyond it a window. Near the window are a round table, armchairs and a small sofa. In the right-hand wall, at the farther end, another door; and on the same side, nearer the footlights, a stove, two easy chairs and a rocking-chair; between the stove and the door, a small table. Engravings on the walls; a cabinet with china and other small objects; a small book-case with well-bound books. The floors are carpeted, and a fire burns in the stove.

It is winter. A bell rings in the hall; shortly afterwards the door is heard to open. Enter NORA, humming a tune and in high spirits. She is in outdoor dress and carries a number of parcels; these she lays on the table to the right. She leaves the outer door open after her, and through it is seen a PORTER who is carrying a Christmas Tree and a basket, which he gives to the MAID who has opened the door.]

Nora: Hide the Christmas Tree carefully, Helen. Be sure the children do not see it until this evening, when it is dressed. *[To the PORTER, taking out her purse.]* How much?

Porter: Sixpence.

Nora: There is a shilling. No, keep the change. *[The PORTER thanks her, and goes out. NORA shuts the door. She is laughing to herself, as she takes off her hat and coat. She takes a packet of macaroons from her pocket and eats one or two; then goes cautiously to her husband's door and listens.]* Yes, he is in. *[Still humming, she goes to the table on the right.]*

Helmer *[calls out from his room]*: Is that my little lark twittering out there?

Nora *[busy opening some of the parcels]*: Yes, it is!

Helmer: Is it my little squirrel bustling about?

Nora: Yes!

Helmer: When did my squirrel come home?

Nora: Just now. *[Puts the bag of macaroons into her pocket and wipes her mouth.]* Come in here, Torvald, and see what I have bought.

Helmer: Don't disturb me. *[A little later, he opens the door and looks into the room, pen in hand.]* Bought, did you say? All these things? Has my little spendthrift been wasting money again?

Nora: Yes but, Torvald, this year we really can let ourselves go a little. This is the first Christmas that we have not needed to economise.

Helmer: Still, you know, we can't spend money recklessly.

Nora: Yes, Torvald, we may be a wee bit more reckless now, mayn't we? Just a tiny wee bit! You are going to have a big salary and earn lots and lots of money.

Helmer: Yes, after the New Year; but then it will be a whole quarter before the salary is due.

Nora: Pooh! we can borrow until then.

Helmer: Nora! *[Goes up to her and takes her playfully by the ear.]* The same little featherhead! Suppose, now, that I borrowed fifty pounds today, and you spent it all in the Christmas week, and then on New Year's Eve a slate fell on my head and killed me, and –

Nora *[putting her hands over his mouth]*: Oh! don't say such horrid things.

Helmer: Still, suppose that happened, – what then?

Nora: If that were to happen, I don't suppose I should care whether I owed money or not.

Helmer: Yes, but what about the people who had lent it?

Nora: They? Who would bother about them? I should not know who they were.

Helmer: That is like a woman! But seriously, Nora, you know what I think about that. No debt, no borrowing. There can be no freedom or beauty about a home life that depends on borrowing and debt. We two have kept bravely on the straight road so far, and we will go on the same way for the short time longer that there need be any struggle.

Nora *[moving towards the stove]*: As you please, Torvald.

Helmer *[following her]*: Come, come, my little skylark must not droop her wings. What is this! Is my little squirrel out of temper? *[Taking out his purse.]* Nora, what do you think I have got here?

Nora *[turning round quickly]*: Money!

Helmer: There you are. *[Gives her some money.]* Do you think I don't know what a lot is wanted for housekeeping at Christmas-time?

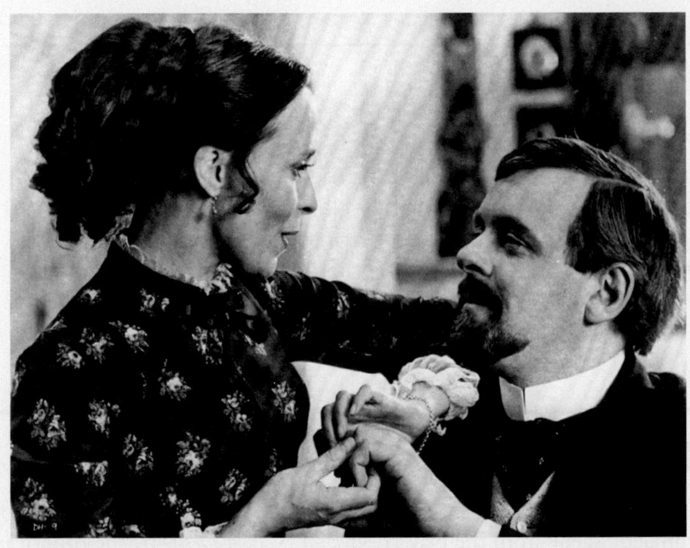

A Doll's House **is a popular text for good reason. You may find the script enjoyable. You may easily find filmed versions of the play online.**

AOE question

How can texts offer insights into other cultures?

A Doll's House (Text 1.41) was originally written in 'Dano-Norwegian', a form of Norwegian heavily influenced by Danish, and set in Norway. Henrik Ibsen, one of Europe's most influential playwrights, was known for commenting on society through his plays. What insights does this opening passage from *A Doll's House* give you into marriages in Norway in the late 19th century, when the play was written?

International mindedness

Reading works in translation, such as *A Doll's House*, is important for broadening your understanding of other cultures and times in history.

11.4 Look back to Unit 1.3 on film and Unit 1.10 on prose fiction. After reading Text 1.41, can you say that playscripts, as a text type, share any qualities with film or prose fiction? If so, how are these text types similar or different? Use a table like this one to map your answers.

Similarities between films and plays	Differences between films and plays
Similarities between stories and plays	**Differences between stories and plays**

CONCEPT

Representation

Activity 11.4 asks you about the differences between films, stories and plays. Is there a literary work that you are reading for class which has two different representations, perhaps through film, stage or prose fiction? You can discuss how the author's ideas are represented differently depending on the media used.

Model text

11.5 Read Text 1.42, a climactic scene from the play *A Streetcar Named Desire* by the American playwright Tennessee Williams. You do not have to know this play or the characters to appreciate the action happening in this scene.

a Get into groups and discuss what you think is happening in this scene. Then, as a group, select a part of the scene that you could perform.

b Assign each person in your group a different character from this scene. If you have more group members than characters, then you have directors as well!

c Imagine you were to freeze your performance of this part of this scene in a kind of '**freeze-frame**'. How would you stand or sit? How would you depict the characters and your part of the scene? Find a quiet area of your school and prepare your group's freeze-frame.

d Present your freeze-frame to your classmates in class. Take a photograph of your freeze-frame for future reference. Ask your classmates to guess which part of Text 1.42 you are depicting. Then explain why you chose the stances, positions and expressions that you did.

TEXT AND CONTEXT

This scene from *A Streetcar Named Desire* includes several characters and quite a lot of action. Blanche DuBois is staying with her sister Stella and Stella's husband Stanley, after having run away from her mysterious past. While Blanche and Stella come from a Southern, aristocratic background, Stanley is a 'working class' man from a Polish background. Stanley does not like the presence of his sister-in-law in his house and questions her reasons for staying with them.

In this scene, he has invited his friends to play poker one evening. Mitch, one of Stanley's friends, has taken a liking to Blanche. Stanley has already told Blanche not to play the radio while he is playing poker with his friends.

Text 1.42

A Streetcar Named Desire

Tennessee Williams 1947

Scene 3

Mitch: What do you teach? What subject?

Blanche: Guess!

Mitch: I bet you teach art or music? (*Blanche laughs delicately.*) Of course I could be wrong. You might teach arithmetic.

Blanche: Never arithmetic, sir; never arithmetic! (*With a laugh.*) I don't even know my multiplication tables! No, I have the misfortune of being an English instructor. I attempt to instil a bunch of bobby-soxers and drug-store Romeos with reverence for Hawthorne and Whitman and Poe!

Mitch: I guess that some of them are more interested in other things.

Blanche: How very right you are! Their literary heritage is not what most of them treasure above all else! But they're sweet things! And in the spring, it's touching to notice them making their first discovery of love! As if nobody had ever known it before!

The bathroom door opens and Stella comes out. Blanche continues talking to Mitch.

Blanche: Oh! Have you finished? Wait – I'll turn on the radio.

She turns the knobs on the radio and it begins to play 'Wien, Wien, nur du allein.' Blanche waltzes to the music with romantic gestures. Mitch is delighted and moves in awkward imitation like a dancing bear. Stanley stalks fiercely through the portieres into the bedroom. He crosses to the small white radio and snatches it off the table. With a shouted oath, he tosses the instrument out of the window.

Stella: Drunk – drunk – animal thing, you! (*She rushes through to the poker table.*) All of you – please go home! If any of you have one spark of decency in you –

Blanche: Stella, watch out, he's –

Stanley charges after Stella.

Men: (*feebly*) Take it easy, Stanley. Easy fellow. – Let's all . . .

Stella: You lay your hands on me and I'll . . .

She backs out of sight. He advances and disappears. There is the sound of a blow. Stella cries out. Blanche screams and runs into the kitchen. The men rush forward and there is grappling and cursing. Something is overturned with a crash.

Blanche: My sister is going to have a baby!

Mitch: This is terrible.

scene number
dialogue
speech directions
interpunctuation
stage directions
entrance
staging
offstage

Blanche: Lunacy, absolute lunacy!

Mitch: Get him in here, men.

Stanley is forced, pinioned by the two men, into the bedroom. He nearly throws them off. Then all at once he subsides and is limp in their grasp. They speak quietly and lovingly to him and he leans his face on one of their shoulders.

Stella (*in a high, unnatural voice, out of sight*): I want to go away, I want to go away!

Mitch: Poker shouldn't be played in a house with women.

A scene from the 1951 film of *A Streetcar Named Desire*, with Marlon Brando (Stanley) and Vivien Leigh (Blanche), depicting the conflict that takes place in the poker-night scene.

Key features explained

11.6 Read the key features of playscripts as explained in this table. Then, in groups, draw a map of a stage for this scene of *A Streetcar Named Desire* (Text 1.42). Include the positions of all of the objects and the movement of the characters throughout the scene. Think about the use of lights as well. You may want to use your freeze-frame (Activity 11.5) as a source of inspiration for doing this activity. Present your map to other groups and explain the decisions you have had to make.

Key features	Examples from Text 1.42
Act and **scene**: Most plays are divided into acts and scenes. Scenes are significant for framing the dramatic action, dialogue and setting.	*A Streetcar Named Desire* does not have acts, only scenes, which is less traditional. Each scene in this play is defined by a different conflict.
Staging: The assembly of **props**, the **set** and the placement of characters in relation to each other and these objects is known as the staging. Staging, in a broader sense, includes **lighting** and **costumes** as well.	This scene relies on a complicated set, as there are multiple rooms, such as a bathroom, kitchen and bedroom. The radio, arguably, is a key prop on this set. It symbolises romanticism and escapism.
Entrance: The way in which an actor comes on to the stage (entrance) and leaves the stage (**exit**) is important to establishing characterisation.	Stella's entrance is an interruption of Blanche's flirting with Mitch. Her entrance into the room with the poker table sets the tone of the scene as well, as she tells all of Stanley's friends to leave.
Dialogue: Dialogue refers to the exchange of words between characters. **Monologue** is when one character speaks for a longer duration for other characters to hear but not for them to necessarily respond. A **soliloquy** refers to a character speaking aloud to himself or herself privately, with the audience listening in. A **dramatic aside** is when a character speaks directly to the audience, conscious and aware of their existence.	The scene starts with a dialogue between Blanche and Mitch, in which the audience can see that they like each other. Interestingly the scene is about Stanley, but he does not say a word. Mitch's last line, 'Poker shouldn't be played in a house with women', does not seem to be directed to anyone in particular. It could be considered a short monologue.
Stage directions: This broad term refers to any text that is not part of the dialogue. They may tell actors where and how to move around the stage.	Tennessee Williams includes several key stage directions in this scene. The directions describe Stanley's violent actions: how he throws the radio out the window, beats his pregnant wife and is held down by his friends.
Speech directions: Stage directions can include speech directions which tell actors how to use inflection, accent or **intonation** in their voice.	Tennessee Williams includes adverbs to describe the ways in which the actors should speak, such as Blanche laughing 'delicately', the men speaking 'feebly' and Stella screaming in a 'high, unnatural voice'.
Sound and **music**: Besides the sound coming from the characters and their actions, stage directions may include instructions to play music or add other noises.	The radio has a large role in this scene, as it seems to be a source of conflict. The song that plays on the radio, 'Wien, Wien, nur du allein', is about Vienna, a faraway city that the singer dreams about. In a sense, it represents Blanche's dreaming of a romantic place. This music is contrasted with the crashing noises of domestic violence coming from the kitchen, moments later.
Offstage: Sometimes action does not happen on the stage for the audience to see but offstage for the audience to imagine.	Much of the violence in this scene happens offstage, though it is not clear from the stage directions how much the audience can see as the characters move from the poker table to the bathroom to the bedroom.

CONCEPT

Representation

The choices that directors and designers make, when staging a play, are about *representation*. How do they represent the playwright's ideas? The director's choices translate the abstract themes and ideas of a play through lighting, costumes, props, characterisation, sets and sound.

Over to you

11.7 If you are reading a playscript for your language and literature course, try staging and acting out a scene from it with a group of classmates. If you are not reading a playscript for your coursework, try writing your own scene based on a passage of prose fiction and stage it for your classmates.

AOE question

How can cultural contexts influence how texts are written and received?

As you think about staging a play for your classmates (Activity 11.7), consider the context in which you live. Compare this context to the context in which the play or novel was originally written.

- How have times changed since the play was written?
- How might you present the play in a different setting or time?
- What decisions must you make, in order to make the scene relevant to a modern audience?

Further reading

- It is recommended that you study and see a play by William Shakespeare at some point in your life, if not during your language and literature course. One big advantage to studying a Shakespeare play, besides being able to find many secondary sources on them, is that you can find different (filmed) performances and interpretations. This can lead to meaningful classroom discussion.
- *How to Read a Play: Script Analysis for Directors* by Damon Kiely offers a practical approach for students, actors and directors who are studying playscripts and trying to bring them to life.

CAS

Creativity is part of CAS. Performing in a staged production of a play is a good activity for your CAS requirement. As you reflect on your role in such a production, consider how creativity is about both self-expression and collaboration.

Extended essay

Did you enjoy studying *A Streetcar Named Desire* and *A Doll's House* in this unit? Category 2 extended essays allow you to compare and contrast a work written in English with a work in translation. These two texts may prove useful for this kind of essay. Any time you compare and contrast works, your level of critical thinking (Criterion C), analysis and evaluation will increase. Comparing and contrasting two texts of the same text type could also prove useful in your extended essay.

Unit 1.12 Poems

Learning objectives

- learn to identify some of the key features of poetry
- develop the skills to analyse and interpret poems, including your critical thinking skills.

What makes English poetic? Are there styles and structures in the English language that naturally appeal to readers' ears? Poetry, after all, is meant to be read aloud. In this unit you will study several poems, reading them aloud. You will discuss what makes poetry 'poetry', analyse several poems and read an essay on a poem. Through this study of poetry, you may come to appreciate how writers use language and structure to articulate some of the more intricate ideas in life.

Word bank

metaphor
simile
imagery
alliteration
assonance
consonance
syllable
metric foot
rhythm
verse
metre
enjambment
stanza
rhyming scheme
prosody
internal rhyme
free verse
blank verse
couplet
English sonnet
volta
caesura
scansion

Getting started

12.1 What *is* poetry? Write your own definition of poetry on a sticky note and display it on a board for your classmates to read. What commonalities do you see between the definitions?

12.2 Read these famous quotations by poets about poetry. How are these definitions similar to or different from your answers to Activity 12.1? What do you think each poet means by their definition?

a 'Poetry is the rhythmical creation of beauty in words.' – Edgar Allan Poe

b 'Poetry is when an emotion has found its thought and the thought has found its words.' – Robert Frost

c 'Poetry comes from the highest happiness or the deepest sorrow.' – A.P.J. Abdul Kalam

d 'Poetry: the best words in the best order.' – Samuel Taylor Coleridge

e 'Poetry is a state of free float.' – Margaret Atwood

f 'Poetry is the lifeblood of rebellion, revolution, and the raising of consciousness.' – Alice Walker

g 'Poetry is the opening and closing of a door, leaving those who look through to guess about what is seen during the moment.' – Carl Sandburg

h 'Poetry, at its best, is the language your soul would speak if you could teach your soul to speak.' – Jim Harrison

i 'Poetry is the spontaneous overflow of powerful feelings: it takes its origin from emotion recollected in tranquillity.' – William Wordsworth

12.3 Here are several lines (a–i) taken from poems, speeches, songs and films. How poetic is each line? In small groups, rate each line, using a five-star scale: five stars being the most poetic and one star not very poetic at all. For each line, discuss how and why you would rate each line. Explain your group's choices to other groups in your class. Comment as a class on the kinds of challenges you faced in doing this activity.

a 'Boom, boom, boom, I want you in my room.' – Vengaboys

b 'Amazing grace, how sweet the sound, that saved a wretch like me.' – John Newton

c 'Life is like a box of chocolates, you never know what you're going to get.' – Forrest Gump

d 'How many roads must a man walk down, before you can call him a man?' – Bob Dylan

e 'Look at me! Look at me! Look at me NOW! It is fun to have fun, But you have to know how.' – Dr. Seuss

f 'Parting is such sweet sorrow, That I shall say good night till it be morrow.' – William Shakespeare

g 'Fly like a butterfly, sting like a bee. The hands can't hit what the eyes can't see.' – Mohammed Ali

h 'How do I love thee? Let me count the ways. I love thee to the depth and breadth and height, My soul can reach, when feeling out of sight, For the ends of being and ideal grace.' – Elizabeth Barrett Browning

i 'As we know, there are known knowns; there are things we know we know. We also know there are known unknowns; that is to say we know there are some things we do not know. But there are also unknown unknowns – the ones we don't know we don't know.' – Donald Rumsfeld

12.4 As a class, and based on your discussions from Activity 12.3, think of several criteria for describing and defining 'poetic language':

- When does language become 'poetic'?
- When does a text become a 'poem'?

International mindedness

Do different cultures find different forms of language more poetic than others? Activity 12.3 asks you to identify poetic forms. Will these be different, depending on your cultural background? Or is poetry absolute and universal? Would you be able to identify poetic language, when read aloud in a foreign language?

12.5 Have you ever wondered why students are asked to study poetry in school? Have you ever discussed with your teacher *how* you should study poetry? Read Text 1.43, a poem about teaching poetry and discuss your answers to these questions:

a How does Billy Collins suggest students should explore poetry?

b How does he use **metaphor** and **simile** to make his point?

c How poetic is his poem? Does it meet one or more of your criteria for poetry from Activity 12.4?

d What kinds of approaches to learning poetry have you taken in English class before?

e How far do you agree with Collins's approach? How do you like to study poetry?

Text 1.43

Introduction to Poetry

Billy Collins 1988

I ask them to take a poem
and hold it up to the light
like a color slide

or press an ear against its hive.

I say drop a mouse into a poem
and watch him probe his way out,

or walk inside the poem's room
and feel the walls for a light switch.

I want them to waterski
across the surface of a poem
waving at the author's name on the shore.

But all they want to do
is tie the poem to a chair with rope
and torture a confession out of it.

They begin beating it with a hose
to find out what it really means.

Billy Collins is an American poet and teacher of poetry, who has been celebrated around the world for his achievements.

TOK

Text 1.43 ends by suggesting that students want to find out what poems 'really mean'.

- How do we ascertain meaning in the arts in general?
- Is it possible to understand the meaning of a poem with any level of certainty? Do you think poets always know the meaning of their own poems?
- How is the word 'meaning' different from 'purpose'?

Discuss these questions as a class.

CONCEPT

Transformation

Does Text 1.43 change your understanding of textual analysis and close reading of poetry? In this course you explore how a text can be 'transformative'. *Transformation* refers to how the reader's outlook on the world changes as the result of what they have read. Does Billy Collins do this for you? Discuss.

Model text

12.6 At home or in a quiet space, record yourself speaking aloud 'Bright Star' by John Keats (Text 1.44) using audio or video. Aim for an effective reading that allows listeners to appreciate Keats's language.

- Listen to your recording. If you are not happy with it, record a new version. Once you are happy with the recording, send it to your teacher.
- Write a 200-word reflection piece in which you comment on the process you took to create this recording. What challenges did you face, and how did you overcome them?
- Share your reflection piece with your teachers and classmates.

No one has to hear your recording unless you are happy to share it with others in the class.

LEARNER PROFILE

Reflective

Activity 12.6 encourages you to write a reflection piece in response to your reading of a poem. The philosopher John Dewey once said that learning is experience plus reflection. After listening to a recording of yourself reading a poem, what have you learnt from the experience?

Text 1.44

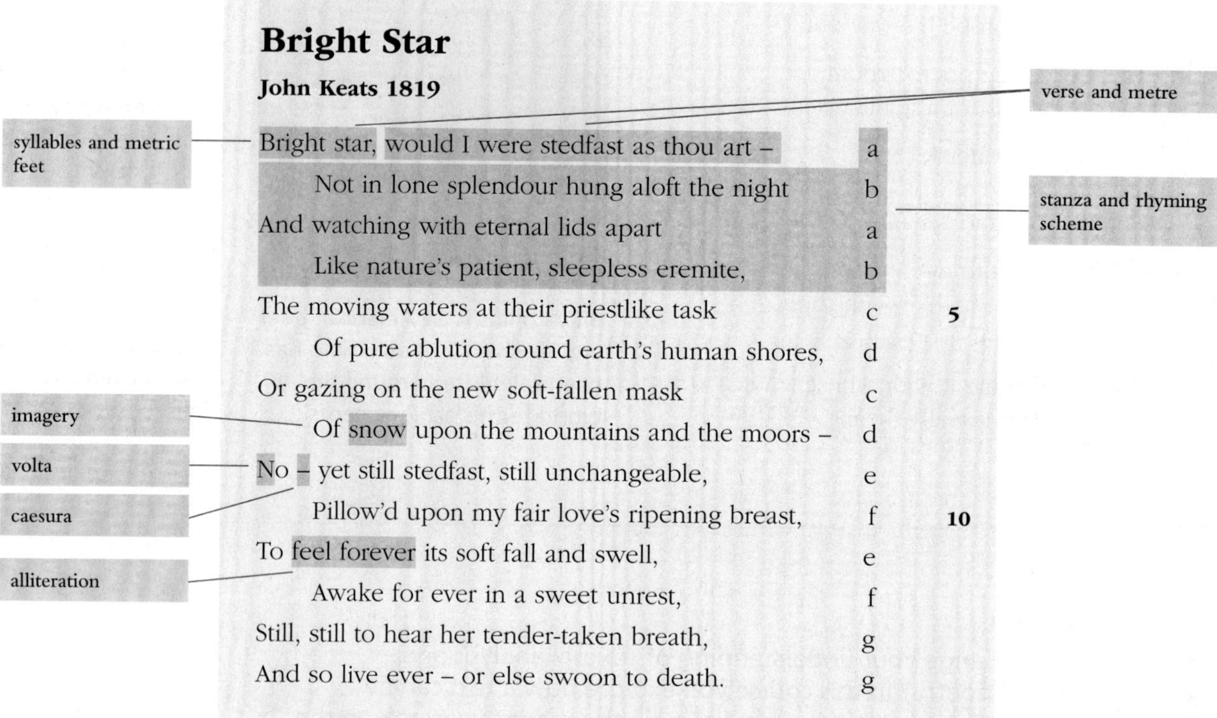

Bright Star

John Keats 1819

Bright star, would I were stedfast as thou art – a
Not in lone splendour hung aloft the night b
And watching with eternal lids apart a
Like nature's patient, sleepless eremite, b
The moving waters at their priestlike task c
Of pure ablution round earth's human shores, d
Or gazing on the new soft-fallen mask c
Of snow upon the mountains and the moors – d
No – yet still stedfast, still unchangeable, e
Pillow'd upon my fair love's ripening breast, f
To feel forever its soft fall and swell, e
Awake for ever in a sweet unrest, f
Still, still to hear her tender-taken breath, g
And so live ever – or else swoon to death. g

TEXT AND CONTEXT

- An eremite is a hermit or recluse, someone living in isolation and devoting themselves to their religious beliefs.
- Ablution means 'washing' or 'cleansing' with the sense of a sacred ritual.

Key features explained

12.7 The key features of poetry are outlined here and highlighted in Text 1.44. Are there any features that you recognise from working on your recording for Activity 12.6? After reading these terms and examples, how would you change your recording of your reading of the poem 'Bright Star' by John Keats?

Key features	Examples from Text 1.44
Imagery: Poems are often full of imagery, as they aim to appeal to the senses to engage the reader.	In 'Bright Star' the narrator paints several pictures in the mind of the reader, by describing snow on the moors and the breathing of his lover.
Alliteration: Poems are meant to be read aloud. Many poems include alliteration, the repetition of a consonant at the beginning of words in sequence. The repetition of the same vowel sound is known as **assonance**. The repetition of consonants in the middle of a word is known as **consonance**.	'feel forever' and 'soft . . . swell' are examples of alliteration; 'pure', 'ablution' and 'human' are examples of assonance with the long 'u' sound. In the line 'watching with eternal lids apart' the 't' sound is repeated throughout the words in the middle or ends of the words. All of these examples make the poem read more fluently and musically.
Syllables and **metric feet**: Every word in English consists of one or more syllables. A syllable is the unit of sound, when speaking a word, which usually has one vowel. Syllables provide the beats of the **rhythm** of a poem. Some syllables are stressed, while others are naturally unstressed. When analysing poetry, you can look for the clusters and patterns of stresses in a line. Each unit of stressed and unstressed sound is known as a metric foot (see Activity 12.8).	Keats opens the poem with the words 'Bright star', two strong syllables that seem to echo throughout the remainder of the poem as the narrator contemplates which characteristics of the star he wants to emulate. The rest of the poem mostly includes iambs, unstressed syllables followed by stressed syllables, which make the poem bounce along in a dream-like way. 'No – yet' is the only interruption in this dream.
Verse and **metre**: Each line of poetry is called a 'verse', which should not be confused with sentences. When a sentence carries on over the end of a line, it is called **enjambment** (or enjambement), which poets may use for artistic reasons. The rhythmic structure of each verse is called metre. It may consist of any number of metric feet (see Activity 12.9).	Generally speaking, 'Bright Star' has five iambic feet in each verse, meaning it uses iambic pentameter (see table with Activity 12.9). This format, traditionally used by poets in the 19th century, was characteristic of Romanticism.
Stanza and **rhyming scheme**: Studying poetry is, to some extent, a study of **prosody**, which refers to the patterns of rhythm and sounds used in poetry. To find patterns, look to the stanzas. Stanzas are to poetry what paragraphs are to prose. They give the reader a sense of structure and organisation. When studying the structure of poems, you may notice the use of rhyme, sometimes within a verse (**internal rhyme**) or at the end of each verse. Many poems, however, do not rhyme at all. **Free verse** does not rhyme. **Blank verse**, which follows a certain metre such as iambic pentameter, also does not rhyme.	Notice how the first line of 'Bright Star' rhymes with the third, the second line rhymes with the fourth, and so forth, until the final two lines (g), which are known as a **couplet**. This is the pattern of an **English sonnet**. This traditional format, inspired by the Italians, was commonly use by Romantic poets.
Volta: Sonnets sometimes take a turn or shift in their message or argument, which is known as a volta.	The narrator is contemplating the kinds of traits of the star that he wants to emulate. Rather than shining like a lonesome hermit, he would rather shine on his lover's breast.
Caesura: Apostrophes, full stops and hyphens can be used to make the reader take a break or pause while reading the poem aloud. This use of caesura allows the reader and listener to contemplate the poet's words.	Keats uses hyphens in lines 1, 8, 9 and 14. The narrator opens the poem by commenting on the steadfast quality of the star. After the caesurae in lines 8 and 9, he returns to the reasons why he wants to shine like a star. And if he cannot shine on his lover and hear her breath, then he would rather die, another sharp contrast indicated by the caesura in the last verse.

12.8 As suggested in the table, there are various kinds of metric feet or patterns of syllables. Analysing the use of metre in poetry, though not an exact science, involves **scansion**. This is the process of scanning a verse to determine its rhythm. You can do this by annotating the poem and placing symbols above the syllables or words. The ◡ symbol can be used to indicate unstressed sound. The / symbol can be used to indicate stressed sound. You can also use italics when editing texts electronically to show which syllables are stressed. Both italics and symbols have been used in this table.

Five sorts of metric feet used in poetry

Name	Pattern	Examples
iamb	◡ / unstressed, *stressed*	◡ / would /
trochee	/ ◡ *stressed*, unstressed	/ ◡ *pil*low'd
spondee	/ / *stressed, stressed*	/ / *Still, still*
anapest	◡ ◡ / unstressed, unstressed, *stressed*	◡ ◡ / ripening *breast*
dactyl	/ ◡ ◡ *stressed*, unstressed, unstressed	eremite

Copy these lines of poetry and annotate them, showing where the stressed and unstressed sounds appear. Break the words and syllables up into feet by using a line '|'. See example 'a'.

a | The *mov* | ing *wa* | ters *at* | their *priest* | like *task*|

a 'The moving waters at their priestlike task' – John Keats

b 'anyone lived in a pretty how town' – E.E. Cummings

c 'If I should die think only this of me' – Rupert Brooke

d 'Sarah Cynthia Sylvia Stout would not take the garbage out' – Shel Silverstein

e 'Now only words in a rhyme' – Carol Ann Duffy

f 'Gas! GAS! Quick, boys! – An ecstasy of fumbling' – Wilfred Owen

12.9 Poetic verse comes in all sizes and shapes. Within the world of poetry there are several types of poems and traditions of poetry writing.

a Get into groups and assign each group a different poetry type from this list. Do some research to find the defining features of your type of poetry.

b Find an example of your poetry type and share it with your classmates. In a short group presentation, comment on the use of rhyming scheme, metre (see table) and other defining characteristics.

- English sonnet
- Italian sonnet
- ode
- villanelle
- limerick
- ballad
- haiku
- epic poem
- elegy.

Rhythmic metres used in poetry

Number of feet	Name of metre	Examples (all iambic)
5	Pentameter	◡ / ◡ / ◡ / ◡ / ◡ / | Of *snow* | up*on* | the *moun* | tains *and* | the *moors* |
4	Tetrameter	◡ / ◡ / ◡ / ◡ / | A*maz* | ing *Grace* | how *sweet* | the *sound* |
3	Trimeter	◡ / ◡ / ◡ / | That *saved* | a *wretch* | like *me* |
2	Dimeter	◡ / ◡ / | be *gone* | be *gone* |

Over to you

12.10 Structural features of poetry are useful, but how do you incorporate these into a meaningful analysis of a poem? As you analyse a poem, you should avoid focusing too much on form, structure and features ('beating it with a hose', in the words of Billy Collins) and not focusing enough on themes, purpose and meaning. As well as identifying and commenting on the features of poetry, it is important to comment on the *effects* these features have on the reader.

a Start by listening to what the poem is telling you. Text 1.45 has been highlighted with four different colours. The student who has highlighted the poem has identified common themes within the text. They have included a colour-coded key to show the commonalities in the text.

b Find a poem that you want to analyse and write about in an essay. Ask your teacher to provide you with a poem if you do not have any ideas. Use four or five different colours and highlight four or five ideas or themes in the poem.

c Create a colour-coded key to accompany your highlights and annotations.

Text 1.45

Seamus Heaney was a Nobel Prize-winning poet from Ireland. 'Blackberry-Picking' is taken from one of his best-known collections of poetry called *Death of a Naturalist* (1966).

Blackberry-Picking

Seamus Heaney 1966

Late August, given heavy rain and sun
For a full week, the blackberries would ripen.
At first, just one, a glossy purple clot
Among others, red, green, hard as a knot.
You ate that first one and its flesh was sweet
Like thickened wine: summer's blood was in it
Leaving stains upon the tongue and lust for
Picking. Then red ones inked up and that hunger
Sent us out with milk cans, pea tins, jam-pots
Where briars scratched and wet grass bleached our boots.
Round hayfields, cornfields and potato-drills
We trekked and picked until the cans were full
Until the tinkling bottom had been covered
With green ones, and on top big dark blobs burned
Like a plate of eyes. Our hands were peppered
With thorn pricks, our palms sticky as Bluebeard's.
We hoarded the fresh berries in the byre.
But when the bath was filled we found a fur,
A rat-grey fungus, glutting on our cache.
The juice was stinking too. Once off the bush
The fruit fermented, the sweet flesh would turn sour.
I always felt like crying. It wasn't fair
That all the lovely canfuls smelt of rot.
Each year I hoped they'd keep, knew they would not.

Colour-coded key

- A sense of eagerness and hope
- Rural images, a celebration of the countryside lifestyle
- Sensual language and imagery that embellishes blackberry-picking
- Hardships and the disappointment of decay

AOE question

How useful is it to describe a work as 'classic'?

You have read three poems in this unit. Is there any reason to attach the label 'classic' to any one of these? The word 'valid' is also interesting, as it relates to logic. How can you validate their 'classic' status? As a class, define the term 'classic' and explain your answers to these questions in a group discussion.

12.11 Text 1.46 is an HL essay that explores 'Blackberry-Picking' by Seamus Heaney (Text 1.45).

a Where, in the essay, do you see literary terms about poetry from this unit?

b Where, in the essay, do you see evidence that background information about the poet, Seamus Heaney, has been researched and incorporated into the essay?

c How are the paragraphs organised and structured? What is the purpose of each paragraph?

d What phrases could you take from this essay and use in an essay that analyses any text?

e Where in the essay do you see evidence of critical thinking?

f How would this essay score as an HL essay? Use the assessment criteria in the introduction to give it marks and a grade. How could it be improved to score a higher mark?

Compare your marks and comments to those of the examiner, provided after the essay.

ATL

Thinking skills

Activity 12.11 asks you to find evidence of critical thinking in the student's HL essay that analyses the poem 'Blackberry-Picking'. *Thinking skills* are part of the approaches to learning in the IB Diploma Programme, and include skills such as:

- analysis
- evaluation
- the ability to find patterns
- the ability to build conceptual knowledge.

Can you find evidence of these skills in the sample HL essay? What do they *look* like?

TIP

You may want to analyse a poem or collection of poetry by the same poet for your HL essay. You could use the sample HL essay provided as a model for your essay.

AOE question

How can texts present challenges and offer insights?

Notice how the line of inquiry for the sample HL essay almost mirrors this question from 'Readers, writers and texts' .For your HL essay, you may wish to 'tweak' one of the questions from one of the areas of exploration, turning it into a 'line of inquiry' which focuses on a text that you have explored in class.

HL Essay – Sample 1

Line of inquiry

How does Seamus Heaney's poem 'Blackberry-Picking' offer insight into the challenges of growing up in rural Ireland?

Essay

Poetry can offer readers a window into the life of a poet. When reading Seamus Heaney's first-published collection of poems, *Death of a Naturalist*, the poem 'Blackberry-Picking' (see Appendix) in particular offers readers a window into the poet's life. It raises the question: 'How does Seamus Heaney's poem 'Blackberry-Picking' offer insight into the challenges of growing up in rural Ireland?' The poem recalls Seamus Heaney's memories of gathering blackberries, giving audiences a better understanding of the life lessons he learnt growing up on a farm. Through the author's use of language and structure, Seamus Heaney shows readers how futile and disappointing it is to cultivate nature.

While it is good to open with a 'hook' or a sentence that grabs your reader's attention, be careful not to overgeneralise. This opening sentence is general but still relevant to the line of inquiry. In fact it sets up the line of inquiry nicely.

If you are analysing a poem, add it as an appendix to your HL essay. 'Blackberry-Picking' is Text 1.45 in this unit.

Try integrating your line of inquiry into the introduction, so as to give your essay a sense of direction.

A good introduction ends with a thesis statement. This thesis statement answers the line of inquiry, comments on the author's purpose and refers to the author's use of 'language and structure'.

In a good piece of textual analysis, examples of linguistic features are given to support any claims or points.

This is an example of an 'integrated' quotation, meaning that the student's ideas include a few words from the primary source. This is good practice.

Notice how the last line of each paragraph does not end with a quotation or illustration. Instead, the last line of a paragraph should link back to the thesis or topic sentence.

The phrase 'through the use of . . . ' is perhaps the most common phrase in students' work. Nevertheless, it is used for good reason, as it allows you to make a connection between form and meaning. That, after all, is what textual analysis is about.

Notice the student's effective use of parentheses, commas, full stops and quotation marks. Including coherent references will help you both on Criteria A and C.

Use language from the line of inquiry in order to keep the essay focused and relevant.

Be careful not to include such ideas as common knowledge. It is important to cite secondary sources where necessary. This essay could use a bibliography to list 'works consulted' and 'works cited'.

The poem 'Blackberry-Picking' carries a sense of eagerness and hope, which Seamus Heaney presumably held as a boy, growing up in rural Ireland. This sense of eagerness is exemplified in his choice of verbs, such as 'sent out' (line 9), 'trekked', 'picked' (line 12) and 'hoarded' (line 17). The use of the past tense suggests that the poem is based on the poet's memory of a regular, recurring activity on the farm. This poem, like many of Heaney's poems in *Death of a Naturalist*, is in the tradition of poetry of William Wordsworth, which takes inspiration from 'emotion recollected in tranquillity'. Furthermore, his heavy use of consonance within these verbs, such as the 't' sound in 'sent out' (line 9), the 'k' sound in 'trekked and picked' (line 12) and the 'd' sound in 'hoarded' (line 17), emphasises his boy-like sense of eagerness. Similarly, the verb 'hoped' in the last line uses two plosives 'p' and 'd' in close proximity, which is not easily pronounced by the reader but easily noticed by the listener. By including this word in the past tense at the end of the poem, it becomes clear that the sense of hope and eagerness would both come and go 'each year' (line 24) for the poet. Seamus Heaney shows the reader how nature provides a recurring sense of hope that dissipates as quickly as it comes.

Through the use of imagery and diction, Seamus Heaney both celebrates rural life and comments on its hardships in his poem 'Blackberry-Picking'. The nouns often point to material objects found around farms, such as 'milk cans', 'pea tins' and 'jam-pots' (line 9), natural elements, such as 'briars', 'wet grass' (line 10), and 'bush' (line 20), and farmland in 'hayfields', 'cornfields' and 'potato-drills' (line 11). These nouns are examples of imagery, as they appeal to the senses and enable the reader to picture rural Ireland and the narrator's lifestyle. In one sense the images are celebratory, as they appear in conjunction with his boyhood eagerness and hope. For example, the natural elements, such as the 'rain and sun' (line 1) would make the blackberries 'ripen' (line 2), and the material objects such as 'the cans' would be 'full' (line 12). In an opposite sense though, the imagery is associated with the hardships of the rural life. The natural elements, such as the 'wet grass' (line 10), would bleach the narrator's boots, and the 'briars' (line 10) would scratch his hands. The 'rat-grey' (line 19) colour of the 'fungus' (line 19) 'fur' (line 18) is perhaps the most striking image in the poem, as it appeals to both tactile and visual senses, with associations of the plague and disease. The fungus symbolises nature's inevitable turn towards decay, with which the narrator must come to terms. With this use of imagery, Seamus Heaney gives the reader insight into both the beauty of rural Ireland and challenges of cultivating nature.

Interestingly, 'Blackberry-Picking' includes sensual language, which is also used to develop the theme of growing up. The poem is full of rich, deep colours such as 'purple' (line 3), 'red' (lines 4 and 8) and 'stains upon the tongue' (line 7), which not only have associations with human sexuality, but also sound quite sensual when spoken. The consonance of the 'l' sound in 'glossy purple clot' rolls off the speaker's tongue in an almost suggestive manner. The fifth verse, 'You ate that first one and its flesh was sweet' (line 5) and the sixth verse, 'summer's blood', seem to refer to the loss of virginity. The sensual language runs parallel with the boy's eagerness to pick the berries, as seen with the use of enjambment in verses seven and eight 'lust for [line break] Picking'. The allusion to Bluebeard is the first sign that sexual discovery, like the excitement of picking blackberries, will eventually fade and spoil. 'Bluebeard' (line 16) is a reference to a French folktale about a wealthy man who marries and kills women habitually. His insatiable appetite for sex was coupled with violence, leaving the women he seduced dead. In a similar way, the narrator and his friends see the result of their picking, 'dark blobs burned Like a plate of eyes' (lines 14–15) and their 'hands were peppered With thorn pricks' (lines 15–16), with astonishment and horror. 'Palms sticky as Bluebeard's' (line 16) suggests that the berry stains on their hands were comparable to the bloodstains on Bluebeard's hands. This juxtaposition of desire and grief is seen throughout the final lines of the poem: 'juice' appears in conjunction with 'stinking' (line 20), 'fruit' with 'fermented' (line 21), 'sweet flesh' with 'sour' (line 21) and 'lovely canfuls' with 'rot' (line 23). This contrast shows the reader that hedonism and delight are paired with sorrow and decay, a life lesson that the narrator learns growing up on the farm in Ireland.

The constant juxtaposition of beauty with hardship, naiveté with experience, and hope with despair is perhaps best observed by studying the structure of Seamus Heaney's poem. While each verse uses pentameter, there is no symmetrical rhyming structure or use of rhythmical feet. The poem begins with a spondee followed by four iambs, '*Late Aug* | ust *gi* | ven *hea* | vy *rain* | and *sun*', followed by a trochee at the end of the second line, '*rip* en,' which seems to throw off its sense of rhythm. Just when the listener senses a rhyming pattern after lines three and four with 'clot' and 'knot,' there are no rhymes until the final two verses. These act as tidy book ends with chaos in between, a juxtaposition that relates to the themes of the poem. The structure of the poem implies that nature cannot be contained or managed by people, as most rhymes are half rhymes, such as 'sweet' (line 5) with 'it' (line 6), 'lust for' (line 7) with 'hunger' (line 8) and 'jam-pots' (line 9) with 'boots' (line 10). Just when the listener is used to this imperfection, the poem ends with a perfect rhyme: 'That all the lovely canfuls smelt of *rot*. Each year I hoped they'd keep, knew they would *not*.' This final word echoes the word 'knot' from verse four, suggesting nature has unravelled the narrator's plans to pick and eat all the berries. This unravelling is first signalled in verse 18 with the word 'But', which acts as a volta, or turning point in the poem: 'But when the bath was filled we found a fur' (line 18). From this point, the disappointment of decay sets in. The 'fungus' (line 19) makes the berries 'rot' (line 23), and the narrator feels like 'crying' (line 22). 'It wasn't fair' (line 22) sounds like the language of a child, rather than the language of a sonnet. This use of language and structure depicts the narrator coming to grips with the hardships of farm life and growing up in rural Ireland. Nature, it seems, taught Seamus Heaney's to deal with and accept the futility of trying to harness nature.

On the surface, the poem 'Blackberry-Picking' depicts Seamus Heaney, the author and narrator, struggling to understand why all of his precious berries would rot each year. However, as the reader digs deeper into this poem, the messages of the poem become more abstract. Eagerness and hope often gravitate towards hardship and despair. Lust leads to disappointment. Nature is full of life but also decay. The author shares these messages with the reader through language and structures that match their sentiment, with regular but irregular rhyming schemes, beautiful but ugly images and sensual but harsh diction. These careful juxtapositions are what make Seamus Heaney's poem timeless and effective, giving readers an understanding of both the author's life and life in general.

Notice how this essay refers to the reader and listener frequently. This is good practice and will help you score well on Criterion B.

Several sentences in this paragraph begin with 'this' or 'that'. Such words point to previous ideas and give the essay coherence.

Do not worry about sounding repetitive by returning to your main points in each paragraph. This gives the essay coherence and unity.

The student's own writing is full of parallelisms and effective stylistic devices. Proofread and edit your writing before you submit your essay to ensure that it is your best work.

HL Essay – Sample 1 – Examiner's marks and comments

Criterion A: Knowledge, understanding and interpretation: 4 out of 5 marks

The essay is very analytical, focusing exclusively on one primary source. The scope of the inquiry on the 'challenges of growing up in rural Ireland' is very broad and therefore difficult to cover entirely. A better line of inquiry might have read: 'How does Seamus Heaney's poem "Blackberry-Picking" offer insight into the challenges that he faced when growing up in rural Ireland?' The student's interpretations of the poem are very focused on Heaney's experiences. References to the poem are integrated effectively into the argument. Arguably, the student's knowledge and understanding of the poem are not based solely on an analysis of the text, meaning that secondary sources should have been referenced.

Extended essay

Perhaps you are inspired by the student's HL essay on 'Blackberry-Picking' to write an extended essay on poetry. You may want to compare the works of two poets (Category 2) or how the poetry of one poet evolves over time (Category 1). Any element of comparison will inevitably increase your level of analysis and marks for critical thinking (Criterion C).

Criterion B: Analysis and evaluation: 5 out of 5 marks

The essay offers a careful analysis of the language of the poem, focusing narrowly on the use of verbs, imagery and diction in constructing meaning. This insightful analysis is consistently relevant to the line of inquiry. The student evaluates the author's use of language and structure, commenting on the effects of juxtaposition, rhyme, allusion and consonance (among other devices) on the poem's reader and listener.

Criterion C: Coherence, focus and organisation: 4 out of 5 marks

A bibliography or 'works cited' section is necessary for this essay. Besides quotations from the primary source, there is also a quotation from William Wordsworth, which needs a citation. Besides this, the essay is organised effectively around different stylistic features. While its focus on the poem is consistent, it loses sight of 'rural Ireland' at times.

Criterion D: Language: 5 out of 5 marks

The essay shows good command of the English language. The essay includes varied sentences, correct use of literary terms and an academic tone.

CAS

Writing your own poetry and performing it at 'slam' poetry events in cafés or clubs is another good way of meeting your CAS requirement. Reflect on how this creative process is transformative for you as both a poet and a student of English.

12.12 After carefully reading this sample HL essay and discussing your answers to the questions from Activity 12.11, try writing your own essay of 1200–1500 words, which analyses a poem in detail (see 'Further reading' for suggested authors). The writing process could take these steps:

- **a** Annotate and highlight the words and lines of a poem with careful detail.
- **b** Create a mind map of ideas that you want to put into your essay.
- **c** Return to the 'key features' section and see if you can find evidence of these in your poem.
- **d** Draft an outline of your essay.
- **e** Write a rough draft of your essay and show it to your teacher. Ask your teacher to comment on the quality of your work, applying the assessment criteria.
- **f** Rewrite your essay, based on your teacher's comments.
- **g** If the essay has been written about a work that you are reading for class at HL, you may wish to submit your essay to the IB as an HL essay.

12.13 Writing essays about poetry is one thing. Writing poetry is another. Have you ever written a poem? Why not give it a try? After carefully reading Seamus Heaney's poem about growing up in Ireland and picking blackberries, you may wish to write a poem about your experiences growing up where you live. What 'life lessons' have you learnt? What messages do you wish to communicate to a wider audience in an artistic, poetic way?

Whether or not you decide to write about 'growing up', write a poem that you could read aloud to your classmates or possibly at a poetry evening at school for family and teachers. Enjoy the process and reflect on its challenges after your reading of your poem with classmates.

LEARNER PROFILE

Risk taker

Does Activity 12.13 sound scary? Writing and performing your own poetry can be intimidating but rewarding. What kind of risks are you taking by doing this? What can you do to overcome your fears and see the value added in writing poetry about your own life?

Further reading

- There are many enjoyable poets and lyricists on the prescribed list of authors for your English A: Language and Literature course, such as: Seamus Heaney, Margaret Atwood, Grace Nichols, Carol Ann Duffy, Elizabeth Barrett Browning, Philip Larkin, Robert Frost, William Shakespeare, John Keats, Bob Dylan, Les Murray, John Lennon, Joni Mitchell, Samuel Taylor Coleridge, William Blake, Emily Dickinson, Edgar Allen Poe, W.H. Auden, Allen Ginsberg, Ted Hughes, Sylvia Plath, William Wordsworth, Judith Wright or William Butler Yeats, to name a few names in no particular order.
- *How to Read Poetry Like a Professor* by Thomas Foster offers a fun approach to reading poetry. It explores verse from Dr. Seuss to Robert Louis Stevenson in a way that is accessible and enlightening.
- *The Poetry Toolkit* by Rhian Williams gives very clear and thorough guidance for students who wish to unpack poetry in more depth. It breaks down poetry into subgenres and analyses the use of many literary devices.

TIP

You can study 15–20 song lyrics by a songwriter as a literary work in the English A: Language and Literature course. Ask your teacher if you can study the lyrics of your favourite artist as a 'freely chosen' work. Remember, when analysing lyrics, terminology from poetry can be relevant. Do not forget to explore other devices, such as chorus, verse and bridge.

REFLECT

Twelve text types have been explored in this chapter by focusing on model texts, explaining their key features and encouraging you to write your own texts. How has this method helped you understand these types of texts better, in preparation for various forms of assessment? How can you use this method to explore other text types?

Make a list of other text types that you would like to explore as a class, and use this method to analyse them effectively. Document your findings in your learner portfolio by creating a section on text types.

Chapter 2

Beliefs and values

How is language used differently by men and women?
How do texts target men and women differently?
What do texts such as advertisements tell us about gender roles in society?
How are narrow definitions of 'beauty' constructed by the media?

In this chapter you will:

- explore representations of women in the media, gender stereotyping and feminism
- discuss how texts put pressure on men and women to act a certain way
- develop skills in visual literacy.

Unit 2.1 Femininity

Learning objectives

- appreciate how a range of texts, from different periods and cultures, show different representations of women
- understand a variety of cultural and temporal contexts in order to engage with the topic of gender stereotyping
- develop skills in analysis, interpretation and evaluation of texts
- develop skills in listening, speaking, reading, writing, viewing, presenting and performing.

Word bank

gender stereotyping
feminism
riddle
sexism
prejudice
discrimination
misogyny
denotation
connotation
representation
association
facial expression
appeal to probability
argumentation fallacy
pronoun
imperative
condescension
parody
tone
anaphora
suffrage
literary theory
feminist literary criticism
free indirect speech
secondary source
primary source
gender equality

How do men and women think and act differently? How feminine or masculine should we be? What occupations and roles are best for men and women in society? These questions are difficult to answer without **gender stereotyping**. Nevertheless, you see implicit answers to these questions regularly in TV commercials, press advertisements or TV shows. Only critical viewers, however, examine how the media construct stereotypes and gender expectations.

This unit asks you to deconstruct various messages about women and explore the idea of **feminism**. You are invited to be critical and analytical as you explore a range of text types, from advertisements to poems.

TIP

This is the first of three chapters which explore global issues. For your language and literature course, you will need to keep track of all your activities, assignments, terms and notes in a learner portfolio. Create sections in your portfolio for each global issue that you explore. Your portfolio will become relevant for the individual oral (Chapter 8).

ATL

Self-management

As the Tip suggests, you will need to maintain and manage a learner portfolio. This will require some *self-management* skills. How will you keep track of the texts that you read and write? How will you 'tag' items so that you can find them later? Will you do this digitally? Discuss methods that work for you with your teacher.

Getting started

1.1 Here is a brief **riddle** for you to discuss with a classmate.

A father and son are in a horrible car crash that kills the dad. The son is rushed to the hospital; just as he's about to go under the knife, the surgeon says, 'I can't operate – that boy is my son!' Explain.

If you were confused when you read this, you were probably working from the assumption that surgeons must be men! Why do people make such assumptions about gender and occupation? Does it mean they are sexist? **Sexism** is **prejudice**, stereotyping or **discrimination**, often against women, on the basis of gender.

Read out the occupations listed here and describe the person you imagine for each: a man or a woman. In response to each item, ask yourself why you imagined each as a man or woman. As a class, discuss how ideas of gender and occupation are constructed by the media.

a nurse	**b** doctor	**c** pilot
d flight attendant	**e** professor	**f** grade school teacher
g hairdresser	**h** security guard	**i** plus-size model.

Text 2.1

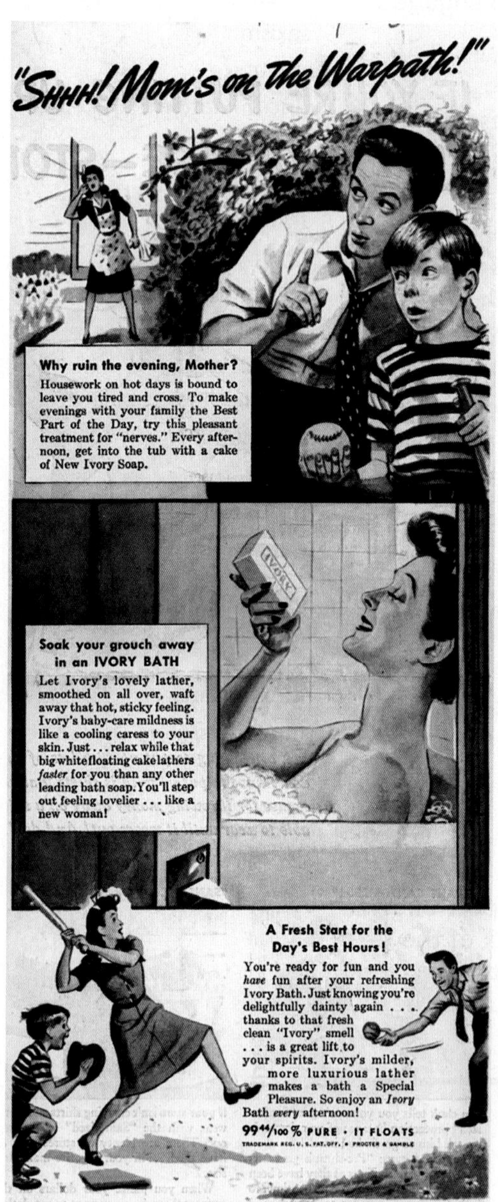

1.2 Is language inherently sexist? Why do phrases a–j sound strange if you replace each noun with the opposite gender? For example, why do people say 'working mother' but not 'working father'? Are these examples of **misogyny** (a dislike of, or contempt for, women)?

- **a** working mother (a mother who works)
- **b** soccer mom (US) (a mother involved in her child's sports)
- **c** mumpreneur (UK) (a mother entrepreneur)
- **d** throw like a girl (not to throw forcefully)
- **e** she wears the pants (US)/trousers (UK) (woman in charge of a relationship)
- **f** housewife (a wife who is not employed)
- **g** mistress (a man's secret lover)
- **h** tomboy (a tough girl)
- **i** catfight (two women fighting)
- **j** mommy wars (US) (two mothers who fight and argue).

1.3 Text 2.1 is an advertisement from another era. Use these questions to start a class discussion on gender and stereotyping:

- **a** Whom does this advertisement target? How do you know this?
- **b** How does it use language to appeal to its audience?
- **c** What are the connotations of the words 'Warpath', 'Mother'? (See TOK feature.) Discuss any other words that seem 'loaded'.
- **d** What is the 'message' of this advertisement? Try articulating the reasoning on which the advertisement is based.
- **e** How does this advertisement use the conventions of comic strips to communicate its message? (See Units 1.4 and 1.5 for further understanding of political cartoons and comic strips.)
- **f** To what extent does this advertisement construct a stereotype? What is the stereotype?
- **g** Do you find this text offensive? Give your reasons.
- **h** Could an advertisement like this be found where you live today? Why, or why not?

CONCEPT

Representation

Representation is a key concept for this course. As you articulate your analyses of various texts, be specific about which social groups are represented, how they are represented and why they are represented in a certain way. It is not sufficient to simply say that an advertisement discriminates against 'women'. Be more specific and refer to the kinds of women who are stereotyped or marginalised.

Readers, writers and texts

1.4 Stereotypes are built through **association**. For example, if TV shows constantly depict male police officers eating doughnuts, then police officers become associated with doughnuts and fatty foods. Consequently, viewers assume that most police officers are overweight men, and a stereotype is born!

Text 2.2, a page from the first edition of *Woman's Weekly* magazine, offers you a glimpse into the past, over a hundred years ago, when women worked very hard, but few were employed. The word 'housewife' does not appear, but how is this stereotype constructed through the use of symbols, **facial expressions**, body language, captions, diction and other stylistic and structural devices? How is this stereotype constructed through association?

See Unit 1.1 on deconstructing images and Unit 1.5 on graphic novels for more useful tools for analysing this text.

1.5 Work in groups of three.

- One of you is a time traveller who has gone back to the year 1911. You find yourself in the office of the chief editor of *Woman's Weekly*.
- One of you is the chief editor who has just published the first edition of this magazine. If fact he personally created Text 2.2. Try to find a male classmate to play this role.
- In his office is a female reader from 1911, who has come to his office to say how happy she is with this new weekly magazine. Try to find a female classmate to play this role.

In your role-playing game, discuss Text 2.2 and how it is helpful or harmful towards mothers. The time traveller may tell the others about the many roles that mothers fulfil in the 'future'.

1.6 Related to 'association' is the **appeal to probability**. Texts often depict and describe situations in which the reader must make various assumptions in order for the text to be meaningful. It is an **argumentation fallacy**, in which something is taken for granted because it would probably be the case. Study Text 2.3 carefully. Consider the attitudes of the readers who would read this advertisement for Heinz Tomato Ketchup in the 1930s. Discuss your answers to these questions with regards to probability, assumptions and stereotypes:

a Why is the text entitled 'How to please a husband'?

b Why does he have a smile on his face as he pours the ketchup?

c Why must a wife be convinced that her husband 'is not unreasonable' or may like 'simple, inexpensive foods'?

TOK

In your Theory of Knowledge course, language is considered a *way of knowing*. In other words, knowledge is acquired through language. But language can be used to manipulate readers into believing something that is not true. Many words have a **denotation**, an exact meaning, and a **connotation**, an emotional association. Words about gender are no different. The words 'mom' or 'mum' denote one's biological or adoptive mother. But the connotations are as diverse and complicated as the kinds of relationships people have with their mothers. Activities 1.1, 1.2 and 1.3 encourage you to think about the various connotations that are communicated through various words and phrases that deal with gender. What are the connotations of the word 'mom' or 'mum' for you? Do you have any, if English is not your 'mother' tongue? Explain.

CAS

Service to others is sometimes centred on those who are marginalised. Think about what you could do to help people who suffer prejudice and discrimination.

d Why is there such a long description about the process of, and the products involved in, making the ketchup?

e Why does it say 'a condiment that men really relish' and not women?

f Why is there a quotation and a signature from President Howard J. Heinz himself?

g Why is this sauce advertised as one of the 57 varieties?

h Why is the bottle depicted twice in the advertisement?

Text 2.2

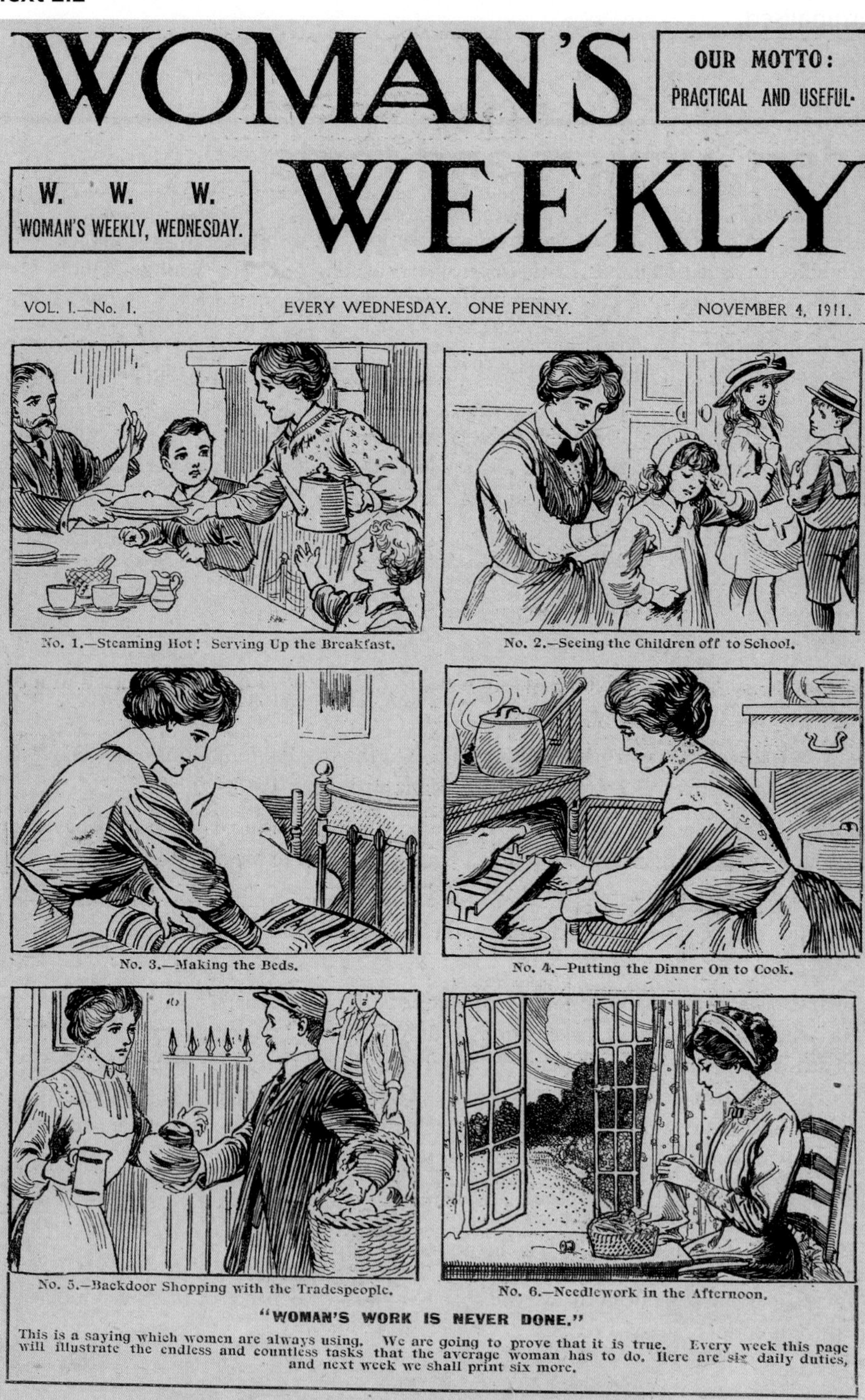

WOMAN'S WEEKLY

OUR MOTTO: PRACTICAL AND USEFUL.

W. W. W. WOMAN'S WEEKLY, WEDNESDAY.

VOL. I.—No. 1. EVERY WEDNESDAY. ONE PENNY. NOVEMBER 4, 1911.

No. 1.—Steaming Hot! Serving Up the Breakfast.

No. 2.—Seeing the Children off to School.

No. 3.—Making the Beds.

No. 4.—Putting the Dinner On to Cook.

No. 5.—Backdoor Shopping with the Tradespeople.

No. 6.—Needlework in the Afternoon.

"WOMAN'S WORK IS NEVER DONE."

This is a saying which women are always using. We are going to prove that it is true. Every week this page will illustrate the endless and countless tasks that the average woman has to do. Here are six daily duties, and next week we shall print six more.

LEARNER PROFILE

Inquirer

Activity 1.6 asks many specific questions about a text. Learning to ask questions about a text is a useful skill in the language and literature course. Can you think of more questions to ask in response to Text 2.3? This is what inquirers do.

Text 2.3

THAT husband of yours isn't unreasonable. You'll find him perfectly satisfied—even delighted—with simple, inexpensive foods, provided only that they are prepared in tasty, appetizing ways. That's why thoughtful housewives are never without a bottle of rich, zestful Heinz Tomato Ketchup. A dash or so adds marvelous savor to pot roasts, stews and hashes. And, of course, tender steaks and chops taste all the better when this tempting sauce is added. Perfect red-ripe tomatoes, the choicest of imported spices, mellow Heinz Vinegar, and artful blending by expert Heinz chefs, go to make a condiment that men really relish. Better order a bottle now, while you think of it.

H. J. HEINZ COMPANY
PITTSBURGH, U. S. A. · TORONTO, CAN. · LONDON, ENG.

"Tasting is a vocation with us. We have a group of employees who have developed a sharp sense of taste. Some are in the kitchens, others serve on our tasting committees, and still another group forms a cross-section of popular taste. Through the average opinion of this group we arrive at conclusions and maintain standards. There is a close relationship between quality and flavor. In the preparation of the 57 Varieties we aim to make it superlatively binding."

Howard Heinz
President, H. J. Heinz Co.

HEINZ TOMATO JUICE · HEINZ CREAM OF TOMATO SOUP · HEINZ CHILI SAUCE

HEINZ *Tomato Ketchup*

THE LARGEST SELLING KETCHUP IN THE WORLD

HEINZ
TOMATO KETCHUP
57

AOE question

How do readers approach texts from different times and different cultures other than their own?

Text 2.3 is very different from advertisements in your time and culture. How would you begin to analyse this advertisement? Perhaps you might consider how the same product, Heinz Tomato Ketchup, is advertised today? It helps to compare target audiences. If this text is pitched towards housewives in the USA in the 1930s, ask yourself how those housewives are different from housewives today.

Continue this discussion by doing an online search for two advertisements for the same product but from a different age.

1.7 What kinds of texts would you think use the second person **pronoun** 'you'? You may expect to find this in instructions, speeches, recipes and textbooks (like this one!), but not in advertisements. Yet you have already seen two advertisements (Texts 2.1 and 2.3) which use 'you', and all of the texts in this unit so far use 'we'. Furthermore, most of the texts have used **imperative** verbs, such as 'come chat' (Text 2.1).

a What is the effect of using 'we' and 'our' or 'you' and 'your' in Texts 2.1–2.3?

b How does the use of pronouns contribute to the construction of gender stereotypes in these texts?

c What is the effect of using imperatives in shaping the reader's response to these texts?

d **Condescension** is the act of belittling someone or speaking down to them. Do you detect condescension in Texts 2.1–2.3? If so, where does it appear? Can you find evidence of it in the text?

Time and space

1.8 Text 2.2 (1911) and Text 2.3 (1930s) may seem rather outdated with their attitudes towards mothers and wives. In the box are adjectives that you can use in the discussion. Which words describe good mothers and wives . . . :

- . . . back then?
- . . . nowadays?
- . . . both then and now?

Complete a copy of this table by writing the adjectives in the correct column.

How have values changed and evolved? Refer to evidence from previous texts or other texts to justify your answers.

independent dependent unquestioning enlightened devoted
hard-working thoughtful cost-conscious obedient agreeable firm
involved attractive self-sacrificing educated graceful meticulous
resourceful smart diligent care-takers

In the early 20th century, good mothers and wives were seen as . . .	Both then and nowadays, good mothers and wives are seen as . . .	Nowadays, good mothers and wives are seen as . . .

1.9 As you discuss the evolving attitudes towards mothers and wives over the past hundred years, it will help if you understand the concept of feminism. What is feminism?

a Write down your own definition of feminism on a piece of paper and give it anonymously to your teacher.

b Ask your teacher to read out everyone's definition of this word.

c Do an online search for the most widely accepted definitions of this word.

d How are these definitions different from your own?

e What is the opposite of feminism? There is no correct answer to this question, only informed responses.

LEARNER PROFILE

Principled

An IB learner is 'principled'. What are the principles of feminism? To what extent are the principles of feminism valued in the country where you live?

1.10 One of the most commonly used symbols of the feminist movement today is Text 2.4. Do an online search for more information about this text and discuss your answers to these questions:

a Why is this image often mistakenly referred to as 'Rosie the Riveter'? Who was that? And why is this not Rosie?

b What type of text is this? What purpose did it once serve? What purpose does it serve these days?

c Explore the use of:

- colour and style of drawing
- body language
- symbols
- the rule of thirds
- other stylistic devices that construct meaning.

d Why do you think this text has become a symbol for the feminist movement?

Text 2.4

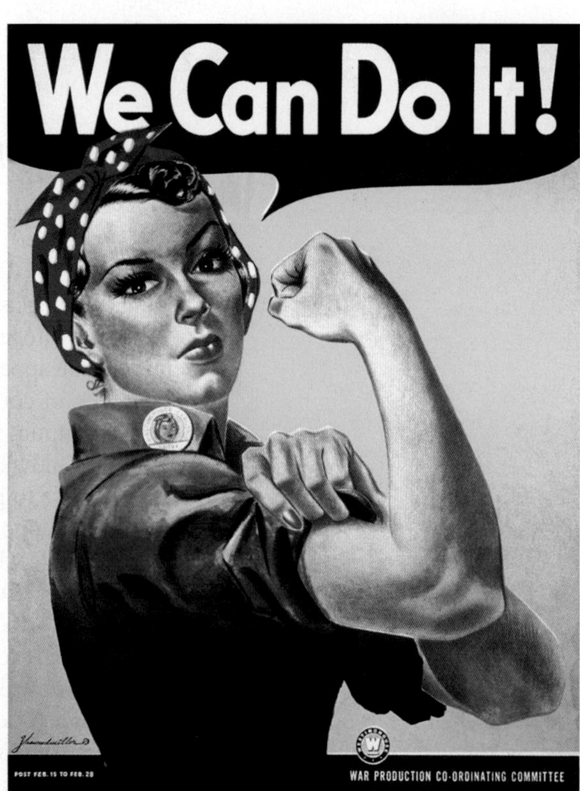

This poster was created by J. Howard Miller in 1943.

1.11 **Parody** is the act of imitating a text's style and structure for a humorous effect. Do an online search for one of the many parodies that have been made of 'We Can Do It!'. In pairs present one of these parodies to your classmates. Ensure that no two pairs present the same parody. In your presentation, explore answers to these questions:

a Why has this parody been created? What is the author's purpose?

b How does it borrow stylistic and structural elements from the original 'We Can Do It!' poster?

c How does the meaning of your parody depend on the target audiences' knowledge of people, places, times and other texts?

d How much of the original message from 'We Can Do It!' is still present in your parody?

AOE question

How can the meaning of a text and its impact change over time?

What if J. Howard Miller could see how people were using Text 2.4 today? What would he say? When considering how the meanings of texts have changed over time, as in Activities 1.10 and 1.11, it's often useful to ask what an author in the past would think of present times. Apply this strategy to your analysis of other texts.

1.12 When discussing texts, we often talk about **tone**. This word describes the writer's attitudes, as expressed through the language of the text. Before you read Text 2.5, look up the definitions of the words listed here (a–k), all of which are associated with tone. You might do this activity with a group of people, with each person responsible for finding the definition of one or two words.

After you have found and understood the meanings of these words, read Text 2.5. Which words describe the tone of this text? What makes you say this? Justify your answers by referring to examples from the text.

a tongue-in-cheek **b** critical **c** biting **d** mocking

e pleasant **f** sarcastic **g** cynical **h** jolly

i subversive **j** ironic **k** complacent.

Text 2.5

Why I Want a Wife

Abridged extract

Judy Syfers 1970

I belong to that classification of people known as wives. I am A Wife.

And, not altogether incidentally, I am a mother. Not too long ago a male friend of mine appeared on the scene fresh from a recent divorce. He had one child, who is, of course, with his ex-wife. He is looking for another wife. As I thought about him while I was ironing one evening, it suddenly occurred to me that I too, would like to have a wife. Why do I want a wife?

I would like to go back to school so that I can become economically independent, support myself, and if need be, support those dependent upon me. I want a wife who will work and send me to school. And while I am going to school I want a wife to take care of my children. I want a wife to keep track of the children's doctor and dentist appointments. And to keep track of mine, too. I want a wife to make sure my children eat properly and are kept clean. I want a wife who will wash the children's clothes and keep them mended. I want a wife who is a good nurturing attendant to my children, who arranges for their schooling, makes sure that they have an adequate social life with their peers, takes them to the park, the zoo, etc. I want a wife who takes care of the children when they are sick, a wife who arranges to be around when the children need special care, because, of course, I cannot miss classes at school. My wife must arrange to lose time at work and not lose the job. It may mean a small cut in my wife's income from time to time, but I guess I can tolerate that. Needless to say, my wife will arrange and pay for the care of the children while my wife is working.

I want a wife who will take care of my physical needs. I want a wife who will keep my house clean. A wife who will pick up after my children, a wife who will pick up after me. I want a wife who will keep my clothes clean, ironed, mended, replaced when need be, and who will see to it that my personal things are kept in their proper place so that I can find what I need the minute I need it. I want a wife who cooks the meals, a wife who is a good cook. I want a wife who will plan the menus, do the necessary grocery shopping, prepare the meals, serve them pleasantly, and then do the cleaning up while I do my studying. I want a wife who will care for me when I am sick and sympathise with my pain and loss of time from school. I want a wife to go along when our family takes a vacation so that someone can continue to care for me and my children when I need a rest and change of scene. I want a wife who will not bother me with rambling complaints about a wife's duties. But I want a wife who will listen to me when I feel the need to explain a rather difficult point I have come across in my course of studies. And I want a wife who will type my papers for me when I have written them. [. . .]

If, by chance, I find another person more suitable as a wife than the wife I already have, I want the liberty to replace my present wife with another one. Naturally, I will expect a fresh, new life; my wife will take the children and be solely responsible for them so that I am left free.

When I am through with school and have a job, I want my wife to quit working and remain at home so that my wife can more fully and completely take care of a wife's duties.

My God, who wouldn't want a wife?

CONCEPT

Transformation

One of the key concepts for this course is *transformation*. Texts can be transformative in the sense that they change your understanding of the way the world works. How does Text 2.5 change the way you see motherhood?

1.13 Do an online search to find out more about the context of Text 2.5.

- **a** When was it written?
- **b** Where was it first read aloud?
- **c** Why did the writer write it?
- **d** To what extent does this text express the ideals of feminism, which you discussed in Activity 1.9?

1.14 Discuss your answers to these questions as a class, referring to Text 2.5.

- **a** Judy Syfers says she 'wants a wife'. But what does she really want?
- **b** What attitudes towards men are expressed in this text? Where do you find evidence of this?
- **c** What is the effect of repeating the words 'I want?' on the audience? This an example of **anaphora**, the repetition of a phrase at the beginning of a sentence. Why is anaphora used here?
- **d** This text was written and read to an audience in 1970. Is Judy Syfers's main message, as expressed in this text, still relevant today? Or is it outdated? What makes you say this?

International mindedness

Text 2.5 explores the meaning of 'wife' and 'mother', and the connotations associated with these words. In countries around the world, the roles of wives and mothers are defined differently according to cultural norms and expectations. These norms and expectations are constantly evolving and changing.

You and your classmates can each choose a different country in the world to research, with examples of developing and developed countries, Anglophone and non-Anglophone countries. Try to find answers to these questions about your chosen country, thinking about the past ten years. Share your findings with your classmates. Don't worry if you haven't been able to find answers to all the questions:

a Until what age do women attend school, on average?

b What is the average age for women to have their first child?

c How many children do women have, on average?

d What is the difference in salaries between women and men?

Intertextuality: connecting texts

1.15 This unit has asked you how definitions of motherhood have changed over time. Texts 2.6 and 2.7 show how the recruitment of women for military service has changed.

a Study both advertisements carefully, thinking about the guiding question: 'In what ways do the linguistic and visual features of these two armed forces recruitment advertisements for the military appeal to different cultural values from different times and places, while trying to achieve a similar purpose?'

b Take notes on both texts, using a copy of this table. Revisit Units 1.1 and 1.2 to inform your response.

c Before you write a comparative analysis of these texts, ask your teacher if you will be assessed on this assignment. Discuss the kinds of criteria that you should use to assess your work.

d Based on your notes and understanding of the assessment criteria, write a comparative analysis of 800–1000 words.

e Show your comparative analysis to your teacher and ask for constructive feedback.

f Rewrite your comparative analysis and place it in your learner portfolio under 'Feminism'.

	Text 2.6	Text 2.7
Target audience and their response		
Author's purpose		
Use of image, including camera angle and symbols (see Unit 1.1)		
Use of layout and structure (see Unit 1.2)		
Author's choice of words (diction)		

Text 2.6

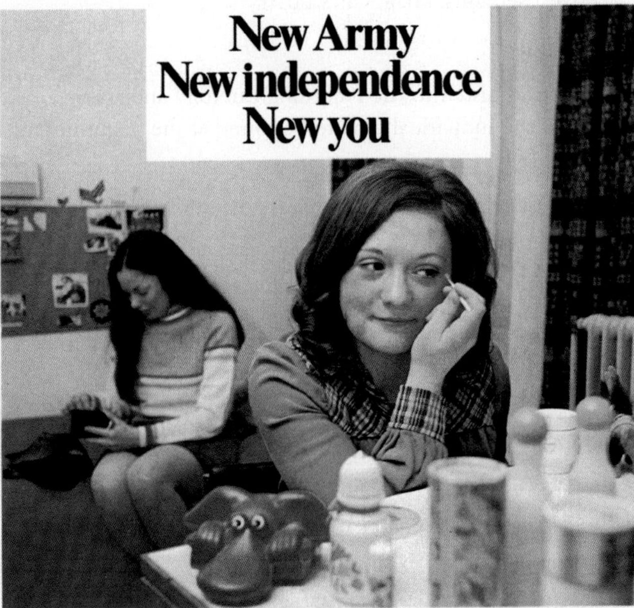

What's new about the Army? Above all, the atmosphere. It's pleasant and relaxed in the Women's Royal Army Corps. The officers and NCOs are friendly and approachable. Part of their job is to help you if you have any problems. There's still discipline, of course. But only enough to help you do your job well. During most evenings and weekends you can be as independent as you like.

There are over 25 different jobs for you in the WRAC! You might be trained as a driver, a stewardess or a policewoman. And this training could be useful to you when you leave (your contract allows you to leave after three years, provided you give 18 months' notice, or when you marry). You'll work hard alongside the men of the Army. But be well paid for doing it – you begin on £17.57 and rise steadily if you do well.

You'll feel at home in the WRAC! You'll share a bright, newly furnished room, usually with three other girls. You can make this room your own. By putting up a few pictures and pin-ups and bringing your record player or radio. Life will never be dull. In the WRAC, you're often on the move. Around Britain. Perhaps over to Germany. Or even away to Cyprus or Hong Kong. But you'll always be among friends. **You'll discover a new you.** The WRAC has everything you want out of life. A chance to get on in a worthwhile job. And the confidence to do it. Variety, travel, friends, and plenty to do with your evenings, weekends and holidays. All this without any worries about fending for yourself, or finding a friendly face to take your troubles to.

So if you want more out of life, send for our booklet now. It could mean a new you.

Start a new life in the New Army

To: WRAC Careers Dept. MP6, Lansdowne House, Berkeley Square, London, W1X 6AA.

Tell me more about life in the New Army.

NAME__________

ADDRESS__________

Date of Birth__________

Applicants must be aged 17–33.

WRAC
WOMEN'S ROYAL ARMY CORPS

Text 2.7

U.S. ARMY
THE BEST PLACE FOR WOMEN IN THE ARMY IS...
EVERYWHERE
U.S.ARMY
To find out more about their incredible accomplishments, go to unsungheroeseducation.com
UNSUNG HEROES

AOE question

How do the conventions of different types of text develop over time?

Text 2.7 was created 45 years after Text 2.6. You can see a clear evolution of structural conventions for this type of text, an advertisement for recruiting women. How have these conventions evolved? Write about this in your comparative analysis (Activity 1.15).

Towards assessment

1.16 For your individual oral, you are asked to explore a literary and a non-literary text on a common global issue. In order to practise your individual oral, prepare and conduct a 10-minute talk in which you compare and contrast Texts 2.8 and 2.9 on the women's **suffrage** movement. Follow these steps:

a Research the movement on women's right to vote in the early 20th century, the origin of the texts and their authors.

b Annotate copies of both texts to highlight the key features. Look at Units 1.1, 1.2 and 1.12 for more about the key features of advertisements, images and poetry.

c Make a bullet-pointed outline with key ideas.

d Record yourself giving this 10-minute talk. Listen to the recording carefully and assess yourself using the assessment criteria for the individual oral, to be found at the beginning of the book.

e If you think you could improve on any aspects of your performance, try recording another attempt.

f Share your final recording with a classmate or your teacher to receive their feedback.

See Chapter 8 for more information on the individual oral.

AOE question

How can different texts offer different perspectives on a topic or theme?

This question from the area of exploration called 'intertextuality' is a good point of departure for an individual oral. Consider how the perspectives of Texts 2.8 and 2.9 are different.

Text 2.8

Females

Charlotte Perkins Gilman 1911

The female fox she is a fox;
The female whale a whale;
The female eagle holds her place
As representative of race
As truly as the male.

The mother hen doth scratch for her chicks,
And scratch for herself beside;
The mother cow doth nurse her calf,
Yet fares as well as her other half
In the pasture far and wide.

The female bird doth soar in air;
The female fish doth swim;
The fleet-foot mare upon the course
Doth hold her own with the flying horse –
Yea and she beateth him!

One female in the world we find
Telling a different tale.
It is the female of our race,
Who holds a parasitic place
Dependent on the male.

Not so, saith she, ye slander me!
No parasite am I.
I earn my living as a wife;
My children take my very life;
Why should I share in human strife,
To plant and build and buy?

The human race holds highest place
In all the world so wide,
Yet these inferior females wive,
And raise their little ones alive,
And feed themselves beside.

The race is higher than the sex,
Though sex be fair and good;
A Human Creature is your state,
And to be human is more great
Than even womanhood!

The female fox she is a fox;
The female whale a whale;
The female eagle holds her place
As representative of race
As truly as the male.

Text 2.9

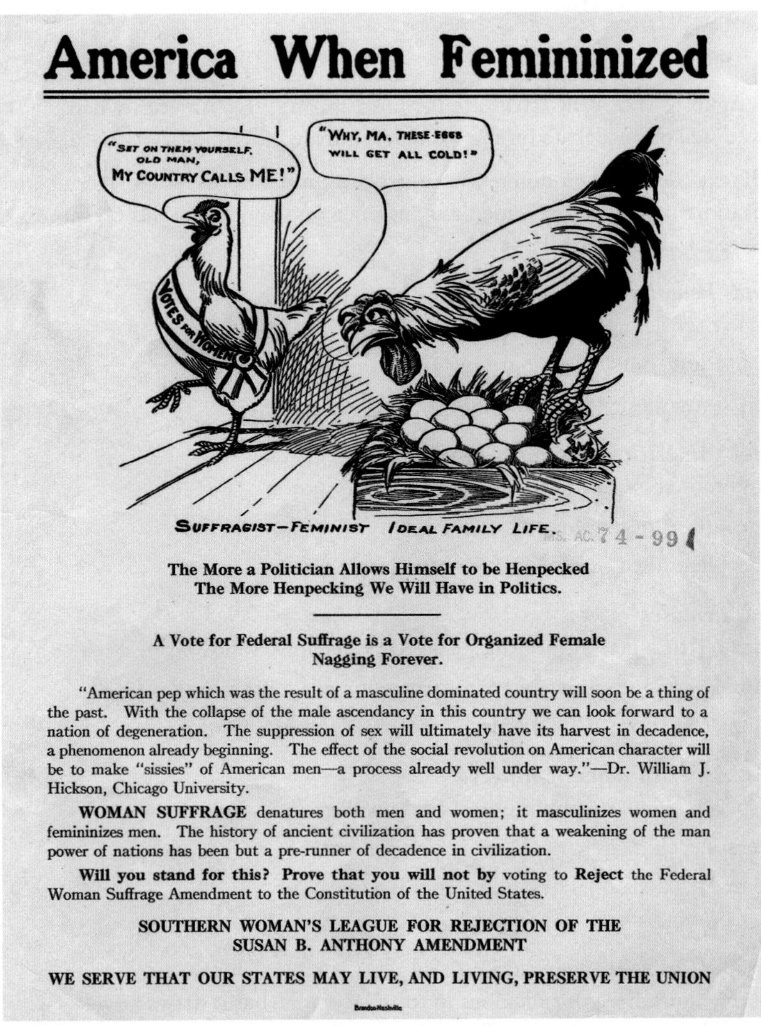

1.17 Whether or not you are reading a literary work about feminism or women's roles in society, you may find one of these four questions appropriate for a practice Paper 2 essay:

a In which ways and for what reasons do two of the literary works that you have read depict a struggle between men and women?

b In what ways and for what reasons do two of the literary works that you have read give women a voice?

c How have the authors of two of the literary works that you have read used language to comment on gender inequality?

d How have two of the literary works that you have read been written and received differently by different audiences?

1.18 Activity 1.16 asks you to develop and deliver a practice individual oral on Texts 2.8 and 2.9. To prepare for this, you should create an outline similar to the example shown here.

- Compare the points in this example outline to your own. How did you organise your individual oral similarly or differently?
- Are there ideas that you can take from this outline, to improve your own performance on these two texts?

Individual oral – Sample 1 – Outline

What is your global issue? Begin with this central organising principle. See Chapter 8 on global issues.

Start your introduction with the 'why'. Briefly explain why your global issue matters to you.

An individual oral should have a thesis statement, just like an essay.

Outlines should include many examples.

Use signs, underlining, italics, bold or other features to structure your outline and help you.

Notice the structure of this outline: switches back and forth between texts, focusing on a common stylistic device. The structure is not required but useful.

Conclusions restate previous points and reiterate the thesis statement.

Be sure to refer to the importance of context in understanding your two texts.

Introduction

Global issue: Women's rights to vote. Why Charlotte Perkins Gilman? Why 'America when feminized'? Both show a side of the debate on the women's suffrage movement.

Thesis statement: Both texts, despite their differences in structure and purpose, use imagery, analogy and direct narration in order to persuade their audience on their viewpoints on the women's suffrage movement in the early 20th century.

Imagery/analogy and 'Females'

Example 1: Eagles, fox, whales → appeal to natural world

Example 2: Wives and 'little ones' → address guilt and responsibility

Example 3: Women as parasites → womanhood is below humankind

Imagery/analogy and 'America When Feminized'

Example 1: Hen and rooster → caricatures of people, shift of power

Example 2: Suffrage sash → overzealous women

Example 3: 'Sissies' → feminised men are perceived as weak

Direct narration and 'Females'

Example 1: 5th stanza: 'I' first-person, 'no parasite am I' → defensive tone

Example 2: 5th stanza: 'wife' and 'children' → irony parasitic relationship

Example 3: 5th stanza: Question: 'Why should I?' → lack of ambition

Direct narration and 'America when feminized'

Example 1: Hen's speech bubble: 'set on them … old man!' → independence

Example 2: Rooster's speech: 'eggs get cold' → responsibility

Example 3: Quote by Dr. William J. Hickson → appeal to authority

Conclusion

Both texts reference the natural world to make a case on what is 'natural' for women and power. 'America when Feminized' seems ridiculous in today's context, but it shows how women once used (visual) language to oppress other women.

Higher level extension

1.19 As you explore literature, you will discover various schools of **literary theory**. You could say that these are lenses through which readers view literary works. One such school of literary theory is **feminist literary criticism**, which is informed by feminist theory and the politics of feminism. This school of literary theory has developed since the early 20th century and approaches literary works by:

- studying the representation of men and women and how they reflect society's pressures and expectations
- analysing the use of language, imagery and narration to construct these gender roles
- examining the balance and significance of female authors in the world of literature.

Read Text 2.10, *The Grass Is Singing* by Doris Lessing, which is set in Southern Rhodesia (now Zimbabwe) in the 1940s. Discuss how a feminist literary critic would analyse the text, especially with regard to these first two bullet points.

Text 2.10

The Grass Is Singing

Extract

Doris Lessing 1950

But all women become conscious, sooner or later, of that impalpable, but steel-strong pressure to get married, and Mary, who was not at all susceptible to atmosphere, or the things people imply, was brought face to face with it suddenly, and most unpleasantly.

She was in the house of a married friend, sitting on the veranda, with a lighted room behind her. She was alone; and heard people talking in low voices, and caught her own name. She rose to go inside and declare herself: it was typical of her that her first thought was, how unpleasant it would be for her friends to know she had overheard. Then she sank down again, and waited for a suitable moment to pretend she had just come in from the garden. This was the conversation she listened to, while her face burned and her hands went clammy.

'She's not fifteen any longer: it is ridiculous! Someone should tell her about her clothes.'

'How old is she?'

'Must be well over thirty. She has been going strong for years. She was working long before I began working and that was a good twelve years ago.'

'Why doesn't she marry? She must have had plenty of chances.'

There was a dry chuckle. 'I don't think so. My husband was keen on her himself once, but he thinks she will never marry. She just isn't like that, isn't like that at all. Something missing somewhere.'

'Oh, I don't know.'

'She's gone off so much, in any case. The other day I caught sight of her in the street and hardly recognized her. It's a fact! The way she plays all those games, her skin is like sandpaper, and she's got so thin.'

'But she's such a nice girl.'

'She'll never set the rivers on fire, though.'

'She'd make someone a good wife. She's a good sort, Mary.'

'She should marry someone years older than herself. A man of fifty would suit her . . . you'll see, she will marry someone old enough to be her father one of these days.'

'One never can tell!'

There was another chuckle, good-hearted enough, but it sounded cruelly malicious to Mary. She was stunned and outraged; but most of all deeply wounded that her friends could discuss her thus. She was so naïve, so unconscious of herself in relation to other people, that it had never entered her head that people could discuss her behind her back. And the things they had said! She sat there writhing, twisting her hands. Then she composed herself and went back into the room to join her treacherous friends, who greeted her as cordially as if they had not just that moment driven knives into her heart and thrown her quite off balance; she could not recognize herself in the picture they had made of her!

AOE question

How do texts engage with local and global issues?

How does Doris Lessing engage with the issue of marriage in *The Grass Is Singing* (Text 2.10)? Do you consider 'marriage' a global or a local issue? Give reasons for your answer.

CONCEPT

Identity

As Mary listens to her friends gossip about her in this passage from *The Grass Is Singing* (Text 2.10), she is confronted with questions about her own *identity* and the role of marriage in shaping that identity. When reading fiction about imaginary characters, readers are asking themselves questions about their own identity.

Have you ever overheard anyone talk about you? Can you relate to Mary's situation? What are your views on marriage? How are those views characteristic of your identity?

1.20 Read Text 2.10 again and discuss your answers to these questions:

a What is the effect of the phrases 'all women' and 'sooner or later' in the opening line of this passage on you, the reader?

b What do these opening lines suggest about the narrator's position on women and marriage?

c What implications are made by the women about the number of years in which a woman should work before getting married? What happens to women, presumably, after they get married?

d What implications are made about the ways women should dress?

e At what age is a woman expected to marry in this society?

f What is the 'something' that is 'missing somewhere'?

g What is meant by the phrase 'to set the rivers on fire'? You may need to look it up.

h What are the qualities of an attractive woman, according to the women?

ATL

Research skills

Activity 1.22 asks you to engage with a **secondary source** and document your findings in your learner portfolio. As you study texts, and document your findings in your portfolio, be sure to understand the difference between **primary sources** and secondary sources. Primary sources are texts that you analyse, such as poems and novels. Secondary sources, such as articles, are intended to inform your analysis of primary sources.

1.21 Notice the use of exclamation marks in the final few lines of Text 2.10. They are characteristic of a form of narration known as **free indirect speech** or *free indirect narration*. Free indirect speech is a form of third-person narration, which shows bias towards the thoughts and emotions of one character.

a Besides the use of exclamation marks, where else does the narrator show bias towards Mary?

b Why does the narrator use this style of narration?

c What is the effect of this style of narration on the reader?

1.22 Look again at the bullet points describing feminist literary criticism in Activity 1.19. The third point explains that feminist literary critics also study the significance of female authors. Do some online research to learn more about the significance of Doris Lessing in the world of literature.

- What have been her contributions?
- What kinds of messages has she voiced?
- How have they been received?

In pairs, find a secondary source on Doris Lessing that you would like to present to your classmates. Ensure that every pair is presenting a different secondary source. In your short presentation, you should explore:

- Doris Lessing's contributions
- her messages
- the responses to her works.

Reflect on your chosen secondary source by explaining to your classmates what you found most interesting about it. Document your findings in your learner portfolio.

Extended essay

For your extended essay, you can explore one or more literary works through the lens of feminism. A good research question may read: 'In what ways do the authors of *The Grass Is Singing* and *Fiela's Child* use narrative technique to explore the feminist perspective in southern Africa during apartheid?' Note: *Fiela's Child* by Dalene Mathhee was originally written in Afrikaans but can be read in English, making this a good Category 2 essay.

Further reading

- If you liked reading Text 2.10 by Doris Lessing, you may want to read more of her works, such as *The Golden Notebook*.
- If you liked Text 2.8, the poem 'Females' by Charlotte Perkins Gilman, you can easily find more of her poems on feminism. Her semi-autobiographical short story 'The Yellow Wallpaper' is studied widely in gender studies classes as a seminal piece for the feminist cause.
- Carol Ann Duffy's poetry is popular for good reason, and most of her poems have a feminist edge.
- *The Handmaid's Tale* by Margaret Atwood, *A Room of One's Own* by Virginia Woolf, *The Awakening* by Kate Chopin and *The Color Purple* by Alice Walker are just a few of many works you may wish to explore in your coursework.
- 'We Should All Be Feminists' by Chimamanda Ngozi Adichie is a longer essay, based on the author's popular TED Talk, which you may also want to watch as a class.

REFLECT

Sit with a classmate of the opposite gender, if possible. Discuss your answers to these questions then recap and share your discussion with your class:

a Which text in this unit did you find most interesting? Why was this?

b To what extent do you consider yourself a feminist? How has this unit contributed to your answer to this question?

c What is the future of motherhood? What will it mean to be a 'wife' in the future?

d Think about what the world will be like in a hundred years. To what extent do you think **gender equality** will be a reality around the world?

Unit 2.2 Masculinity

Word bank

manliness
masculinity
camera shot
socialisation
expression
linguistic determinism
gender bias
social constructs
syntax
readership
male chauvinism
spoof
culture jamming
subvertising
parody
pastiche
hypermasculinity
Bechdel test
patriarchy
role models
role reversal
awareness campaign
counterstereotypes
progressive
dadvertising

Learning objectives

- understand how gender roles have been constructed differently in different temporal contexts
- develop skills for analysing the stylistic and structural features of visual texts and moving images, such as advertisements and commercials
- become more aware of the issues of gender stereotype, and the pressures on men to be 'manly' or masculine
- develop creative skills by making your own advertisement.

In the previous unit you explored ways in which gender stereotypes are constructed, using the examples of stereotypes of mothers and wives. This unit continues to explore the problems of gender stereotyping, but in relation to men. What expectations are created for men by narrow definitions of '**manliness**' in the mass media? According to many dictionaries, 'manliness' includes such traits as 'tough', 'powerful' or 'rugged'. Where do these ideas come from?

In this unit you will consider how these definitions of manliness are constructed. You will study a range of texts, developing your skills of critical analysis and questioning gender stereotypes.

Getting started

2.1 What associations can you think of for the word '**masculinity**'?

a On a sheet of paper, write down three things that come to mind when you hear this word. Do not write your name on the paper.

b Give this paper to your teacher, who will read out your class's responses.

c What are the differences between 'masculinity' and 'manliness'? Discuss these differences as a class.

International mindedness

To what degree are your definitions of masculinity determined by the culture in which you were raised? Review your answers to Activity 2.1 and discuss how these definitions reflect your class's cultural backgrounds.

2.2 Read Text 2.11 which is a transcript of the Old Spice commercial. Watch the commercial online by searching for: 'Old Spice' and 'The Man Your Man Could Smell Like' or 'Smell Like a Man, Man'. Discuss your answers to these questions:

a To what degree does this commercial promote your class's associations of masculinity which previously you wrote down for your teacher (Activity 2.1)?

b What are the effects of its language on the audience? Consider its use of diction, images, symbols, **camera shot** and camera angle. Discuss your answers as a class. See Unit 1.3 on analysing film to support your discussion.

c Whom does this commercial target – men or women? What makes you say this? How might men and women respond differently to this commercial?

Text 2.11

Hello, ladies, look at your man, now back to me, now back at your man, now back to me. Sadly, he isn't me, but if he stopped using ladies' scented body wash and switched to Old Spice, he could smell like he's me. Look down, back up, where are you? You're on a boat with the man your man could smell like. What's in your hand? Back at me. I have it. It's an oyster with two tickets to that thing you love. Look again, the tickets are now diamonds. Anything is possible when your man smells like Old Spice and not a lady. I'm on a horse.

AOE question

How can texts present challenges and offer insights?

In response to Text 2.11, write a list of 'insights' and another list of 'challenges' with regard to:

- gender roles
- stereotypes
- gender equality.

2.3 **Socialisation** is the process of learning to behave in a way that is acceptable to society. It is the result of interactions between people, and the messages that you receive through various media in everyday life. How are young men and boys socialised through the use of various **expressions**? An expression is a turn of phrase that is commonly used. Here are some expressions that create unrealistic expectations of boys and men. They can be damaging to society and to relationships. Have you heard such phrases used before? Look up the meanings of any of these phrases you do not know. As a class, discuss these questions:

- Why might these phrases be thought offensive?
- Why are they problematic for society?
- What do they imply about manhood?

a Nice guys finish last.

b to man up

c Boys don't cry.

d to grow a pair

e Men are pigs.

f mummy's boy

g Boys will be boys.

h to wear the pants/trousers

i That's so gay.

TOK

Is language a *description* of real-life experiences, or does language structure our understanding of real life? This is a question often asked in TOK. The idea that language shapes our understanding of reality is known as **linguistic determinism.**

If the phrase 'that's so gay' is used to mean 'that's so stupid', then people will equate homosexuality with intellectual inferiority. This is why such phrases and others from Activity 2.3 can be harmful and offensive. Can you think of other examples of how language determines your understanding of gender roles?

2.4 Gender bias is the act of appealing to one gender over the other. Here are two job descriptions for an engineering job. The first one uses vocabulary that might appeal to a male audience. The second one might appeal to a female audience. Assign every italicised word in the job descriptions to a different person in your class. Individually, look up the meaning of your word or words (if you have been assigned more than one). Explain to your classmates why you think these words show a particular bias towards men or women.

Text 2.12

Engineering job descriptions

Barbara Annis and Richard Nesbitt 2017

	Male-themed words used in an engineering job description	Female-themed words used in an engineering job description
Company description	We are a *dominant* engineering firm that *boasts* many *leading* clients. We are *determined* to *stand apart* from the *competition*.	We are a *community* of engineers who have effective *relationships* with many *satisfied* clients. We are *committed to understanding* the engineer sector *intimately*.
Qualifications	*Strong* communication and *influencing* skills. Ability to *perform individually* in a *competitive* environment. *Superior* ability to *satisfy* customers and manage the company's association with them.	*Proficient* oral and written communication skills. Collaborates well in a *team* environment. *Sensitive* to clients' needs, can *develop warm* client *relationships*.
Responsibilities	*Direct* project groups to *manage* project *progress* and ensure accurate task *control. Determine compliance* with clients' *objectives*.	Provide general *support* to the project team in a manner that's complementary to the company. *Helps* client with construction *activities*.

From *Results at the Top: Using Gender Intelligence to Create Breakthrough Growth*

CONCEPT

Culture

Text 2.12, two job descriptions for the same job, gives you an insight into *culture*. It shows you how engineering firms view the role of men and women differently. How are gender roles expressed differently in job advertisements in the culture where you live?

2.5 Based on your discussions from the previous activities and your own experiences, describe the types of **social construct** that have been created by the media for men and boys. A social construct is a representation of a person, place or thing, collectively created by society through social interaction and the mass media. Complete these sentences. Share your answers with your classmates. How similar or different are your answers? How have the girls in your class answered differently from the boys?

a In my society, there are pressures on men to be . . .

b A 'good' father is one who . . .

c People usually find men attractive when they . . .

d Certain characteristics of men that are not valued by society include . . .

Readers, writers and texts

2.6 You are going to read Text 2.13, an editorial from a men's magazine which comments on what it means to be 'a man'. After reading the editorial, consider the statement: 'An ideal man, according to Text 2.13, is . . .'. What evidence can you find in the text to support these endings (a–g) to this statement? Discuss your answers as a class.

a . . . a gentleman.
b . . . apolitical.
c . . . a provider.
d . . . sensitive.
e . . . tough.
f . . . heterosexual.
g . . . knowledgeable.
h . . . resourceful.
i . . . responsible.
j . . . honest.
k . . . rigorous.
l . . . disciplined.

AOE question

How can texts present challenges and offer insights?

Do you remember this question? It was asked in response to Text 2.11 earlier in this unit. Return to your lists of insights and challenges in response to Text 2.11. After reading Text 2.13, are there any points you would add to your lists?

Text 2.13

What Is a Man?

Tom Chiarella for *Esquire* 2015

A man carries cash. A man looks out for those around him – woman, friend, stranger. A man can cook eggs. A man can always find something good to watch on television. A man makes things – a rock wall, a table, the tuition money. Or he rebuilds – engines, watches, fortunes. He passes along expertise, one man to the next. Know-how survives him. This is immortality. A man can speak to dogs. A man fantasizes that kung fu lives deep inside him somewhere. A man is good at his job. Not his work, not his avocation, not his hobby. Not his career. His job. It doesn't matter what his job is, because if a man doesn't like his job, he gets a new one.

A man can look you up and down and figure some things out. Before you say a word, he makes you. From your suitcase, from your watch, from your posture. A man infers.

A man owns up. That's why Mark McGwire is not a man. A man grasps his mistakes. He lays claim to who he is, and what he was, whether he likes them or not.

Some mistakes, though, he lets pass if no one notices. Like dropping the steak in the dirt.

A man doesn't point out that he did the dishes.

A man looks out for children. Makes them stand behind him.

A man knows how to bust balls.

A man has had liquor enough in his life that he can order a drink without sounding breathless, clueless, or obtuse. When he doesn't want to think, he orders bourbon or something on tap.

Never the sauvignon blanc.

A man welcomes the coming of age. It frees him. It allows him to assume the upper hand and teaches him when to step aside.

Maybe he never has, and maybe he never will, but a man figures he can knock someone, somewhere, on his ass.

He does not rely on rationalizations or explanations. He doesn't winnow, winnow, winnow until truths can be humbly categorized, or intellectualized, until behavior can be written off with an explanation. He doesn't see himself lost in some great maw of humanity, some grand sweep. That's the liberal thread; it's why men won't line up as liberals.

A man gets the door. Without thinking.

He stops traffic when he must.

A man resists formulations, questions belief, embraces ambiguity without making a fetish out of it. A man revisits his beliefs. Continually. That's why men won't forever line up with conservatives, either.

A man knows his tools and how to use them – just the ones he needs. Knows which saw is for what, how to find the stud, when to use galvanized nails.

A miter saw, incidentally, is the kind that sits on a table, has a circular blade, and is used for cutting at precise angles. Very satisfying saw.

A man knows how to lose an afternoon. Drinking, playing Grand Theft Auto, driving aimlessly, shooting pool.

He knows how to lose a month, also.

A man loves driving alone most of all.

Style – a man has that. No matter how eccentric that style is, it is uncontrived. It's a set of rules.

He understands the basic mechanics of the planet. Or he can close one eye, look up at the sun, and tell you what time of day it is. Or where north is. He can tell you where you might find something to eat or where the fish run. He understands electricity or the internal-combustion engine, the mechanics of flight or how to figure a pitcher's ERA.

A man does not know everything. He doesn't try. He likes what other men know.

A man can tell you he was wrong. That he did wrong. That he planned to. He can tell you when he is lost. He can apologize, even if sometimes it's just to put an end to the bickering.

A man does not wither at the thought of dancing. But it is generally to be avoided.

A man watches. Sometimes he goes and sits at an auction knowing he won't spend a dime, witnessing the temptation and the maneuvering of others. Sometimes he stands on the street corner watching stuff. This is not about quietude so much as collection. It is not about meditation so much as considering. A man refracts his vision and gains acuity. This serves him in every way. No one taught him this – to be quiet, to cipher, to watch. In this way, in these moments, the man is like a zoo animal: both captive and free. You cannot take your eyes off a man when he is like that. You shouldn't. The hell if you know what he is thinking, who he is, or what he will do next.

A man listens, and that's how he argues. He crafts opinions. He can pound the table, take the floor. It's not that he must. It's that he can.

A man is comfortable being alone. Loves being alone, actually. He sleeps.

Or he stands watch. He interrupts trouble. This is the state policeman. This is the poet. Men, both of them.

LEARNER PROFILE

To what degree does the 'man' described in Text 2.13 exemplify the character traits of the IB learner profile: open-minded, balanced, caring, knowledgeable, principled, thinker, communicator, inquirer, reflective, risk taker?

CONCEPT

Identity

Text 2.13 deals very much with *identity*. Why do you think Tom Chiarella wrote this text about what it means to be a 'man'? To what degree are his readers searching for answers about their own identity? Do you think the author is trying to define his own identity by writing this text? If you are a young man, think about the degree to which this text influences your own sense of identity.

TEXT AND CONTEXT

- Mark McGwire is an American baseball player who eventually admitted to using muscle-enhancing drugs.
- Grand Theft Auto is a violent computer game.
- ERA is an acronym for earned run average, a concept used to measure the ability of a baseball pitcher.

2.7 **Syntax** refers to the order in which words are written and the use of punctuation.

a The syntax in Text 2.13 is not always grammatically correct, as some sentences lack nouns. Why do you think the author chose this use of syntax?

b You could argue that the syntax of this text relies on short sentences and excessive use of punctuation. Why has the author written the text in this way?

c How does syntax contribute to the tone of the piece?

2.8 The term '**readership**' refers to the target audience of a particular newspaper, magazine or other frequently published text.

a Research the readership of *Esquire*, the magazine in which Text 2.13 was published. Read a few of its articles online.

b What words would you use to describe the audience that typically reads *Esquire*?

c To what degree does Text 2.13 appeal to that audience?

Find evidence to support your answers. Discuss your answers as a class.

Time and space

2.9 How have car advertisements changed over the past decades? Specifically, how do these changes reflect cultural shifts in gender roles and social constructs? Study Text 2.14 and discuss your answers to these questions:

a The tagline reads 'Only Mustang makes it happen!' What does 'it' refer to? What is the effect of the word 'only'?

b How does the copy of this advertisement use pun or a play on words, specifically with the word 'dig', which can mean 'like' and 'excavate'?

c 'Identity' is one of the key concepts for this course. How does this advertisement appeal to and comment on 'identity'?

d Look up the definition of the phrase '**male chauvinism**'. Is this an example of male chauvinism? Refer to this text to support your answers.

e This advertisement is from 1968. Could a similar advertisement appear today?

Text 2.14

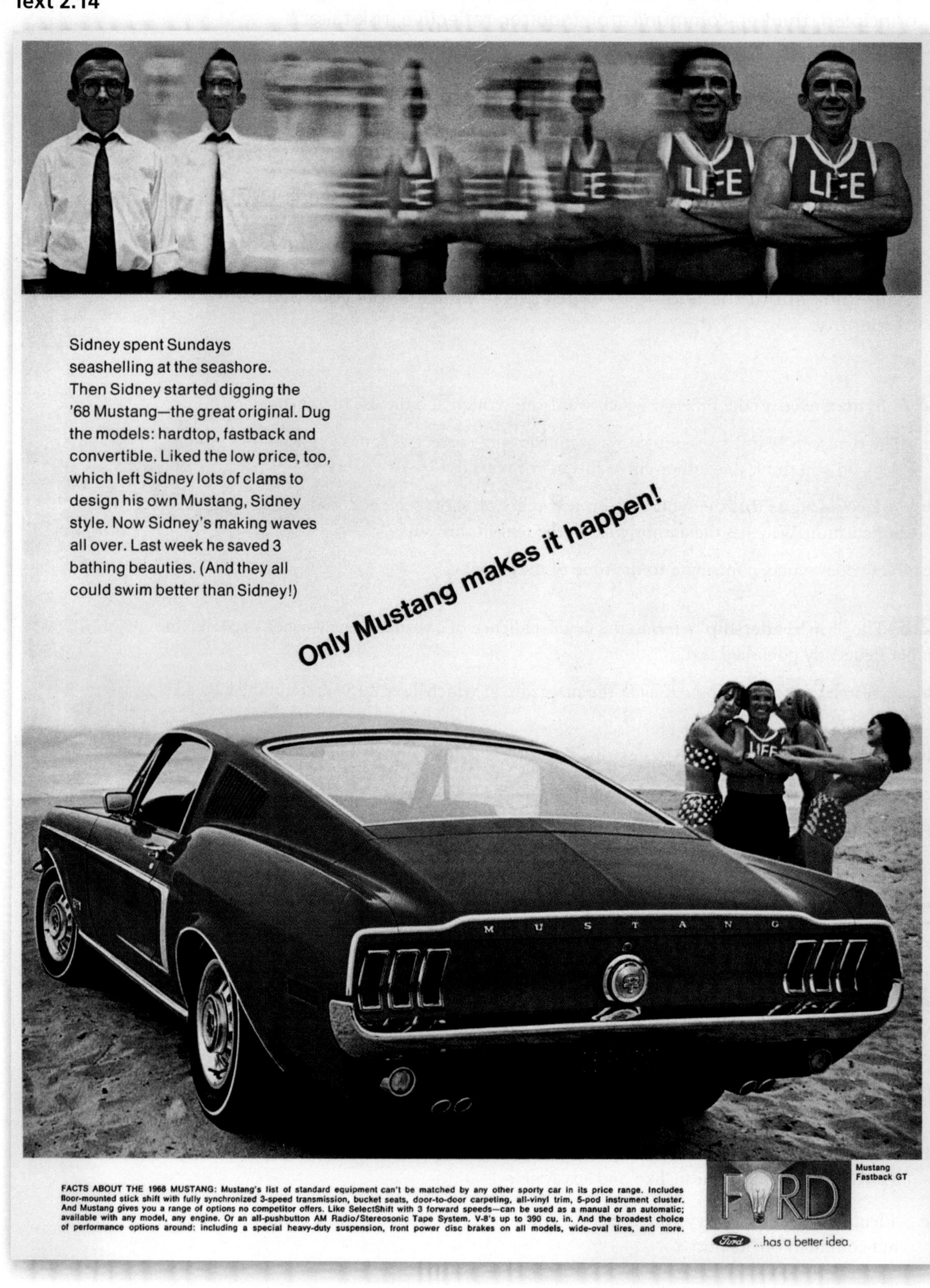

AOE question

How can cultural contexts influence how texts are written and received?

The Ford Mustang (Text 2.14) is a type of car, often called a 'muscle car', which has more horsepower and is lower to the ground than the average car. In the cultural context of muscle cars, this advertisement and the Dodge commercial (Text 2.15) may be highly effective in targeting their audience. What about the cultural contexts of other vehicles?

a Find and compare advertisements for plug-in hybrids, minivans, utility vehicles or trucks.

b How do these target a different demographic?

c How has cultural context helped shape the production and reception of these texts?

2.10 In order to view Text 2.15, you need to do an online search for 'Man's Last Stand', a Dodge Charger commercial that aired during the 2010 Super Bowl. The Super Bowl is the championship game of the National Football League in the USA. American football is often seen as a 'tough' and 'masculine' sport. While both men and women watch the Super Bowl every year, many of the commercials appeal to a male audience. After watching the commercial as a class, discuss your answers to these questions:

a Compare the titles of Text 2.14, 'Only Mustang makes it happen', and Text 2.15, 'Man's Last Stand'. How do these titles reflect different cultural contexts?

b How does the context of Text 2.15, which aired in the USA during the Super Bowl in 2010, determine how it was received?

c How does this commercial reflect cultural values that are similar to or different from those expressed in Text 2.14?

d How do the implicit messages of Text 2.15 comment on masculinity and marriage? How appropriate are these messages in the context in which you live?

Text 2.15

Man's Last Stand, 2010

Do an online search for the Dodge Charger Super Bowl commercial from 2010, using the search term 'Man's Last Stand'.

2.11 The previous activities asked you to compare and contrast advertisements for the same product from different times. Think of products that are typically marketed to men, such as lawn mowers or beer.

Do an online search for advertisements for these products from different eras. As a class, make a 'then and now' wall where you place copies of these advertisements side by side for your classmates to see. Discuss how notions of what it means to be a man have changed over time.

Record your findings in your learner portfolio.

AOE question

How do the conventions of different types of text develop over time?

While Text 2.14 is a print advertisement and Text 2.15 is a TV commercial, focus on the convention of using masculinity to sell 'muscle cars' in both texts. How have gender roles and relations shifted in the years between the texts? Where do you see evidence of this shift in these texts?

Intertextuality: connecting texts

2.12 Text 2.15, the Dodge Charger commercial, was met with criticism after it aired in 2010. Criticism is sometimes best expressed through '**spoof**'. A spoof is a way of making fun of a particular text by imitating its style and structure for a different purpose. Do an online search for spoofs of the Dodge Charger commercial, using search terms such as 'Women's Last Stand' or 'Dodge Charger spoof ad'. Choose one of these spoof ads, and discuss your answers to these questions with your classmates:

a What is the main message of your spoof commercial? Why do you agree or disagree with this message?

b How does this spoof make you more conscious of how harmful the original commercial is towards women?

c How does this spoof achieve its purpose by using the same stylistic and structural features of the original commercial?

2.13 Spoof advertisements and commercials, like the ones you explored in the previous activity, are examples of **culture jamming**, or **subvertising.** These are tactics used to disrupt or subvert mainstream media and the messages they construct. Subvertising aims to expose the methods used in advertising by large corporations. It makes people think about the adverse messages that they frequently send. **Parody** and spoof are closely related to **pastiche** – a type of text that imitates the style of another text. Unlike spoof, which mocks a particular text, or parody, which mocks a genre of texts, pastiche does not mock the text on which it is based or the intentions of its author. Instead, pastiche draws inspiration from the original text and continues in a similar style.

In this activity you will consider one example of a pastiche:

a Divide into two groups and go into separate rooms.

b The first group reads the poem *Broetry* by Brian McGackin (Text 2.16) and prepares a short presentation. In the presentation, explore the purpose of the author, his use of language and how readers may interpret his poem.

c The second group reads both *Broetry* (Text 2.16) and 'This is Just to Say' by William Carlos Williams, a poem which you can find through an online search. This group also researches common interpretations of Williams's poem and prepares a presentation on *Broetry* (Text 2.16), exploring the author's purpose, use of language and the readers' response in the light of Williams's poem.

d Both groups then come together in one room. The first group should present first. After the second group has presented, discuss how the analyses were different. How was the second group's interpretation different from that of the first group? How was the second group's interpretation affected by the knowledge that *Broetry* is a pastiche?

Text 2.16

Cover poem from *Broetry*

Brian McGackin 2011

I have finished
the beer
that was in
the icebox

and which
you were probably
saving
for Friday

Forgive me
this girl came over
so sweet
and so hot.

AOE question

How can comparing and interpreting texts transform readers?

Activity 2.13 shows how interpretations of the same poem can be different, especially when one interpretation is informed by an interpretation of another poem. You can do this type of activity with other pastiches or parodies.

Towards assessment

2.14 In 2013, psychologists Megan Vokey, Bruce Tefft and Chris Tysiaczny at the University of Manitoba published a paper about the problems of **hypermasculinity**. Hypermasculinity, according to them, is underpinned by four beliefs:

- Danger is exciting.
- Toughness is a form of emotional self-control.
- Violence is manly.
- It's fine to be callous about women and sex.

The researchers studied over 500 advertisements in several mainstream men's magazines from 2007 to 2008 and concluded that over 50% of advertisements promoted one or more of these four beliefs of hypermasculinity. Conduct your own research, using similar methods.

a Find several magazines (in print) that generally appeal to a male readership.

b For each advertisement, check to see if there is evidence of one or more of the beliefs that underpin hypermasculinity.

c Record the number of advertisements that you have studied in each magazine and the number of advertisements that depict hypermasculinity. Which magazines run these advertisements the most?

d Select one advertisement from one magazine and share it with your classmates. Prepare a short presentation on it, using the following guiding question: 'To what degree is hypermasculinity depicted in this advertisement, and what adverse effects might such advertisements have on their target audience?'

e Listen to everyone's presentation and record your findings in your learner portfolio.

CONCEPT

Representation

As you present your advertisement for Activity 2.14, keep in mind that one of the key concepts for this course is *representation*. How are notions of masculinity represented or misrepresented in the advertisement that you have selected?

Extended essay

For your extended essay, you may wish to analyse the depiction of men in TV commercials as a Category 3 essay. You may want to compare older commercials to newer ones, analysing how gender roles and social constructs have changed over time. You may want to compare the depiction of men and women in one commercial. If you decide to write this type of essay, be sure to:

- keep your focus on only a few commercials
- engage with a meaningful topic, such as gender stereotyping
- refer to secondary sources
- make specific reference to the primary sources, including the use of dialogue, setting or character depiction, symbols, music and use of cinematography.

Higher level extension

2.15 In this unit so far, you have explored narrow definitions of masculinity as constructed by various texts. Most likely, you have seen narrowly defined social constructs in popular films as well. How gender-biased are films these days?

The **Bechdel test** is a simple set of three criteria to determine if a film is not overly biased towards men. The Bechdel test is named after Alison Bechdel, who introduced this test in her comic strip, *Dykes to Watch Out For*. A film passes the Bechdel test if it:

- features at least two, named women . . .
- who have a meaningful conversation at some point during the film . . .
- about something other than a man.

a Think of the most recent film you watched in the cinema, at home or anywhere. Does it pass the Bechdel test?

b As a class, write a list of everyone's results. How many films pass the test?

c Discuss your results as a class. Should you be concerned about these results?

2.16 Do an online search for a TED Talk by Colin Stokes entitled 'How movies teach manhood'. Watch this talk and discuss your answers to these questions as a class:

a How familiar are you with the two films that Colin Stokes compares and contrasts: *The Wizard of Oz* and *Star Wars – A New Hope*? If you are familiar with these films, can you say whether his observations and analysis are accurate? If you are familiar with the more recent Star Wars films, have they made a departure from previous Star Wars films in the ways they represent men and women?

b Do you agree with his statement that boys these days need to learn how to defend themselves against 'the **patriarchy**'? Patriarchy is an interesting choice of words. It refers to a hierarchy in which men hold the power and exclude women from gaining power. Colin Stokes argues that films provide more examples of girls and women who challenge established patriarchies than they do of boys who battle this system.

c Colin Stokes quotes a study that says one in five women in America have been sexually assaulted at some time in their life. He wonders if these sexual assailants are influenced by modern films. Do you think they are? Can he prove this?

d Colin Stokes's talk is from 2011. Are the ideas from his talk outdated or more relevant than ever? Do you think that films include better **role models** for girls, boys, women and men these days than they used to? Discuss how progressive films are today. Give examples to prove your points.

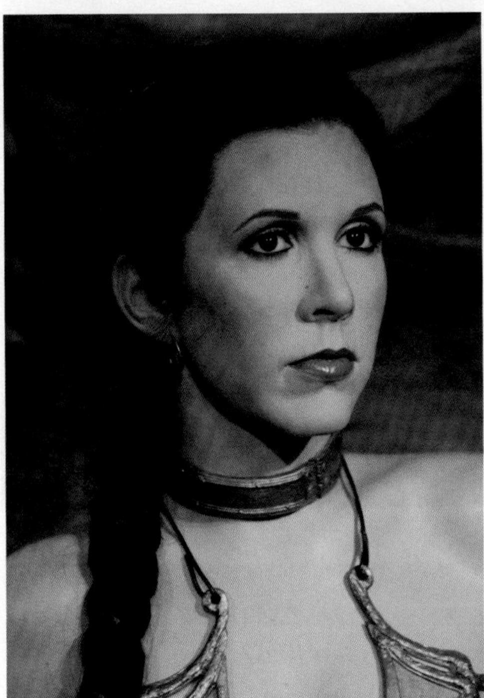

Has the depiction of women in films progressed over the years? Compare Princess Leia (1976) to Rey (2015) from the Star Wars films. Are films portraying stronger leading women these days? Are such portrayals of 'tough' women problematic or progressive for gender equality?

2.17 This unit has identified the problems of narrow definitions of masculinity in advertising. The next question is: what can be done to solve this problem? Activities 2.12 and 2.13 introduced you to spoof, parody and subvertising as ways of spreading awareness about this issue.

Role reversal is another strategy often used by organisations to raise awareness about the unrealistic depictions of men and women in the media. Role reversal places men where women would usually appear or vice versa. Text 2.17 is an example of this. Study Text 2.17 and discuss your answers to these questions as a class:

a Kookai is a women's fashion company, and yet Text 2.17 does not depict their clothing. How does this advertisement achieve its purpose of selling their product, nonetheless?

b How does this advertisement use colour, body language, camera angle and other stylistic features of visual texts to construct meaning? See Unit 1.1 on analysing images and Unit 1.2 on analysing advertisements for further information and support about these text types.

c In your opinion, how successful is this advertisement in spreading awareness about gender inequality?

Text 2.17

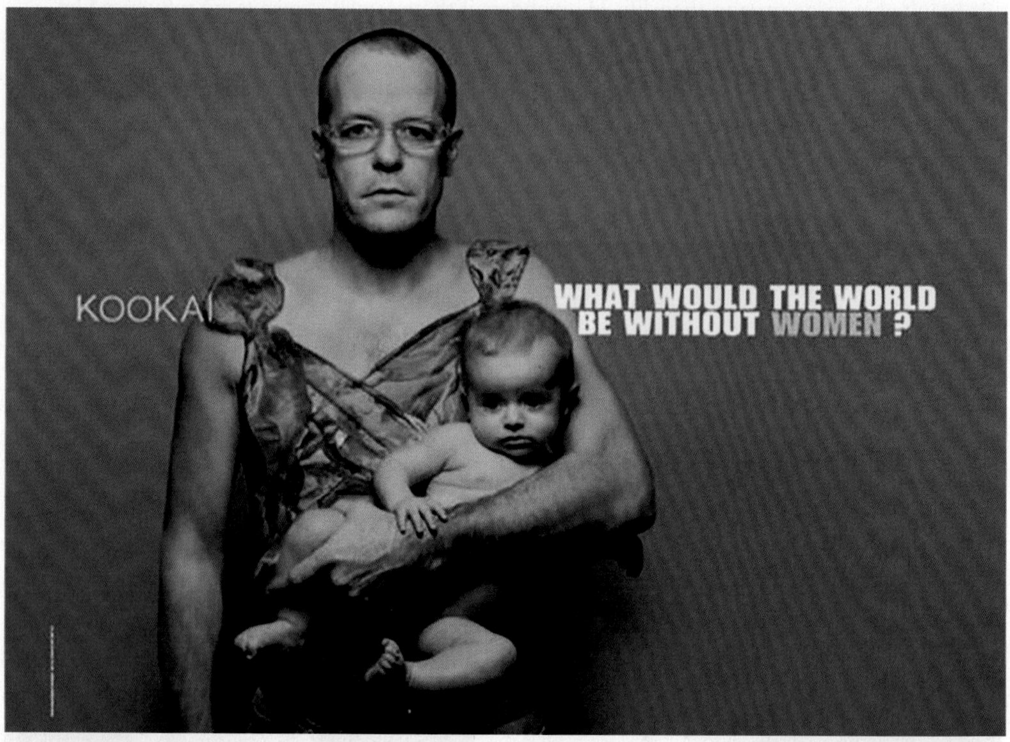

AOE question

How can language represent social differences and identities?

Consider this question with regard to Text 2.17. By 'language' consider the use of colour, lighting, facial expression, body language symbols and role reversal (Activities 2.17–2.18).

Research skills

Activity 2.18 asks you to find an example of role reversal in advertising by searching online. When you research images, try to identify the original creator or source of the image. As many images are repurposed or copied on the web, finding the original source will help you comment on the creator's intention more accurately.

2.18 Do an online search for images related to 'role reversal in advertising'. You may find some funny examples. Choose an image and share this with your classmates. Discuss your answers to these questions as a class:

a What is the main message of your image?

b What contextual knowledge must the reader have in order to understand the image?

c Is your image an advertisement, an **awareness campaign**, a spoof, a parody, a pastiche or a combination of these text types?

d How is your image similar to or different from Text 2.17?

e How effective is your image in spreading awareness about gender roles in advertising?

2.19 A similar but different technique from role reversal is the use of **counterstereotype** – an unexpected representation of a person. Text 2.18 includes counterstereotypes of what you expect of nurses. Analyse the text and discuss your answers to these questions as a class:

a Look back to Text 2.12, which advertises a job vacancy in ways that might appeal to men and women differently. Compare the language of the male-biased version of Text 2.12 to that used in Text 2.18. How do they appeal to similar values of strength, dominance and masculinity?

b Look at the list of potentially offensive phrases from Activity 2.3 (e.g. 'to man up'). To be 'man enough', the expression used in the heading of Text 2.18, is not listed there. Should it be? Do you consider this heading offensive?

c What social constructs or stereotypes of manhood does Text 2.18 reinforce? How does it do this?

d Is Text 2.18 **progressive**? This term means advocating for social change and promoting equality.

e Can you think of other examples of counterstereotyping in the media? Do an online search for more examples. These may include the depiction of:

- a successful person from an ethnic minority
- a man in a caring role (sometimes called '**dadvertising**')
- a woman in a position of power.

These depictions may be in advertisements, films, commercials or brochures. Share your example with your classmates. Discuss the effectiveness of your example of counterstereotyping in promoting equality.

> **AOE question**
>
> *How do the conventions of different types of text develop over time?*
>
> To answer this question with regard to Text 2.18, you may want to look for older advertisements which aim to recruit nurses. How has this type of text evolved over past decades?

Text 2.18

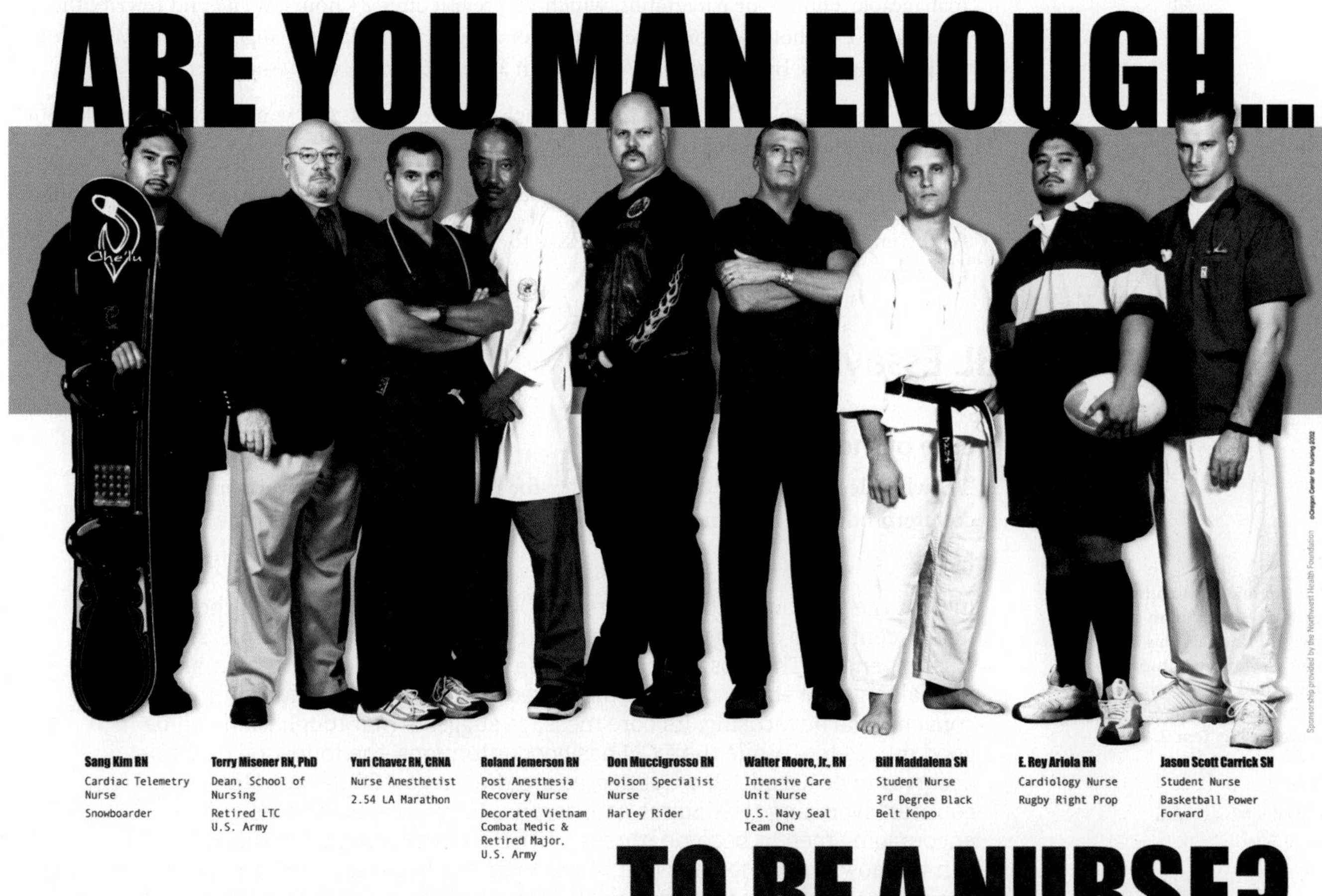

2.20 At higher level you must write an HL essay on a literary or non-literary text. You may wish to write this piece of coursework on a text that you have explored in Units 2.1 and 2.2, focusing on stereotypes, social constructs, feminism and masculinity. Follow these steps to develop your own HL essay:

a Read Chapter 7 if you have not done so already. Read the assessment criteria for the HL essay (in the introduction), so that you know what is expected from you on this form of assessment.

b Read this sample HL essay and the examiner's marks and comments.

c Find a text, an advertisement, commercial or poem, which pressures men and women to be more masculine or feminine. You may choose a text from this unit, such as the Old Spice or Dodge Charger commercials.

d Think of your own 'line of inquiry' which can be similar to the line of inquiry followed in these units, for example: 'To what extent are women or men misrepresented by narrow definitions of femininity and/or masculinity in Text X?' Be sure that the text that you select has enough content and depth to enable you to write a 1200–1500-word essay.

e Write a thesis statement and create a mind map to visualise the ideas that you want to include in your HL essay. Discuss these ideas with your teacher before you start writing the essay.

f Turn your mind map into a linear outline and start writing your essay. Break the writing into manageable 'chunks' or paragraphs, which you revisit after 24 hours. Write and rewrite these paragraphs in 1-hour sessions spread out over a few days, making changes to what you wrote on previous days. But do not take more than a week to write your essay.

g Submit your complete HL essay to your teacher for feedback. Ask your teacher to mark your work using the assessment criteria.

h Use your teacher's comments to rewrite your essay. Keep your essay in your learner portfolio.

i At the end of your course, revisit this essay to see if you want to submit it as your best HL essay.

HL Essay – Sample 1

Line of inquiry

'To what degree are the Oregon Center for Nursing's counteradvertising techniques counterproductive in achieving its goal of encouraging men to become nurses?'

Essay

You can include an advertisement, poem or extract as an appendix to your HL essay. This makes the focus of your essay more easily understood for the examiner. The appendix in the context of this coursebook is Text 2.18.

In 2002 the Oregon Center for Nursing (OCN) created a poster for schools and health centres to change the perception of men in the nursing profession (see Appendix). This poster is an example of counteradvertising, as it aims to challenge the status quo and the stereotypical representations of men in conventional advertising. Its core message suggests that tough men can be good nurses too. While the OCN has good intentions, the following question deserves to be asked: 'To what degree are the Oregon Center for Nursing's counteradvertising techniques counterproductive in achieving its goal of encouraging men to become nurses?' Upon a closer analysis of this poster, it can be shown how the depiction of the men, the heading, subheadings and the use of labels actually reinforce existing stereotypes about manliness.

Good textual analysis always uses the present tense, even if the text was created long ago.

First of all, the depiction of the men, including their clothing, their body expressions and facial expressions, all reinforce the notion that men should be tough, competitive and emotionless. The black and white photographs of the men have been taken from a low-angle shot so that the men look down on the viewer, making them appear strong and domineering. The full body shots show them taking a stance and posing for the camera, aware of its presence. This awareness makes them appear in control. In response to the camera, they have broadened their chests or crossed their arms and placed their feet at shoulder width, positions that exude power and strength. Whether they hide behind a snowboard or have their hands in their pockets, they seem ready for combat. While some of them are wearing nursing attire, others are wearing street clothes, sporting gear or a suit. This suggests to the reader that their identity is not exclusively defined by the profession of nursing, but also by any sports, hobbies or military service that they may have had. Unfortunately, these sports are competitive, tough-guy sports, such as karate, rugby and basketball. Toughness and competitiveness are juxtaposed with the profession of nursing, which is often associated with caring and kindness. Similarly, their facial expressions lack the warm, outgoing attitude that is expected of nurses in a care-taking role. While the OCN intentionally juxtaposes these tough looks with the reader's expectations of nursing in order to raise interest in the nursing profession, it also reinforces stereotypes that men must be competitive, tough and strong in order to be successful in any profession.

Furthermore, OCN uses a heading and subheading to reinforce social constructs of how men should be and behave. The phrase 'Are you man enough . . . to be a nurse?' uses a question, ellipsis and the second-person pronoun to intrigue the male reader and make him consider nursing as a career path. The expression 'to be man enough', however, can be considered sexist. It implies that manhood is equated with strength and toughness. If one is not strong enough, then one is not 'man enough' in this line of hurtful logic. This sexist question undermines the message of the advertisement, which aims to redefine gender roles in the nursing profession. The subheadings, with the bold font and italics, capture the reader's attention and appeal to character traits that are often associated with manly men. 'Courage', for example, equates heroism and bravery with manliness. 'Skill', 'career' and 'unlimited opportunity', which should appeal to both women and men, are used here to target a male audience exclusively. It is unfortunate that these traits are thought to attract men to the profession of nursing. Other character traits or ideals, such as 'compassion', 'collaboration' or 'grace', may have been more appropriate traits for the profession of nursing. Unfortunately, the layout of the poster suggests that these character traits form the foundation on which men should stand, as they appear under the men at the footer of the poster. Again, the reader reads a conflicting message. On the one hand, readers should be open to the idea that men too can be nurses. On the other hand, they are told that only manly, high-achieving men should apply. In other words, the poster tries to challenge the stereotypes of nursing while reinforcing social constructs of manliness.

Finally, the poster uses labels to construct narrow definitions of manliness, which have the counterproductive effect of pressuring men. Under each photographed man, two labels appear: the first describes the man's job in the nursing profession and the second describes the man's hobby, sport or military history. The medical labels beside each name include such acronyms as RN (Registered Nurse) or PhD (Doctor of Philosophy), which give the men a sense of professionalism and distinction. Understandably this is important in making the nursing profession seem distinguished and attractive to men who are attracted to status. Their job titles are equally impressive, as they include professional jargon such as 'Cardiac Telemetry' or 'Post Anaesthesia Recovery Nurse' which mystifies the reader and sounds quite specialised. While it is commendable that the nursing profession offers such job opportunities, it is unfortunate that they are accompanied by other labels, such as 'Harley Rider', 'Decorated Vietnam Combat Medic' or 'Basketball

The verbs 'appear', 'suggest', 'seem' and 'show' all work well for textual analysis of a visual text.

Notice that this paragraph has three illustrations: body language, dress and facial expressions. Each illustration is followed by an explanation or analysis of its significance.

Notice how the final sentence of this paragraph reflects the first paragraph of this essay. It is important to return to the ideas that you outlined in your thesis statement and topic sentences.

This topic sentence, like the first one, connects a linguistic feature, such as headings, with meaning, such as comments on manliness.

Use relevant quotations from a primary source in your HL essay. It will help you on Criterion A. Notice how the first paragraph, analysing visual text, paraphrases and describes the images that it analyses. This too is good practice.

Phrases such as 'on the one hand . . . on the other hand' are good for the 'flow' of your essay. They act as signposts for the reader and indicate the relationships between ideas.

This essay has three large body paragraphs, an introduction and conclusion. While the 'five paragraph essay' may or may not work for your topic and text, it is advisable to write in depth about carefully selected stylistic features.

Power Forward'. These labels suggest that it is not enough for the men to be specialised nurses, or teachers and students of nursing. It suggests that 'real men' must be specialists in multiple fields. It is not enough, for example, for one man to be labelled 'marathon runner'. Instead the OCN has written the man's marathon time and event '2.54 LA Marathon', which is a very impressive time. It is not enough for one man to be in the US Navy. Instead he is a 'US Navy Seal Team One', which sounds like an elite position. The man who practices karate is a '3rd Degree Black Belt Kengo', which suggests a high level of mastery. With all of these labels, readers are sent a message that men must be specialised, skilled, experienced and strong in order to be successful nurses. What's worse, it suggests that work, sport and military are the only meaningful definitions of men's identity, excluding other roles related to family and friendship. These labels place an unwanted social pressure on its target audience by narrowly defining success in life and work. It sends the wrong message that the nursing profession only wants high-level achievers in competitive sports or military service, which could prove counterproductive in recruiting the right people for the job.

Although 'to conclude' may sound boring, it is effective. Do not be afraid to use standard phrases if they work well.

To conclude, the OCN creates unrealistic definitions of manliness and uses existing stereotypes of masculinity in its 2002 poster in order to achieve its purpose of recruiting male nurses. It is interesting to note how the OCN later made changes to this poster by creating a colour version with smiling men, wearing their nursing attire, looking less intimidating and friendlier. The labels were changed from '2.54 LA Marathon' to 'long distance runner', for example. It seems as if the OCN was aware of the problems that they had created in their original advertisement. Unfortunately the headline 'Are you man enough . . . to be a nurse?' was kept. Such use of sexist language deserves to be challenged more often in advertising, as it sets unrealistic expectations on its target audiences to fulfil roles that cannot be fulfilled. Not every man can be expected to be a high achieving athlete or a decorated military hero. This poster shows how advertisements can be counterproductive in their purpose. By trying to challenge the stereotypes of gender roles in nursing, it actually reinforces social constructs that men must be powerful, skilled and high achievers if they are to be successful in life and work.

Although this is a good essay, there is certainly a missed opportunity here, as the student could have analysed the improved colour poster with more depth and compared it to the black and white original.

HL Essay – Sample 1 – Examiner's marks and comments

Criterion A: Knowledge, understanding and interpretation: 5 out of 5 marks

The student's interpretation of this poster is very relevant to the line of inquiry. While the essay could have compared this poster to newer versions of it, it is effective in answering the line of inquiry. Consulting secondary sources would have given the student even more understanding of the OCN's intentions and their responses to criticism, though this approach is not required by such a narrow line of inquiry. References to the text are integrated effectively and are consistently relevant to the thesis that the counteradvertising techniques are counterproductive.

Criterion B: Analysis and evaluation: 5 out of 5 marks

The student has, in a very perceptive analysis, noticed that the OCN sends a conflicting message to men through the (visual) language of this recruitment poster. The analyses of body language, medical jargon, clothing, facial expressions and labels are very insightful. This essay shows appreciation for the richness of the stimulus text.

Criterion C: Coherence, focus and organisation: 5 out of 5 marks

The body paragraphs are organised effectively, connecting the stylistic features of the text to the stereotypes that the OCN poster reinforces. The essay consistently focuses on the poster's inability to achieve its aims and address social constructs.

Criterion D: Language – 5 out of 5

The language of this essay is spot on! The student seems equipped with subject-appropriate vocabulary, using semantic fields such as 'heroism', 'manliness' and 'power'. The language of several sentences is very effective in capturing the essence of the ideas, such as: 'Such use of sexist language deserves to be challenged more often in advertising, as it sets unrealistic expectations on its target audiences to fulfil roles that cannot be fulfilled.'

CONCEPT

Communication

You have explored a range of text types in this unit, including awareness campaigns, parodies, pastiches, spoofs, commercials and poetry. *Communication*, it seems, is an art form. Are some text types richer in their use of language than others? Activity 2.20 asks you to think carefully about a primary source for your HL essay. Which forms of communication lend themselves best to deeper analysis?

Further resources

- *The Mask You Live In* by Jennifer Siebel Newsom is a documentary about the pressures on men and hypermasculinity.
- Jackson Katz in an interesting author and speaker. His TED Talk, documentary (*Tough Guise*) and books provide a good understanding of the 'macho paradox' and male violence against women.
- Both the book and the documentary called *Guyland*, by Michael Kimmel, offer insight into social pressures on young men and how these are constructed in the media.

REFLECT

Sit in pairs with someone of the opposite gender, if possible, and discuss your answers to these questions before holding a classroom discussion:

a Was there a text in this unit that you found particularly interesting? Explain why.

b Is there an equal misrepresentation of men and women in the media? Or is one gender group more misrepresented than the other?

c What can you do to spread awareness about the problems of gender bias in the media?

Unit 2.3 Beauty

Word bank

digital retouching
airbrushing
truncated sentence
capitalisation
self-esteem
purpose-driven content marketing
shockvertising
anti-advertising
spoof
awareness campaign
thinspiration
self-image
sex in advertising
taboo
role reversal
objectification
degradation
metonymy
allusion
rape myth
surrealism
hashtag
anaphora
anecdote
enumeration
parallelism
polysyndeton

Learning objectives

- explore a range of texts that deal with narrow definitions of 'sex' and 'beauty'
- develop skills in visual literacy, analysing advertisements and awareness campaigns
- become proficient with terms and concepts that are relevant to the topic and text types.

In this chapter, you have discussed the various social pressures on men and women to fit narrow definitions of gender. You have explored notions of motherhood, fatherhood, wifehood, husbandhood, femininity and masculinity.

This unit continues to ask how the mass media puts pressure on men and women by constructing narrow definitions of 'beauty'. It also explores social problems that are created by unrealistic depictions of beauty and sex, such as eating disorders and sexual harassment. You will explore this topic through a range of texts, from poems to advertisements.

Getting started

3.1 Text 2.19 is an advertisement for make-up featuring Aishwarya Rai Bachchan, an Indian actress, model and the winner of the 1994 Miss World pageant. The accompanying image is a photograph of the model without **digital retouching** or **airbrushing**. Digital retouching is a commonly used stylistic feature of visual texts these days.

Text 2.19

a How has digital retouching been used in this advertisement (Text 2.19)?

b Why do you think these changes have been made?

c What are the effects of digital retouching on the viewer of this advertisement?

3.2 Now study Text 2.20, an awareness campaign by Adbusters, and discuss your answers to these questions:

a The text begins with the line, 'She's pretty isn't she?' Do you think she is pretty? How do you think your definitions of beauty are formed? Are they biological? Or have your definitions of beauty been shaped by the media, as Text 2.20 suggests?

b What does the author of this text mean by 'beauty is averageness'?

c There are several words missing from some of the sentences in this text. The words in italics here would make these sentences complete. '*Do* you wish you looked like her?' or '*It is a* pity *that* she doesn't exist.' This stylistic device is known as the **truncated sentence**. Do you see more examples in Text 2.20? What is the effect of including truncated sentences instead of complete sentences?

d Why does the author use white text boxes over the image? Comment on the use of font, italics and **capitalisation** as stylistic features.

e Who is 'we' in this text? Who are 'you'? How does the use of pronouns help deliver the message of this text?

f What type of text is Text 2.20? Where would it appear?

Text 2.20

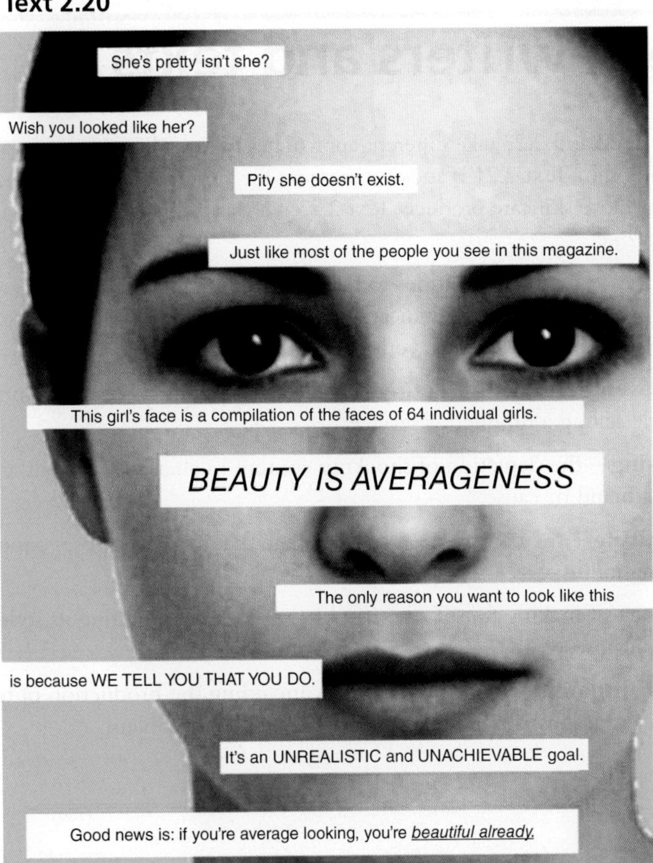

TOK

As you explore the arts as an 'area of knowledge' in TOK, you will come across questions such as 'what is beauty?' or 'how can we define "beautiful"?' Are there universally accepted qualities that we look for in a 'beautiful' magazine model?

Text 2.20 seems to suggest that the ideal 'pretty' face does not even exist in the real world. But if 'pretty' models are the fabrications of the fashion industry, why do people aspire to be like them? How do you 'know' when someone is 'beautiful'? Discuss your answers to these questions as a class.

AOE question

What are the different ways in which people are affected by texts?

Activity 3.2 and Text 2.20 invite you to ask how young women may be affected by texts that narrowly define 'beauty' through the use of digital retouching.

3.3 By digital retouching, advertisements can construct unrealistic definitions of beauty. Many young people around the world consume hundreds of such advertisements every day. This helps to explain why so many people suffer from depression, low **self-esteem** and eating disorders. The line of logic goes: if consumers want to appear like the models they see in the advertisements, and they cannot be like those models, then they become frustrated with their own physical shortcomings. Even the model Cindy Crawford once said, 'I wish I could look like Cindy Crawford'. Discuss your answers to these questions:

a Do you think that problems such as low self-esteem, depression and eating disorders are caused by unrealistic depictions of beauty in the media, as explained in this text? Are people really influenced so much by the media around them?

b Do these problems affect women and men equally?

c What kinds of initiatives and campaigns can address these problems?

d Why would Cindy Crawford say 'I wish I could look like Cindy Crawford'? What does she mean by this?

Readers, writers and texts

3.4 Texts 2.21, 2.22 and 2.23 take different approaches to spreading awareness about the pressures on women to look slim. Text 2.21 is an advertisement for a modelling agency. Text 2.22 is an advertisement for Dove skincare products. Text 2.23 is a campaign by Adbusters, a progressive website and magazine.

Here are several key terms and definitions to help you understand the approaches taken by these three texts. After studying these texts, indicate which terms are relevant to each text. Terms may be relevant to more than one text. Discuss your answers with your classmates.

- **Purpose-driven content marketing** – the act of building a brand around a social purpose or cause while selling a product or service.
- **Shockvertising** – the depiction of shocking content in an advertisement, in order to draw attention to a brand or cause.
- **Anti-advertising** – the construction of a message that clearly opposes common messages in the advertising industry.
- **Spoof** – the act of making fun of a text and its message by imitating its style and structure to an opposite purpose.
- **Awareness campaign** – a range of activities, including the production of texts, in an effort to raise public awareness about a particular issue or social problem.

Text 2.21

Text 2.22

fat?
fit?
Does true beauty only squeeze into size 8?
campaignforrealbeauty.co.uk
Dove

Text 2.23

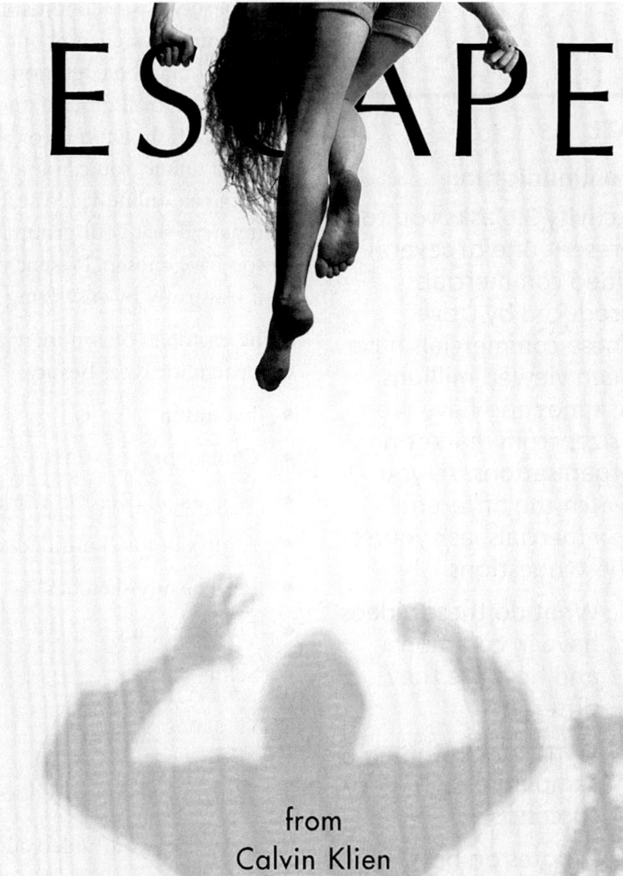

3.5 Anorexia nervosa and bulimia are eating disorders, where a person fasts, or uses vomiting or laxatives after binge eating, usually in an effort to become skinnier. Those who suffer from these health disorders often look to images of fashion models for '**thinspiration**' (inspiration to look thin). Look again at Texts 2.21–2.23 and discuss how you think someone with anorexia or bulimia might respond to these texts. Would these texts provide them with thinspiration? Why do you think this might be?

CONCEPT

Identity

Our *identity* is affected by our **self-image**. Self-image is the way we imagine ourselves in terms of appearance and personality. Some people form their self-image by comparing themselves to people they either know or see in the media. The 'Real Beauty Sketches' by Dove are a reminder that our self-image is not always accurate. How critical are you of your own appearance? And to what extent do you compare yourself to others?

ATL

Communication

Activity 3.6 asks you to present one of several video commercials produced by Dove. These commercials have been viewed millions of times and have won prizes from marketing organisations. As you watch the different commercials, ask yourself these questions:

- What do these videos have in common and how are they different?
- What makes this campaign so successful?

Take notes on how your classmates use various presentation skills to present their commercial. Consider:

- Do they analyse freeze-frames or stills from their videos?
- Do they answer the questions from the activity?
- Do they read from notes?

Developing your own *communication skills* is about observing and listening to others carefully.

3.6 Text 2.22, from Dove's Campaign for Real Beauty, has been remarkably successful in spreading awareness about social issues, increasing brand recognition and selling more products. In small groups, study one of Dove's commercials shown here or a similar one that you find online. You can find your commercial by doing an online video search for the commercial that your group has been assigned or you have chosen. Present your video to your classmates by answering questions a–e.

Some examples of commercials from Dove's Campaign for Real Beauty:

- Evolution
- Onslaught
- Women all over the world make a choice
- A girl's beauty confidence starts with you
- Real beauty sketches
- Free being me
- Selfie.

Dove's Campaign for Real Beauty has run several commercials over the years which you can research and analyse (Activity 3.6).

a What social concern does your video explore?

b How does your video address issues created by the media's narrow definition of 'beauty'?

c How does your video use camera angle, mise en scène, lighting, symbols and sound to create meaning and convey a message? See Unit 1.3 for more information on these terms.

d What is the effect of these film techniques on their viewers? How do you think your video has been received? Try to find a secondary source that reviews your video and comments on its reception by a larger audience.

e Can you find any criticisms of the Dove Campaign for Real Beauty? What kinds of criticisms have been voiced about this campaign, and are they relevant to your video?

3.7 In this unit you have explored the adverse effects of digital retouching and the effect of skinny models on young women's physical and mental health. What happens when women or men are portrayed as objects of sexual desire? What are the effects of these images on women and men, and how do they set expectations for real-life relationships?

Sex appeal or '**sex in advertising**' is a kind of persuasion technique which usually includes nudity or suggestion. It subscribes to the axiom 'sex sells', and suggests that the inclusion of sex in advertising will lead to more sales of products or services.

Think of a print or television advert that you have seen which uses sex to sell a product. Present your advertisement to your classmates, analysing the way it alludes to sex to sell a product. As a class, discuss the commonalities and trends you see among the advertisements you have each chosen. Record your findings in your learner portfolio.

International mindedness

Sex in advertising is a cultural issue. People all around the world feel differently about this topic. In some cultures, advertisements such as Text 2.24 may be considered artistic. In others, they are **taboo**.

Activity 3.8 invites you to discuss how this text might be received in your own culture. Be sure not to generalise when speaking about entire countries or parts of the world. Consider people's religious affiliations. Consider where people live in relation to rural or urban areas. Internationally minded learners understand that not everyone will share their view of the world. Keep this in mind as you discuss the texts in this unit with your classmates and teacher.

Time and space

3.8 Text 2.24 appeared in fashion magazines around the world in 2007. Discuss your answers to these questions:

a How similar to or different from the one you researched in Activity 3.7 is Text 2.24? Do you see similar or different forms of sex in advertising, as introduced in Activity 3.7?

b Think of popular fashion magazines that you can buy. Would you see such advertisements as Text 2.24 in magazines in your country or region? Why might these advertisements be available or unavailable in the context in which you live?

c Text 2.24 is one of many advertisements for the fashion company Dolce & Gabbana that use sexually provocative or erotic imagery. Research how this or other Dolce & Gabbana advertisements have been received around the world. Have they ever had to pull an advertisement or apologise to anyone? Find out more about any conflict surrounding advertisements from this company in the past and share your findings with your classmates.

d Does sex sell? How effective is sex in advertising in selling products or services? Find out more about the research that has been done on this topic and share your findings with your classmates. Were you surprised by your findings?

Text 2.24

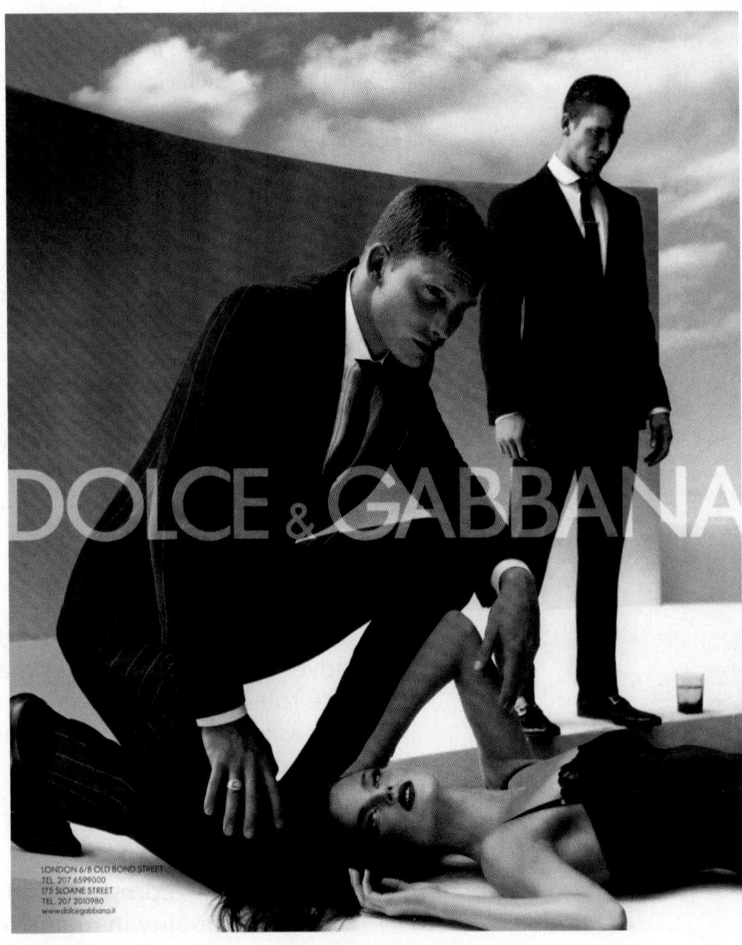

AOE question

How can language represent social differences and identities?

This question is particularly relevant to the Dolce & Gabbana advertisement (Text 2.24).

- Who are these people? How does their body language, way of dressing and gaze represent who they are?
- How are they similar to fictional characters in a novel?
- How can their target audience relate to them?
- Do they represent a certain social class, occupation, role or purpose?

Intertextuality: connecting texts

3.9 What if men had to pose for advertisements in the ways that women are asked to? Is it possible to objectify men in the same way as women?

a Do an online search for a spoof advertisement that makes use of **role reversal**. Many of these spoofs are placed alongside the original advertisement that they imitate.

b Bring your spoof advertisement to class and share it with your classmates.

c Explain, in a short presentation, how the use of role reversal makes the viewer more aware of the problems of gender representation and the **objectification** of women in advertising. Compare the spoof to the original advertisement.

d Are men objectified in advertisements, as well as women? Can you find examples of this in real advertisements (rather than in spoofs)? Is the objectification of men another form of gender equality or gender **degradation**? Discuss.

CONCEPT

Representation

In this unit you have explored the ways in which women are represented in advertisements and other mass media texts. Activity 3.9 encourages you to use role reversal as a way to see if these representations of women are fair. It asks you to consider if the objectification of men is another form of gender equality.

- How has the *representation* of men in advertising changed over the past 50 years?
- How has this representation changed with more inclusion and acceptance of homosexuality in mainstream Western media in that time? Find examples to prove your points.

3.10 Text 2.25 is an awareness campaign from the Salvation Army in South Africa. Discuss your answers to these questions as a class:

a How does Text 2.25 borrow stylistic and structural features from other advertisements that depict and objectify women? Explore features such as body language, gaze, camera angle, lighting and copy. See Units 1.1 and 1.2 for further support for analysing images and advertisements.

b The text makes a reference to 'black and blue', which is an example of **metonymy**. Metonymy is a stylist device where an aspect, such as colour, stands for a greater phenomenon or thing, such as domestic violence. Why has the author used metonymy here?

c The white and gold dress is an **allusion** to an optical illusion that is widely debated. An allusion is a reference to another text for a particular effect. Do an online search for 'white and gold dress illusion' and discuss how this information adds to your understanding of Text 2.25.

d Do you believe there is a connection between domestic violence and mass media that objectifies and sexualises women? How is Text 2.25 connected to other texts, such as Text 2.24?

e How effective is this campaign in raising awareness of domestic violence? Describe how it makes you feel. Research how others have reacted to this campaign.

Text 2.25

3.11 Domestic violence is only one form of violence against women. Groping, sexual assault and rape are, unfortunately, also problems around the world. The visual language of commercials, advertisements and billboards may enable assailants to objectify women by subscribing to various rape myths. A **rape myth** is a kind of scenario or story that both perpetrators and victims believe explains why sexual assault happens. Some of the most common rape myths include:

- The victim's way of dressing was an invitation for rape.
- Intoxication justifies any unwanted sexual advances, or intoxication is an invitation for sex.
- Sexual intercourse is reciprocation for paying for dinner or a date.
- It is not technically rape unless the victim resists.
- More often than not, victims lie about being raped and therefore no one can fairly make such claims.
- Unwanted sex is not a violent crime.

Text 2.26 exploits one of these rape myths in an effort to raise awareness against sexual assault. Discuss your answers to these questions with your classmates:

a How does this text work? What type of text is it? What devices does it use to communicate its message? How effectively does it use these devices? Explain your answers.

b Compare Text 2.25 to Text 2.26, both of which aim to raise awareness about violence, but in different ways. Discuss their similarities and differences.

c Looking back at other texts from this unit, comment on and explain how one of them might promote a rape myth among its viewers.

Text 2.26

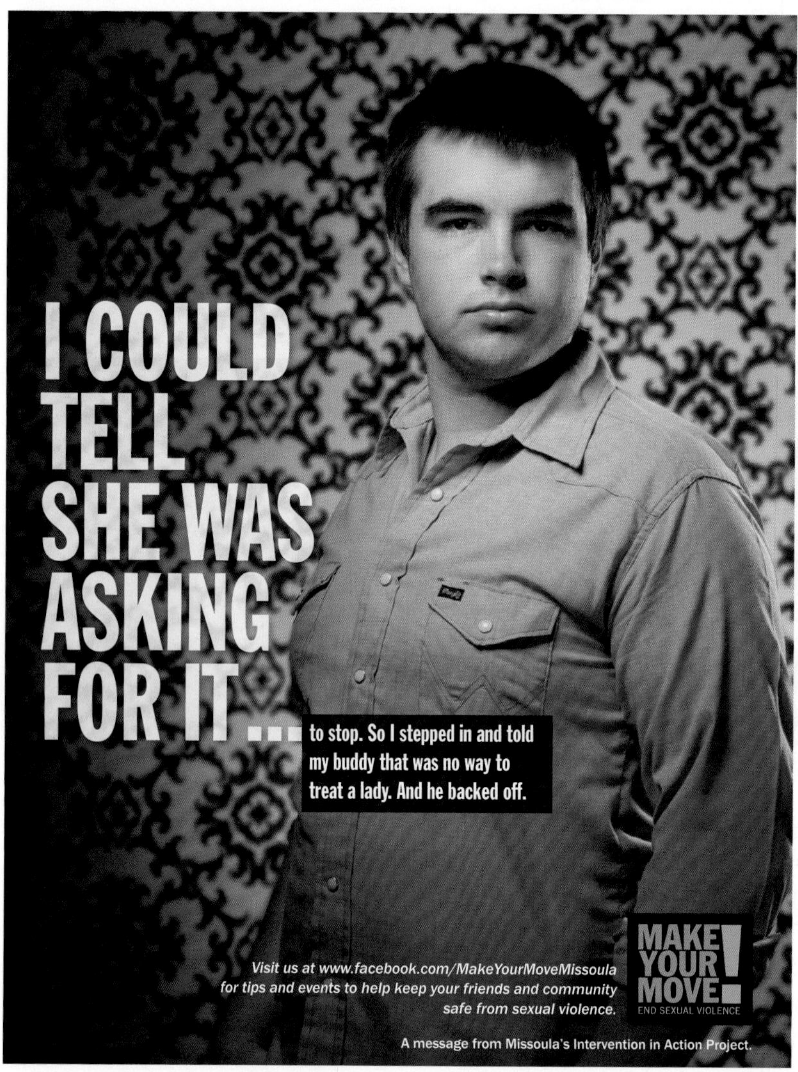

AOE question

How can different texts offer different perspectives on a topic or theme?

Text 2.25 depicts a woman. Text 2.26 depicts a man. Their common issue is physical abuse. How do they compare in achieving their purpose by depicting different people and targeting different audiences?

Towards assessment

3.12 So far in this unit you have explored unrealistic depictions of women, the objectification of women and sexual assault. This activity encourages you to build on that knowledge and demonstrate your understanding of two texts in a practice individual oral that you prepare both individually and as a class. Text 2.27 is a poem by Carol Ann Duffy. Text 2.28 is an advertisement for a diet product.

You may find it helpful to follow these steps for your practice individual oral:

a What do you need to know to plan an individual oral? See Chapter 8 for an understanding of what is expected in this form of assessment. The assessment criteria for an individual oral can be found in the introduction to this coursebook.

b As a class, discuss the global issues that connect Texts 2.27 and 2.28. Which issues could you explore in an individual oral? Agree on *one* global issue that you would like to explore in this practice oral. Chapter 8 includes more information on the term 'global issue'. Here, 'anorexia' or 'dieting' may be considered 'global issues' in the context of this course.

c On your own, create an outline for an individual oral on Texts 2.27 and 2.28. Ask your teacher to create one as well. See the model outlines provided in Unit 2.1 and in Chapter 8.

d Anonymously display everyone's outlines for their individual oral on these two texts.

e Study all the outlines carefully. Create a new and improved outline for yourself, sharing the best ideas from your classmates and teacher.

f Outside class, plan and prepare an individual oral on Texts 2.27 and 2.28. You may want to use some of the suggested words and phrases in the box shown here.

g Record yourself delivering a 10-minute oral on these texts and their common global issue.

h Assess your own performance, using the assessment criteria for the individual oral. Write examiner-style comments on each of the four criteria, referring to examples from your own performance. Listen to your recording to inform your marking.

i Share your recording and your own assessment of your performance with your teacher, and ask them to listen to it and give you feedback. Do you generally agree or disagree with the marks that you gave yourself? What would you need to do to improve your individual oral?

j Add your outline, recording, marks and comments to your learner portfolio. Revisit these when you prepare your next individual oral.

In your practice oral, you may include some of the phrases and key terms in the box, which are relevant to either the poem or the topic. The list is neither exhaustive nor prescriptive.

anorexia nervosa   personification   **surrealism***   imagery   irony   social pressures
self-image   self-esteem   unrealistic definitions of beauty   thinspiration
digital enhancing   fashion industry   models   awareness campaigns   stanzas

* **Surrealism** is an artistic style which encourages readers to imagine unreal or bizarre stories.

TIP

Activity 3.12 encourages you to share ideas with classmates and your teacher in preparation for an individual oral. This is not to encourage collusion in the actual exam. However, you should take advantage of group discussions and shared knowledge by preparing a practice assessment together.

TIP

Activity 3.12 encourages you to engage in self-assessment. It may be helpful to do this after listening to a recording of another student's practice oral. You can then compare your marks with those awarded to that performance, and read the comments that were written about it. Be fair on yourself when assessing your performance, and do not be afraid to identify areas for improvement.

Text 2.27

The Diet

Carol Ann Duffy 2002

The diet worked like a dream. No sugar,
salt, dairy, fat, protein, starch or alcohol.
By the end of week one, she was half a stone
shy of ten and shrinking, skipping breakfast,
lunch, dinner, thinner; a fortnight in, she was
eight stone; by the end of the month, she was skin
and bone.

She starved on, stayed in, stared in
the mirror, svelter, slimmer. The last apple
aged in the fruit bowl, untouched. The skimmed milk
soured in the fridge, unsupped. Her skeleton preened
under its tight flesh dress. She was all eyes,
all cheekbones, had guns for hips. Not a stitch
in the wardrobe fitted.

What passed her lips? Air,
water. She was Anorexia's true daughter, a slip
of a girl, a shadow, dwindling away. One day,
the width of a stick, she started to grow smaller –
child-sized, doll-sized, the height of a thimble.
She sat at her open window and the wind
blew her away.

Seed small, she was out and about,
looking for home. An empty beer bottle rolled
in the gutter. She crawled in, got drunk on the dregs,
started to sing, down, out, nobody's love. Tiny others
joined in. They raved all night. She woke alone,
head splitting, mouth dry, hungry and cold, and made
for the light.

She found she could fly on the wind,
could breathe, if it rained, underwater. That night,
she went to a hotel bar that she knew and floated into
the barman's eye. She slept for hours, left at dawn
in a blink, in a wink, drifted away on a breeze.
Minute, she could suit herself from here on in, go
where she pleased.

She stayed near people,
lay in the tent of a nostril like a germ, dwelled
in the caves of an ear. She lived in a tear, swam
clear, moved south to a mouth, kipped in the chap
of a lip. She loved flesh and blood, wallowed
in mud under fingernails, dossed in a fold of fat
on a waist.

But when she squatted on the tip of a tongue,
she was gulped, swallowed, sent down the hatch
in a river of wine, bottoms up, cheers, fetched up
in a stomach just before lunch. She crouched
in the lining, hearing the avalanche munch of food,
then it was carrots, peas, courgettes, potatoes,
gravy and meat.

Then it was sweet. Then it was stilton,
roquefort, weisslacker-kase, gex; it was smoked salmon
with scrambled eggs, hot boiled ham, plum flan, frogs'
legs. She knew where she was all right, clambered
onto the greasy breast of a goose, opened wide, then
chomped and chewed and gorged; inside the Fat Woman now,
trying to get out.

Text 2.28

You know why she's wearing the sweatshirt, don't you.

It's a classic case of cold feet.

Beneath that floppy sweatshirt she's a little overweight.

You knew that.

Because right now, you're a little overweight, too. That's bad.

This year's bathing suits hide nothing.

Unless you start losing some, you may spend your summer in a sweatshirt, too.

Face it, you've got to stop eating.

Talking about dieting is easy. But dieting isn't.

Because it seems like everything that tastes good is fattening, right?

Not any more.

Shape.® It's new from Metrecal.®

We've invented a new diet food, a powder and liquid, that really tastes good. It's different than the old ones were.

Shape has no cyclamate, no saccharin.

Shape has no artificial sweeteners.

It's made only with natural sugars and wholesome ingredients. Which play a role in its superior taste.

In taste tests chocolate Shape was preferred significantly over leading competitors' chocolates.

And that's the name of the game.

Because no diet product ever works any better than it tastes.

Shape powder or Shape liquid.

Our mix-with-milk powder comes fresh packed. In a coffee-type canister. Enough for ten meals.

Our liquid comes ready-to-drink.

Either way, Shape is rich with the vitamins, minerals and protein needed for health.

So you can substitute Shape for one or two meals a day.

Or, if you're really serious, four Shape meals a day for a while. And no other food.

And that's where Shape's flavor helps you most.

It tastes good enough that you can stay with it long enough to lose.

If we made Shape taste any better, you might start sneaking it now and then, and you would get fat on it.

Try it.

Shape liquid. And Shape powder.

They do taste good enough to help you stop eating.

Stop eating.

Extended essay

Are you interested in writing your extended essay on provocative advertisements, like the ones you have seen in this unit? If so, be sure to narrow your focus to one or two campaigns. You may want to comment critically on how they have been received differently over time.

A good Category 3 research question might read: 'In what ways and for what reasons have the advertising campaigns of Dolce & Gabbana evolved over the past 40 years with regard to the sexualisation and objectification of men and women?'

AOE questions

What can diverse texts have in common?

Texts 2.27 and 2.28 are very diverse texts, written in different times and places for different purposes. Nevertheless, they both explore the topics of anorexia, dieting and self-esteem. In their own way they invite you to imagine how a victim of anorexia might think. Keep this AOE question in mind when finding texts and preparing for your individual oral.

3.13 Diet advertisements from different times and places are not difficult to find online. Find a diet advertisement with a significant amount of language, both visual and written, which would be appropriate for a Paper 1 analysis. Ask your teacher for approval of your text before you write a Paper 1-style analysis of it. You may wish to write this practice paper outside class time, as coursework.

Share your analysis with your classmates to create a 'database' of analyses on diet advertisements. Go through these scripts and find some of your class's 'best bits of analysis'. Create a top-five list of 'best bits of analysis' and add this to your learner portfolio.

Higher level extension

Oprah Winfrey speaking at the Golden Globe awards in 2018.

3.14 Text 2.29 is a speech delivered by TV celebrity Oprah Winfrey, upon accepting the Golden Globe's Cecil B. DeMille Award. Read through the speech and do a 'See, Think, Wonder' routine by filling in a table like the one shown. After you have completed the table, share your answers with your classmates. Then watch a recording of the speech online.

See – What images come to mind when you *see* and read this text?	**Think** – What abstract ideas do you *think* about in response to these concrete images?	**Wonder** – In response to these concrete images and abstract ideas, what do you *wonder*? What questions do you have?

Text 2.29

Their time is up

Oprah Winfrey 2018

In 1964, I was a little girl sitting on the linoleum floor of my mother's house in Milwaukee watching Anne Bancroft present the Oscar for Best Actor at the 36th Academy Awards. She opened the envelope, and said five words that literally made history: 'The winner is Sidney Poitier.' Up to the stage came the most elegant man I had ever seen. I remember his tie was white and, of course, his skin was black. And I'd never seen a black man being celebrated like that. And I have tried many, many, many times to explain what a moment like that means to a little girl, a kid watching from the cheap seats as my mom came through the door, bone tired from cleaning other people's houses. But all I can do is quote and say that the explanation in Sidney's performance in *Lilies of the Field*, 'Amen, amen. Amen, amen'.

In 1982, Sidney received the Cecil B. DeMille Award right here at the Golden Globes, and it is not lost on me that at this moment, there are some little girls watching as I become the first black woman to be given this same award.

It is an honor – it is an honor and it is a privilege to share the evening with all of them and also with the incredible men and women who inspire me, who challenge me, who sustain me and made my journey to this stage possible. Dennis Swanson, who took a chance on me for AM Chicago. Quincy Jones, who saw me on that show and said to Steven Spielberg, 'Yes, she is Sofia in *The Color Purple*'. Gayle, who has been the definition of what a friend is. And Stedman, who has been my rock. Just a few to name.

I'd like to thank the Hollywood Foreign Press Association because we all know that the press is under siege these days, but we also know that it is the insatiable dedication to uncovering the absolute truth that keeps us from turning a blind eye to corruption and to injustice – to tyrants and victims and secrets and lies. I want to say that I value the press more than ever before as we try to navigate these complicated times, which brings me to this: what I know for sure is that speaking your truth is the most powerful tool we all have. And I'm especially proud and inspired by all the women who have felt strong enough and empowered enough to speak up and share their personal stories. Each of us in this room are celebrated because of the stories that we tell. And this year we became the story. But it's not just a story affecting the

TEXT AND CONTEXT

- NAACP is the National Association for the Advancement of Colored People, an organisation in the USA committed to improving human rights.
- 'Me too' is a reference to a movement which started in 2017, after several powerful men, including the President of the United States, were accused of sexually harassing many women. Their victims used the **hashtag** #metoo on Twitter and social media platforms to come forward and find solidarity.

entertainment industry. It's one that transcends any culture, geography, race, religion, politics or workplace. So I want tonight to express gratitude to all the women who have endured years of abuse and assault because they, like my mother, had children to feed and bills to pay and dreams to pursue.

They're the women whose names we'll never know. They are domestic workers and farm workers. They are working in factories, and they work in restaurants, and they're in academia and engineering and medicine and science. They're part of the world of tech and politics and business. They are athletes in the Olympics, and they are soldiers in the military.

And there's someone else: Recy Taylor, a name I know and I think you should know too. In 1944, Recy Taylor was a young wife and a mother. She was just walking home from the church service she'd attended in Abbeville, Alabama, when she was abducted by six armed white men, raped, and left blindfolded by the side of the road coming home from church. They threatened to kill her if she ever told anyone, but her story was reported to the NAACP, where a young worker by the name of Rosa Parks became the lead investigator on her case. And together they sought justice. But justice wasn't an option in the era of Jim Crow. The men who tried to destroy her were never persecuted. Recy Taylor died 10 days ago, just shy of her 98th birthday. She lived as we all have lived, too many years in a culture broken by brutally powerful men. For too long, women have not been heard or believed if they dared to speak their truth to the power of those men, but their time is up.

Their time is up. Their time is up. And I just hope – I just hope that Recy Taylor died knowing that her truth, like the truth of so many other women who were tormented in those years and even now tormented, goes marching on. It was somewhere in Rosa Parks' heart almost 11 years later when she made the decision to stay seated on that bus in Montgomery. And it's here with every woman who chooses to say, 'Me too' and every man, every man who chooses to listen.

In my career what I've always tried my best to do, whether on television or through film, is to say something about how men and women really behave, to say how we experience shame, how we love and how we rage, how we fail, how we retreat, persevere and how we overcome. I've interviewed and portrayed people who have withstood some of the ugliest things life can throw at you, but the one quality all of them seem to share is an ability to maintain hope for a brighter morning, even during our darkest nights. So I want all the girls watching here now to know that a new day is on the horizon.

And when that new day finally dawns, it will be because of a lot of magnificent women, many of whom are right here in this room tonight, and some pretty phenomenal men fighting hard to make sure that they become the leaders who take us to the time when nobody ever has to say, 'Me too' again. Thank you.

3.15 Text 2.29 contains several key characteristics and rhetorical devices of good speeches. Can you find examples of the stylistic devices from the list in the speech? For each device and example, describe its effect on the reader. Are there any other stylistic features or rhetorical devices that you can find in this text?

- **Allusion** – a reference to another text.
- **Anaphora** – the repetition of a word or phrase at the beginning of a sentence.
- **Anecdote** – a short story describing a real-life event, often used to illustrate a greater point or abstract idea.
- **Enumeration** – making a point by listing items, events or actions in detail.
- **Parallelism** – a use of syntax with repeated words or grammatical structures.
- **Polysyndeton** – a technique in which conjunctions ('and' or 'but') are used frequently creating a sense of a list.

3.16 The hashtag (#) is a popular way to tag and filter content on social media. It can be argued that it is a stylistic feature, since its use has an effect on readers by highlighting catchphrases or key words. If you were to retweet Oprah's speech (Text 2.29) or find responses to it, what catchphrases or key words from her speech would you use? Write a short list and share them with your classmates. Then research the kinds of hashtags that were actually used after her speech on social media. Were your guesses accurate?

3.17 Try writing an HL essay on Oprah Winfrey's 2018 speech (Text 2.29). Before you write your essay, you will need a 'line of inquiry'. In order to find one, think about the aspects listed here. Remember: a line of inquiry is like a research question for the extended essay – it should have the right scope and focus for exploring the text and the topic. The HL essay should be 1200–1500 words, and the one you write for this assignment may or may not be the one you submit to the IB. Assess your work using the criteria. Read Chapter 7 on the HL essay for further guidance.

Your line of inquiry might explore:

- the ways in which Winfrey's speech was received (secondary texts)
- her choice of words and stylistic features (language)
- what was happening in history during the time of her speech (context)
- what gives the speaker the right to speak (ethos, biographical approach).

AOE question

How do texts engage with local and global issues?

For your HL essay, you may want to apply this question to a text that you have read.

Further reading

- *Buyology* by Martin Lindstrom provides an understanding of the neuroscience behind purchasing decisions, brand loyalty and the effects of sex in advertising. The conclusions of his research are quite astonishing.
- *Killing Us Softly* is a series of talks and documentaries by Jean Kilbourne which explores the problems of sex in advertising and unrealistic depictions of beauty.
- *Me Too* is a documentary by social activist Tarana Burke. It was inspired by the events of 2017 when many women spoke out about the sexual harassment that they had experienced.

REFLECT

Look back through Chapter 2 on language and gender. Skim through the texts and glance over the activities.

- On a large board in your classroom, write 'language and gender'. Divide the board into two halves. On the top of the left half, write: 'I used to think . . .'. On the top of the right half of the board, write: 'Now I think . . .'.
- On a large sticky note, write one sentence describing what you used to think about any one of the topics explored in these units (such as gender stereotyping, feminism, masculinity, skinny models in advertising or the objectification of women).
- On another sticky note, write what you think *now* about one of these topics, after having worked through this chapter.
- Place your sticky notes on their respective sides of the board and read what your classmates have posted as well.
- Discuss these reflections as a class.

Chapter 3

Identity, culture and community

How has language been used in the past and present to construct racial stereotypes, propagate colonialism and discriminate against immigrants?
How do different communities use language differently?
How do texts challenge racist, colonial and xenophobic ideas?

In this chapter you will:

- analyse racist, colonial and xenophobic texts
- explore a range of texts that comment critically on racism, colonialism and xenophobia
- discuss how context shapes both the interpretation and the composition of texts.

Unit 3.1 Racism

Word bank

racism
xenophobia
racial bias
idiolect
Englishes
dialect
African American Vernacular English (AAVE)
colloquialism
racial profiling
civil rights
apartheid
emancipation
positive discrimination
ethnic diversity
persona
narrator
memoir
stereotype

Learning objectives

- develop an awareness of language variation
- engage with a range of different texts that deal with racism
- speak and write about the topic of racism, exploring different perspectives and making comparison between texts.

Racism is the act of discriminating against someone on the basis of their race. Racism is unfortunately a reality in many parts of the world today. Researchers such as Tim Wise have shown that people of colour, in predominantly 'white' societies, are less likely to be successful when applying for jobs, more often overcharged, pulled over on the road more frequently by the police and sentenced to prison for longer sentences than their white counterparts.

Racism is a form of social injustice and inequality which can lead to other social problems such as crime. In this unit you will see how racism is addressed in a range of texts, from song lyrics to speeches, seeing how language is used to spread awareness and promote racial equality.

International mindedness

Part of being internationally minded is being able to work with people of all races. How often do you engage with people of another race, country or culture? During the course of your Diploma Programme, try to create an opportunity for yourself to interact with people from other places in the world.

CAS

Activity 1.1 asks you how post-racist your world is. What can you do to ensure that social organisations, such as your school, are more conscious of racism? How can you become involved in programmes that encourage equal opportunities for all people? Consider these questions when designing a CAS project.

Getting started

1.1 Discuss your answers to these questions:

a To what extent is **xenophobia** a problem in your part of the world? Xenophobia is the fear of people who are perceived as different.

b Is racism a problem where you live? How has the history of your country or town shaped these race relations?

c To what degree is white privilege a problem where you live? White privilege refers to structural advantages that are enjoyed by white people in a society.

d Do you think you live in a post-racist world, where race no longer plays a role in work, politics and education? To what extent are people 'colour blind' or 'colour conscious' in your country? What makes you say this?

TOK

Are people racist by nature? Or is racism something we are taught from a young age by the people and messages around us? Is there a biological or psychological explanation for **racial bias**? Might racism, in some cases, even be useful?

Do an online search for a TED Talk by Paul Bloom entitled 'Can prejudice ever be a good thing?' and try to find answers to this question and others that you might have about racism.

1.2 Do you think Text 3.1, an advertisement for Aunt Jemima's Pancake Mix, is racist? What makes you say this? Analyse the use of language, both written and visual, to inform your answers to these questions. Discuss your answers with your classmates.

1.3 How is racism related to language? Look carefully at Text 3.1. Aunt Jemima speaks differently from the white people in the advertisement. She drops letters, pronounces words differently, conjugates verbs differently ('pancake days is happy days') and even dresses differently.

Arguably, everyone speaks English in their own way (an idea known as **idiolect**) just as everyone dresses differently. But just as some groups of people dress similarly, so too do groups of people speak similarly, perhaps because they have a common race, religion or background. For this reason there are many **Englishes** or **dialects** of the English language. Aunt Jemima's dialect is also known as **African American Vernacular English (AAVE)** and the way she uses it in this advertisement affects the way African Americans are viewed by others.

Here are just a few characteristics of AAVE. What do you associate with people who speak this way? Where do you think these associations came from?

Form of language	Explanation	Example
Double negatives	Two negative words used in combination	'I don't have none.'
Vocabulary	Choice of words	'I am not' becomes 'I ain't' or 'ask' becomes 'aks'
Pronunciation and dropping consonants	Some parts of words are not voiced or they are conflated with other words	'What do you want?' becomes: 'Whatcha want?' 'For' and 'your' become 'fo' and 'yo'.
Subject–verb agreement	One verb form for single and plural subjects	'I don't' and 'he don't'

Text 3.1

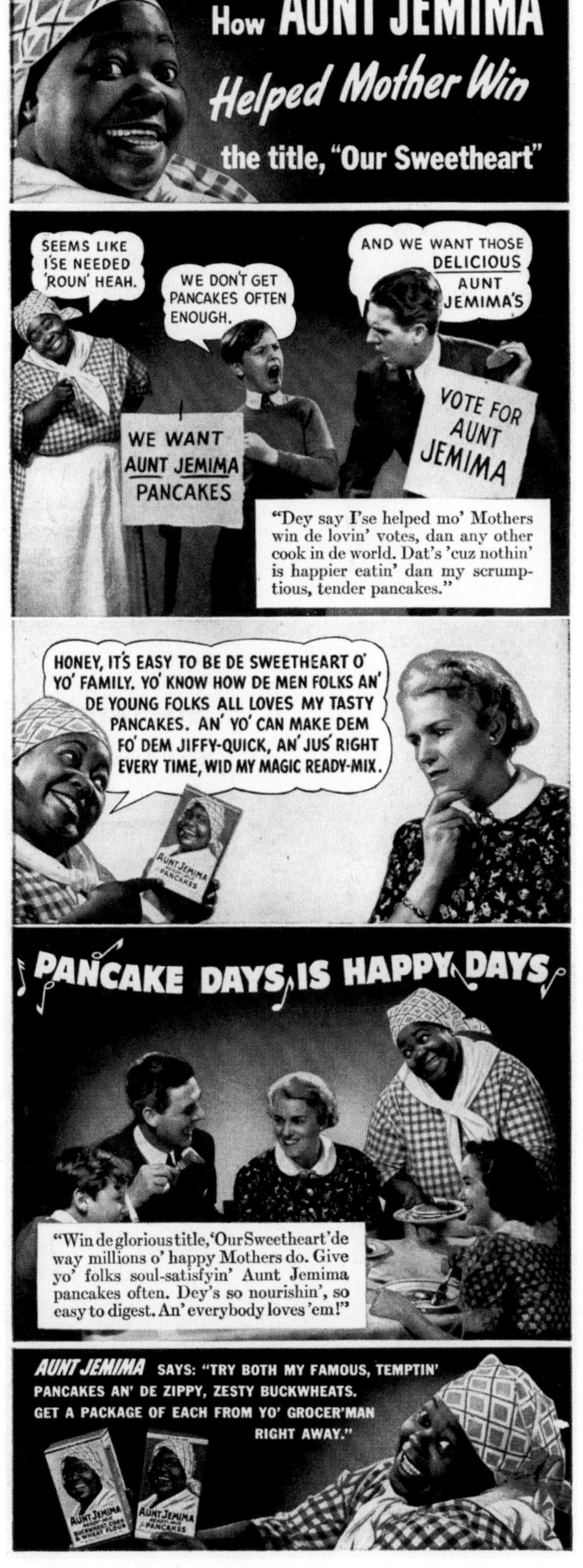

Readers, writers and texts

1.4 What does AAVE sound like? How can it be used to express someone's identity and comment critically on racism?

a Read Text 3.2 carefully. Draw a picture that depicts the setting and characters of the poem.

b Now go online, search for a reading of the poem then listen to it.

c What can you add to your drawing of the setting and the characters of the poem?

d Display everyone's drawings in your class, and discuss the similarities and differences between the drawings. How do these differences in drawings show differences in your understandings of the poem?

AOE question

How and why do people study language and literature?

How do you study a poem that is difficult to understand because of its use of dialect? Can poetry written in dialect be considered 'literature'? Should schools be allowed to teach dialect and teach through the use of dialect? Discuss your answers to these questions as a class.

Text 3.2

Speakin' At De Cou't-House

Paul Laurence Dunbar 1903

Dey been speakin' at de cou't-house,
An' laws-a-massy me,
'T was de beatness kin' o' doin's
Dat evah I did see.
Of cose I had to be dah
In de middle o' de crowd,
An' I hallohed wid de othahs,
Wen de speakah riz and bowed.

I was kind o' disapp'inted
At de smallness of de man,
Case I 'd allus pictered great folks
On a mo' expansive plan;
But I t'ought I could respect him
An' tek in de wo'ds he said,
Fu' dey sho was somp'n knowin'
In de bald spot on his haid.

But hit did seem so't o' funny
Aftah waitin' fu' a week
Dat de people kep' on shoutin'
So de man des could n't speak;
De ho'ns dey blared a little,
Den dey let loose on de drums,–.
Some one toll me dey was playin'
"See de conkerin' hero comes."

"Well," says I, "you all is white folks,
    But you 's sutny actin' queer,
What's de use of heroes comin'
    Ef dey cain't talk w'en dey's here?"
Aftah while dey let him open,
    An' dat man he waded in,
An' he fit de wahs all ovah
    Winnin' victeries lak sin.

Wen he come down to de present,
    Den he made de feathahs fly.
He des waded in on money,
    An' he played de ta'iff high.
An' he said de colah question,
    Hit was ovah, solved, an' done,
Dat de dahky was his brothah,
    Evah blessed mothah's son.

Well he settled all de trouble
    Dat's been pesterin' de lan',
Den he set down mid de cheerin'
    An' de playin' of de ban'.
I was feelin' moughty happy
    'Twell I hyeahed somebody speak,
"Well, dat's his side of de bus'ness,
    But you wait for Jones nex' week."

CONCEPT

In what ways is Text 3.2 about both racism and *identity*? How does Paul Laurence Dunbar use language to express his identity and comment on the progress of race relations in the USA at the end of the 19th century?

1.5 Reread the poem 'Speakin' at de Cou't-House'. Highlight the words and phrases that you find difficult to understand. Dunbar uses key characteristics of AAVE such as 'dey's' to mean 'they is' (or 'they are'). He also writes words phonetically based on AAVE pronunciation and not standardised spelling. Furthermore, he uses **colloquialisms** such as 'laws-a-massy me' which means 'lord have mercy on me'. Colloquialisms are phrases or words that are informal and figurative, typical of a region or social group. Why do you think he has chosen to write his poem this way? As a class, discuss the author's choice of style, referring to the words that you have highlighted.

1.6 What is the main message of Text 3.2? On a sticky note, write down the main idea of the poem and stick it on a wall where you can read what your classmates have written as well. Read everyone's version of the poem's message. How similar or different are your class's ideas? How does Dunbar use language to construct this message? Discuss your answer to these questions as a class.

Time and space

1.7 Here is a 'Text and context' box on Text 3.2. How does this information give you a better understanding of the poem?

TEXT AND CONTEXT

- Paul Laurence Dunbar was born in 1872 in Dayton, Ohio, and died, aged 33, in 1906.
- His parents had been enslaved in the South before the American Civil War.
- His father had escaped from slavery to fight for the North in this war.
- One of the North's objectives in winning the American Civil War was to end slavery in the USA.
- After the North won the Civil War, African Americans in the USA were still not granted many civil rights, and segregation and employment discrimination were not banned until 1964.

AOE question

How can cultural contexts influence how texts are written and received?

The 'Text and context' box on this page is a list of historic facts. But what is the cultural context of Text 3.2? How is this text a product of a particular culture?

1.8 Text 3.3 is a photograph. Do you know what is going on in it? In your class:

a Who claims to know nothing about the photograph? Ask them what they think is going on but do not say whether they are correct or not.

b Who wants to make an educated guess about what is going on in the photograph? What makes them think that?

c Who knows with certainty what is going on in the photograph? How certain are they?

d How accurate is your class' understanding of the photograph? Go to the Wikipedia page for the 1968 Olympics Black Power salute and read about it. How does this information change your understanding of the photograph?

e Search online for images of Colin Kaepernick, a former quarterback for the San Francisco 49ers, kneeling during the national anthem. Find out why he did this. How similar to or different from that of Tommie Smith and John Carlos (Text 3.3) was his situation?

f Hold a class debate on the claim that 'International sports events should not be an arena for public debate on civil rights', with half of you in favour and the other half against. Research Text 3.3, the Kaepernick case and other examples (such as the 1936 Olympics) to inform your arguments. If you find yourself arguing for the side you do not believe in, just consider it a good exercise in empathy.

AOE Question

How does a text engage with local and global issues?

Do an online search for a print advertisement run by Nike, which features Colin Kaepernick, title 'Believe in something. Even if it means sacrificing everything.' This advertisement has been met with much controversy. Why is this? How can such a seemingly innocent text create such debate?

Text 3.3

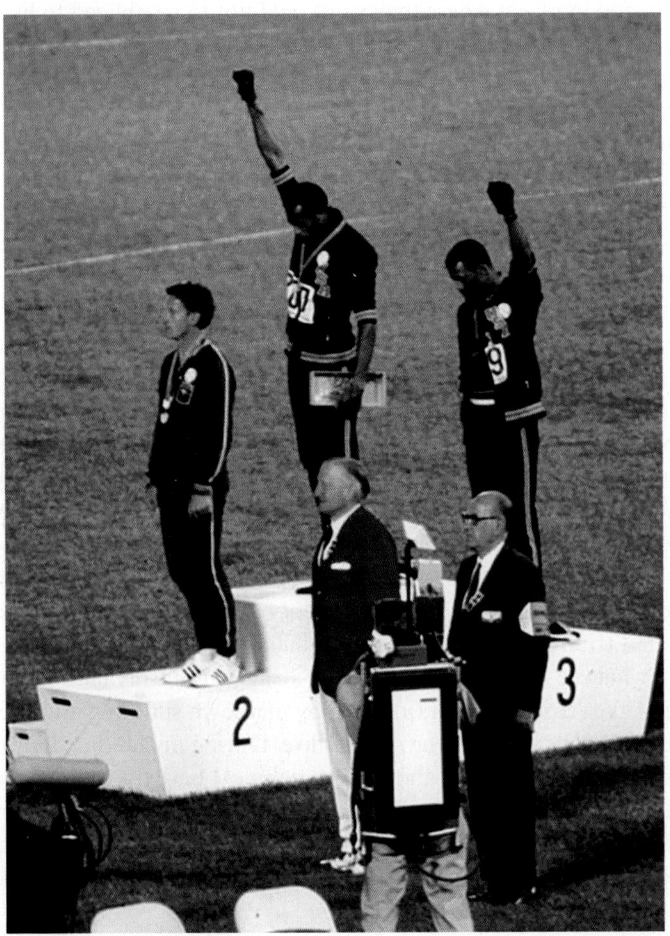

1.9 So far in this unit you have explored texts from the USA and the struggle for civil rights. How has the fight against racism been similar or different in other parts of the world? The name of the speaker, its year of publication, and other contextual information of Text 3.4 have been removed. Read it carefully and give educated guesses to these questions:

- **a** Who is the speaker?
- **b** When and where did they say these words?
- **c** Why are they speaking?
- **d** To whom are they speaking?
- **e** What has been going on in their country, before giving this speech?
- **f** How do you think this speech was received by the person or people listening?

Text 3.4

An ideal for which I am prepared to die

Abridged extract

Africans want to be paid a living wage. Africans want to perform work which they are capable of doing, and not work which the government declares them to be capable of. Africans want to be allowed to live where they obtain work, and not be endorsed out of an area because they were not born there. Africans want to be allowed to own land in places where they work, and not to be obliged to live in rented houses which they can never call their own. Africans want to be part of the general population, and not confined to living in their own ghettoes.

African men want to have their wives and children to live with them where they work, and not be forced into an unnatural existence in men's hostels. African women want to be with their menfolk and not be left permanently widowed in the reserves. Africans want to be allowed out after 11 o'clock at night and not to be confined to their rooms like little children. Africans want to be allowed to travel in their own country and to seek work where they want to and not where the labour bureau tells them to. Africans want a just share in the whole of South Africa; they want security and a stake in society.

Above all, we want equal political rights, because without them our disabilities will be permanent. I know this sounds revolutionary to the whites in this country, because the majority of voters will be Africans. This makes the white man fear democracy. But this fear cannot be allowed to stand in the way of the only solution which will guarantee racial harmony and freedom for all. It is not true that the enfranchisement of all will result in racial domination. Political division, based on colour, is entirely artificial and, when it disappears, so will the domination of one colour group by another. The ANC has spent half a century fighting against racialism. When it triumphs it will not change that policy.

This then is what the ANC is fighting. Their struggle is a truly national one. It is a struggle of the African people, inspired by their own suffering and their own experience. It is a struggle for the right to live. During my lifetime I have dedicated myself to this struggle of the African people. I have fought against white domination, and I have fought against black domination. I have cherished the ideal of a democratic and free society in which all persons live together in harmony and with equal opportunities. It is an ideal which I hope to live for and to achieve. But if needs be, it is an ideal for which I am prepared to die.

ATL

Research

Activity 1.10 asks you to research the context of Nelson Mandela's speech (Text 3.4) after having read it. The Diploma Programme aims to help you develop your *research skills*. One way to keep your research focused is to ask questions about a primary source, such as: 'why was it written?' 'where was it written?' or 'for whom was it written?'

1.10 Now do some research on Nelson Mandela, **apartheid**, the African National Congress (ANC) and the speech's title, 'An ideal for which I am prepared to die'. Find answers to the questions from Activity 1.9. How does this information change your understanding of the speech?

Intertextuality: connecting texts

1.11 Text 3.4 was spoken by Nelson Mandela 30 years before he spoke the words of Text 3.5, a speech he gave before his inauguration as the first black President of South Africa. Compare Text 3.4 to Text 3.5 and discuss your answers to these questions:

a What has happened between speeches? How is this evident from the speeches?

b How do the different contexts of the speeches (Text 3.4 and Text 3.5) shape their style, structure and use of syntax?

c Which speech do you prefer? What makes you say this?

d What have you learnt about the history of South Africa by studying these speeches?

A younger Nelson Mandela, before he was sentenced to prison.

CONCEPTS

Which key concepts from this course are relevant to Nelson Mandela's inauguration speech (Text 3.5)? Explain how each relevant concept is relevant by referring to the language of the speech:

- identity
- culture
- creativity
- communication
- perspective
- transformation
- representation.

Nelson Mandela in 1994 before his inauguration as President of the Republic of South Africa.

Text 3.5

Inaugural Speech, Pretoria

Extract

Nelson Mandela 1994

The time for the healing of the wounds has come.

The moment to bridge the chasms that divide us has come.

The time to build is upon us.

We have, at last, achieved our political **emancipation**. We pledge ourselves to liberate all our people from the continuing bondage of poverty, deprivation, suffering, gender and other discrimination.

We succeeded to take our last steps to freedom in conditions of relative peace. We commit ourselves to the construction of a complete, just and lasting peace.

We have triumphed in the effort to implant hope in the breasts of the millions of our people. We enter into a covenant that we shall build the society in which all South Africans, both black and white, will be able to walk tall, without any fear in their hearts, assured of their inalienable right to human dignity – a rainbow nation at peace with itself and the world.

As a token of its commitment to the renewal of our country, the new Interim Government of National Unity will, as a matter of urgency, address the issue of amnesty for various categories of our people who are currently serving terms of imprisonment.

We dedicate this day to all the heroes and heroines in this country and the rest of the world who sacrificed in many ways and surrendered their lives so that we could be free.

Their dreams have become reality. Freedom is their reward.

We are both humbled and elevated by the honour and privilege that you, the people of South Africa, have bestowed on us, as the first President of a united, democratic, non-racial and non-sexist South Africa, to lead our country out of the valley of darkness.

We understand it still that there is no easy road to freedom.

We know it well that none of us acting alone can achieve success.

We must therefore act together as a united people, for national reconciliation, for nation building, for the birth of a new world.

Let there be justice for all.

Let there be peace for all.

Let there be work, bread, water and salt for all.

Let each know that for each the body, the mind and the soul have been freed to fulfil themselves.

Never, never and never again shall it be that this beautiful land will again experience the oppression of one by another and suffer the indignity of being the skunk of the world.

The sun shall never set on so glorious a human achievement!

Let freedom reign.

God bless Africa!

I thank you!

1.12 Nelson Mandela was not the only great leader to address race relations in his speeches. The Reverend Dr Martin Luther King was a well-known orator on the topic of civil rights in the 1960s. Study this extract from his famous speech 'I have a dream' (Text 3.6) and make a list of how he uses language similarly to Nelson Mandela in Text 3.5. How are they using language? What are they accomplishing through words and rhetorical devices?

Read Unit 1.7, on speeches and rhetoric, to help you identify some of the devices that they use to achieve their purpose. Use a table like the one here to connect the common rhetorical devices to their common purposes.

Common rhetorical devices in Text 3.5 and Text 3.6	Why do the speakers include each rhetorical device?

Text 3.6

I have a dream

Abridged extract

Martin Luther King 1963

I am happy to join with you today in what will go down in history as the greatest demonstration for freedom in the history of our nation.

Five score years ago, a great American, in whose symbolic shadow we stand today, signed the **Emancipation** Proclamation. This momentous decree came as a great beacon light of hope to millions of Negro slaves who had been seared in the flames of withering injustice. It came as a joyous daybreak to end the long night of their captivity.

But one hundred years later, the Negro still is not free. One hundred years later, the life of the Negro is still sadly crippled by the manacles of segregation and the chains of discrimination. One hundred years later, the Negro lives on a lonely island of poverty in the midst of a vast ocean of material prosperity. One hundred years later, the Negro is still languishing in the corners of American society and finds himself an exile in his own land. So we have come here today to dramatize a shameful condition. [. . .]

We must forever conduct our struggle on the high plane of dignity and discipline. We must not allow our creative protest to degenerate into physical violence. Again and again we must rise to the majestic heights of meeting physical force with soul force. The marvelous new militancy which has engulfed the Negro community must not lead us to distrust of all white people, for many of our white brothers, as evidenced by their presence here today, have come to realize that their destiny is tied up with our destiny and their freedom is inextricably bound to our freedom. We cannot walk alone. [. . .]

I have a dream that one day this nation will rise up and live out the true meaning of its creed: "We hold these truths to be self-evident: that all men are created equal."

I have a dream that one day on the red hills of Georgia the sons of former slaves and the sons of former slave owners will be able to sit down together at the table of brotherhood.

I have a dream that one day even the state of Mississippi, a state sweltering with the heat of injustice, sweltering with the heat of oppression, will be transformed into an oasis of freedom and justice.

I have a dream that my four little children will one day live in a nation where they will not be judged by the color of their skin but by the content of their character.

I have a dream today.

I have a dream that one day, down in Alabama, with its vicious racists, with its governor having his lips dripping with the words of interposition and nullification; one day right there in Alabama, little black boys and black girls will be able to join hands with little white boys and white girls as sisters and brothers.

I have a dream today.

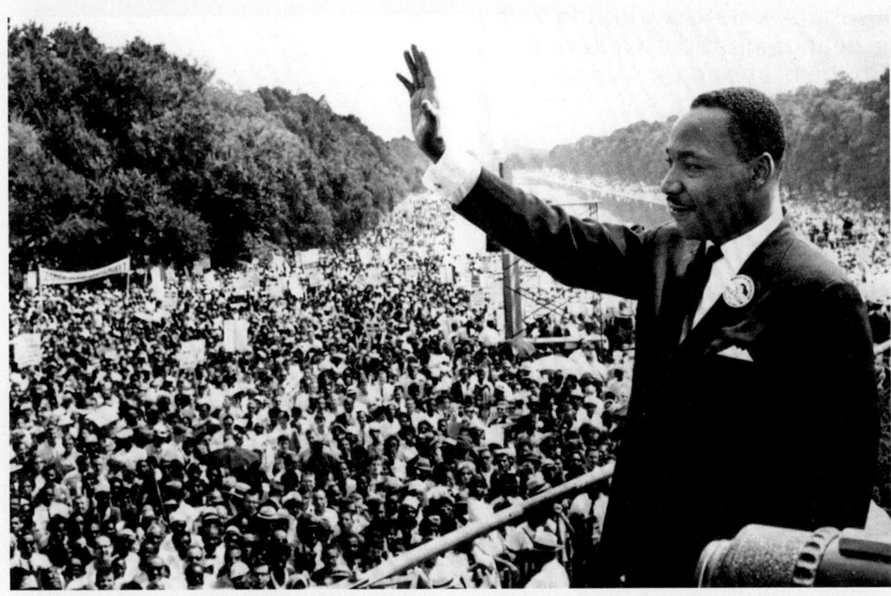

1.13 Watch the entire 'I have a dream' speech (Text 3.6) online. Find a transcript of the full speech, or watch it with subtitles. Martin Luther King's speech is full of allusion and references to other texts, such as the Bible, folk songs, the US Declaration of Independence, news stories from his times and the Emancipation Proclamation.

a Individually, research the various allusions and references that have been listed in this table.

b Using a copy of the table, explain what each reference or allusion means, and why you think Martin Luther King chose to use it.

c Compare your table to a classmate's. How were your experiences researching this assignment similar or different?

d What sources did you both consult, and how were your results and analyses different?

e Display your table for all your classmates to read and discuss the power of allusion in the speech 'I have a dream' (Text 3.6).

TIP

Activity 1.13 asks you to research the context of several allusions and references from Text 3.6, 'I have a dream'. You may want to check out genius.com for a detailed analysis of the entire speech.

References and allusions in 'I have a dream' (Text 3.6)	What do these mean? Why does Dr Martin Luther King use each allusion or reference?
• Five score years ago, a great American	
• Emancipation Proclamation	
• We hold these truths to be self-evident: that all men are created equal.	
• The marvelous new militancy which has engulfed the Negro community	
• Mississippi, a state sweltering with the heat of injustice, sweltering with the heat of oppression	
• in Alabama, with its vicious racists, with its governor having his lips dripping with the words of interposition and nullification	

1.14 Research the term 'affirmative action' (US) or '**positive discrimination**' (UK). This is a policy that aims to help people who have been discriminated against by giving them an advantage in society. It's the act of offering people positions at university or job opportunities by setting a quota of people who must come from ethnic minorities. How successful have such measures been in addressing racism in different parts of the world? Find a text that is related to this topic and include it in your learner portfolio.

Towards assessment

1.15 Follow the steps listed here to practise your writing skills for Paper 1.

a Read Chapter 7 on Paper 1, if you have not already done so, and make sure you are familiar with the assessment criteria.

b Search online for an image using the search terms 'the man on the left' and 'ACLU', which should produce a 'wanted'-style poster featuring photographs of Martin Luther King and Charles Manson. Study this public awareness advertisement carefully and read the student's Paper 1-style response to it then the examiner's marks and comments, to inform your understanding.

c Return to another text in this unit which you found particularly interesting. You may also ask your teacher for another interesting stimulus text that explores race through language. Or use a text of your own choice or analysis.

d Write a 'guiding question' which is appropriate for your selected text. Discuss this question with your teacher and ask for feedback. Change the question if necessary.

e Once you have read the sample student's response, understood the requirements and agreed on a stimulus text and question, write an outline or a plan for your Paper 1 response. Meet with your teacher again to discuss your outline and ask for feedback.

f Write a Paper 1-style commentary on your chosen text, answering the guiding question.

g Assess your own work using the assessment criteria for Paper 1, before your teacher assesses your work. Are there any areas where it could have been improved? What can you do to make those improvements?

h Add your work to your learner portfolio.

Extended essay

'How racist is a chosen text?' This question could be the starting point for a Category 3 extended essay. It is recommended that you discuss the *evolution* of texts in your essay.

Text 3.1, the Aunt Jemima advertisement, was from the 1930s. How has that product been advertised differently over the past decades? How have other brands changed their marketing to be less racist over the years? A good research question might read: 'How has Disney's portrayal of race changed over time through its use of characterisation and animation?' This question would be a good starting point for research on an interesting topic. Be sure to refer to particular examples from specific films.

Paper 1 – Sample 1

Guiding question

How does this poster from the ACLU use visual structures to make readers more aware of racial inequality? Note that the 'man on the left' is civil rights activist Dr Martin Luther King and 'the man on the right' is a convicted serial murderer, Charles Manson.

Analysis

This poster is an advertisement from an awareness campaign by the American Civil Liberties Union. It borrows visual structures from a wanted poster, such as font, colour and layout, to make its readers more aware of the problems of racial profiling in America.

The layout of this advertisement is essential in constructing meaning and making its audience aware of the problem of racial profiling. The 'man on the left' is Dr Martin Luther King. Even though he is a good man, who has fought peacefully for civil rights, he is '75 times more likely to be stopped by the police while driving' than the white serial killer, Charles Manson, on the right. This is because King is black. The two black and white headshots, the weathered edges of the poster and the nails that appear to keep it in place, make the poster look like something from a Wild West scene, such as a 'wanted' poster. To suggest that Martin Luther King is a criminal is a false accusation, and this is what shocks the readers. This effect makes them think more about the injustice of the police stopping black and Hispanic people without reason.

In the introduction to your analysis, identify the type of text that you are analysing.

Your thesis statement should comment on the author's purpose, answer the guiding question and identify the key features that will be explored in the analysis.

It is important to state the obvious in a Paper 1 analysis. Constantly ask yourself 'why' readers feel the way they feel.

Secondly, the poster uses the same fonts and font sizes as a wanted poster, which makes readers intrigued by its message. The heading, which includes a statistic, captures the reader's attention in the same way that a sensational heading of a wanted poster would. It uses a serif font that is similar to those of the Wild West days, which makes the reader think that the men in the pictures are criminals who are wanted 'dead or alive'. The black lines above and below the heading add gravitas to its meaning and reinforce the 'wanted poster' analogy. The very small font under the photographs suggests that the copy of this advertisement will be detailed. The problem of racial profiling in the context of Florida is explained here in detail: 'Police stop people based on their skin color, rather than for the way they are driving.' It is shocking to learn that 80% of people pulled over are black or Hispanic, even though they constitute only 5% of all drivers. There is a call to action, in this text with the fine print, which recommends that readers support the ACLU.

It is not good to finish a paragraph with an illustration or quotation. Why has this call to action been written with a small font? It is not clear.

The use of colour contributes further to the text's purpose of making readers think about racism as a problem. The various shades of brown and the curled up corners make the poster appear as if it has been weathered and bleached by the sun. It suggests that the criminals in the poster have been at large for a long time. In effect it suggests that racial profiling has remained an unsolved problem in America for a very long time. The black and white headshots imitate those of a wanted poster as well, as these posters are cheaply made for mass production. This suggests that racial profiling is a widespread problem, just as crime is. Ironically the text uses a text type commonly created by the police, in order to be critical of the police. The colours of this wanted poster trigger a response from the reader that makes them think about justice and their rights.

Strong topic sentences, like this one, connect a stylistic feature with the text's purpose.

The last sentence of a paragraph should link back to the point of the first sentence of the paragraph and the thesis statement.

All in all the ACLU poster borrows the visual structures of a wanted poster in an effort to make readers more aware of the problems of racial profiling. By alluding to Martin Luther King and Charles Manson, it makes readers question why black people should be falsely accused of crimes. The use of fonts, colour and layout are used effectively by the ACLU to spread awareness about racial profiling and remind them of their rights as American citizens.

Use words from your thesis statement in your conclusion.

In your conclusion, mention the main features that you have explored in your analysis.

Return to the author's purpose in the conclusion as well.

Paper 1 – Sample 1 – Examiner's marks and comments

Criterion A: Knowledge, understanding and interpretation: 4 out of 5 marks

The student's interpretation of this poster is based on inferences from the stimulus text. It is stated quite clearly that the poster makes readers 'think more about the injustice of the police stopping black and Hispanic people without reason'. This kind of sentence articulates the purpose of the text clearly. Multiple references to the stimulus text support the analysis's main claims. Quotations are integrated into the student's argument.

Criterion B: Analysis and evaluation: 5 out of 5 marks

The student is very perceptive in analysing the visual features of the text, such as the 'weathered edges', 'nails' and 'headshots'. The effects of these features are also articulated clearly and concisely, as they 'add gravitas' and 'make readers more aware of the problems of racial profiling in America'. Even the relationship between the small font and the detailed explanation is established effectively.

Criterion C: Coherence, focus and organisation: 5 out of 5 marks

The analysis is organised coherently and effectively. Although it is rather short in extent, it is very focused and structured. Body paragraphs are organised around three stylistic features – 'layout', 'fonts' and 'colour' – which are connected to the text's call to action and spreading of awareness.

Criterion D: Language: 5 out of 5 marks

Sentence structures are varied, vocabulary is appropriate and the register is academic. Words such as 'analogy', 'allusion' and 'mass production' are very accurate in capturing the essence of the stimulus text and how it uses language to construct meaning.

TIP

You will have 1 hour and 15 minutes at standard level to analyse one text, 2 hours and 15 minutes at higher level to analyse two separate texts. How will you manage your time? Activity 1.15 encourages you to write a practice Paper 1 as coursework, in your own time. Write an amount of text that you think you could potentially write during exam conditions. Practise writing this amount of text more often in response to texts, so that you can actually do it under exam conditions.

1.16 Do an online search for Benetton's advertisements on race by Oliviero Toscani from the 1990s. Text 3.7 is an example of one of these advertisements. At the time they were received with praise, shock and criticism. Benetton aimed to spread awareness about racism as a problem and celebrate **ethnic diversity**. Others claimed that the advertisements were counterproductive and actually incited racism.

As a class, search for more advertisements from this campaign. Assign each class member a different advertisement from the collection. Give a short presentation on the advertisement that you have been assigned. In your presentation, explain how the visual language of your text is used by Toscani to do one or more of the following:

- express the importance of race to a person's identity
- spread awareness about, and comment critically on, racism
- celebrate ethnic diversity
- incite racism.

Research and explain how these advertisements were received in the 1990s. Compare this response to how they might be received today. Refer to Units 1.1 and 1.2 on how to deconstruct images and advertisements.

Text 3.7

AOE question

How do texts follow or move away from the conventions associated with different types of text?

Oliviero Toscani's campaign on diversity and race for Benetton in the early 1990s broke many of the conventions of advertising. Compare the advertisements that you have studied here for Activity 1.16 with the traditional conventions of advertising as described in Unit 1.2. How are the Benetton advertisements different?

1.17 Text 3.8 is a piece of student writing in response to three Benetton advertisements from the 1990s. The student has adopted a **persona** and constructed arguments, which are not his own, to write a letter of complaint to Oliviero Toscani about these advertisements.

a Read the letter carefully. It has been annotated to help you understand the conventions for writing a letter of complaint.

b Do an online search for an advertisement that might be considered racist or denigrating to a particular group of people. While this unit has predominantly explored African Americans in the USA and blacks in South Africa, you may want to find advertisements that unfairly represent other ethnic minority groups.

c Write a letter of complaint to the producer of your racist advertisement. You may wish to use Text 3.8 to become familiar with the structure and features of a letter. Discuss your letter with your teacher and add it to your learner portfolio.

Text 3.8

Addresses. Include your own first, followed by the address of person you are writing to.

Bradford Hilltop
76 King Street
London, United Kingdom

Oliviero Toscani
Via Asconio Sforza
Milan, Italy

Date

12 December 1991

Greeting

Dear Mr Toscani,

Context: give your letter context by describing when and where you came across the controversial text.

Direct opening: why are you writing? State this clearly.

Opinion: include your opinion in the introduction as a statement.

As a person who travels regularly on the London Underground, I have noticed the shocking advertisements that you have created for the United Colors of Benetton. With this letter I would like to express my deep concerns that you are trivialising British values and stirring controversy in the United Kingdom.

I understand that shock advertising creates brand awareness and sells products, but I think you have crossed a line and gone too far. My problem with your advertisements also lies in the lack of sensitivity you have shown for racial issues in our country.

I realise that your depiction of two children hugging, one black and one white, is meant to make people stop and think about race. These young models, however, are not old enough to know what they are promoting or what messages they are sending to the world. The black child in this ad appears to have devil's horns, while the white child has the golden locks of an angel. The black child's face looks sinister and serious, while the white child's looks innocent and happy. Rather than promoting racial equality, it sends the opposite message: it reinforces the stereotypes of the black child as the aggressor and the white child as the sheepish victim.

Textual analysis: if you complain about a text, explain why it is offensive.

For similar reasons, your ad that depicts two mating horses is also disturbing and inappropriate. In England, sex is an act between two people who care intimately and deeply for each other. This image simply trivialises the act of making love altogether, and it has nothing to do with the clothing of Benetton. It also fails to promote racial equality. Why must it be the *black* horse that mounts the white horse? Again, this advertisement reinforces the stereotype of the beastly, black aggressor against the innocent white person. Although you may not have intended to suggest this message, I feel it my duty to point out that it can be interpreted this way.

Adjectives: use adjectives to comment on the effects of the original text on you, the reader.

Your most disturbing ad in this campaign must be the one depicting a white baby feeding from a black woman's breast. British people are not accustomed to seeing bare breasts in advertising. Breast-feeding is regarded as a private matter in the UK. It is not something we show off frivolously for the sake of selling a jumper. But what is most horrific about this ad, once again, is the comment it makes on racial stereotypes and the history of Great Britain. It is a reminder of colonialism and the days when black servants and slaves wet-nursed the children of their owners and the ruling elite. In the UK we are not proud of this past and we do not wish to be reminded of it on billboards around the country.

For the reasons I have mentioned, I ask you to consider the social values of the British people and show more cultural sensitivity, before releasing such campaigns in the UK again.

Call to action: what do you want the reader of your letter to do?

Kind regards,

Closing salutation

Bradford Hilltop

Signature

CONCEPT

Creativity

Text 3.8 is a piece of creative writing. The student adopts a persona, follows the conventions of a text type and synthesises his knowledge of three stimulus advertisements into one meaningful letter. Writing responses to texts will help you understand text types and better develop your own powers of creativity.

International mindedness

Pretending to write a letter from another person's perspective is a great way to practise international mindedness. It allows you to empathise with other people's ideas.

Higher level extension

1.18 You are about to read Text 3.9, an extract from Richard Wright's *Black Boy*, which describes a scene from his childhood. Discuss your answers to these questions with your classmates:

a Why does the author use quotation marks around 'white' and 'black'?

b The **narrator** claims: 'My grandmother, who was white as any "white" person, had never looked "white" to me.' What does he mean by this?

c The narrator asks: 'And did not all fathers, like my father, have the right to beat their children?' Does the narrator really believe that fathers have the right to beat their children? If not, why does the narrator ask this?

d What is the role of the mother in this passage? What are the challenges that she faces in raising Richard?

e The passage ends with the line: 'Whenever I saw "white" people now I stared at them, wondering what they were really like.' What is the effect of this line on the reader? What does it say about the character Richard Wright versus the narrator Richard Wright? Why might this line be considered humorous?

AOE question

How can language represent social differences and identities?

This question is from the 'time and space' part of your language and literature course. The questions in Activity 1.18 are essentially variations of this question. How do other words from Text 3.9, such as 'whip' or 'beat', represent social distinctions and identities?

Text 3.9

Richard Wright was an American author who wrote about race.

Black Boy

Extract

Richard Wright 1945

I soon made myself a nuisance by asking far too many questions of everybody. Every happening in the neighborhood, no matter how trivial, became my business. It was in this manner that I first stumbled upon the relations between whites and blacks, and what I learned frightened me. Though I had long known that there were people called 'white' people, it had never meant anything to me emotionally. I had seen white men and women upon the streets a thousand times, but they had never looked particularly 'white.' To me they were merely people like other people, yet somehow strangely different because I had never come in close touch with any of them. For the most part I never thought of them; they simply existed somewhere in the background of the city as a whole. It might have been that my tardiness in learning to sense white people as 'white' people came from the fact that many of my relatives were 'white'-looking people. My grandmother, who was white as any 'white' person, had never looked 'white' to me. And when word circulated among the black people of the neighborhood that a 'black' boy had been severely beaten by a 'white' man, I felt that the 'white' man had had a right to beat the 'black' boy, for I naively assumed that the 'white' man must have been the 'black' boy's father. And did not all fathers, like my father, have the right to beat their children? A paternal right was the only right, to my understanding, that a man had to beat a child. But when my mother told me that the 'white' man was not the father of the 'black' boy, was no kin to him at all, I was puzzled.

'Then why did the "white" man whip the "black" boy?' I asked my mother.

'The "white" man did not whip the "black" boy,' my mother told me. 'He beat the "black" boy.'

'But why?'

'You're too young to understand.'

'I'm not going to let anyone beat me,' I said stoutly.

'Then stop running wild in the streets,' my mother said.

I brooded for a long time about the seemingly causeless beating of the 'black' boy by the 'white' man and the more questions I asked the more bewildering it all became. Whenever I saw 'white' people now I stared at them, wondering what they were really like.

AOE question

How can cultural contexts influence how texts are written and received?

As you explore how 'time and space' affect the meaning of a text, you will consider this question. Memoirs such as Richard Wright's *Black Boy* (Text 3.9) are interesting for this reason. How does his cultural context shape the way he wrote this text? How might it have been received when it was published in the USA in 1945? How does your context shape the way you read it today?

1.19 How would you describe Richard as a character in this memoir? Think of one adjective to describe him and write this on a sticky note. Place your sticky notes on a wall for everyone in your class to see. Then each person should take a turn explaining why they chose this adjective. Refer back to the text when doing this.

1.20 For your learner portfolio, find another non-literary or literary text that sheds light on the problem of racism in some part of the Anglophone world. Discuss your chosen text with your teacher, include it in your portfolio and write a paragraph or two that answers these questions:

a How is race represented in your text?

b How is language used to construct this ?

c How does your text reflect the cultural context of another time and place, which is different from your own?

d How does your text compare to another text that you have explored in this unit or elsewhere?

LEARNER PROFILE

What aspects of the learner profile does Richard exemplify? Remember – an IB learner is an *inquirer*, a *thinker*, a *risk taker* and a *communicator*. An IB learner is *balanced*, *knowledgeable*, *reflective*, *caring*, *principled* and *open-minded*. Give evidence from Text 3.9 to support your answer. This question can be discussed with Activity 1.19.

CONCEPT

Representation

Representation has been a key concept throughout this unit. How do people use visual or written language to represent an entire race and relationships across races? Do these representations reinforce **stereotypes**? These questions might be helpful to explore in your learner portfolio in preparation for your individual oral.

Tim Wise is a public speaker and author who spreads awareness about racism in the USA. You may find an extract from his book or documentary *White Like Me* useful for Activity 1.20.

Further reading

- *Born a Crime* is Trevor Noah's autobiography about growing up in South Africa during and after apartheid.
- Harper Lee's *To Kill a Mockingbird*, Kathryn Stockett's *The Help*, Toni Morrison's *The Bluest Eye* and Alice Walker's *The Color Purple* are popular novels about racial discrimination in the US South.
- *White Like Me* by Tim Wise is a book and documentary about the current state of racism in the USA.
- Rap lyrics of several artists make for interesting study of language, race and culture. Big L's song 'Ebonics' is about AAVE. Tupac Shakur and Kendrick Lamar also have lyrics that you may want to analyse in an individual oral.

REFLECT

Return to the key terms in the word bank at the beginning of this unit.

- Which terms were new for you?
- How have you come to know those terms better by working through this unit?
- For the terms that are not directly related to racism, such as persona, idiolect or memoir, state how they were made relevant to racism in this unit.
- How have the texts and activities in this unit made you think differently about racism today?

Unit 3.2 Colonialism

Learning objectives

- explore how context affects the ways in which texts are written and received
- compare and contrast texts from different times and places
- explore colonialism and post-colonial readings.

Word bank

empire
colonialism
cultural appropriation
cultural sensitivity
colonial discourse
patronising
othering
noble savage
hegemony
manga
post-colonial reading
politically correct
enjambment
allusion
facetious
voice-over
ethnography
cultural bias

Cultural appropriation is the adoption of a minority culture by a dominant culture in an insensitive way. Wearing a traditional Native American headdress in this fashion is not respectful.

It was once said that the sun never set on the British Empire, as Great Britain had colonies around the globe at that time. Although the days of '**empire**' may be over, there is evidence of it all around the world, from the tunnels of Gibraltar to the cricket fields of Singapore. The legacy of the British Empire has affected people all around the world. Its mark in history is evident in many cultures and forms of literature. It is the reason why the Anglophone world is so large.

In this unit you will study texts from colonial and post-colonial times to gain a better understanding of how **colonialism** has affected so many people.

International mindedness

Part of being internationally minded is showing **cultural sensitivity**. This is to say that you consider your audience, their culture and history, before you make generalisations about them.

CONCEPT

Culture

How has your *culture* been shaped by the forces of colonialism? Even if you do not live in an Anglophone country, you may find influences from colonial forces. The Spanish, Portuguese, French and Dutch, for example, also colonised large parts of the world. What evidence of a colonial past can you find in your daily lives?

Getting started

2.1 Without looking up the meaning of the word, how would you define 'colonialism'? Write your definition on a sticky note and put it on a wall for your classmates to read. What similarities and differences can you see between your definition and those of others in your class?

2.2 Look up a definition of colonialism. How different is it from your definitions from Activity 2.1? Where in Text 3.10 do you see evidence of colonialism? How does the author express a colonial mentality?

Text 3.10

The Niger and the West Sudan

Captain A.J.N. Tremearne 1910

What a wonderful fascination there is in the name of West Africa, the most mysterious part of that very mysterious continent! What visions of cannibals, 'jujus' and sacrifices it conjures up; what thoughts of conquests of new countries and new peoples; what desires of travel and exploration! There are other things – fever, for instance – which will come later and tend to shatter some of the virgin illusions, but in spite of everything there will always remain some attraction about this land which one will never shake off. It is said that when once a man has the call of the bush in his blood he will continue to answer to it until he leaves his bones there – unless by some lucky chance he be invalided in time to die at home.

AOE question

How can texts present challenges and offer insights?

Text 3.10 may give you insight into the mindset of a coloniser. What challenges does it present you with?

- What words must you check the meanings of?
- Which ideas seem foreign, and why might this be?
- What were the challenges of the author?

Readers, writers and texts

2.3 Return to Text 3.10, and, trying to make inferences from the text and its title, discuss your answers to these questions:

a Who wrote this text?

b Why did he write it?

c For whom was it written?

d What type of text is it?

2.4 In your study of Text 3.10, you may have noticed a way of speaking about exploring new places and encountering new people. This language, used by the colonisers about the colonies and the people they colonised, can be called **colonial discourse**, a term coined by Edward Said in *Orientalism* (see 'Further reading' at the end of this unit). This discourse, or use of colonial language, often took a **patronising** tone. It aimed to justify colonial control, define indigenous peoples and silence the colonised.

Read Text 3.11, taken from *Heart of Darkness* by Joseph Conrad. It is about a man, Charles Marlow, travelling on the Congo River in his steamboat with his crew, searching for the infamous ivory trader Mr Kurtz. On his journey he encounters indigenous people. Discuss your answers to these questions:

a How does the author use language to create a sense of 'us and them', known as '**othering**'?

b Is there evidence in Marlow's narrative that he condones or supports the notion of 'empire'?

c In colonial times, literature would often depict the idea of a '**noble savage**', where indigenous people were portrayed as 'pure' in their uncivilised ways. How are the indigenous people portrayed in Text 3.11?

d How is power exerted through language?

e *Heart of Darkness* is considered classic English literature by some and racist propaganda by others. Based on your reading of this passage, do you think it should be studied as English literature, or banned from schools? Give evidence to support your opinion.

f How is Text 3.11 similar to or different from Text 3.10? Compare and contrast their use of language and the purposes of these texts.

TIP

In this unit you will see several literary texts. While you may not be reading these works to meet your reading requirements, it is good to study extracts from a range of literary works in order to inform your understanding of global issues for the learner portfolio. For your 'freely chosen' literary work, you may ask your teacher for permission to explore one of the extracts from this unit in its entirety.

CONCEPT

Perspective

Question 'a' in Activity 2.4 asks about 'othering' in relation to Conrad's *Heart of Darkness* (Text 3.11). *Perspective* is an important concept when reading and writing about colonialism. While the narrator writes about the people that he encounters along the Congo River, the text says much more about his perspective on colonialism. Do an online search for book covers for *Heart of Darkness* that publishers have created over the years. How does each book cover offer a different perspective on the novel and colonialism in general?

Text 3.11

Heart of Darkness

Joseph Conrad 1899

Trees, trees, millions of trees, massive, immense, running up high; and at their foot, hugging the bank against the stream, crept the little begrimed steamboat, like a sluggish beetle crawling on the floor of a lofty portico. It made you feel very small, very lost, and yet it was not altogether depressing, that feeling. After all, if you were small, the grimy beetle crawled on – which was just what you wanted it to do. Where the pilgrims imagined it crawled to I don't know. To some place where they expected to get something, I bet! For me it crawled towards Kurtz – exclusively; but when the steam-pipes started leaking we crawled very slow.

The reaches opened before us and closed behind, as if the forest had stepped leisurely across the water to bar the way for our return. We penetrated deeper and deeper into the heart of darkness. It was very quiet there. At night sometimes the roll of drums behind the curtain of trees would run up the river and remain sustained faintly, as if hovering in the air high over our heads, till the first break of day. Whether it meant war, peace, or prayer we could not tell. The dawns were heralded by the descent of a chill stillness; the wood-cutters slept, their fires burned low; the snapping of a twig would make you start. We were wanderers on prehistoric earth, on an earth that wore the aspect of an unknown planet. We could have fancied ourselves the first of men taking possession of an accursed inheritance, to be subdued at the cost of profound anguish and of excessive toil. But suddenly, as we struggled round a bend, there would be a glimpse of rush walls, of peaked grass-roofs, a burst of yells, a whirl of black limbs, a mass of hands clapping, of feet stamping, of bodies swaying, of eyes rolling, under the droop of heavy and motionless foliage. The steamer toiled along slowly on the edge of a black and incomprehensible frenzy. The prehistoric man was cursing us, praying to us, welcoming us – who could tell? We were cut off from the comprehension of our surroundings; we glided past like phantoms, wondering and secretly appalled, as sane men would be before an enthusiastic outbreak in a madhouse. We could not understand because we were too far and could not remember, because we were travelling in the night of first ages, of those ages that are gone, leaving hardly a sign – and no memories.

The earth seemed unearthly. We are accustomed to look upon the shackled form of a conquered monster, but there – you could look at a thing monstrous and free. It was unearthly, and the men were – No, they were not inhuman. Well, you know, that was the worst of it – this suspicion of their not being inhuman. It would come slowly to one. They howled and leaped, and spun, and made horrid faces; but what thrilled you was just the thought of their humanity – like yours – the thought of your remote kinship with this wild and passionate uproar. Ugly. Yes, it was ugly enough; but if you were man enough you would admit to yourself that there was in you just the faintest trace of a response to the terrible frankness of that noise, a dim suspicion of there being a meaning in it which you – you so remote from the night of the first ages – could comprehend.

AOE question

How and why do people study language and literature?

If *Heart of Darkness* (Text 3.11) is deemed racist, why might it still be worth studying? Can Conrad's writing style be considered literary, while his treatment of another culture is demeaning?

2.5 Here is a list of adjectives (a–o) that could be used to describe the use of tone in a text. Look up any meanings you do not already know. Which words apply to this passage from *Heart of Darkness* (Text 3.11)? Why have you selected these words? Give evidence from the text to support your answers:

a enigmatic	**b** optimistic	**c** dark	**d** evasive
e pensive	**f** sentimental	**g** tongue-in-cheek	**h** confused
i objective	**j** indignant	**k** macabre	**l** imploring
m condescending	**n** instructive	**o** cautionary.	

Time and space

2.6 When analysing works of literature from colonial times, it is important to consider the relationships between characters and how 'power' plays a role in these. **Hegemony** refers to the ways in which a ruling power's authority is accepted by those who are ruled. When people fail to question why the ruling powers have the right to rule, there is evidence of hegemony. It's the idea that everyone in a society accepts an unfair distribution of wealth or power. It is an important concept for understanding colonialism and colonial literature.

Text 3.12 is a passage from the play *The Tempest*, written by William Shakespeare at the beginning of the 17th century. Read the passage carefully and discuss your answers to these questions:

a How did Caliban welcome Prospero and his daughter Miranda when they arrived on the island?

b How did Prospero gain power over Caliban? What gives him the right to rule over Caliban?

c Caliban tried to rape Prospero's daughter, Miranda ('thou didst seek to violate / The honour of my child'). What is the result of this? How does this affect your understanding of his character?

d Would you say there is hegemony on this island? What makes you say this?

Text 3.12

The Tempest

William Shakespeare 1611

CALIBAN

I must eat my dinner.
This island's mine, by Sycorax my mother,
Which thou takest from me. When thou camest first,
Thou strokedst me and madest much of me, wouldst give me
Water with berries in't, and teach me how
To name the bigger light, and how the less,
That burn by day and night: and then I loved thee
And show'd thee all the qualities o' the isle,
The fresh springs, brine-pits, barren place and fertile:
Cursed be I that did so! All the charms
Of Sycorax, toads, beetles, bats, light on you!
For I am all the subjects that you have,
Which first was mine own king: and here you sty me
In this hard rock, whiles you do keep from me
The rest o' the island.

PROSPERO

Thou most lying slave,
Whom stripes may move, not kindness! I have used thee,
Filth as thou art, with human care, and lodged thee
In mine own cell, till thou didst seek to violate
The honour of my child.

CALIBAN
O ho, O ho! would't had been done!
Thou didst prevent me; I had peopled else
This isle with Calibans.

PROSPERO
Abhorred slave,
Which any print of goodness wilt not take,
Being capable of all ill! I pitied thee,
Took pains to make thee speak, taught thee each hour
One thing or other: when thou didst not, savage,
Know thine own meaning, but wouldst gabble like
A thing most brutish, I endow'd thy purposes
With words that made them known. But thy vile race,
Though thou didst learn, had that in't which
good natures
Could not abide to be with; therefore wast thou
Deservedly confined into this rock,
Who hadst deserved more than a prison.

CALIBAN
You taught me language; and my profit on't
Is, I know how to curse. The red plague rid you
For learning me your language!

PROSPERO
Hag-seed, hence!
Fetch us in fuel; and be quick, thou'rt best,
To answer other business. Shrug'st thou, malice?
If thou neglect'st or dost unwillingly
What I command, I'll rack thee with old cramps,
Fill all thy bones with aches, make thee roar
That beasts shall tremble at thy din.

CALIBAN
No, pray thee.
Aside
I must obey: his art is of such power,
It would control my dam's god, Setebos,
and make a vassal of him.

PROSPERO
So, slave; hence!

AOE question

How do texts engage with local and global issues?

Activity 2.7 asks you about the context of *The Tempest* and how William Shakespeare engaged the audiences of his time with the issues of colonialism. With all of these questions, keep in mind that the dialogue spoken by their characters is a way for playwrights to engage their audience.

2.7 *The Tempest* was written in the early 17th century, during Europe's exploration of what was known as the 'New World'. Find secondary sources that help you answer the following questions. You may wish to split up the research questions among groups and report to the class on your findings:

a How much would London audiences in the early 17th century have known about the 'New World' and the indigenous populations there? How would this knowledge have influenced their understanding of *The Tempest*?

b How was Caliban most likely portrayed on the stage in Shakespeare's time? What do you think he would have looked like? How is slavery an issue here?

c To what extent do scholars consider William Shakespeare an advocate of colonialism and a supporter of 'empire' through their analysis of *The Tempest*?

d How is *The Tempest* significantly different from other plays written by William Shakespeare?

2.8 Based on your understanding of Text 3.12 and its characters, how would you stage this scene of *The Tempest* for a modern-day audience? Describe the set that you would create, the costumes you would design, the directions you would give the actors and the ways you would have them perform their lines. What decisions have you made, and why have you made them? Explain the rationale behind your modern-day production of this scene from *The Tempest* to your classmates. Refer to your analysis of the text from Activity 2.6 and your research from Activity 2.7.

CONCEPT

Representation

Representation is a key concept in this language and literature course. Activity 2.8 asks you to design a set and costumes for a modern-day performance of *The Tempest*. Essentially, this activity asks you how the characters and playwright's ideas should be represented in order to appeal to a contemporary audience. Producers of theatrical productions deal with the question of *representation* all the time.

AOE question

How can comparing and interpreting texts transform readers?

Through an online search, find a filmed performance of a scene from *The Tempest* or any other Shakespeare play. Read the scene from the play first before viewing the filmed performance of it.

After you have viewed this scene, ask yourself how the performance has transformed your interpretation of the text. Compare the filmed version to the written version, and discuss what is added and what is lost through the process of performing and filming it.

2.9 After you have discussed how you would stage Text 3.12, do an online search for images of Caliban and Prospero, as they have appeared in various stage or film productions. A few have been included here.

a What choices have producers made when depicting these characters?

b How do these choices reflect the producer's understanding of the author's intentions and their audience's expectations?

c How do these images compare to what you had in mind in Activity 2.8?

Djimon Hounsou as Caliban in the 2010 film of *The Tempest.*

A drawing of Caliban by Charles A. Buchel in 1904.

David Suchet as Caliban in this 1978 stage production by the Royal Shakespeare Company.

CONCEPT

Transformation

Transformation is a key concept in this course. Activity 2.10 asks how Shakespeare's play *The Tempest* has been transformed into a manga graphic novel. Try working with more *transformations* of texts in order to understand them better. For example, novels are often transformed into films.

Intertextuality: connecting texts

2.10 What if you were to turn *The Tempest* into a manga or a graphic novel? Study Text 3.13, which is a manga version of the scene from Text 3.12. Write a letter to its author, Richard Appignanesi, and its illustrator, Paul Duffield. In your letter, praise and/or criticise their efforts to transpose Shakespeare's ideas into a different text type for a different audience in a different time. Comment on how the author and illustrator have circumnavigated the problems of colonialism in their work. Read Unit 1.5 for a better understanding of graphic novels.

AOE question

What can diverse texts have in common?

Studying both a performance and a **manga** edition of a Shakespeare play can help you answer this question. The 'points of similarity' can be characters or dialogue.

Text 3.13

ATL

In the Diploma Programme you work on your *self-management skills*, which include *organisational skills*. Your responses to Activities 2.10 and 2.11 can be used for your learner portfolio. As you continue to do activities like these for your portfolio, ask yourself how the portfolio can help you develop your organisational skills. Are you:

- organising your entries by theme or global issue?
- building a collection of your own imaginative writing?
- curating interesting primary sources?

Discuss various methods of organising your portfolio with your teacher and classmates.

Towards assessment

2.11 We live in a post-colonial age. This is to say that most people today believe everyone has a right to live in a sovereign nation state that governs itself, without the influence of a foreign empire or colonial power. Because of this, people read texts differently now from the way they did a hundred years ago.

Text 3.14

DELIGHTFUL DURBAN

CHARMINGLY different, this gem-like Riviera in the Garden Province of South Africa . . . Gay, colorful, joyful Durban . . . Here health and pleasure prosper in a setting of sparkling sunshine, zestful climate, the amazing blue of the Southern sky, the dancing waters of the Indian ocean.

Luxurious hotels overlook spacious stretches of beach and a beautiful harbor alive with white-bellied sails of pleasure craft, with warships, whalers, windjammers . . . Delightful golf and yachting clubs . . . Sailing, sea bathing, surfing, angling, polo, cricket, horse-racing, motoring, high-class concerts, theatres . . . all catering happily to the lovers of sport, recreation, leisure.

Durban's attractions provide an exquisite interval in a tour of South Africa's many wonders . . . Matchless Victoria Falls . . . Zimbabwe's mysterious ruins . . . Kimberley's famous diamond mines . . . Marvelous Cango Caves . . . The gold mines of the Rand . . . Drakensberg Mountains . . . The Valley of a Thousand Hills . . . The great Kruger Big Game Preserve . . . and Historic Good Hope, the "Cape Beautiful."

Send for fully illustrated booklet to

SOUTH AFRICAN GOVERNMENT RAILWAYS

11 Broadway, New York City

a In small groups, discuss a **post-colonial reading** of Text 3.14, using the concepts and questions presented in the table. Fill in the third column on a copy of the table. Present your analysis to your classmates.

b As a group, do an online search for another text that can be used to explore colonialism by applying a post-colonial reading. This list gives some suggestions for the types of text you might search for:

- poetry or literature that celebrates the idea of empire
- travel posters for journeys to the colonies
- travel logs or journals from colonists or explorers
- charts or official documents from colonial times
- old advertisements that are no longer considered **politically correct**, such as those for Aunt Jemima's Pancake Mix (Unit 3.1), Uncle Ben's rice or Mrs Butterworth's syrup.

c Complete the fourth column in the table. Present your findings to your class in a group presentation.

Concepts	Questions	Answers in relation to Text 3.14	Answers in relation to a text of your choice
Power	How is power exerted through language?		
Empire	How does the author condone or support 'empire'?		
Voice	In what ways are some people given a voice while others are silenced within the text?		
Othering	How are people's differences depicted?		
Hegemony	To what degree is the rule of one over another accepted?		

2.12 Whether or not you are reading literary works about colonialism for your language and literature course, you may find it useful to practise essay writing for Paper 2 by answering *one* of these four questions. You should compare and contrast *two* literary works in your response. See Chapter 6 for guidance on Paper 2 and writing comparative essays on literary works.

a How is power distributed among the characters in two literary works that you have read? How is language used in these works to comment on these power relationships?

b With regard to two literary texts that you have read, how have they been interpreted differently over time?

c How and for what reasons have some characters been silenced, excluded or marginalised within two literary texts that you have read?

d In what ways and for what reasons do two of your literary works comment critically on racism or colonialism?

Higher level extension

2.13 To what degree do you understand the mindset of colonisers? A good example of insight into the colonial mindset is Rudyard Kipling's poem 'The White Man's Burden' (Text 3.15). Read the poem carefully. Where in the text do you see evidence that supports these claims?

a Without the white man's intervention, much of the world would slip into chaos, famine and sin.

b While bringing peace and order to the world is not an easy task, it is a noble one.

c Colonisers should not expect rewards or appreciation for their hard work.

Text 3.15

The White Man's Burden

Rudyard Kipling

TAKE up the White Man's burden –
Send forth the best ye breed –
Go bind your sons to exile
To serve your captives' need;
To wait in heavy harness
On fluttered folk and wild –
Your new-caught sullen peoples,
Half devil and half child.

Take up the White Man's burden –
In patience to abide
To veil the threat of terror
And check the show of pride;
By open speech and simple,
An hundred times made plain,
To seek another's profit,
And work another's gain.

Take up the White Man's burden –
The savage wars of peace –
Fill full the mouth of famine
And bid the sickness cease;
And when your goal is nearest
The end for others sought,
Watch Sloth and heathen Folly
Bring all your hopes to nought.

Take up the White Man's burden –
No tawdry rule of kings,
But toil of serf and sweeper –
The tale of common things.
The ports ye shall not enter,
The roads ye shall not tread,
Go make them with your living,
And mark them with your dead!

Take up the White Man's burden –
And reap his old reward,
The blame of those ye better,
The hate of those ye guard –
The cry of hosts ye humour
(Ah slowly !) towards the light:-
'Why brought ye us from bondage,
'Our loved Egyptian night?'

Take up the White Man's burden –
Ye dare not stoop to less –
Nor call too loud on Freedom
To cloak your weariness;
By all ye cry or whisper,
By all ye leave or do,
The silent sullen peoples
Shall weigh your gods and you.

Take up the White Man's burden –
Have done with childish days –
The lightly proffered laurel,
The easy, ungrudged praise.
Comes now, to search your manhood
Through all the thankless years,
Cold-edged with dear-bought wisdom,
The judgement of your peers.

LEARNER PROFILE

Inquirer

As a student of the IB Diploma Programme, you should take an inquisitive approach in general. Activity 2.15 asks several questions about Text 3.15 and its author. Can you think of more questions? More important than knowing 'the right' interpretation of a poem is the ability to ask the right questions about it.

2.14 What kinds of rhythm, metre and rhyme are used in Text 3.15? Why has the author chosen this structure? Look specifically at the use of iambic feet. Read Unit 1.12 for more information about the use of metre in poetry.

2.15 Find out more about the author Rudyard Kipling and his poem 'The White Man's Burden'.

a Why did Kipling write this poem?

b How has his place in the English canon changed since post-colonial times?

c Can you make a connection between 'The White Man's Burden' and what you have read about him?

d How does this poem reflect his life and times?

e Text 3.16 appeared in the satirical magazine *Judge* in 1899, at the time of the Philippine-American War, in response to Kipling's poem. How does it illustrate the ideas that he expresses in his poem? How does it use language to reinforce or challenge the colonial mindset?

f Text 3.17 is a cartoon from *Life* magazine (1899), also titled 'The White Man's Burden'. Like Text 3.16, it depicts the symbolic characters of John Bull and Uncle Sam. How is the narrative of this cartoon different from Text 3.16 and Kipling's poem (Text 3.15)?

Text 3.16

Text 3.17

TIP

You can practise for the individual oral by working with 'The White Man's Burden' and one of these cartoons, with 'colonialism' as the connecting global issue.

2.16 Compare Text 3.15 to Text 3.18 with your classmates. The class splits into two: one group will focus on the similarities and the other will focus on differences. Each group takes turns stating a similarity or a difference between the two poems. Each statement must be original. The originality of your statement can be judged by your teacher. If your group has run out of statements, then the other group has won!

AOE question

How do the style and structure of a text affect its meaning?

Activity 2.16 asks you to compare and contrast two very different poems. How do these differences contribute to their different meanings?

CONCEPT

Identity

Texts 3.15 and 3.18 are very much about *identity*, one of the key concepts in this course. How do the identities of the narrators of Texts 3.15 and 3.18 reflect their attitudes towards empire? When analysing poetry, discuss whether or not you believe the narrator to be the poet.

Text 3.18

From 'Wings of a Dove' in *Rights of Passage*

Edward Kamau Brathwaite 1967

Brother Man the Rasta
man, beard full of lichen
brain full of lice
watched the mice
come up through the floor-
boards of his down-
town, shanty-town kitchen,
and smiled. Blessed are the poor
in health, he mumbled,
that they should inherit this
wealth. Blessed are the meek
hearted, he grumbled,
for theirs is this stealth.

Brother Man the Rasta
man, hair full of lichen
head hot as ice
watched the mice
walk into his poor
hole, reached for his peace and the pipe of his ganja
and smiled how the mice
eyes, hot pumice
pieces, glowed into his room
like ruby, like rhinestone
and suddenly startled like
diamond

And I
Rastafar-I
in Babylon's boom
town, crazed by the moon
and the peace of this chalice, I
prophet and singer, scourge
of the gutter, guardian
Trench Town, the Dungle and Young's
Town, rise and walk through the now silent
streets of affection, hawk's eyes
hard with fear, with
affection for my people
cry, my people
shout:

Down down
white

man con
man brown
man down

down full
man, frown-
ing fat
man that
white black
man that
lives in
the town

Rise rise
locks-
man, Solo-
man wise
man, rise
rise rise
leh we
laugh
dem mock
dem stop
dem kill
dem an' go
back back
to the black
man lan'
back back
to Af-
rica

TEXT AND CONTEXT

- Rastafaris are a religious group primarily living in the Caribbean Islands.
- Dungle Town is another name for Kingston, Jamaica.
- Trench Town is a neighbourhood in Kingston, Jamaica.
- Young's Town is a brand of canned sardines.
- 'Blessed are the poor' is a passage from the Bible (Matthew 5:3), in which Jesus suggests that the poor can be wealthy in spirit if not in worldly, material terms.
- The word 'dem' is vernacular for 'them'.
- The word 'lan" is vernacular for 'land'.
- The word 'locks' refers to dreadlocks, a hairstyle worn by Rastafaris.

2.17 Assign each person in your class one of the literary terms in this box. In turns, each person explains the relevance of his or her term in relation to Text 3.18. You should explain:

- *why* you think the author applied this literary feature
- what the effect of this literary feature is on the reader.

Look up the definitions of features you may not know.

enjambment	repetition	alliteration	juxtaposition	rhyme	vernacular	
imagery	volta	point of view	diction	hyphen	simile	imperative	**allusion**

2.18 You are going to read Text 3.19: 'How to write about Africa'. Binyavanga Wainaina wrote this piece for the magazine *Granta* in 2006. Before you read the text, make sure you understand the pairs of terms listed here. After reading Text 3.19, explain which term in each pair is most relevant to this text. Explain why you made this choice:

a parody / satire
b **facetious** / sarcastic
c foreign / familiar
d essay / instruction
e Western / African
f sweeping / specific
g offensive / humorous
h confronting / elusive
i condescending / empowering.

AOE question

How do the style and structure of a text affect its meaning?

Answering this question in relation to Text 3.19 will help you discuss the relevant terms from Activity 2.18.

Text 3.19

How to write about Africa

Binyavanga Wainaina for *Granta* 2006

Always use the word 'Africa' or 'Darkness' or 'Safari' in your title. Subtitles may include the words 'Zanzibar', 'Masai', 'Zulu', 'Zambezi', 'Congo', 'Nile', 'Big', 'Sky', 'Shadow', 'Drum', 'Sun' or 'Bygone'. Also useful are words such as 'Guerrillas', 'Timeless', 'Primordial' and 'Tribal'. Note that 'People' means Africans who are not black, while 'The People' means black Africans.

Never have a picture of a well-adjusted African on the cover of your book, or in it, unless that African has won the Nobel Prize. An AK-47, prominent ribs, naked breasts: use these. If you must include an African, make sure you get one in Masai or Zulu or Dogon dress.

In your text, treat Africa as if it were one country. It is hot and dusty with rolling grasslands and huge herds of animals and tall, thin people who are starving. Or it is hot and steamy with very short people who eat primates. Don't get bogged down with precise descriptions. Africa is big: fifty-four countries, 900 million people who are too busy starving and dying and warring and emigrating

to read your book. The continent is full of deserts, jungles, highlands, savannahs and many other things, but your reader doesn't care about all that, so keep your descriptions romantic and evocative and unparticular.

Make sure you show how Africans have music and rhythm deep in their souls, and eat things no other humans eat. Do not mention rice and beef and wheat; monkey-brain is an African's cuisine of choice, along with goat, snake, worms and grubs and all manner of game meat. Make sure you show that you are able to eat such food without flinching, and describe how you learn to enjoy it – because you care.

Taboo subjects: ordinary domestic scenes, love between Africans (unless a death is involved), references to African writers or intellectuals, mention of school-going children who are not suffering from yaws or Ebola fever or female genital mutilation.

Throughout the book, adopt a *sotto* voice, in conspiracy with the reader, and a sad *I-expected-so-much* tone. Establish early on that your liberalism is impeccable, and mention near the beginning how much you love Africa, how you fell in love with the place and can't live without her. Africa is the only continent you can love – take advantage of this. If you are a man, thrust yourself into her warm virgin forests. If you are a woman, treat Africa as a man who wears a bush jacket and disappears off into the sunset. Africa is to be pitied, worshipped or dominated. Whichever angle you take, be sure to leave the strong impression that without your intervention and your important book, Africa is doomed.

Your African characters may include naked warriors, loyal servants, diviners and seers, ancient wise men living in hermitic splendour. Or corrupt politicians, inept polygamous travel-guides, and prostitutes you have slept with. The Loyal Servant always behaves like a seven-year-old and needs a firm hand; he is scared of snakes, good with children, and always involving you in his complex domestic dramas. The Ancient Wise Man always comes from a noble tribe (not the money-grubbing tribes like the Gikuyu, the Igbo or the Shona). He has rheumy eyes and is close to the Earth. The Modern African is a fat man who steals and works in the visa office, refusing to give work permits to qualified Westerners who really care about Africa. He is an enemy of development, always using his government job to make it difficult for pragmatic and good-hearted expats to set up NGOs or Legal Conservation Areas. Or he is an Oxford-educated intellectual turned serial-killing politician in a Savile Row suit. He is a cannibal who likes Cristal champagne, and his mother is a rich witch-doctor who really runs the country.

Among your characters you must always include The Starving African, who wanders the refugee camp nearly naked, and waits for the benevolence of the West. Her children have flies on their eyelids and pot bellies, and her breasts are flat and empty. She must look utterly helpless. She can have no past, no history; such diversions ruin the dramatic moment. Moans are good. She must never say anything about herself in the dialogue except to speak of her (unspeakable) suffering. Also be sure to include a warm and motherly woman who has a rolling laugh and who is concerned for your well-being. Just call her Mama. Her children are all delinquent. These characters should buzz around your main hero, making him look good. Your hero can teach them, bathe them, feed them; he carries lots of babies and has seen Death. Your hero is you (if reportage), or a beautiful, tragic international celebrity/aristocrat who now cares for animals (if fiction).

Bad Western characters may include children of Tory cabinet ministers, Afrikaners, employees of the World Bank. When talking about exploitation by foreigners mention the Chinese and Indian traders. Blame the West for Africa's situation. But do not be too specific.

Broad brushstrokes throughout are good. Avoid having the African characters laugh, or struggle to educate their kids, or just make do in mundane circumstances. Have them illuminate something about Europe or America in Africa. African characters should be colourful, exotic, larger than life – but empty inside, with no dialogue, no conflicts or resolutions in their stories, no depth or quirks to confuse the cause.

Describe, in detail, naked breasts (young, old, conservative, recently raped, big, small) or mutilated genitals, or enhanced genitals. Or any kind of genitals. And dead bodies. Or, better, naked dead bodies. And especially rotting naked dead bodies. Remember, any work you submit in which people look filthy and miserable will be referred to as the 'real Africa', and you want that on your dust jacket. Do not feel queasy about this: you are trying to help them to get aid from the West. The biggest taboo in writing about Africa is to describe or show dead or suffering white people.

Animals, on the other hand, must be treated as well rounded, complex characters. They speak (or grunt while tossing their manes proudly) and have names, ambitions and desires. They also have family values: *see how lions teach their children?* Elephants are caring, and are good feminists or dignified patriarchs. So are gorillas. Never, ever say anything negative about an elephant or a gorilla. Elephants may attack people's property, destroy their crops, and even kill them. Always take the side of the elephant. Big cats have public-school accents. Hyenas are fair game and have vaguely Middle Eastern accents. Any short Africans who live in the jungle or desert may be portrayed with good humour (unless they are in conflict with an elephant or chimpanzee or gorilla, in which case they are pure evil).

After celebrity activists and aid workers, conservationists are Africa's most important people. Do not offend them. You need them to invite you to their 30,000-acre game ranch or 'conservation area', and this is the only way you will get to interview the celebrity activist. Often a book cover with a heroic-looking conservationist on it works magic for sales. Anybody white, tanned and wearing khaki who once had a pet antelope or a farm is a conservationist, one who is preserving Africa's rich heritage. When interviewing him or her, do not ask how much funding they have; do not ask how much money they make off their game. Never ask how much they pay their employees.

Readers will be put off if you don't mention the light in Africa. And sunsets, the African sunset is a must. It is always big and red. There is always a big sky. Wide empty spaces and game are critical – Africa is the Land of Wide Empty Spaces. When writing about the plight of flora and fauna, make sure you mention that Africa is overpopulated. When your main character is in a desert or jungle living with indigenous peoples (anybody short) it is okay to mention that Africa has been severely depopulated by Aids and War (use caps).

You'll also need a nightclub called Tropicana, where mercenaries, evil nouveau riche Africans and prostitutes and guerrillas and expats hang out.

Always end your book with Nelson Mandela saying something about rainbows or renaissances. Because you care.

2.19 At higher level, you are asked to write a 1200–1500-word essay, known as the higher level essay. Text 3.19 is a good, non-literary stimulus for writing such an essay. You may want to practise your essay writing skills by writing an HL essay about this text. You will need a 'line of inquiry', which explores several key concepts from this course.

Here are several lines of inquiry (a–d), which you may find useful for your essay. Compare your essay with a classmate's essay and apply the assessment criteria for this component to your work, before asking your teacher to look at it:

a To what extent does Binyavanga Wainaina use language in 'How to write about Africa' to sketch an image of 'Africa' that confronts Western readers with their own biased attitudes?

b How is the meaning of Binyavanga Wainaina's 'How to write about Africa' rooted in popular Western films about 'Africa' such as *Out of Africa*, *Blood Diamond*, *The Last King of Scotland* and *The Constant Gardener*?

c To what extent is satire an effective medium for Binyavanga wainaina's message in 'How to write about Africa'?

d In what ways and for what reasons might 'How to write about Africa' by Binyavanga Wainaina be considered offensive by both Western and African readers?

Turn to Chapter 7 for further guidance about how to write a higher level essay.

Extended essay

Question 'b' from Activity 2.19 could be the starting point for a research question for an extended essay. For your extended essay, you may want to focus on how notions of 'power', 'empire', 'voice' and 'hegemony' are represented in one or two films about African nations. Comparing an older film to a newer film may prove fruitful for analysis. Be sure to focus on how film techniques are used to construct meaning in this Category 3 essay.

This still from *Out of Africa*, starring Meryl Streep, may be the kind of depiction of Africans that inspired Binyavanga Wainaina to write his piece 'How to write about Africa'.

CONCEPTS

In your higher level essay you are asked to explore a line of inquiry, like those presented in Activity 2.19, and several key concepts from this course. Which of the seven concepts (*creativity, communication, perspective, transformation, representation, identity, culture*) are relevant to an analysis of Text 3.19?

2.20 Text 3.20 is the **voice-over** from a South African film called *The Gods Must Be Crazy* by Jamie Uys.

a Ask one person from your class to read the text aloud. After every few sentences, stop reading the text aloud and discuss what images or scenes would be depicted in the film to accompany that part of the voice-over.

b If you can, watch the first part of the movie. How are the images that you imagined different from the actual scenes in the movie?

A still from the movie *The Gods Must Be Crazy* in which the arrival of a Coke bottle seems to disrupt the harmony of these Kalahari Bushmen.

Text 3.20

The Gods Must Be Crazy

Jamie Uys 1980

It looks like a paradise, but it is the most treacherous desert in the world: the Kalahari. After the short rainy season there are many water holes, and even rivers. But after a few weeks, the water sinks away into the deep Kalahari sand.

The water holes dry up, and the rivers stop flowing. The grass fades to a beautiful, blond colour that offers excellent grazing. But for the next nine months, there'll be no water to drink. So most of the animals move away, leaving the blond grass uneaten.

Humans avoid the Kalahari like the plague because man must have water to live.

So the beautiful landscapes are devoid of people. Except for the little people of the Kalahari. Pretty, dainty, small and graceful: the Bushmen.

Where any other person would die of thirst in a few days they live quite contentedly in this desert that doesn't look like a desert. They know where to dig for roots and bugs and tubers and which berries and pods are good to eat.

And of course they know what to do about water. For instance, in the early morning, you can collect dewdrops from leaves that were carefully laid out the previous evening.

Or a plume of grass can be a reservoir. And if you have the know-how, an insignificant clump of twigs can tell you where to dig and you come to light with an enormous tuber.

You scrape shavings off it with a stick that is split to give it a sharp edge. You take a handful of the shavings, point your thumb at your mouth and squeeze.

They must be the most contented people in the world. They have no crime, no punishment, no violence, no laws, no police, judges, rulers or bosses. They believe that the gods put only good and useful things on the earth for them to use. In this world of theirs, nothing is bad or evil. Even a poisonous snake is not bad. You just have to keep away from the sharp end. Actually, a snake is very good. In fact, it's delicious. And the skin makes a fine pouch.

They live in the vastness of the Kalahari in small family groups. One family of Bushmen might meet up with another once in a few years. But for the most part, they live in complete isolation, quite unaware that there are other people in the world.

In the deep Kalahari, there are Bushmen who have never seen nor heard of civilised man.

Sometimes they hear a thundering sound when there are no clouds in the sky. They assume the gods have eaten too much and their tummies are rumbling up there. Sometimes they can even see the evidence of the gods' flatulence. Their language has an idiosyncrasy of its own. It seems to consist mainly of clicking sounds.

They're very gentle people. They'll never punish a child or even speak harshly to it. So, of course, their kids are extremely well-behaved. And their games are cute and inventive.

When the family needs meat the hunter dips his arrow in a brew that acts as a tranquilliser. So when he shoots a buck, it only feels a sting and the arrow drops out.

The buck runs away, but soon it gets drowsy and it stops running. After a while, it goes to sleep. And the hunter apologises to his prey. He explains that his family needs the meat. The one characteristic which really makes the Bushmen different from all other races on Earth is that they have no sense of ownership at all. Where they live, there's really nothing you can own. Only trees and grass and animals. In fact, these Bushmen have never seen a stone or a rock in their lives. The hardest things they know are wood and bone. They live in a gentle world, where nothing is as hard as rock or steel or concrete. Only 600 miles to the south, there's a vast city. And here you find civilised man.

Civilised man refused to adapt himself to his environment. Instead he adapted his environment to suit him. So he built cities, roads, vehicles, machinery.

And he put up power lines to run his labour-saving devices. But somehow he didn't know when to stop. The more he improved his surroundings to make life easier, the more complicated he made it. So now his children are sentenced to 10 to15 years of school, just to learn how to survive in this complex and hazardous habitat they were born into.

TOK

One of the Reflection questions asks you about your own **cultural bias.** This refers to our natural tendency to favour our own culture over the cultures of others. Think about a time you travelled abroad. How did you see other cultures through the lens of your own? Do you think colonisers were any different when voyaging to far corners of the world? What can you do to become more conscious of your own cultural bias?

2.21 After reading Text 3.20 *The Gods Must Be Crazy*, discuss your answers to these questions:

a The term **ethnography** is used by anthropologists to describe people and culture in a scientific way. To what extent is the narrator's ethnography of the Kalahari Bushmen 'scientific'? Is it possible to describe another culture or people in a scientific way?

b To what extent does *The Gods Must Be Crazy* promote the notion of 'the noble savage'?

c Compare Text 3.20 to Text 3.19. How do they use language similarly or differently to 'write about Africa'?

d How do you think Binyavanga Wainaina would respond to *The Gods Must Be Crazy*?

Further reading

- Christopher O'Reilly's *Post-Colonial Literature* is a collection of writing about the experience of the British Empire by writers from formerly colonised countries.
- *Orientalism* by Edward Said is a seminal work in its field, read by many college students of anthropology and cultural studies. It discusses the way that the West represents Asia, North Africa and the Middle East.
- *Things Fall Apart* by Chinua Achebe is a popular novel that explores the problems of colonialism.

REFLECT

Reflect on what you have learnt in this unit by discussing with your classmates your answers to these questions. Write your answers in your learner portfolio:

a In what ways have you become more conscious of your own cultural bias in this unit?

b How have the texts in this unit made you more aware of the effects of colonialism on social groups around the world?

c Are there texts in this unit that you might be able to use for your individual oral? How do these texts lend themselves well to another text that you have studied? How might you connect these texts to the global issue of colonialism?

Unit 3.3 Immigration

Learning objectives

- learn more about immigration and people's attitudes towards immigrants
- analyse a range of texts that deal with the topic of immigration and the experiences of immigrants
- write and speak about the topic of immigration.

The rise of globalisation has been accompanied by a rise in migration. People who leave their country are known as *emigrants* and people who arrive in a country are known as *immigrants*. While emigration is an interesting topic, immigration is hotly debated. Some people fear that immigrants will take their jobs, spoil their neighbourhoods or ruin their schools. These sentiments are related to the 'fear of the other' that is explored in Units 3.1 and 3.2. Other people see immigration as an opportunity to exchange knowledge, diversify cultures and build new businesses.

Before judgement is passed on immigrants, it is worth asking why they have left their homes. There is a big difference between moving voluntarily and moving involuntarily. Unfortunately, the number of asylum seekers and refugees has grown over the past decades because of war, drought, political turmoil or lack of employment opportunities.

In this unit you will analyse and explore a range of texts that deal with the issues that surround immigration, considering why people emigrate and how immigrants are viewed and discussed.

International mindedness

Internationally minded people realise that we are all immigrants in some sense, even though some people are fortunate enough to be born in prosperous nation states. Everyone deserves equal rights and decent standards of living. What are your responsibilities towards other people who are less fortunate than you, even if they are not from your country?

Getting started

3.1 Study Text 3.21, a cartoon by David Horsey, and discuss your answers to these questions:

a Why has this man built a wall?

b Why are Muslims, Mexicans and refugees not welcome within his wall?

c Why has the cartoonist created this cartoon?

d Why has David Horsey given his character beady eyes, a long nose and a cap with the letters 'USA' on? Why has he given him these speech bubbles?

e Why might this cartoon be considered humorous?

Word bank

speech bubble
situational irony
pronoun
imagery
enjambment
metaphor
personification
propaganda
fearmongering
hate speech
stock image
hyperbole
sensationalism
rhetorical question
ellipsis
teasers
weasel word
newsworthiness
negativity bias
appeal to authority
hypophora
anecdote

CAS

For CAS you are encouraged to have intercultural experiences, where you meet and collaborate with people from other cultures. You may not have to travel far to meet someone from another culture. You may find refugees, asylum seekers or immigrants close to where you live. How can you help them navigate the culture of your country? Can you get involved in projects to help them?

Text 3.21

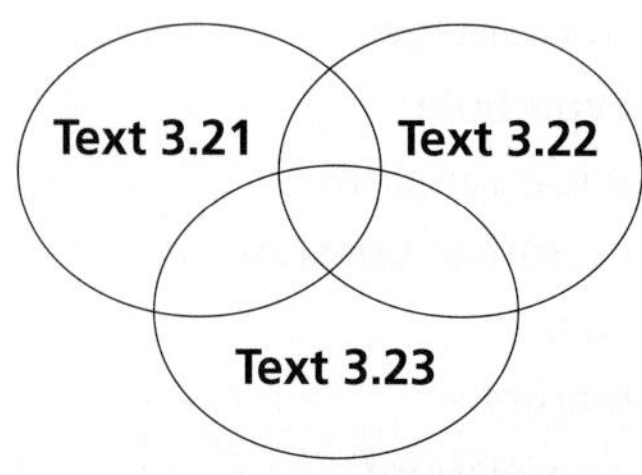

Use a three-way Venn diagram like this one to compare and contrast Texts 3.21–3.23.

3.2 Draw a very large three-way Venn diagram on a board. Each circle of the Venn diagram represents one of the texts: Text 3.21, Text 3.22 and Text 3.23. On a sticky note write a statement of analysis about one, two or all three of the texts and place it on the corresponding part of the diagram.

For example, a statement such as 'These cartoons all use walls as a symbol to represent protectionism' could go in the middle of the Venn diagram, where all three circles overlap. But another statement, such as 'These cartoons use **situational irony** to make people see the futility of walls', might go on the overlapping part between the bubbles for Text 3.21 and Text 3.22.

As a class, take turns placing sticky notes on the diagram and presenting your point to your classmates. Refer to the stylistic features and devices of cartoons and comics found in Unit 1.5.

Text 3.22

'You fellas need a job?'

Text 3.23

'A crying need for general repairs?'

3.3 Looking back on your discussion from Activities 3.1 and 3.2, make a list of 'issues surrounding immigration' as a class.

Readers, writers and texts

3.4 One person in your class (perhaps your teacher) is going to read aloud Text 3.24. While they read, close your eyes. Do not read the text. Just listen. Then open your eyes, and work on a copy of this 'See, Think, Wonder' table – a teaching and learning strategy developed by Harvard's Project Zero. Share your table with your classmates and discuss everyone's table as a class.

What do you *see*? What concrete images come to mind?	What do these images make you *think* about? What abstract ideas come from these concrete visuals?	What do these things make you *wonder*? What questions do you have about the author and the text?

AOE question

What are the different ways in which people are affected by texts?

How does Text 3.24 affect you? How does the 'See, Think, Wonder' strategy (Activity 3.4) help you to see how everyone in your class is affected in different ways? Try using this visible thinking strategy with poems and other texts.

Text 3.24

Home

Warsan Shire 2016

No one leaves home
unless home is the mouth of a shark.

You only run for the border
when you see the whole city
running as well.

Your neighbours running faster than you,
the boy you went to school with
who kissed you dizzy behind
the old tin factory
is holding a gun bigger than his body,
you only leave home
when home won't let you stay.

No one would leave home unless home
chased you, fire under feet,
hot blood in your belly.

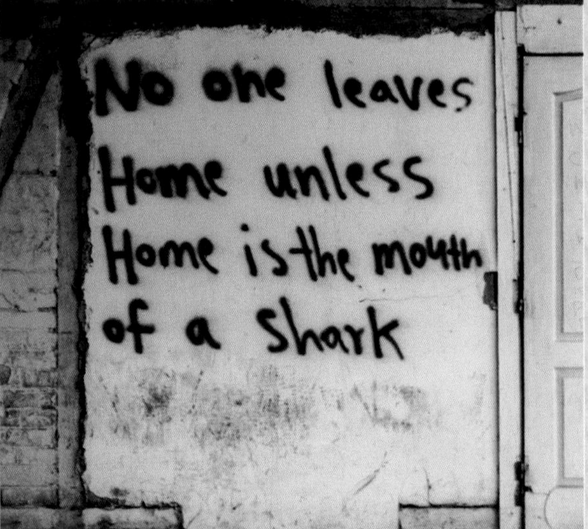

This photograph depicts the opening lines from Warsan Shire's poem Home. This line from her poem, 'home is the mouth of a shark', became a kind of battle cry for Syrian refugees. You may use an image like this or others for Activity 3.7.

It's not something you ever thought about
doing, and so when you did –
you carried the anthem under your breath,
waiting until the airport toilet
to tear up the passport and swallow –
each mouthful making it clear that
you would not be going back.

You must understand,
no one puts their children in a boat
unless the water is safer than the land.

Who would choose days and nights
in the stomach of a truck,
unless the miles travelled
meant something more than journey.

No one would choose to crawl under fences,
be beaten until your shadow leaves you
raped, then drowned, forced to the bottom of
a boat because you are darker, be sold,
starved, shot at the border like a sick animal,
be pitied, lose your name, lose your family,
make a refugee camp a home for a year or two or ten
stripped and searched, find prison everywhere
and if you survive
and you are greeted on the other side
go home blacks, refugees
dirty immigrants, asylum seekers
sucking our country dry of milk,
dark, with their hands out
smell strange, savage –
look what they've done to their own countries,
what will they do to ours?

The dirty looks in the street
feel softer than a limb torn off,
the indignity of everyday life more tender
than fourteen men who look like your father,
Between your legs. Insults easier to swallow
than rubble, than your child's body
in pieces - for now, forget about pride
your survival is more important.

I want to go home,
but home is the mouth of a shark
home is the barrel of the gun
and no one would leave home
unless home chased you to the shore
unless home tells you to
leave what you could not behind,
even if it's human.

No one leaves home until home
is a damp voice in your ear saying
leave, run now, I don't know what
I've become.

CONCEPT

Perspective

Text 3.24 offers you a *perspective* on immigration from a migrant's point of view. Warsan Shire herself was a year old when her Somali parents migrated from Kenya to the UK. How has this context given you the kind of perspective necessary to write a poem like this?

3.5 Discuss your answers to these questions about Text 3.24:

a Comment on the author's use of **pronouns**, such as 'I' and 'you'. What effect do these have on the reader and listener?

b **Imagery** is language that appeals to the senses. The author's use of imagery is most likely what instigated your discussion in Activity 3.4. How does the language of the poem appeal to your senses?

c How does the use of line breaks or **enjambment** affect your reading of the poem?

d 'Home is the mouth of a shark.' This line is repeated twice. What is the effect of repeating this metaphor? Can you find other **metaphors**? What is the effect of these on the reader?

e How does the author's use of punctuation or lack of it contribute to her message and the reader's experience?

f The poem ends with an example of **personification**, as the 'home' whispers something in the speaker's ear. What is the effect of this on the reader at the end of the poem?

3.6 Read Text 3.24 and refer back to your list of 'issues surrounding immigration' from Activity 3.3. How are some of these issues expressed and explored in this poem?

3.7 Make a collage of images and text to go with Text 3.24. Present your collage to your classmates. Why did you select these images and words?

3.8 Do an online search for the poem 'What they took with them', by Jenifer Toksvig, as performed by Cate Blanchett and other actors for the United Nations High Commissioner for Refugees (UNHCR). You could watch this online while reading a transcript of the poem. What is the effect of this poem on you? How do the actors use their voices to create an effect on the listener?

Try reading Text 3.24 aloud with a group of students in a similar way so that your audience is moved. What kinds of decisions do you have to make before reading this poem aloud?

Time and space

3.9 Read Text 3.25, a poem by Emma Lazarus. Without doing any research about it, try to work out what the text is about by discussing your answers to these questions. You can look up the meanings of words from the poem that you do not know:

a Why has the author written this text?

b For whom did she write it?

c Where would this poem be read?

d Why has she used capital letters for 'MOTHER OF EXILES'?

e What do you think of her use of diction, style and structure?

Text 3.25

The New Colossus

Emma Lazarus 1883

Not like the brazen giant of Greek fame,
With conquering limbs astride from land to land;
Here at our sea-washed, sunset gates shall stand
A mighty woman with a torch, whose flame
Is the imprisoned lightning, and her name
MOTHER OF EXILES. From her beacon-hand
Glows world-wide welcome; her mild eyes command
The air-bridged harbor that twin cities frame.

'Keep, ancient lands, your storied pomp!' cries she
With silent lips. 'Give me your tired, your poor,
Your huddled masses yearning to breathe free,
The wretched refuse of your teeming shore.
Send these, the homeless, tempest-tost to me,
I lift my lamp beside the golden door!'

3.10 Did you work out what this poem is about? It can be found at the Statue of Liberty in New York. For this next activity you will work as a class on a 'Know, Want, Learn (KWL)' table like this one. You may want to do this as an online document that everyone in the class can edit in real time.

First, for the left column, make a summary of what you already know about this poem, 'The New Colossus', based on your discussion from Activity 3.9. Then, as a class, make a list of things you want to find out about the poem. Make a list of research questions and assign everyone a different question to answer. After your research, write a list of what you have learnt.

What I already *know* about Text 3.25:	What I *want* to find out about Text 3.25:	What I *learn* about Text 3.25:

LEARNER PROFILE

Principled

An IB learner is principled. Which principles are expressed in the poem 'The New Colossus'? Are these principles that you share with the author of the poem?

3.11 Reread the poem now that you know more about it. How is your experience, reading it with this background knowledge and understanding, different from the first time you read it in Activity 3.8? How does context add to or take away from your response?

Intertextuality: connecting texts

3.12 How is Text 3.25, 'The New Colossus', similar to or different from Text 3.24 'Home'? In pairs, write some notes on a table like this one. Discuss your tables as a class.

	Similarities between Texts 3.24 and 3.25	Differences between Texts 3.24 and 3.25
Context		
Message		
Purpose		
Use of language		

Emma Lazarus's sonnet 'The New Colossus' is engraved on a plaque at the Statue of Liberty. Why is this?

AOE question

How useful is it to describe a work as 'classic'?

This question from the 'intertextuality' part of the syllabus is particularly relevant to Text 3.25, Emma Lazarus's sonnet. What makes it a classic, if it truly is one? Will Warsan Shire's poem (Text 3.24) be read over a hundred years from now? What makes you think this?

AOE question

How can the meaning of a text and its impact change over time?

Do an online search for lyrics of the song 'The Snake', as read aloud by Donald Trump during his campaign for President of the USA in 2016. It was originally written by civil rights activist Oscar Brown in 1963, based on 'The Farmer and the Viper', a fable by the Greek writer Aesop. How has Donald Trump's use of the poem changed its meaning?

3.13 Immigration is political. Text 3.26 is a billboard by the UK Independence Party (UKIP) about immigration and the Brexit referendum of 2016. Discuss your answers to these questions:

a How does this billboard use **propaganda** techniques to persuade people to vote to leave the EU?

b Why do you think this billboard was considered controversial?

c Look up the definition of **fearmongering**. Is this an example of that?

d In many countries, it is illegal to incite racial hatred. Look up the definition of 'inciting racial hatred' or '**hate speech**' and say whether you think this is an example of it.

e The photograph in the billboard was taken by a journalist who was documenting a group of Syrian refugees travelling from Slovenia to Croatia. He did not give UKIP direct permission to use this photograph for the billboard. He had made it available as a **stock image** on a popular website where advertisers and publishers can purchase photographs. The people that he photographed also did not know that their faces would appear on the UKIP billboard. Is UKIP's use of the photograph ethical? Give reasons for your answer.

Extended essay

On 23 June 2016 the UK voted in a referendum to leave the European Union (EU) (an event which came to be known as 'Brexit'). As you can see from Text 3.26, the topic of immigration played a role in persuading people to vote to leave the EU. You may want to research a series of primary sources that politicised immigration in an effort to sway voters. A good research question might read: 'To what extent did the *Sun* newspaper make the Brexit referendum about immigration in the months leading up to the vote?'

CONCEPT

Transformation

Activity 3.13 draws your attention to the fact that the UKIP billboard makes use of a stock image. This kind of *transformation* of a stock image into a billboard, awareness campaign or advertisement happens frequently. As a class, try looking at stock images to see how everyone can turn them into different kinds of text by simply adding words.

Text 3.26

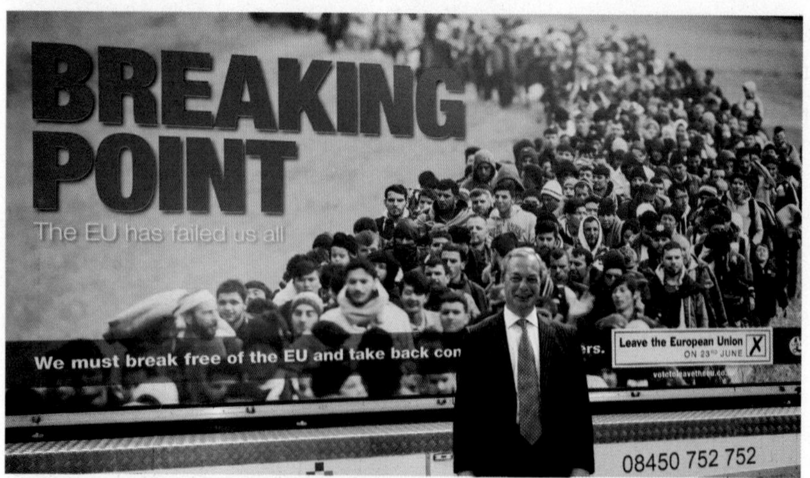

3.14 Text 3.27 includes a still from a Nazi propaganda film from the 1930s. The voice-over that accompanies this image reads: '[Refugees], who flooded Europe's cities after the last war – parasites, undermining their host countries.' Discuss your answers to these questions:

a How does Text 3.26 borrow structural features of Text 3.27, even though one is a photograph and the other a film?

b How is UKIP's message similar to or different from the Nazis' message?

c Is it fair to UKIP to make such a comparison between their billboard and the Nazi propaganda film?

Text 3.27

AOE question

How can comparing and interpreting texts transform readers?

Has seeing the image from the Nazi propaganda film changed your perception of the UKIP billboard?

3.15 How do newspapers report on migration? Study Text 3.28, from the front page of the UK newspaper the *Daily Mail*. It uses many linguistic devices that are typical of biased reporting. Look up the definitions of the terms listed here if they are not familiar to you. Find an example of each device in Text 3.28 and state why you think the newspaper chose to use such devices. What are their effects on the reader?

a **hyperbole**

b **sensationalism**

c **rhetorical question**

d **ellipsis**

e single quotation marks to suggest that something is alleged, supposed or so-called

f **teasers** in newspapers

g **weasel words**.

Text 3.28

As numbers break all records ...

MIGRANTS: HOW MANY MORE CAN WE TAKE?

By **Steve Doughty, Ian Drury** and **John Stevens**

THE true scale of the immigration crisis was laid bare last night as damning figures revealed net migration had surged to a record 330,000 – a rise of 40 per cent in one year.

It is a humiliating blow to David Cameron after his 'no ifs, no buts' pledge to reduce the number to 'tens of thousands'. Incredibly, yesterday's figures do not include illegal immigrants in the UK, estimated at 1.1 million.

The devastating statistics came as thousands of migrants yesterday flooded across the Hungarian border into central Europe. Many will now head to Calais to join those trying to sneak into Britain.

In other developments:

■ Britain's foreign-born population has passed 8 million for the first time – meaning one person in every

Turn to Page 4

COMMENT

Is David Cameron's 'ambition' to slash immigration merely hot air to be wafted around at election time?

SEE PAGE 16

Text 3.29

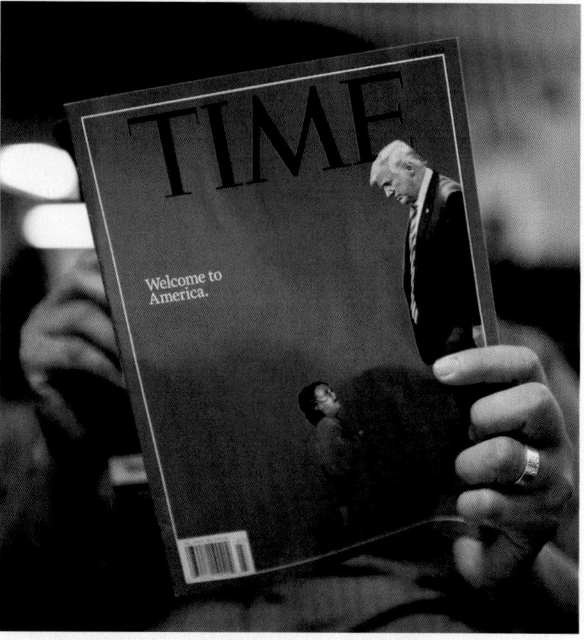

TOK

In your TOK course you learn that language is a way of knowing (WOK). How much can you learn or know from language that is ambiguous or biased? While Text 3.28 refers to numbers and facts, where do you see language that is misleading?

3.16 How is immigration depicted by news media? How are immigrants represented by the mass media? In the summer of 2018 the USA separated many immigrant children from their parents at the Mexican border and detained them. Do an online search for the *Time Magazine* cover from 2 July 2018 (Text 3.29). What can you find out about the context of this visual text? Who is the Honduran girl and how does she represent a larger group of people? How is meaning constructed in this visual text? How does contextual information affect your interpretation of it?

3.17 Which stories are deemed to have **newsworthiness** by newspapers and news magazines? There are three criteria for determining the newsworthiness of a story. For a story to appear on the front page of a newspaper or news magazine, it should meet one or more of these criteria. How does the story of the Honduran girl, as depicted in *Time Magazine* (Text 3.29), meet one or more of these criteria?

a *Extraordinary* – how special, original, unique, spectacular or extraordinary is the story?

b *Relevance* – how relevant is the story to the lives of the readers?

c *Negativity* – how bad is it? People have a bad news bias, also known as a **negativity bias**. This means that a negative story attracts our attention more than a positive story. The saying in the media world is: 'If it bleeds, it leads', meaning that death and destruction come before other stories in the presentation of the news.

3.18 The photograph of the Honduran girl at the Mexico–US border was published and went viral all over the world in June 2018. Since then, journalists and politicians have referenced or used this image for different purposes in different texts.

With your school's permission, do an online search for the 'Honduran girl border photo' to find how the story has been presented in different ways. Coordinate your search with classmates, so that you each study a unique text. These texts may be from other magazines, newspapers, websites or videos.

Present your text to your class. In your presentation, comment on the following in relation to your chosen text:

- message
- purpose
- context
- audience
- tone
- mood
- style
- structure.

3.19 Do an online search for a video called 'Most Shocking Second a Day Video' by the charity organisation Save the Children. The video uses a technique called 'role reversal', where the main character, a white British girl living in the UK, becomes a refugee.

For your learner portfolio, write a reflective statement on how this video makes you feel. Focus on your personal response and initial reaction. What makes you feel this way? In your portfolio entry, describe how this video created this effect on you. Read Unit 1.3 on film and commercials for more information on how a moving image constructs meaning.

ATL

Thinking

Comparing different versions of the same story is a good way to develop your thinking skills. Activity 3.18 asks you to explore multiple representations of the story of the Honduran girl at the Mexico–US border in various texts. Activity 3.17 asks you to think about the newsworthiness of stories in newspapers and magazines, which also requires thinking skills.

Towards assessment

3.20 In order to prepare for your individual oral, it is useful to listen to another student's response:

a How familiar are you with the requirements for the individual oral? Read Chapter 8 to gain a better understanding of global issues, outlines and the individual oral. You can find the assessment criteria for the individual oral in the introduction of this coursebook.

b Study Text 3.30, a three-image poster titled 'We the People', and reread Text 3.24, the poem called 'Home'. As a class, discuss how you would prepare an individual oral on these two texts and 'immigration' as a global issue. Collectively, make a one-page outline that would support an effective individual oral on this issue.

c Read the sample individual oral. The outline for this oral has not been provided here. As a class, try to recreate the outline that the student would have used to deliver this oral.

d Compare the outline that you recreated for the sample student oral (in step c) to the one that you had previously made as a class (in step b). Where do you see similarities and differences? How would the student have benefitted from your outline? How would your outline have benefitted from the student's ideas?

e Give this individual oral marks on all four criteria, which you can find in the introduction of this coursebook. Take both the 10-minute presentation and the 5-minute follow-up discussion into consideration. Compare your marks and comments with those of the teacher, provided after the transcript.

Text 3.30

Individual oral – Sample 1

Global issue

Immigration

Transcript

In your introduction you should define your global issue and put your texts into context.

Student: For this individual oral I'll be analysing two texts in relation to the global issue of immigration. The first text is called 'We the People'. It's a famous poster by Shepard Fairey from 2017. The second text is a poem called 'Home' by Warsan Shire, which is from a similar time in history, 2016. During this time, immigration and fear of immigrants were big issues around the world. They played a big role in determining the Brexit vote and the US Presidential vote for Donald Trump. I selected these texts because they're so different. Not only are they very different text types, but they also look at different aspects of immigration. While 'We the People' uses allusion, colour and symbolism to argue that America should be open-minded, 'Home' uses repetition and imagery to make readers understand why immigrants immigrate in the first place.

This thesis statement treats the two texts separately, which is fine. You do not have to compare and contrast in your individual oral.

Use signposting like this throughout your individual oral, to make the structure clear.

I'm going to start with the 'We the People' text, and I'd like to show how these three devices, symbolism, colour and allusion, all make viewers think more about what makes America 'America'. It's a country of immigrants, of course, and this text reminds people of just that. The woman depicted in this image is a Muslim woman with a headscarf, which is made from the American flag. Below her, it reads 'We the People', the first words of the US constitution. And below that is the phrase 'are greater than fear'. This poster is Shepard Fairey's political message, that America should welcome immigrants and it should not let fear of the other dictate American politics.

You may want to explore a visual text in your individual oral. Be sure to comment on the use of colour, symbols and the other features of visual texts. See Unit 1.1 for further support on analysing different types of visual text.

First of all, this meaning can be derived from the use of colour. The reds and blues are probably the first thing the viewer notices when they see this image, and most people in the USA would recognise them as the colours from Obama's 'Hope' poster from 2008, which was also created by Shepard Fairey. This 'We the People' poster borrows all of the same structural elements from the 'Hope' poster. Back then he created a two-tone, stylised photo of Obama so as to make him look really iconic. Obama had once said that there were no red states or blue states but the 'United States' of America. So just to explain how the 'Hope' poster worked: red stood for the Republican Party, and blue stood for the Democratic Party. By including both red and blue in equal amounts, the 'Hope' poster pitched Obama as the moderate candidate. So now, by using the same red and blue colour scheme here in this 'We the People' ad – I mean poster – Fairey is calling for more moderation in the debate on immigration. It's like he's reminding everyone of the hope that was promised during the Obama era. He's saying that they should still be hopeful and balanced in this debate on whether America should allow more immigrants, especially from Muslim countries.

Besides using reds and blues, Fairey uses the symbol of the American flag and the symbol of the headscarf. In fact he conflates them into one thing, which is precisely what makes the image so controversial. In America, Muslims are, unfortunately, sometimes associated with terrorism. But, it's exactly this line of reasoning that Shepard Fairey is trying to challenge by creating this poster. He is saying that it *is* possible, in a country of immigrants, for Muslims to be pro-American. And it *is* possible for America to be pro-Muslim. The American flag wrapped around her head as a headscarf communicates this message very succinctly. It conflates two symbols into one: the flag, of course, representing freedom and the USA, and the headscarf representing Islam.

This leads up to the last thing that I want to say about this poster, before I move on to the poem. It alludes to the first words of the US Constitution, which reads: 'We the People'. Most Americans will recognise this immediately. And most Americans will know that these words were chosen as the opening of the Constitution by the founding fathers as a way of showing how the citizens of this new country were united against British rule. The phrase, 'We the People', for most Americans, stands for independence, freedom, democracy and justice. So, to pair this phrase with the Muslim woman, wearing the headscarf, shows that she too could and should be included in the American dream. It was and still is a country of immigrants, after all. The poster is saying that America has a duty or responsibility to accept her as one of its citizens.

The second phrase 'are greater than fear' is not taken from the US Constitution. In fact, it's a surprising twist for the reader. It makes the reader wonder if 'fear' is driving American politics during and after the Trump elections. At this time there was a lot of fear in America: fear of Muslims, fear of immigrants and fear of the other. This was being used to manipulate people and the way they voted. But by saying that 'we the people' of the United States are 'greater' than fear, Fairey is saying, once again, that there is hope for them not to be manipulated by politicians and fear mongers.

So, to conclude this part of my individual oral, it's clear that Shepard Fairey is challenging the fear and bigotry in American politics by creating this poster. He does this by alluding to the US Constitution and the Obama poster. And he uses the two symbols of the American flag and the headscarf in one. And he uses the reds and blues from the iconic 'Hope' poster. All in all, these features construct a message that says America should accept Muslims and immigrants from Muslim countries as Americans and not be afraid of them.

The second text that I'd like to analyse is the first 40 lines from the poem called 'Home' by Warsan Shire. She is the daughter of Somalian immigrants. She was born in Kenya and moved at the age of one to the UK with her parents. This poem, like a lot of her poetry, is inspired by the lives of people she's close to, like her parents. Although she's never been to Somalia, she has talked to many refugees and immigrants from there. Her poem uses repetition and imagery to make readers empathise with immigrants and understand the hardships that they have had to endure.

When preparing your oral, think about the kinds of verbs you will use to describe the author's purpose.

Remember to use inflection and emphasis in your voice when delivering your individual oral.

TIP

Notice that this individual oral is on a poem, **'Home'**, that would not fit onto one page in its entirety. Your extract from one of your literary works should be roughly 40 lines. For this reason, the student only refers to the first 40 lines of the poem.

This student refers frequently to the reader and the viewer. This is good practice and will help to gain a good score on Criterion B.

The use of phrases such as 'all in all' or 'to conclude' are effective in giving the teacher and moderator a sense of organisation.

The title of the poem, 'Home', is repeated throughout the poem as a kind of anchor point. You could even say it's the point of reference, which she keeps returning to, like a home. But this 'home' is not something one would want to return to. Instead, it is the kind of 'home' that she has to explain or describe to anti-immigrant people who keep telling her to go back home. 'Home' is repeated most frequently in the verse that reads: 'home is the mouth of a shark', This is a metaphor, which makes you think of refugees in a boat being chased by a shark. 'Home' is scary and threatening and dangerous. Her use of the word changes the whole meaning of the word for the reader. For the reader, the word 'home' probably has warm connotations. But this poem makes them realise that if 'home' is a scary monster, then risking everything to make it to a developed Western country is one's only choice.

While you should avoid sounding repetitive, it is important to have a few key words to use during your individual oral. The student uses the word 'hardships' effectively throughout this part of the oral.

Make sure you have quotes to support the points you want to make. You can then make quick and effective reference to the text.

The other word that is repeated very frequently is 'no one'. It serves a purpose to make the reader realise that refugees are just like 'every one', including the reader herself. Throughout the poem, it is emphasised that 'no one' would endure these hardships of running away 'unless the miles travelled meant something more than journey', as the poem states in lines 28–29. 'No one', she states in lines 24 to 36, wants to spend 'days and nights in the stomach of a truck' or put 'their children in a boat' or be 'sold' or 'crawl under fences' or 'be beaten' or 'choose refugee camps'. The repetition of 'no one' in combination with these hardships stresses to the reader that refugees do not have a choice. Readers realise, through the use of this repetition, that refugees are just like everyone. They make the same choices that the reader would make if they were put into such dangerous situations.

This section is rather confusing because the student changes focus from imagery to figurative language to pronouns, to hyperbole. It is more effective to focus on one literary device at a time.

Besides the use of repetition, the author uses a lot of imagery and figurative language to make readers empathise with refugees. This imagery is paired with the second-person pronoun 'you' quite frequently, so that the reader can imagine what it is like to be in the refugee's shoes. For example, lines 3–11 paint a picture in the mind of the reader as she says: 'you only run for the border / when you see the whole city / running as well / Your neighbours running faster than you / the boy you went to school with / who kissed you dizzy / behind the old tin factory / is holding a gun bigger than his body'. This use of language and hyperbole appeal to the reader's visual senses, as you imagine a flood of people running away from an angry teenage boy with a giant gun. And, curiously, he's the same boy that 'you' once kissed behind an old factory.

Finish your oral by relating your text back to the global issue.

There are, of course, more examples of imagery in this poem, but I see I'm running out of time. So, to wrap it up: Warsan Shire uses both imagery and repetition to explain to her reader why refugees run away from home and endure hardships. This poem, hopefully, makes readers empathise with immigrants and refugees more.

Teacher: OK, that was great, thanks. I think you've chosen two interesting texts to discuss here. You're right: immigration is a very topical discussion. Let's talk about the first text, the one with the American flag as a headscarf. You said that America was a country of immigrants and you suggested that she was an immigrant. Where, in this poster, do you see that she is an immigrant?

Student: Well, that's a good question. I suppose you don't see that she's an immigrant at first sight. But this poster is from a series of posters that came out around the same time that Trump was running for president. And the other two showed an African American girl and a Latino woman. I think the point was that they were not pictures of angry white men. It was at a time when Trump was wearing his 'Make America Great Again' hat and people were turning to nationalism. These Shepard Fairey posters were a contrast to that. They were more about internationalism and open-mindedness. I think he was trying to make a statement about all of the anti-immigrant talk that was going on at the time.

Teacher: Ah, that's interesting. So it's more about diversity really than immigration.

Student: Yeah, I guess.

Teacher: No, that's OK. It's just interesting to see that they're connected.

Student: I guess that, because, you know, you see so many refugees leaving Islamic countries, like Syria, you kind of assume that she must have left an Islamic country too. And she is now in America and wants to be accepted there as a citizen. So this may be why she wears the headscarf. And I did a little research on this. And there are not that many Muslims living in the United States. It's only like 1% of the population. So this poster makes a big statement. By picturing her in the flag, it's like saying she has as much say as every other minority in the States.

Teacher: Yes, it is. It ties in nicely to what you said about democracy earlier.

Student: Yeah, I think that's emphasised especially through the phrase 'We the People'. It's an allusion to the Constitution and it suggests that Americans have equal rights.

Teacher: Yes, that's interesting. And it makes sense, especially if it appeared alongside two other posters of minority groups, like you said. But before you go, I'd like to ask a few questions about the poem too.

Student: Sure.

Teacher: You said that repetition was used throughout the poem to make the reader experience the immigrant's 'hardships'. As a reader, can you comment more on your experience reading the poem? How did it make you feel when you first read it? Or how did you feel when we listened to someone reading it in class?

Student: Well, I mean, it's a very emotional poem. When I first heard it, I thought: Wow! Heavy. It hit me, you know. Like I was being punched hard.

Teacher: And why do you think that was?

Student: It's the language, I guess. It just sounds harsh and not very poetic or lyrical. Words like 'refugee camps' have a really rough sound, I suppose. 'Refugee camps!' You don't hear that in a poem every day.

Teacher: No, I don't imagine you do.

Student: But it's also the imagery, you know. You can almost see the immigrant crawling under a fence. Or you can imagine this immigrant tearing up a passport in a bathroom stall at the airport and then trying to swallow the hard paper. It feels awful and horrible. That's why it hits you so hard, I think. It's the tone of the poem and the imagery.

TIP

Notice how the student relates the poster to other posters by the same author (Shepard Fairey). Unfortunately, the poem was not related to other poems by the same poet (Warsan Shire). Be sure to relate your extracts to other texts from the same 'body of work' when analysing them in your individual oral.

Teacher: Oh, I'd love to talk more about the tone of the poem, but I see it's time. Is there anything else you'd like to add?

Student: No, that's it. I think I said it all anyway. It was a good activity. I liked it.

Teacher: OK, good. Thanks for that.

Student: Thank you.

Individual oral – Sample 1 – Teacher's marks and comments

Criterion A: Knowledge, understanding and interpretation: 8 out of 10 marks

There is good knowledge of the contexts of both texts. References to the Brexit vote and the Trump vote help give the texts meaning. While interpretations are not consistently relevant to the global issue of 'immigration', they are insightful and effective. There are frequent and appropriate references to the source texts throughout the oral.

Criterion B: Analysis and evaluation: 8 out of 10 marks

The oral clearly focuses on how meaning is constructed through language. The student's analysis of the texts is stronger than their evaluation of the texts, meaning that their effectiveness in commenting on immigration is not always explored in depth. Comments on layout, structure and colour, in relation to the poster, are especially insightful.

Criterion C: Coherence, focus and organisation: 8 out of 10 marks

There is a clear thesis statement and sense of organisation. At times, the oral seems to wander off topic, such as the example about the Obama poster. Nevertheless, it regains focus quickly. The analysis of the poem is not as thorough as the analysis of the poster. It feels rushed when the student explores a list of quotations and stylistic devices.

Criterion D: Language: 9 out of 10 marks

The language is fluent, proficient, appropriate and accurate. At times, simplistic language slips into the oral, such as 'Wow! Heavy. It hit me, you know. Like I was being punched hard.' This happens more in the dialogue than in the presentation part of the oral. For the most part, however, the use of language is very effective in delivering the student's message.

3.21 In preparation for Paper 2, you may or may not be reading literary works about immigration. In either case, you may find one of these four questions a useful stimulus for Paper 2 practice:

a In what ways and for what purposes does the notion 'journey' play a role in two works that you have read?

b Authors often depict characters who happen to be in the wrong place at the wrong time. With respect to two works that you have read, explain how and why such depictions have been made.

c 'Fear of the other' is a common theme in literary works. In what ways and for what reasons is this theme explored in two works that you have read?

d It has often been said that literature is a voice for the oppressed. Explain how this is relevant in two works that you have read.

Higher level extension

3.22 Most of the texts in this unit share the same purpose of creating sympathy for the plight of refugees and asylum seekers. But what about the anti-immigration perspective? As a class, list arguments against open borders and open immigration policies.

3.23 Read Text 3.31, a famous speech made by the British Conservative politician Enoch Powell in 1968. How does he use language to express ideas a–j? For each idea, explain why the author uses these words and phrases. Find examples from the text to support your answers:

- **a** He realises that his message may not be considered politically correct.
- **b** He has a responsibility to represent his constituency.
- **c** He is not fabricating untrue stories.
- **d** Immigrants will not live in all communities in equal numbers.
- **e** Parliament can improve the prospects for the future by changing immigration laws in the present.
- **f** Parliament should not allow any more immigrants to enter the country and should dismiss or deport existing immigrants.
- **g** A small group of immigrants has had an adverse effect on the entire population.
- **h** The immigrants should be happy that they have a job, rather than complain about their rights to practise their customs.
- **i** The legislation suggested by Parliament will only enable the immigrants to organise themselves better and dominate the British population.
- **j** Powell believes it is his duty to express his observations.

Text 3.31

The Birmingham Speech

Abridged extract

Enoch Powell 1968

A week or two ago I fell into conversation with a constituent, a middle-aged, quite ordinary working man employed in one of our nationalised industries.

After a sentence or two about the weather, he suddenly said: 'If I had the money to go, I wouldn't stay in this country.' I made some deprecatory reply to the effect that even this government wouldn't last for ever; but he took no notice, and continued: 'I have three children, all of them been through grammar school and two of them married now, with family. I shan't be satisfied till I have seen them all settled overseas. In this country in 15 or 20 years' time the black man will have the whip hand over the white man.'

I can already hear the chorus of execration. How dare I say such a horrible thing? How dare I stir up trouble and inflame feelings by repeating such a conversation?

The answer is that I do not have the right not to do so. Here is a decent, ordinary fellow Englishman, who in broad daylight in my own town says to me, his Member of Parliament, that his country will not be worth living in for his children.

Conservative Member of Parliament Enoch Powell in 1968.

I simply do not have the right to shrug my shoulders and think about something else. What he is saying, thousands and hundreds of thousands are saying and thinking – not throughout Great Britain, perhaps, but in the areas that are already undergoing the total transformation to which there is no parallel in a thousand years of English history.

In 15 or 20 years, on present trends, there will be in this country three and a half million Commonwealth immigrants and their descendants. That is not my figure. That is the official figure given to parliament by the spokesman of the Registrar General's Office.

There is no comparable official figure for the year 2000, but it must be in the region of five to seven million, approximately one-tenth of the whole population, and approaching that of Greater London. Of course, it will not be evenly distributed from Margate to Aberystwyth and from Penzance to Aberdeen. Whole areas, towns and parts of towns across England will be occupied by sections of the immigrant and immigrant-descended population.

As time goes on, the proportion of this total who are immigrant descendants, those born in England, who arrived here by exactly the same route as the rest of us, will rapidly increase. Already by 1985 the native-born would constitute the majority. It is this fact which creates the extreme urgency of action now, of just that kind of action which is hardest for politicians to take, action where the difficulties lie in the present but the evils to be prevented or minimised lie several parliaments ahead.

The natural and rational first question with a nation confronted by such a prospect is to ask: 'How can its dimensions be reduced?' Granted it be not wholly preventable, can it be limited, bearing in mind that numbers are of the essence: the significance and consequences of an alien element introduced into a country or population are profoundly different according to whether that element is 1 per cent or 10 per cent.

The answers to the simple and rational question are equally simple and rational: by stopping, or virtually stopping, further inflow, and by promoting the maximum outflow. Both answers are part of the official policy of the Conservative Party. [. . .]

Now we are seeing the growth of positive forces acting against integration, of vested interests in the preservation and sharpening of racial and religious differences, with a view to the exercise of actual domination, first over fellow-immigrants and then over the rest of the population. The cloud no bigger than a man's hand, that can so rapidly overcast the sky, has been visible recently in Wolverhampton and has shown signs of spreading quickly. The words I am about to use, verbatim as they appeared in the local press on 17 February, are not mine, but those of a Labour Member of Parliament who is a minister in the present government:

'The Sikh communities' campaign to maintain customs inappropriate in Britain is much to be regretted. Working in Britain, particularly in the public services, they should be prepared to accept the terms and conditions of their employment. To claim special communal rights (or should one say rites?) leads to a dangerous fragmentation within society. This communalism is a canker; whether practised by one colour or another it is to be strongly condemned.'

All credit to John Stonehouse for having had the insight to perceive that, and the courage to say it.

For these dangerous and divisive elements the legislation proposed in the Race Relations Bill is the very pabulum they need to flourish. Here is the means of showing that the immigrant communities can organise to consolidate their members, to agitate and campaign against their fellow citizens, and to overawe and dominate the rest with the legal weapons which the ignorant and the ill-informed have provided. As I look ahead, I am filled with foreboding; like the Roman, I seem to see 'the River Tiber foaming with much blood'.

That tragic and intractable phenomenon which we watch with horror on the other side of the Atlantic but which there is interwoven with the history and existence of the States itself, is coming upon us here by our own volition and our own neglect. Indeed, it has all but come. In numerical terms, it will be of American proportions long before the end of the century.

Only resolute and urgent action will avert it even now. Whether there will be the public will to demand and obtain that action, I do not know. All I know is that to see, and not to speak, would be the great betrayal.

3.24 Where in Text 3.31 do you see examples of these stylistic and rhetorical devices? Why do you think Powell used each of these devices? What are the effects of each device on the audience? You may need to look up the meanings of devices that you do not already know.

a **appeal to authority** b **hypophora** c simile d **anecdote**

e allusion f imagery g play on words.

3.25 Return to your list of arguments used against immigration from Activity 3.22. Does Enoch Powell voice any of these in his speech (Text 3.31)?

3.26 Were Enoch Powell's predictions about immigration accurate?

a Research the number of children currently born to foreign parents in the UK.

b Research the present number of foreign-born population living in the UK.

c Can you find out more about the distribution of these people across the UK? How equal or unequal is this?

d How do these numbers compare to the numbers of foreign-born people living in other Anglophone countries such as Australia or Canada?

e In your opinion, were Enoch Powell's fears justified? What kind of questions do you need to ask in order to find out whether Powell's comments were accurate and justified?

3.27 Find two or three students in your class to volunteer to perform a reading of Text 3.32, 'Telephone Conversation' by Wole Soyinka. One person can be the landlady and the other two can divide up part of the narration and dialogue. Highlight the lines in three different colours if necessary. Then the rest of the class can interview the performers, asking them to explain how they prepared their performance and what decisions they had to make when performing the poem.

Extended essay

Activity 3.26 asks you to research secondary sources on immigration that would be relevant to a primary source, Text 3.31. This may be a stepping-stone for a Category 3 extended essay that compares the speeches of Enoch Powell and another politician, such as Nigel Farage. A good research question might be: 'To what extent does the language of British politicians Enoch Powell and Nigel Farage rely on fearmongering to advance their political position?'

Text 3.32

Do an online search for 'Telephone Conversation' by Wole Soyinka.

LEARNER PROFILE

Look back at the units in this chapter, on racism, colonialism and immigration. Select *one* of the ten traits from the IB learner profile and say how you have worked directly or indirectly on developing it while working through these units. Remember, an IB learner is: knowledgeable, caring, principled, balanced, reflective and open-minded. An IB learner is a thinker, inquirer, communicator and risk taker.

CONCEPT

Identity

How does Wole Soyinka express *identity* in his poem? What kind of person is the narrator, based on your analysis of this poem?

3.28 Look at the key terms in the word banks at the beginning of the three units in this chapter. Find one term that you find particularly applicable to Text 3.32. Prepare a short explanation of how your key term is relevant to the poem. Everyone in the class should have a chance to present. When it is your turn to present, be sure to refer to the text. Comment on how language is used to construct meaning. Describe the effects of the language on the reader.

3.29 Go to genius.com and search for 'Telephone Conversation' by Wole Soyinka. Read the annotations on this poem, line for line. Were there ideas and analyses that you did not already notice as a class in Activities 3.27 and 3.28? What have you learnt from this website?

Further reading

- *House of Sand and Fog* by Andre Dubus III tells the story of an Iranian immigrant family, living in California.
- *The Arrival* by Shaun Tan is a graphic novel without words. It lends itself well to critical analysis of images and visual narration. As a creative writing assignment, you could add captions to each page.
- *Persepolis* by Marjane Satrapi is a popular graphic novel, originally written in French, that tells the author's story of growing up during the Iran–Iraq war in the 1980s before emigrating to Austria.
- Rodolfo Gonzales's epic poem 'I am Joaquin' captures the sentiments of a Mexican immigrant in the USA.
- 'Land of the Free' by The Killers has an interesting music video, directed by Spike Lee, which can be found online. It depicts life on the border between Mexico and the USA. This visual text, together with the lyrics, is rich material for an HL essay.

REFLECT

In this unit you have explored immigration and the language used by poets, photographers, journalists and cartoonists to discuss this issue. Look back at the range of texts that you studied.

- Which text or texts did you find most interesting? Explain your reasons to your classmates.
- Might you consider using one or more of these texts to prepare your individual oral?
- What do you need to add to your learner portfolio before you feel confident talking about a literary and non-literary text on immigration as a global issue?

Chapter 4

Politics, power and justice

How do politicians and poets write about war?
How do people use language to protest social inequality?
How is language used in election campaigns, public speeches and signs to promote political ideas?

In this chapter you will:

- analyse how language is used for various purposes, such as campaigning for political office, warmongering or protesting in the streets
- discuss the representation and misrepresentation of politicians and political ideas through various media
- analyse the use of rhetorical devices and argumentation fallacies by politicians.

Unit 4.1 War

Word bank

propaganda
assertion
false dichotomy
name calling
appeal to fear
glittering generalities
appeal to authority
argumentation fallacy
disinformation
hindsight bias
war mongering
mood
atmosphere
euphemism
ambient advertising
mural
sonnet
iambic pentameter
onomatopoeia
allusion
cacophony
censorship

Learning objectives

- study a broad range of text types, comparing their stylistic and structural elements
- explore different contexts of war, from the trenches of the First World War to Sierra Leone, from Iraq to the Middle East
- develop your skills of textual analysis and your ability to articulate your analyses.

How do we talk about war? Literally, what kind of language do we use to recruit soldiers, describe bombings, discuss death or label terrorists? War could not be waged or understood without language.

This unit includes a broad range of texts that deal with the topic of war in different ways. You will find propaganda posters, a speech, a photograph, a piece of street art, an advertisement, a mural, a passage from a memoir and a poem. The language of these primary sources is brought to you by journalists, soldiers, politicians, advertisers, artists and protesters. They are real people who care about the fate of humanity and have constructed these texts to persuade and inform a broader public about their cause.

Throughout the unit, you are encouraged to think critically about the texts and their contexts, and the lessons that can be learnt from them.

International mindedness

How much do you know about wars that are going on in the world right now? Reading about military conflict from news sources will give you more insight into international relations, and better understanding of them. Internationally minded people understand the importance of diplomacy over military action.

Getting started

1.1 Discuss your answers to these questions:

a Do you know anyone who has fought in a war or has been affected by war? What do their experiences tell you about the nature of war?

b Can a war ever be 'just'? If so, can you give an example of a 'just' war in recent times or the past?

c Do you know of any active war zones today? Why did these wars start?

d Is there more or less war and military violence in the world than there was 50 or 100 years ago? Why do you think this?

e Will there ever be a time in the future when there is no more war? Why do you think this?

1.2 Study Texts 4.1–4.4, four **propaganda** posters whose purpose was to recruit soldiers to fight in the First World War. Discuss your answers to these questions:

a What kind of techniques are used in these posters to persuade young men to enlist in the military? Besides referring to any propaganda techniques that you know of, refer to the use of colour, symbolism, font, language and artistic style.

b How do you think young men at this time responded to these stylistic and propaganda techniques?

c How are young men and women recruited to fight in wars today? What media are used? How do these techniques compare to those of 1915?

d Posters from the First and Second World Wars are easy to find online. Search for one that you find particularly interesting and give a short presentation on it. Comment on how it uses various propaganda techniques and stylistic devices to achieve a particular purpose.

Text 4.1

British poster from 1915.

Text 4.2

Australian poster from 1915.

Text 4.3

Canadian poster from 1915.

Text 4.4

This British poster taps into the public outrage after the RMS *Lusitania* was torpedoed by a German U-boat in 1915.

1.3 What is propaganda? Can you define this term in your own words? Write your definition on a sticky note and place it on a wall for all of your classmates to see. How is your definition different from or similar to your classmates' definitions? Look up a definition online. How are your class's definitions different from those found online?

Readers, writers and texts

1.4 Here are the definitions of several propaganda techniques. Can you find an example of each technique in Text 4.5, an extract from a speech made by US President George W. Bush in 2003, before the USA invaded Iraq? Several techniques may be relevant to single phrases or lines from the speech.

a **Assertion** – a bold statement or claim presented as truth, and it cannot be questioned. It is to be taken on the speaker's authority, and is not open for discussion.

b **False dichotomy** – when you are presented with only two solutions to a problem. In an effort to convince you that one solution is better, you are faced with a false dilemma. In reality there may be more solutions.

c **Name calling** – labelling people or calling your enemy names is a way of simplifying matters and rallying support against someone or a group of people.

d **Appeal to fear** – trying to persuade people by appealing to their fears.

e **Glittering generalities** – some ideals and values, such as justice, freedom or democracy, are difficult to argue against. Speakers sometimes use glittering generalities to establish broad agreement.

f **Appeal to authority** – some people assume that people in power are inherently right. An appeal to authority can convince people to listen to their leaders, just because they are the leaders.

TOK

Many propaganda techniques are versions of **argumentation fallacies.** An argumentation fallacy is an argument which is not valid, because the truth of its conclusion does not rest on the truth of its premises.

ATL

Thinking skills

Critical thinkers can distinguish an invalid argument from a valid one. Learning to identify argumentation fallacies and propaganda techniques will help you become a more empowered citizen and critical thinker.

Extended essay

Text 4.5 raises an interesting point about war and propaganda, which could be explored further in a Category 3 extended essay: 'To what extent did the rhetoric of George W. Bush and Fox News convince Americans that an invasion of Iraq was a suitable response to the terrorist attacks of 9 September 2001?' There is certainly evidence that the American public was misled in 2003 through argumentation fallacies and **disinformation**.

Text 4.5

The State of the Union Address

Abridged extract

George W. Bush 2003

George W. Bush calling for a war in Iraq in his 2003 State of the Union Address.

Mr Speaker, Vice President Cheney, members of Congress, distinguished citizens and fellow citizens: every year, by law and by custom, we meet here to consider the state of the union. This year, we gather in this chamber deeply aware of decisive days that lie ahead.

You and I serve our country in a time of great consequence. During this session of Congress, we have the duty to reform domestic programs vital to our country; we have the opportunity to save millions of lives abroad from a terrible disease. We will work for a prosperity that is broadly shared, and we will answer every danger and every enemy that threatens the American people.

In all these days of promise and days of reckoning, we can be confident. In a whirlwind of change and hope and peril, our faith is sure, our resolve is firm, and our union is strong.

This country has many challenges. We will not deny, we will not ignore, we will not pass along our problems to other Congresses, to other presidents, and other generations.

We will confront them with focus and clarity and courage. [. . .]

There are days when our fellow citizens do not hear news about the war on terror. There's never a day when I do not learn of another threat, or receive reports of operations in progress, or give an order in this global war against a scattered network of killers. The war goes on, and we are winning. [. . .]

We have the terrorists on the run. We're keeping them on the run. One by one, the terrorists are learning the meaning of American justice. [. . .]

Our war against terror is a contest of will in which perseverance is power. In the ruins of two towers, at the western wall of the Pentagon, on a field in Pennsylvania, this nation made a pledge, and we renew that pledge tonight: whatever the duration of this struggle, and whatever the difficulties, we will not permit the triumph of violence in the affairs of men – free people will set the course of history.

Today, the gravest danger in the war on terror, the gravest danger facing America and the world, is outlaw regimes that seek and possess nuclear, chemical, and biological weapons. These regimes could use such weapons for blackmail, terror, and mass murder. They could also give or sell those weapons to terrorist allies, who would use them without the least hesitation. [. . .]

1.5 Do an online search for a video recording of George W. Bush's 2003 State of the Union Address. Watch specifically the part on which Text 4.5 is based. Discuss your answers to these questions:

a How does his audience in the House of Congress seem to receive his speech?

b Do you find his speech persuasive or convincing? What makes you say this?

c What words or phrases strike you as the most important in constructing George W. Bush's message?

d Read the first few paragraphs of the Wikipedia page on the Iraq War. How does this change your understanding of Bush's speech?

TOK

Activity 1.5 asks you to research the Iraq War in order to critique George W. Bush's speech. When historians analyse primary sources, they have to be careful of **hindsight bias,** also known as the 'knew-it-all-along' effect. In the light of what you know about the current state of Iraq, Syria and the Middle East, it is easy to dismiss Bush's speech as **war-mongering**. Remember, however, the context of 9/11, the terrorist attack on the USA in 2001, and take this into consideration when analysing his speech.

CONCEPT

Perspective

The choice of words by George W. Bush in Text 4.5 says a lot about his *perspective*. One person's 'terrorist' may be another person's 'freedom fighter'. One person's 'government' may be another person's 'regime'. Another person's 'war' may be someone else's 'conflict'. As you discuss the language of war, keep in mind that every battle has two sides and thus two different perspectives and two different uses of language.

1.6 Analysing a photograph is very different from analysing a speech (Text 4.5) or propaganda posters (Texts 4.1–4.4). Study Text 4.6 and create a list of five words that describe the **mood** of the photograph. Remember, 'mood' describes the **atmosphere** of the text as created by the author (or, in this case, photographer).

After you have created your list of mood words, read them out to your classmates. Then, one classmate will ask you about one of the words from your list. The kinds of questions you may ask your classmates include:

- 'What made you use that word?'
- 'Why did you say that?'
- 'How did the photographer give you that impression?'

Give everyone a chance to explain one mood word from his or her list.

Text 4.6

AOE question

How can texts present challenges and offer insights?

Make a short list of insights and another list of challenges in response to Text 4.6. Study the photograph carefully. Use the word 'challenges' to refer to anything which you do not understand about the photograph.

1.7 Activity 1.6 helps you to understand the kinds of techniques and devices that photographers use to construct meaning. As a class, make a list of 'aspects that photographers consider when taking photographs'.

1.8 Imagine that Text 4.6 hung in a gallery for the general public to view. Write a caption that explains to the viewer what they are looking at. This caption or description should be about 100–150 words long. You need not know the exact context to do this assignment. Make up the caption using your imagination and your own interpretation of the photograph. Compare your caption to those of your classmates.

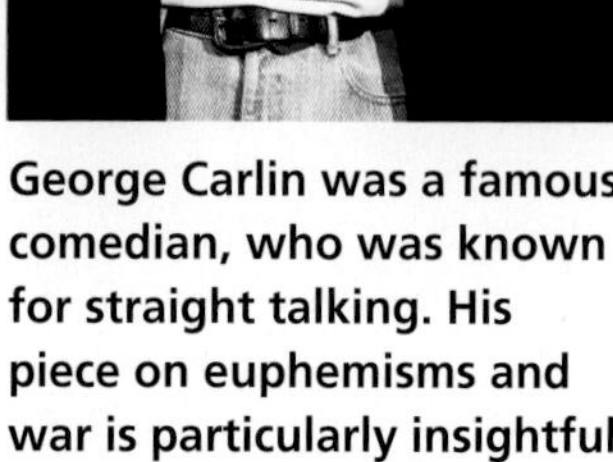

George Carlin was a famous comedian, who was known for straight talking. His piece on euphemisms and war is particularly insightful.

1.9 Do an online search for 'George Carlin' and '**euphemisms**'. Euphemisms are words that make ideas or things sound more acceptable than they really are. They are especially relevant during wartime. Watch George Carlin's act and then discuss what you think these war-related euphemisms *really* mean. Then look up their meanings through an online search:

- collateral damage
- enhanced interrogation techniques
- soft targets
- surgical strikes
- campaign
- protective custody
- conflict
- boots on the ground
- pacification
- enemy noncombatant
- neutralise
- regime change.

1.10 An author's message and purpose are connected. An author's *message* is a kind of statement or claim. This reflects the author's *purpose* of communicating to an audience. The author's *technique* is the way in which this message is constructed. These three aspects (message, purpose and technique) correlate to the 'why', 'what' and 'how' of communication theory.

Here is an example of message, purpose and technique for Text 4.7, a piece of street art made by Banksy in Israel in 2007.

Message (what)	Purpose (why)	Technique (how)
In Text 4.7, Banksy claims that Israeli soldiers' unwarranted frisking of Palestinians is a violation of their rights.	Banksy aims to make Israelis more conscious of their abuse of military dominance over Palestinians.	He achieves this by depicting an innocent girl frisking an Israeli soldier, a strange reversal of power roles.

a As a class, do an online search for more Banksy art from the Middle East from 2007, and select one. In groups of two, analyse your piece of street art using the 'message, purpose, technique' method. Be sure that each pair of students in your class is working on a different piece of street art from Banksy's trip to the Middle East in 2007.

b Prepare a short presentation of your work to your classmates, making sure that it is informed by research on the conflict between Israelis and Palestinians in Gaza and the West Bank (Palestinian Territories). This will help you understand the artist's purpose and message.

Text 4.7

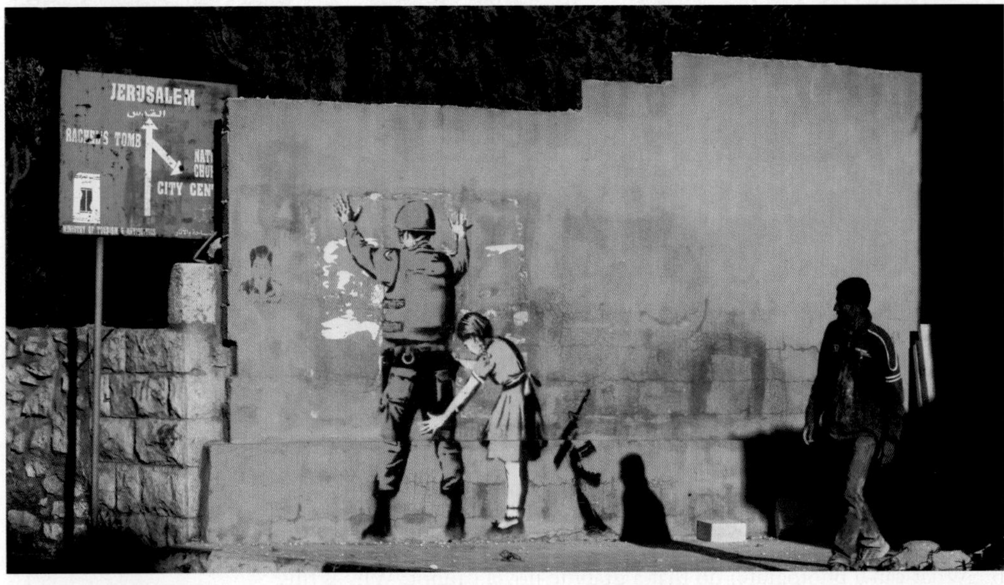

Intertextuality

1.11 Return to Activity 1.6 and your list of mood words to describe the award-winning photograph (Text 4.6). Could you use the same list of words to describe Text 4.8, a page from Joe Sacco's graphic novel *Palestine*? Can you think of other mood words that are only applicable to Text 4.8? Complete a copy of this table.

Mood words shared by Texts 4.6 and 4.8	Mood words that only describe the mood of Text 4.8

Text 4.8

AOE question

What can diverse texts have in common?

Can you answer this question with regard to Texts 4.6 and 4.8?

1.12 Look at your list of words from Activity 1.11. What accounts for these differences? Compare the two texts and discuss your answers to these questions:

a What can a graphic novel do that a photograph cannot? Why is this?

b What can a photograph do that a graphic novel cannot? Why is this?

c What are the differences between a graphic novel and a comic book?

d To what extent do the creators of Texts 4.6 and 4.8 share a similar purpose?

e Does the graphic novel, as a medium, lend itself effectively to the author's purpose in Text 4.8? How?

1.13 This boxed list shows the techniques used by graphic novels, photographs or both media. Make a copy of the table and write each technique in one of the columns. Look up the meanings of any words that you do not already know. Discuss their application and relevance to Texts 4.6 and 4.8. You may wish to refer to Units 1.1 and 1.5 for more guidance on analysing visual texts and graphic novels.

CONCEPT

Representation

Artists such as Joe Sacco (Text 4.8) and Banksy (Text 4.7) must make choices about how they depict people to make them recognisable to their audiences. *Representation* is a key concept in this course. With any depiction of people in works of art, you should consider if they are fairly represented. Is it fair for the Israeli soldier to symbolise Israelis? Is it fair for the weeping mother to represent Palestinians?

blank space, exposure, colour, rule of thirds, camera angle, gutter, lighting, depth, voice-over, symbols, panels, gaze, emanata, speech bubble, composition, subject, depth, shutter speed, contrast, texture, cartoonification, abstraction

Techniques to construct meaning in photographs *only*	Techniques for constructing meaning in *both* graphic novels and photographs	Techniques to construct meaning in graphic novels *only*

1.14 Take one word from Activity 1.13 and explain to your classmates the effect on the reader or viewer of using this technique or device in *either* Text 4.6 or Text 4.8.

1.15 Text 4.9 is a type of text called '**ambient advertising**'. This is a kind of advertisement whose meaning is dependent on its physical surroundings. The transparent glass structure of the poster shown in Text 4.9 gives the impression that a child soldier is sitting on the pavement beside the viewer. It originally appeared in cities in Switzerland in 2006.

Text 4.10 is another public text type: a **mural**. It was painted in Derry, Northern Ireland in 1994. It commemorates the Battle of the Bogside in August 1969, a riot that occurred near the beginning of 'the Troubles', the period of sectarian violence between Catholics and Protestants between 1968 and 1998.

Text 4.9

Text 4.10

Both texts depict a child and both comment on conflict. Discuss your answers to these questions as a class:

a Do the texts treat the topic of child soldiers similarly or differently? How are their aims different?

b How are they different or similar in terms of style and structure?

c What do you think the people of Derry would say if someone placed Text 4.9 in their town? What do you think the people of Switzerland would say if someone placed Text 4.10 in Geneva or Zurich? What makes you say this? How is meaning dependent on context?

d What is the effect of each text on you? How does each text make you think about child soldiers?

Towards assessment

1.16 For your individual oral, you will analyse an extract from a literary text and a non-literary text in relation to a common global issue.

a Read Chapter 8 on the individual oral and make sure you are familiar with the expectations of this form of assessment, including the assessment criteria.

b Read Text 4.11, a passage from a literary text, *A Long Way Gone* by Ishmael Beah. Read more about the text online to learn about the author, why he wrote this memoir and how it was received.

c Find a non-literary text which you can use in conjunction with Text 4.11 to explore the global issue of child soldiers. You may want to choose from one of the text types listed:

- an awareness campaign on child soldiers by a non-profit organisation such as Amnesty International (see Text 4.9)
- a speech given by someone who is knowledgeable on the topic of child soldiers (Ishmael Beah has also given speeches)
- an informative page from the website of an organisation such as Human Rights Watch
- a news article or report about child soldiers
- an interview with a former child soldier or someone else who has experience with this issue.

d Write a thesis statement and make an outline for an individual oral that explores the global issue of child soldiers. Follow the format for an outline that is suggested in Chapter 8. With reference to Text 4.11, you may want to focus on one or more of the stylistic and structural features listed:

- memoir
- point of view
- narration
- dialogue
- diction
- tone
- mood.

e Show your outline and thesis statement to your teacher and ask for feedback on it. Make improvements where they are deemed necessary.

f Make a 10-minute recording of yourself speaking about Text 4.11 and your chosen non-literary text. How do they construct meaning and engage with a common global issue?

g Once you have made your 10-minute recording, let another student listen to it. Assess each other's recordings using the assessment criteria for the individual oral, which you can find in the introduction of this coursebook. Ask your teacher to assess your recording as well, as a 'mock' individual oral. Add any comments on your oral to your learner portfolio.

1.17 As a class, discuss your answers to these questions:

a How effective was your selection of a non-literary text on the global issue of child soldiers? How effective was your text selection, compared to the selections made by other students?

b Did your classmates approach Text 4.11 similarly to or differently from you?

c Based on Text 4.11, did you know enough about *A Long Way Gone* to sustain a 10-minute analysis on it? What more did you need to know?

d How did you find the experience of recording yourself? How different would it have been with your teacher sitting across from you?

e What would you have done differently? Why? What were the strengths and weaknesses of your recording? How could you improve your performance? What do you still need to do to prepare for your real individual oral?

Text 4.11

A Long Way Gone

Extract

Ishmael Beah 2007

Ishmael Beah, author of *A Long Way Gone*, also gives talks about the problem of child soldiers in the world.

'I left town to look for my family,' the old man said in a frightened voice, as he managed to catch his breath. The rebel with the semiautomatic machine gun, who had been standing against a tree smoking a cigarette, furiously walked toward the old man and pointed his gun between the old man's legs.

'You left Mattru Jong because you don't like us.' He put his gun on the old man's forehead and continued. 'You left because you are against our cause as freedom fighters. Right?'

The old man closed his eyes tightly and began to sob.

What cause? I thought. I used the only freedom that I had then, my thought. They couldn't see it. While the interrogation went on, one of the rebels painted RUF on all the walls of the houses in the village. He was the sloppiest painter I have ever seen. I don't think he even knew his alphabet. Rather, he only knew what R, U, and F looked like. When he was done painting, he walked up to the old man and placed his gun to the old man's head.

'Do you have any last words to say?' The old man at this point was unable to speak. His lips trembled, but he couldn't get a word out. The rebel pulled the trigger, and like lightning, I saw the spark of fire that came from the muzzle. I turned my face to the ground. My knees started trembling and my heartbeat grew faster and louder. When I looked back, the old man was circling around like a dog trying to catch a fly on its tail. He kept screaming, 'My head! My brains!' The rebels laughed at him. Finally, he stopped and slowly raised his hands toward his face like a person hesitant to look in a mirror. 'I can see! I can hear!' he cried out, and fainted. It turned out that the rebels hadn't shot him but had fired at close range near his head. They were very amused at the old man's reaction.

The rebels now faced us and announced that they were going to select some people among us to be recruited, as it was the sole reason for their patrol. They ordered everyone to line up: men, women, even children younger than I. They walked up and down the line trying to make eye contact with people. First, they chose Khalilou, and then myself, then a few others. Each person that was chosen was asked to stand in a different line facing the previous one. Junior wasn't chosen, and I stood facing him on the other side of the crowd, on my way to becoming a rebel. I looked at him, but he avoided eye contact, putting his head down. It seemed as if our worlds were different now and our connection was breaking. Fortunately, for some reason the rebels decided to do a fresh pick. One of them said that they had chosen wrongly, since most of us who had been chosen were trembling and that meant we were sissies.

'We want strong recruits, not weak ones.' The rebel pushed us back to the other side of the crowd. Junior edged next to me. He gave me a soft poke. I looked up at him and he nodded and rubbed my head.

'Stand still for the final pick,' one of the rebels screamed. Junior stopped rubbing my head. During the second pick, Junior was chosen. The rest of us weren't needed, so they escorted us to the river followed by the chosen ones. Sweeping an arm in our direction, one of the rebels announced, 'We are going to initiate all of you by killing these people in front of you. We have to do this to show you blood and make you strong. You'll never see any of these people again, unless you believe in life after death.' He punched his chest with his fist and laughed.

I turned around and looked at Junior, whose eyes were red because he was trying to hold back his tears. He clenched his fists to keep his hands from trembling. I began to cry quietly and all of a sudden felt dizzy. One of the chosen boys vomited. A rebel pushed him to join us by smashing him in the face with the butt of his gun. The boy's face was bleeding as we continued on.

LEARNER PROFILE

Risk taker; Communicator

Ishmael Beah survived his youth in Sierra Leone and emigrated to the USA. There he learnt English and met people who helped him heal and tell his story to the world. You might consider Ishmael Beah to be a *risk taker* and a *communicator* for writing his memoir.

1.18 Whether or not you have read literary works about war, you may find it helpful to explore one of these questions in preparation for Paper 2:

- **a** It is often said that literature is about the human struggle to find peace. With regard to two works that you have read, explain how this is true.
- **b** With regard to two works that you have read, discuss the significance of narration and the reliability of the narrator in constructing meaning for the reader.
- **c** Literature has the power to give readers new experiences, make them feel deeper emotions and show them the best and worst of human nature. How have two works that you have read done this?
- **d** In what ways and for what reasons do two literary works that you have read gravitate towards an inevitable tragedy?

When preparing your practice Paper 2 essay, you may find it helpful to follow these steps:

- Unpack the question by creating a mind map.
- Create an outline for your response.

- Write your essay.
- Assess your finished essay using the assessment criteria for Paper 2 in the introduction to this book.
- Share your essay with your teacher and ask for feedback based on the Paper 2 assessment criteria.
- Identify the strengths and weaknesses of your essay. How could it be improved to gain more marks? What can you do to improve your essay writing to prepare for Paper 2?

Higher level extension

1.19 Do an online video search for 'Dulce et Decorum Est by Wilfred Owen: read by Christopher Eccleston' by Docs On 4. Do not look ahead to Text 4.12; simply watch Christopher Eccleston recite this poem. After your classroom viewing, discuss your answers to these questions:

a What kinds of sounds do you remember hearing?

b How does Christopher Eccleston bring this poem to life, making the viewer experience Wilfred Owen's poem?

c Does his reading sound like a poem or does it sound like a different type of text, such as a story, a song, a conversation, a soliloquy or a speech? Explain why it might sound like one or more of these text types?

d For the viewer, what is the effect of the cinematography, including the lighting, shot length, panning, camera angle, zoom, location, colour and contrast? (Read Unit 1.3 for further guidance on how to analyse film.)

e What images from the poem do you see in your mind after viewing Christopher Eccleston's performance? Were these images built around prior knowledge that you may have had about the First World War and trench warfare?

f How would your experience of this poem have been different if you only listened to Christopher Eccleston's reading, without seeing his performance?

TIP

Reading a poem aloud makes you think more about the meanings of its words and the sounds they make. As you study poetry in class, take the opportunity to prepare and deliver a reading of a poem. If you are exploring the global issue of war, you can easily find poetry about war, especially poems from and about the First World War.

1.20 After your classroom discussion on Activity 1.19, read the poem, 'Dulce et Decorum Est' silently by yourself. Then annotate a copy of the poem, as if you were preparing an essay or oral commentary on it, focusing on how meaning is constructed through language. Use different coloured pens, highlighters or other tools.

- In the margins of your page, write comments and questions about the poem.
- In the poem, underline any key words. Circle phrases or even individual letters.
- Draw lines to connect words, phrases or verses.
- Identify key literary devices and their effects on the reader.

Then everyone in your class should display their annotated poem on a wall, for everyone to see. Discuss the similarities and differences among the annotations.

Text 4.12

Wilfred Owen is one of many young British soldiers who wrote poetry during the First World War.

Dulce et Decorum Est

Wilfred Owen 1918

Bent double, like old beggars under sacks,
Knock-kneed, coughing like hags, we cursed through sludge,
Till on the haunting flares we turned our backs,
And towards our distant rest began to trudge.
Men marched asleep. Many had lost their boots,
But limped on, blood-shod. All went lame; all blind;
Drunk with fatigue; deaf even to the hoots
Of gas-shells dropping softly behind.

Gas! GAS! Quick, boys! – An ecstasy of fumbling
Fitting the clumsy helmets just in time,
But someone still was yelling out and stumbling
And flound'ring like a man in fire or lime . . .
Dim through the misty panes and thick green light,
As under a green sea, I saw him drowning.

In all my dreams before my helpless sight,
He plunges at me, guttering, choking, drowning.

If in some smothering dreams, you too could pace
Behind the wagon that we flung him in,
And watch the white eyes writhing in his face,
His hanging face, like a devil's sick of sin;
If you could hear, at every jolt, the blood
Come gargling from the froth-corrupted lungs,
Obscene as cancer, bitter as the cud
Of vile, incurable sores on innocent tongues, –
My friend, you would not tell with such high zest
To children ardent for some desperate glory,
The old Lie: *Dulce et decorum est*
Pro patria mori.

AOE question

How do texts follow or move away from the conventions associated with different types of text?

It is interesting to consider the extent to which Wilfred Owen's poem is a typical or atypical **sonnet**. Why would he follow the conventions of a sonnet at the beginning of this poem and then break them?

1.21 Assign everyone in your class a different stylistic or structural device from the list shown here. Find evidence of your device in 'Dulce et Decorum Est' (Text 4.12) and explain to your classmates its effect on the reader and why you think Wilfred Owen used this device. You may find a definition of your device online or in the glossary of this coursebook.

a **iambic pentameter**
b **onomatopoeia**
c imagery
d volta
e point of view
f repetition
g rhyming scheme
h sonnet
i enjambment
j **allusion** (to Horace's 'The Odes')
k second-person pronoun
l alliteration
m caesura
n parataxis
o ellipsis
p asyndeton
q consonance
r hyphen or dash
s **cacophony**
t capitalisation.

1.22 Return to your wall of annotated poems from Activity 1.20. Can you find any evidence that one or more of your classmates had already noticed the significance of your chosen stylistic device? How has your understanding of this poem evolved from listening to it (Activity 1.19) to annotating it (Activity 1.20) and then analysing it (Activity 1.21)?

1.23 Compare Wilfred Owen's poem 'Dulce et Decorum Est' to the propaganda posters for the First World War at the beginning of this unit (Texts 4.1–4.4). How is the message of his poem different from the messages of these posters? What accounts for these differences?

1.24 In all of your discussions on language and war, it is important not only to consider the words and images that are included in a text, but also those that are excluded. What does **censorship** mean, and how is it relevant during wartime?

After studying the First World War, you may wish to do an online search for images that were censored from the general public at that time. Do an online search for images that there have been unsuccessful attempts to censor from the general public at some point in the past. Make sure every student (or every pair of students) in your class is working on a different image. Present your chosen image to your classmates and explain why it was originally censored from the general public.

Further reading

Many literary works have been written about war and its effects. Besides *Palestine* (Text 4.8) by Joe Sacco, *A Long Way Gone* by Ishmael Beah (Text 4.11) and poetry from the First World War (Text 4.12), you may be interested in these texts:

- *Maus* by Art Spiegelman
- *Slaughterhouse Five* by Kurt Vonnegut
- *If This Is a Man* (originally in Italian) by Primo Levi

- *Catch-22* by Joseph Heller
- *The Things They Carried* by Tim O'Brien
- *All Quiet on the Western Front* by Erich Maria Remarque (originally written in German)
- the poetry of Mahmoud Darwish, which captures the sentiments of displaced people in the Middle East. As a work in translation, his poems are very accessible, meaningful and rich in language.

REFLECT

This unit has approached the topic of war through a broad range of texts: propaganda posters, a speech, a photograph, a page from a graphic novel, a piece of street art, an ambient advertisement, a mural, a passage from a memoir and a poem.

- Which text did you find most interesting?
- Which text type was new for you?
- Which text seemed richest in meaning?
- Which text gave you the most insight into the topic of war?
- What other texts could you add to this collection and include in your learner portfolio?

Unit 4.2
Protest

Learning objectives

- become familiar with a range of texts that deal with protest against injustices or social inequality
- learn about the contexts where protests have occurred in different places and times in history
- understand the different traditions of literary criticism.

Word bank

graphic art
reader-response criticism
literary theory
conflict
protagonist
antagonist
Marxist literary criticism
formalism
biographical criticism
protest sign
allusion
pun
sarcasm
irony
symbolism
slogan
manifesto
ethos
logos
pathos

How is language used to protest against social inequality? There are as many answers to this question as there are texts with this purpose. For centuries people have written songs, books, stories, poems and speeches, and produced posters to speak out against injustices and social inequality.

This unit introduces you to a range of protest texts from different times and places. It invites you to think about your own context and how you can use language to change your world.

International mindedness

Internationally minded people question the status quo. As you explore this unit on 'protest', ask yourself why and how individuals have challenged societies.

Getting started

2.1 Study Texts 4.13–4.16 carefully and discuss your answers to these questions:

a What is the difference between propaganda posters, protest posters, **graphic art** and visual art? What text types are these texts examples of?

b What stylistic and structural features do these texts have in common? Comment on their use of both visual language and words.

c Without using the title of the poster, what is the message of each poster? What are they really saying?

d How do they use symbols and icons to construct their message? (See Unit 1.1 for further help on the use of symbols in images and graphic art.)

e What do you know about the context of each text? How does this affect your understanding of the message of each one?

f What do you think you need to know before you can properly understand each text?

Text 4.13

Text 4.15

Text 4.14

Text 4.16

AOE question

How can the 'meaning' of a text be constructed, negotiated, expressed and interpreted by readers and writers?

Discuss your class's answers to this question in response to Texts 4.13–4.16. What can you learn about Keith Haring, Angela Davis, the Labour Party and the hippie movement by studying these images on their own? What can you learn without researching any contextual information and analysing them?

2.2 Texts 4.13-4.16 may seem outdated in today's world. Do people still create protest posters? What issues are people protesting about today, and what media or text types do they use to do this? Can you find an example of a modern-day text whose purpose is to protest against something? Bring it into class and discuss how it uses language to serve its purpose.

2.3 Create a piece of graphic art to protest about a current problem in the world. You do not have to be a skilled artist to do this. You can draw stick figures or copy images from the web. Share your creation with your classmates and explain the choices you made when designing your protest poster.

CONCEPT

Creativity

Activity 2.3 asks you to create your own protest poster. *Creativity*, it can be said, is a higher-order thinking skill. In order to create it, you have to consider how your poster will be received and how you will construct your message using language, symbols, colour and layout. As a result, you will be more analytical when viewing other posters.

CAS

How can you make the world a better place? Use this question for guidance when developing a CAS project. While CAS is an opportunity to work on self-fulfilment, you can make positive contributions to your community at the same time. Think about the 'protest' theme in this unit and how you could make a difference.

Readers, writers and texts

2.4 Text 4.17 is a short story which can be seen as a kind of a riddle. For this activity, let's turn the roles around. Rather than answer discussion questions from this coursebook, think of five questions that you would ask your classmates about this text. These questions should require close reading and textual analysis.

Write each question on a sticky note and display them on a wall. Read everyone's questions and take down five questions *that you did not write*. Write a short answer on the back of each sticky note in response to each question. Take turns reading aloud the answers to the questions that you selected. How many of you had similar questions and answers?

Text 4.17

Sitting

H.E. Francis 1983

In the morning the man and woman were sitting on his front steps. They sat all day. They would not move. With metronomic regularity he peered at them through the pane in the front door. They did not leave at dark. He wondered when they ate or slept or did their duties. At dawn they were still there. They sat through sun and rain.

At first only the immediate neighbours called: Who are they? What are they doing there? He did not know. Then neighbours from farther down the street called. People who passed and saw the couple called. He never heard the man or woman talk. When he started getting calls from all over the city, from strangers and city fathers, professionals and clerks, garbage and utilities men, and the postman, who had to walk around them to deliver letters, he had to do something. He asked them to leave. They said nothing. They sat. They sat. They stared, indifferent. He said he would call the police. The police gave them a talking to, explained the limits of their rights, and took them away in the police car. In the morning they were back. The next time the police said they would put them in jail if the jails were not so full, though they would have to find a place for them somewhere, if he insisted. That is your problem, he said. No, it is really yours, the police told him, but they removed the pair.

When he looked out the next morning, the man and the woman were sitting on the steps. They sat there every day for years. Winters he expected them to die from the cold.

But he died.

He had no relative, so the house went to the city.

The man and woman went on sitting there.

When the city threatened to remove the man and the woman, neighbours and citizens brought a suit against the city: after sitting there so long, the man and the woman deserved the house.

In the morning strange men and women were sitting on front steps all over the city.

2.5 Throughout your studies of language and literature, you will be asked to respond to texts. You may be tempted to think there is one 'correct' interpretation of a text. Indeed, some readings are more informed than others. You could also say that every individual reader is entitled to his or her own unique interpretation of a text. This kind of thinking is characteristic of **reader-response criticism**, a school of **literary theory** that focuses on the reader's experience of a text.

Return to your sticky notes from Activity 2.4. Can you state briefly what you think Text 4.17 means? Write down your interpretation of Text 4.17 on a new sticky note and place it on a board for your classmates to see. Discuss the similarities and differences. What accounts for these similar and different interpretations?

AOE question

What are the different ways in which people are affected by texts?

This question is asked in reader-response criticism of literature (Activity 2.5). It is comparable to the visual arts, where people say that meaning is in the eye of the beholder. Think of a literary text that you are reading together in class. Ask everyone how it has affected them. How different are everyone's responses?

2.6 When analysing literary texts, it is important to look at the relevance of the term '**conflict**'. Conflict in literature can be defined as the core problem or struggle, which the reader hopes to see the **protagonist** resolve. The protagonist is the character who makes the action of a story progress. While conflict comes in many shapes and forms, it may fall into one or more of these categories:

- Individual versus society – it may seem that the whole world is against the protagonist. Many novels are centred on an individual who struggles against an oppressive society.
- Individual against another individual – the person standing in the way of the protagonist is usually the **antagonist**. The struggles between protagonists and antagonists usually symbolise a greater ideological struggle.

- Individual versus circumstances – sometimes the protagonist just seems to be in the wrong place at the wrong time. There may be natural disasters, accidents, twists of fate or random incidents that reflect the adverse circumstances that life can throw at you.
- Individual versus himself or herself – sometimes the protagonist is his or her own worst enemy. He or she may be a 'flawed' character, meaning they have a harmful trait or characteristic. Part of the plot may involve the protagonist reflecting on events and making changes.

Look back to 'Sitting' (Text 4.17) and ask yourself how one or more of these four types of conflict are represented. Refer to specific lines from the text in your analysis.

2.7 Sometimes it helps to look at literature through a lens. Let's look at Text 4.17 through the lens of **Marxist literary criticism**, another school of literary theory.

Marxist literary criticism explores literature by:

- focusing on the depiction of social class and the power struggles between characters and classes, especially with regard to the rise of the proletariat against the ruling class
- considering the significance of a literary work as an impetus for social change or an expression of progressive ideas
- treating literary works in the context of the author's times and an expression of the author's political views.

Return to Text 4.17 and ask yourself how a Marxist literary critic might read the story. You may want to research Marxist literary criticism further before doing this. Does your understanding of the story change when you look at it through this lens?

CONCEPT

Representation

What do the 'man' and 'woman' in Text 4.17 stand for? Are they the 'proletariat' as suggested in Activity 2.7? In your language and literature course you will explore the concept of *representation*. As you study literary works, consider how characters may represent broader ideas.

2.8 Read Text 4.18, a poem by Percy Bysshe Shelley, written 200 years ago. Your class should divide into three groups.

- Group 1 – you will take a reader-response approach to the poem. Describe how it makes you feel. What personal associations do you have with the language of the poem? You need not do any online research on this poem.
- Group 2 – you will use **formalism** to approach the poem. This is to say that you will focus on the style and structure of the poem, and determine how its meaning can be understood by analysing the author's use of these devices. You may want to research the poem's use of rhyme and metre. It may be helpful to find out more about the meaning of formalism with respect to literature.
- Group 3 – you will take a Marxist approach to the poem. Use the three bullet points from Activity 2.7 to inform your interpretation of the poem. You may research Marxist literary criticism further and apply your understanding of it to the poem.

After you have discussed your approach to the poem and your interpretation of it, report back to the rest of your class. How is the nature of each group's presentation different? Is any single method or approach more effective than the other in determining meaning?

Text 4.18

Percy Bysshe Shelley (1792–1822) is one of the more revered English poets of the Romantic period. His works have influenced many progressive thinkers and writers.

A Song: 'Men of England'

Percy Bysshe Shelley 1819

Men of England, wherefore plough
For the lords who lay ye low?
Wherefore weave with toil and care
The rich robes your tyrants wear?

Wherefore feed and clothe and save
From the cradle to the grave
Those ungrateful drones who would
Drain your sweat – nay, drink your blood?

Wherefore, Bees of England, forge
Many a weapon, chain, and scourge,
That these stingless drones may spoil
The forced produce of your toil?

Have ye leisure, comfort, calm,
Shelter, food, love's gentle balm?
Or what is it ye buy so dear
With your pain and with your fear?

The seed ye sow, another reaps;
The wealth ye find, another keeps;
The robes ye weave, another wears;
The arms ye forge, another bears.

Sow seed – but let no tyrant reap:
Find wealth – let no imposter heap:
Weave robes – let not the idle wear:
Forge arms – in your defence to bear.

Shrink to your cellars, holes, and cells –
In hall ye deck another dwells.
Why shake the chains ye wrought? Ye see
The steel ye tempered glance on ye.

With plough and spade and hoe and loom
Trace your grave and build your tomb
And weave your winding-sheet – till fair
England be your Sepulchre.

Time and space

2.9 Another approach to analysing literary texts is **biographical criticism**. This approach suggests that it is difficult to understand and appreciate a text without knowledge of the author's life and times.

Try to find answers to these questions. How do their answers inform your understanding of Text 4.18? Which sources did you find most useful in your research? Why?

- a Who was Percy Bysshe Shelley?
- b What kinds of political ideas did Shelley propagate?
- c What kind of life did he lead?
- d What else did he write?
- e How were influential leaders such as Karl Marx and Mahatma Gandhi influenced by Shelley?

2.10 Place a copy of Shelley's poem (Text 4.18) in your learner portfolio and add your own annotations to it. Include any other clippings that you came across in your research for Activities 2.8 and 2.9. How can you connect this poem to 'protest' as a global issue? How could you use this text in preparation for an individual oral?

2.11 Text 4.19 is a famous speech by Mahatma Gandhi from 1942. The annotations ask questions about the context of the speech. In pairs, research the answers to these questions and then discuss as a class:

- a Could you understand the speech without knowing the answers to the questions in the annotations ? Why, or why not?
- b How was your understanding of Gandhi's speech affected by what you already knew about him and his cause, before you started researching answers to the questions?
- c What were your answers to the questions in the annotations?
- d What sources did you find valuable in helping you answer the annotation questions?
- e Why do you think this speech is often cited as one of the most important speeches of the 20th century?

AOE question

How do readers approach texts from different times and different cultures from their own?

Text 4.19 might seem like an artefact from a different time and place. By asking questions about the text, as has been done in the annotations, we have a starting point for researching its context. Apply this method to other texts that you may not understand.

LEARNER PROFILE

Inquirer

An IB learner is an *inquirer*. To become a better inquirer, get into the habit of asking questions of texts by annotating them, as has been done with Text 4.19.

ATL

Research

Effective research starts by asking appropriate questions. The annotations to Text 4.19 show you how to ask questions of primary sources. These types of questions should guide you on your search for secondary sources, when analysing texts.

Text 4.19

Quit India

Mahatma Gandhi 1942

Mahatma Gandhi sought India's independence from Great Britain through non-violent protest.

Before you discuss the resolution, let me place before you one or two things. I want you to understand two things very clearly and to consider them from the same point of view from which I am placing them before you. I ask you to consider it from my point of view, because if you approve of it, you will be enjoined to carry out all I say. It will be a great responsibility. There are people who ask me whether I am the same man that I was in 1920, or whether there has been any change in me. You are right in asking that question.

Let me, however, hasten to assure that I am the same Gandhi as I was in 1920. I have not changed in any fundamental respect. I attach the same importance to non-violence that I did then. If at all, my emphasis on it has grown stronger. There is no real contradiction between the present resolution and my previous writings and utterances.

Occasions like the present do not occur in everybody's and but rarely in anybody's life. I want you to know and feel that there is nothing but purest Ahimsa in all that I am saying and doing today. The draft resolution of the Working Committee is based on Ahimsa, the contemplated struggle similarly has its roots in Ahimsa. If, therefore, there is any among you who has lost faith in Ahimsa or is wearied of it, let him not vote for this resolution. Let me explain my position clearly. God has vouchsafed to me a priceless gift in the weapon of Ahimsa. I and my Ahimsa are on our trail today. If in the present crisis, when the earth is being scorched by the flames of Himsa and crying for deliverance, I failed to make use of the God-given talent, God will not forgive me and I shall be judged unworthy of the great gift. I must act now. I may not hesitate and merely look on, when Russia and China are threatened.

Ours is not a drive for power, but purely a non-violent fight for India's independence. In a violent struggle, a successful general has been often known to

Who is 'you'?

Which resolution?

What is his 'point of view'? Who is Mahatma Gandhi at this point in history?

Who has questioned him, and why?

What were his previous writings and utterances?

What is Ahimsa?

What is Himsa?

India's independence from whom?

effect a military coup and to set up a dictatorship. But under the Congress scheme of things, essentially non-violent as it is, there can be no room for dictatorship. A non-violent soldier of freedom will covet nothing for himself, he fights only for the freedom of his country. The Congress is unconcerned as to who will rule, when freedom is attained. The power, when it comes, will belong to the people of India, and it will be for them to decide to whom it placed in the entrusted. May be that the reins will be placed in the hands of the Parsis, for instance – as I would love to see happen – or they may be handed to some others whose names are not heard in the Congress today. It will not be for you then to object saying, 'This community is microscopic. That party did not play its due part in the freedom's struggle; why should it have all the power?' Ever since its inception the Congress has kept itself meticulously free of the communal taint. It has thought always in terms of the whole nation and has acted accordingly . . . I know how imperfect our Ahimsa is and how far away we are still from the ideal, but in Ahimsa there is no final failure or defeat. I have faith, therefore, that if, in spite of our shortcomings, the big thing does happen, it will be because God wanted to help us by crowning with success our silent, unremitting Sadhana for the last twenty-two years.

I believe that in the history of the world, there has not been a more genuinely democratic struggle for freedom than ours. I read Carlyle's French Revolution while I was in prison, and Pandit Jawaharlal has told me something about the Russian revolution. But it is my conviction that inasmuch as these struggles were fought with the weapon of violence they failed to realise the democratic ideal. In the democracy which I have envisaged, a democracy established by non-violence, there will be equal freedom for all. Everybody will be his own master. It is to join a struggle for such democracy that I invite you today. Once you realise this you will forget the differences between the Hindus and Muslims, and think of yourselves as Indians only, engaged in the common struggle for independence.

Then, there is the question of your attitude towards the British. I have noticed that there is hatred towards the British among the people. The people say they are disgusted with their behaviour. The people make no distinction between British imperialism and the British people. To them, the two are one. This hatred would even make them welcome the Japanese. It is most dangerous. It means that they will exchange one slavery for another. We must get rid of this feeling. Our quarrel is not with the British people, we fight their imperialism. The proposal for the withdrawal of British power did not come out of anger. It came to enable India to play its due part at the present critical juncture. It is not a happy position for a big country like India to be merely helping with money and material obtained willy-nilly from her while the United Nations are conducting the war. We cannot evoke the true spirit of sacrifice and valour, so long as we are not free. I know the British Government will not be able to withhold freedom from us, when we have made enough self-sacrifice. We must, therefore, purge ourselves of hatred. Speaking for myself, I can say that I have never felt any hatred. As a matter of fact, I feel myself to be a greater friend of the British now than ever before. One reason is that they are today in distress. My very friendship, therefore, demands that I should try to save them from their mistakes. As I view the situation, they are on the brink of an abyss. It, therefore, becomes my duty to warn them of their danger even though it may, for the time being, anger them to the point of cutting off the friendly hand that is stretched out to help them. People may laugh, nevertheless that is my claim. At a time when I may have to launch the biggest struggle of my life, I may not harbour hatred against anybody.

Who are the 'Parsis'?

Why would Gandhi say his Congress is 'imperfect'?

What is Sadhana?

Why was he in prison?

Is there a problem with Hindus and Muslims?

What is this 'present critical juncture'?

Why are the British in 'distress'? Why does Gandhi care about their distress?

Why are the British on the 'brink of an abyss'?

What is the biggest struggle of his life?

Intertextuality: connecting texts

2.12 An interesting type of text for analysis is the **protest sign**. These are often homemade products of cardboard, pens, glue and tape. Their use of language must be concise and punchy in order to be effective. Furthermore, they often express criticism through the use of:

- **allusion**, which is a reference to another text
- **pun**, a kind of play on words
- other linguistic devices, such as **sarcasm**, **irony** or **symbolism**.

Text 4.20 is a photograph taken during an anti-Trump rally in the UK in July 2018. This protest sign borrows elements from another text that you have already studied, the Second World War 'We Can Do It!' poster (Text 2.4 from Unit 2.1). Study these two images and discuss your answers to these questions:

a How does the 'We Can Do It!' poster (Text 2.4) add meaning to the anti-Trump protest sign (Text 4.20)?

b Besides alluding to the 'We Can Do It!' poster, how else is meaning constructed? What are the effects of colour, punctuation, font and layout on her audience?

c The raised fist is a common symbol of protest. What can you find out about this symbol? Where does it come from? How has it been used before? Why do you think the protester has used it here?

d How do other symbols construct meaning in this protest sign?

e The woman's T-shirt also protests against Brexit. What does Brexit (the UK's 'exit' from the European Union) have to do with an anti-Trump rally? Research the parallels between these two issues.

f When you think of the word 'protester', is this woman the kind of person who comes to mind? What makes you say that? Has she changed your associations with the word 'protester'?

Text 4.20

2.13 As well as using images, protest signs often include words. Here are several phrases that have been used on signs to protest about the presidency of Donald Trump in the USA. You may find them confusing without much contextual knowledge.

Assign each person in your class a different phrase. Do an online search to learn more about the contexts in which your phrase was used. Try to find how your text is connected to another text or texts of some kind. The phrases allude to statements that President Trump has used, other famous protest signs or **slogans** from other campaigns. Explain how the meaning of your protest sign's text is dependent on another text and context. Present your findings to your classmates.

a We shall overcome.

b Keep your tiny hands off my rights.

c No you can't.

d Pussies grab back.

e Nope.

f I wish this were fake news.

g 40% approval. Sad!

h Resist bigly.

i Trump: bad hombre for the whole world.

j Are we winning yet? I was told there would be winning.

k Make love not walls.

l You're fired.

m Nasty women vote.

n Lock him up.

o Make Russia Great Again.

AOE question

How can comparing and interpreting texts transform readers?

As you research the language of the signs that protest against Donald Trump (Activity 2.13) you may learn something about US politics, presidential campaigns and the 45th President of the United States. What have you learnt from your research?

Towards assessment

2.14 In small groups, select a protest movement from these options or think of another one that you would like to research:

- women's suffrage movement
- protest against the war in Vietnam
- UK coal miners' strike in 1984–85

- anti-apartheid movement in South Africa
- Occupy (Wall Street) movement
- Arab Spring
- Black Lives Matter
- #Metoo
- The Umbrella movement in Hong Kong
- March for Our Lives.

a Find a primary source of any kind (for example, a poem, poster, pamphlet, cartoon or **manifesto**) in English, which is relevant to the movement or protest that you have chosen.

b Give a copy of this text to another group. Ask them to analyse it without any contextual knowledge about the text.

- Ask the other group how the meaning of the text is constructed through its use of language.
- Ask them to suggest how the text may have been received by readers and viewers in its time.
- Give them contextual information about the movement and the text's author to help them understand its meaning better.

Prepare notes on your text and keep a record of your group's discussion in your learner portfolio.

2.15 Text 4.21 is a political cartoon. Political cartoons may appear on your Paper 1 exam at either higher or standard level. Remember, Paper 1 is a guided analysis, meaning that the stimulus text for analysis is accompanied by a guiding question. Text 4.21 is an example of the kind of stimulus text on a Paper 1 exam. An example guiding question for Text 4.21 has been included below the cartoon as a caption. Below the cartoon and its guiding question are the 'marking notes' to examiners who would mark students' Paper 1 analyses of Text 4.21. Like all marking notes, they list the kinds of responses that examiners expect for 'good' marks or 'excellent' marks, regardless of the assessment criteria.

a If you have not already done so, read Chapter 5 on Paper 1 to gain a better understanding of this form of assessment. Study the assessment criteria in the introduction of this coursebook as well.

b Read the Paper 1 marking notes for Text 4.21 carefully. Use these marking notes and the guiding question to write your own guided analysis of Text 4.21. You do not have to write this analysis under exam conditions, but it should be the same length as an analysis written in the exam. You may use words and phrases from the marking notes in your own analysis. You do not have to limit yourself to the ideas expressed in the marking notes.

c Ask your teacher or a fellow student to mark your analysis using the assessment criteria in the introduction to this coursebook.

d Identify the strengths and weaknesses of your analysis. Are there any areas where your response could have been improved? How could you improve your performance in these areas?

e Keep your analysis of Text 4.21 in your learner portfolio under both Paper 1 and the global issue of 'protest'.

TIP

You may be tempted to check online or other sources for information about some of the less familiar phrases in Text 4.21, such as 'the Glass–Steagall Act' or 'corporate personhood'. During your actual Paper 1 exam you will not be able to do this. While some background information may be provided, you will have to make inferences from the text. Your ability to make informed claims about the context of the text will help you earn marks on Criterion A.

Text 4.21

Guiding question

How does this cartoon comment on the role of the media in political protest?

> **TIP**
>
> Activity 2.15 asks you to write an analysis of a text based on the examiner's marking notes. This may seem like answering a question with an answer that someone else has given you. Marking notes, however, are not analytical essays. See the tips and examples in Chapter 5 on how to write coherently and effectively. Once you know *what* you will write, then think about *how* you will write it.

AOE question

How do the style and structure of a text affect its meaning?

This AOE question captures the essence of most guiding questions that will appear on your Paper 1 exam. See Chapter 5 for more information on analysing texts using MAPS (Meaning = Audience + Purpose + Style).

Paper 1 – Marking notes for Text 4.21

The marking notes (notes for examiners) are intended only as guidelines to assist marking. They are not offered as an exhaustive and fixed set of responses or approaches to which all answers must rigidly adhere. Good ideas and approaches not offered here will be acknowledged and rewarded as appropriate. Similarly, answers which do not include all the ideas or approaches suggested here will not be penalised so as to distort appreciation of individuality.

Guiding question

How does this cartoon comment on the role of the media in political protest?

A good analysis will:

- identify the cartoon's criticism of the media for listening to wealthy bankers instead of protest groups

- comment on the use of the cartoon's style and structure in conveying this message, for example, the use of symbols such as dollar signs and peace signs
- explore the language of the protest signs in constructing the message that Wall Street and the banks are greedy and irresponsible
- comment on the style of the cartoonist's drawings
- explore how this cartoon may make readers laugh.

An excellent analysis will:

- articulate David Hurwitt's criticism of the media for not representing 99% of the population and instead reporting what the wealthiest 1% dictate to them
- analyse the cartoon's use of symbols such as the peace sign, dollar sign, top hat, radio equipment and pillars in order to comment on abstract ideas such as democracy, wealth, transparency and the press
- explore the protest signs' use of language, such as imperative verbs, to express the anger towards corporations and the government for unfair distribution of wealth
- analyse the drawing style of the cartoonist, which uses details such as well-groomed hair, big lips and fake eyelashes in order to make the reporter appear unintelligent and uncritical
- comment on how readers might respond to this cartoon by both laughing at the reporter's lack of reporting and questioning the bankers' involvement in controlling the media.

TIP

Notice how the 'good to excellent' marking notes require more in-depth analysis from students. What aspect of textual analysis is each of the points really asking you to explore: audience, purpose, style, structure, tone, mood or message?

2.16 By writing your own set of marking notes, you will understand what examiners are looking for.

a Find a non-literary text that would be interesting as a stimulus text on a Paper 1 exam and relevant for this global issue on 'protest'. You may want to find a political cartoon, protest sign, street art, political speech or web page.

b Write your own set of 'marking notes' for this text. Study the marking notes in this unit and Chapter 5 to help you write your own notes.

c Exchange texts and marking notes with a classmate. Discuss ways in which the marking notes could be improved. Make changes to your marking notes, taking your classmate's ideas into consideration.

d Add your text and marking notes to your learner portfolio and revisit them before your actual Paper 1 exam.

2.17 You may be reading literary works for your English Language course that relate to themes of social equality, injustices and human rights. You might want to practise writing a Paper 2 essay on one of these four questions:

a Dr Martin Luther King once said that 'the arc of the moral universe is long, but it bends toward justice'. To what extent and for what reasons do two literary works that you have read show humankind's long but inevitable arc towards justice?

b To what extent were two of the literary works that you have read written as a response to the social injustices that their authors have experienced?

c To what extent do two literary works that you have read show individuals struggling against society?

d How have the authors of two of the works you have read used language to make their readers care more about a cause that they find important?

Extended essay

Song lyrics are considered poetry by the IB and are studied as literature. It is possible to write a Category 1 essay on song lyrics. A good research question might read: 'To what extent were the lyrics of several Beatles songs a voice for the hippie movement?' This might be a successful research question, provided that you analyse The Beatles's lyrics in the context of events in the late 1960s. Its success will also depend on the kinds of secondary sources that you consult.

Higher level extension

2.18 Here are several quotations about democracy. From these quotations, select:

- the one that you *agree* with most
- the one that you *disagree* with most
- one that you find confusing
- one that you find funny.

For each quote that you have chosen, explain to your classmates why you agree or disagree with it or find it confusing or funny. Then find out more about the person who said *one* of these things and explain to your classmate why you think he or she may have said this:

a 'Democracy is the art and science of running the circus from the monkey cage.' – H.L. Mencken

b 'Democracy is good. I say this because other systems are worse.' – Jawaharlal Nehru

c 'There cannot be true democracy unless women's voices are heard.' – Hillary Clinton

d 'The best argument against democracy is a five-minute conversation with the average voter.' – Winston Churchill

e 'Democracy cannot succeed unless those who express their choice are prepared to choose wisely. The real safeguard of democracy, therefore, is education.' – Franklin D. Roosevelt

f 'Democracy must be something more than two wolves and a sheep voting on what to have for dinner.' – James Bovard

g 'Democracy is the road to socialism.' – Karl Marx

h 'Democracy is a device that insures we shall be governed no better than we deserve.' – George Bernard Shaw

i 'A mature society understands that at the heart of democracy is argument.' – Salman Rushdie

j 'Without God, democracy will not and cannot long endure.' – Ronald Reagan

k 'Republics decline into democracies and democracies degenerate into despotisms.' - Aristotle

l 'If you have a sense of purpose and a sense of direction, I believe people will follow you. Democracy isn't just about deducing what the people want. Democracy is leading the people as well.' – Margaret Thatcher

AOE question

How can different texts offer different perspectives on a topic or theme?

Activity 2.18 offers several different perspectives on a single topic: democracy. For any other topic that you are studying, find a range of interesting quotations, discuss them and write about them in your learner portfolio.

2.19 If you and your classmates could 'take over' the United Nations for a day, and be able to voice your opinions on how to make the world a better place, what would you say? As a class, make a list of key global issues for the UN to address to ensure that the world becomes a safer, more prosperous place for everyone.

2.20 In 2013 there was a 'Youth Takeover' of the United Nations, in which Malala Yousafzai spoke about her fight for education and women's rights. Text 4.22 is the speech that she delivered to the UN on this day. **Ethos, pathos** and **logos** are three of the key ingredients for a good speech. You can learn more about the key features of speeches in Unit 1.7.

a Split your class into *three* groups with each group being responsible for *one* of these characteristics (ethos, pathos or logos).

b Read the speech carefully and then, in your group, prepare a short group presentation on your chosen characteristic. In your presentation, you should explain this characteristic, giving examples from Malala's speech. Comment on the effects of these examples on her target audience.

c Take notes on each group's presentation, using a table like this.

	Ethos	Pathos	Logos
Definition			
Examples from Text 4.22			
Effect of this language on the audience			

LEARNER PROFILE

As you read Malala Yousafzai's speech, look for evidence of the IB learner profile. Which traits does she exemplify and promote? Give evidence to support each claim. Remember IB learners are:

- inquirers
- knowledgeable
- thinkers
- communicators
- principled
- open-minded
- caring
- risk takers
- balanced
- reflective.

Text 4.22

Malala Yousafzai's speech at the Youth Takeover of the United Nations

Extract

Malala Yousafzai 2013

Malala Yousafzai speaking at the Youth Takeover of the United Nations in 2013.

There are hundreds of human rights activists and social workers who are not only speaking for human rights, but who are struggling to achieve their goals of education, peace and equality. Thousands of people have been killed by the terrorists and millions have been injured. I am just one of them.

So here I stand . . . one girl among many.

I speak – not for myself, but for all girls and boys.

I raise up my voice – not so that I can shout, but so that those without a voice can be heard.

Those who have fought for their rights:
Their right to live in peace.
Their right to be treated with dignity.
Their right to equality of opportunity.
Their right to be educated.

Dear Friends, on the 9th of October 2012, the Taliban shot me on the left side of my forehead. They shot my friends too. They thought that the bullets would silence us. But they failed. And then, out of that silence came thousands of voices. The terrorists thought that they would change our aims and stop our ambitions but nothing changed in my life except this: Weakness, fear and hopelessness died. Strength, power and courage were born. I am the same Malala. My ambitions are the same. My hopes are the same. My dreams are the same.

Dear sisters and brothers, I am not against anyone. Neither am I here to speak in terms of personal revenge against the Taliban or any other terrorist group. I am here to speak up for the right of education of every child. I want education for the sons and the daughters of all the extremists, especially the Taliban.

I do not even hate the Talib who shot me. Even if there is a gun in my hand and he stands in front of me, I would not shoot him. This is the compassion that I have learnt from Muhammad, the prophet of mercy, Jesus Christ and Lord Buddha. This is the legacy of change that I have inherited from Martin Luther King, Nelson Mandela and Muhammad Ali Jinnah. This is the philosophy of non-violence that I have learnt from Gandhiji, Bacha Khan and Mother Teresa. And this is the forgiveness that I have learnt from my mother and father. This is what my soul is telling me, be peaceful and love everyone.

Dear sisters and brothers, we realise the importance of light when we see darkness. We realise the importance of our voice when we are silenced. In the same way, when we were in Swat, the north of Pakistan, we realised the importance of pens and books when we saw the guns.

The wise saying 'The pen is mightier than [the] sword' was true. The extremists are afraid of books and pens. The power of education frightens them. They are afraid of women. The power of the voice of women frightens them. And that is why they killed 14 innocent medical students in the recent attack in Quetta. And that is why they killed many female teachers and polio workers in Khyber Pakhtunkhwa and FATA. That is why they are blasting schools every day. Because they were and they are afraid of change, afraid of the equality that we will bring into our society.

I remember that there was a boy in our school who was asked by a journalist, 'Why are the Taliban against education?' He answered very simply. By pointing to his book he said, 'A Talib doesn't know what is written inside this book.' They think that God is a tiny, little conservative being who would send girls to hell just because of going to school. The terrorists are misusing the name of Islam and Pashtun society for their own personal benefits. Pakistan is a peace-loving democratic country. Pashtuns want education for their daughters and sons. And Islam is a religion of peace, humanity and brotherhood. Islam says that it is not only each child's right to get education, rather it is their duty and responsibility.

Honourable Secretary General, peace is necessary for education. In many parts of the world, especially Pakistan and Afghanistan, terrorism, wars and conflicts stop children going to their schools. We are really tired of these wars. Women and children are suffering in many parts of the world in many ways. In India, innocent and poor children are victims of child labour. Many schools have been destroyed in Nigeria. People in Afghanistan have been affected by the hurdles of extremism for decades. Young girls have to do domestic child labour and are forced to get married at an early age. Poverty, ignorance, injustice, racism and the deprivation of basic rights are the main problems faced by both men and women.

Dear fellows, today I am focusing on women's rights and girls' education because they are suffering the most. There was a time when women social activists asked men to stand up for their rights. But, this time, we will do it by ourselves. I am not telling men to step away from speaking for women's rights, rather I am focusing on women to be independent to fight for themselves.

Dear sisters and brothers, now it's time to speak up.

So today, we call upon the world leaders to change their strategic policies in favour of peace and prosperity.

TOK

Malala Yousafzai makes several claims in her speech. Based on her words, how do you know that the claims (a–e) are 'true'? What are the premises for these conclusions? Use reasoning to answer these questions.

a 'The pen is mightier than the sword.'

b 'Knowledge is power.

c 'Islam is a religion of peace, humanity and brotherhood.'

d 'Our words can change the world.'

e 'Education is the only solution. Education First.'

- We call upon the world leaders that all the peace deals must protect women and children's rights. A deal that goes against the dignity of women and their rights is unacceptable.
- We call upon all governments to ensure free compulsory education for every child all over the world.
- We call upon all governments to fight against terrorism and violence, to protect children from brutality and harm.
- We call upon the developed nations to support the expansion of educational opportunities for girls in the developing world.
- We call upon all communities to be tolerant – to reject prejudice based on cast, creed, sect, religion or gender. To ensure freedom and equality for women so that they can flourish. We cannot all succeed when half of us are held back.
- We call upon our sisters around the world to be brave – to embrace the strength within themselves and realise their full potential.

Dear brothers and sisters, we want schools and education for every child's bright future. We will continue our journey to our destination of peace and education for everyone. No one can stop us. We will speak for our rights and we will bring change through our voice. We must believe in the power and the strength of our words. Our words can change the world.

Because we are all together, united for the cause of education. And if we want to achieve our goal, then let us empower ourselves with the weapon of knowledge and let us shield ourselves with unity and togetherness.

Dear brothers and sisters, we must not forget that millions of people are suffering from poverty, injustice and ignorance. We must not forget that millions of children are out of schools. We must not forget that our sisters and brothers are waiting for a bright peaceful future.

So let us wage a global struggle against illiteracy, poverty and terrorism and let us pick up our books and pens. They are our most powerful weapons.

One child, one teacher, one pen and one book can change the world.

Education is the only solution. Education First.

CONCEPT

Perspective

How does Malala Yousafzai's experience with the Taliban give you *perspective* on terrorism and fundamentalism? How should you consider her opinions on Islam and the Taliban, as a Muslim and a victim of a terrorist attack? How does this relate to the use of ethos in her speech?

2.21 After your short presentation on ethos, pathos or logos, as represented in Malala Yousafzai's speech (Text 4.22), watch an online video of her delivering her full speech. As a class, discuss your answers to these questions:

a How effective is Malala Yousafzai in achieving her purpose through her use of language?

b Is there a line in her speech that you find most powerful? Which line is this? Why do you think this is so powerful?

c If you could interview Malala Yousafzai, what would you ask her? Why would you ask her this?

d In what ways is her speech similar to, or different from, Mahatma Gandhi's speech (Text 4.19)? Make a list of similarities and differences.

2.22 In Activity 2.19 you were asked to make a list of global issues that you found particularly important. Choose *one* of these issues and write a speech about it, which you might deliver at a Youth Takeover of the United Nations. You may adopt a persona (pretending to be someone you are not). Or you may write from your own perspective. Refer to real-life situations, current events and statistics. Your speech should be between 800 and 1000 words. As a school, you may wish to organise an event where speeches are read aloud for friends and parents. Or you may simply read your speech to your classmates in class. Look to Unit 1.7 and other speeches in this coursebook, such as Text 4.22, for inspiration.

Further reading

- *Kiss of the Spider Woman* is a highly acclaimed novel by Manuel Puig, originally in Spanish, about two cellmates in an Argentinean prison.
- *Nineteen Eighty-Four* by George Orwell is a classic novel – and for good reasons. It details all aspects of an imaginary oppressive regime through the eyes of Winston Smith, who is tasked with rewriting history for the Ministry of Truth.
- Martin Luther King's speeches and letters may also be studied as 'prose other than fiction' as a literary text for your English language and literature course. These texts will give you an excellent insight into the mind of a revolutionary.
- *Letters from Robben Island* by Achmed Kathrada is an excellent account of the African National Congress's struggle against apartheid in South Africa in the 1960s.
- There are many songwriters on the Prescribed Reading List (PRL) who have sung songs of protest. Joni Mitchell, John Lennon and Bob Dylan are a few that you can choose from. Lyrics from a protest song are appropriate for the individual oral, in which you analyse both a literary text and a non-literary text in relation to a global issue.

REFLECT

Do an online search for a video called 'The Power of Words', by Andrea Gardner for Purple Feather, which features a woman helping a blind man. What do you think of this video?

Look back at the texts you have read in this unit from Mahatma Gandhi to Percy Bysshe Shelley, from Keith Haring to Malala Yousafzai. To what extent have these people been successful in changing the world through their words? Give a short answer to this question with regard to at least *one* of the texts studied in this unit. As a class, discuss how you can change the world using words.

Unit 4.3 Politics

Word bank

metaphor
language framing
referendum
negative campaigning
attack ad
argument ad hominem
name calling
contrast ad
false dichotomy
fearmongering
deontology
dystopia
euphemism
dirty tricks

LEARNER PROFILE

Caring, principled

How political are you? IB learners are political because they are *caring* and *principled*. If you think about your local government, what policies are currently debated? What kinds of principles guide these debates?

Learning objectives

- learn how the language of different text types, such as magazine covers, advertisements, commercials and political speeches, is used to persuade audiences
- become familiar with the contexts of various political campaigns from previous decades and how they shaped the political language of their time
- develop your skills of textual analysis and essay writing by writing a mock Paper 1 and HL essay.

Have you ever noticed that politicians use language in a particular way? There is even an expression in English: 'spoken like a true politician'. What does this mean? Is it a way of making an unpopular idea sound agreeable? Does it suggest that politicians cannot be trusted? Policies, election campaigns, public speeches, polls and voting signs all use language to various political ends.

As language and literature students, you will find that elections provide you with a wealth of texts to study. This unit will explore several text types, such as magazine covers, speeches, essays, advertisements and commercials, showing how language has been used for political purposes. While the texts are taken from various times and places, you are encouraged to find comparable texts from modern-day contexts. You should think critically about the language used by politicians and policies, especially concerning those issues that affect you and your future.

International mindedness

In order to think about politics, policies and international mindedness, you may want to join a Model United Nations (MUN) club at your school or elsewhere. MUN encourages groups of young people to represent countries at conferences and simulate the United Nations's activities, such as the International Court of Justice, the Security Council and the General Assembly.

Getting started

3.1 Here are two texts – 4.23a and 4.23b. Half of your class will read Text 4.23a in Group 1. The other half will read Text 4.23b in Group 2, if possible in separate rooms. Read your text silently. Then answer the question in Activity 3.2.

Text 4.23a

Metaphors We Think With: The Role of Metaphor in Reasoning

Paul H. Thibodeau and Lera Boroditsky 2011

Crime is a virus infecting the city of Addison. Five years ago Addison was in good shape, with no obvious vulnerabilities. Unfortunately, in the past five years the city's defense systems have weakened, and the city has succumbed to crime. Today, there are more than 55,000 criminal incidents a year – up by more than 10,000 per year. There is a worry that if the city does not regain its strength soon, even more serious problems may start to develop.

Text 4.23b

Metaphors We Think With: The Role of Metaphor in Reasoning

Paul H. Thibodeau and Lera Boroditsky 2011

Crime is a beast preying on the city of Addison. Five years ago Addison was in good shape, with no obvious vulnerabilities. Unfortunately, in the past five years the city's defense systems have weakened, and the city has succumbed to crime. Today, there are more than 55,000 criminal incidents a year – up by more than 10,000 per year. There is a worry that if the city does not regain its strength soon, even more serious problems may start to develop.

3.2 After having read your text (Text 4.23a or Text 4.23b), give your answer to this question:

Imagine that the city of Addison has consulted you about the crime problem. You have the resources to investigate one of the four issues. Select one from the list:

a the education system and availability of youth programmes

b the economic system including the poverty level and employment rate

c the size and charge of the police force

d the correctional facilities, including the methods by which convicted criminals are punished.

3.3 Come together as a class and make a list of everyone's answers to Activity 3.2.

- Did Group 1 (Text 4.23a) favour answers 'a' and 'b', which focused on education, youth programmes, poverty levels and employment rates?
- Did Group 2 (Text 4.23b) favour answers 'c' and 'd', which focused on police force, correctional facilities and the punishment of criminals?

Read both texts carefully. What is the only difference between them? Do you see the **metaphor**? How did this difference in language affect your answers, if at all?

AOE question

How can texts present challenges and offer insights?

How did the two texts about crime in the fictional town of Addison (Texts 4.23a and 4.23b) and Activities 3.2–3.3 offer insight into the power of metaphor?

3.4 Texts 4.23a and 4.23b are versions of texts used by Paul H. Thibodeau and Lera Boroditsky in their 2011 experiment, which investigated (in a more scientific way than presented here) the degree to which people's decisions are influenced by language and metaphors. More specifically, they were concerned by the language of politicians and how it affected voter behaviour. In linguistics and the social sciences, this phenomenon is referred to as **language framing**. Discuss your answers to these questions as a class:

a To what extent are your political views influenced by the language of politicians and the mass media?

b To what extent is it possible for a **referendum** to be worded in a neutral, non-biased way? Do you think that proposals for new laws should be put to a referendum vote for all people in a country?

c To what extent do social media platforms, such as Facebook, only give you the kinds of political messages you want to hear, instead of opposing and balanced views?

Readers, writers and texts

3.5 As we continue to ask how language influences voters, it is important to consider visual language as well. Politics, for better or worse, can be about personalities and power, as people want strong political leaders. But what do powerful people look like? How do various media construct power?

a Study Texts 4.24–27, four magazine covers on which Margaret Thatcher appears. These were created throughout her career – before, during and after her time as Prime Minister of the UK.

b Place the magazine covers in a sequence from least to most powerful. On which cover is Thatcher depicted as the least powerful? On which cover is she depicted as most powerful? Take all aspects of the texts into consideration.

c Compare your sequence of texts to your classmates' sequences. How do they compare? Were your opinions similar or different?

d Based on your sequences, how would you define or describe a strong political leader? How might this definition differ for men or women in positions of political power?

e As a class, list the textual features of the text type 'magazine cover' that are used to construct meaning. How are these features used to construct the notion of 'power'?

f After you have listed your features, read Unit 1.1 on analysing images and magazine covers. Would you change your analysis of the Margaret Thatcher covers now?

g To what extent has 'context' played a role in your analysis of these Margaret Thatcher covers?

Text 4.24

Text 4.25

OBSERVER
magazine
DECEMBER 1990
'I think male prime ministers will one day come back into fashion'

Text 4.26

Tuesday 09.04.13
Published in London and Manchester
£1.40

Inside: unique 16-page supplement including Mikhail Gorbachev, Shirley Williams, Lech Walesa
Plus Ian McEwan on Lady Thatcher's legacy, page 5

theguardian

"She became harder than hard"

Hugo Young on Margaret Thatcher, 1925 - 2013

Days before he died in 2003 Young, Guardian columnist and Thatcher biographer, wrote an epitaph for the prime minister who changed Britain for ever

The first time I met Margaret Thatcher, I swear she was wearing gloves. But without any question, sitting behind her desk, she was wearing a hat.

Being a woman is undoubtedly one of the features, possibly the most potent, that makes her ascent to power memorable.

The woman, however, changed. The gender remained, its artefacts deployed with calculation. But it was overlaid by the supposedly masculine virtues, sometimes more manly than the men could ever assemble. She became harder than hard. Sent Bobby Sands to an Irish hero's grave without a blink. Faced down trade union leaders after her early years - apprentice years, when Jim Callaghan's Britain was falling apart - in which the commonest fear was that the little lady would not be able to deal with them across the table.

Thatcher became a supremely self-confident leader. No gloves, or hats, except for royalty or at funerals, but feet on the table, whisky glass at hand, into the small hours of solitude, for want of male cronies in the masculine world she dominated for all her 11 years in power.

I think by far her greatest virtue, in retrospect, is how little she cared if people liked her. Britain was battered out of the somnolent conservatism that had held back progress and, arguably, prosperity. This is what we mean by the Thatcher revolution, imposing on Britain, for better or for worse, some of the liberalisation that the major continental economies know, 20 years later, they still need. I think on balance, it was for the better, and so, plainly did Thatcher's chief successor, Tony Blair. If a leader's record is to be measured by the willingness of the other side to decide it cannot turn back the clock, then Thatcher bulks big in history.

But this didn't come without a price. Thatcher left a dark legacy that, like her successes, has still not disappeared behind the historical horizon. What happened at the hands of this woman's indifference to sentiment and good sense in the early 1980s brought unnecessary calamity to the lives of several million people who lost their jobs. It led to riots that nobody needed. More insidiously, it fathered a mood of tolerated harshness. Materialistic individualism was blessed as a virtue, the driver of national success. Everything was justified as long as it made money - and this, too, is still with us.

2-15

Read the full text on pages 2-3 »

Text 4.27

The Economist
APRIL 13TH–19TH 2013
Economist.com
America's enterprising immigrants
Blaming Germany
Will Abenomics work?
Digital cash: the Bitcoin bubble
What women want
Freedom fighter

CONCEPT

Identity

Who *was* Margaret Thatcher? Based on your analysis of these four magazine covers, is it possible for you to comment on her character? To what extent do these magazine covers reflect her *identity*?

3.6 Can you think of a current political leader from an Anglophone country, who has appeared on several magazine covers?

a Do an online search for magazine covers, finding one that depicts a male political leader and another that depicts a female political leader.

b Prepare a 5-minute comparative analysis that explores power, politics and gender, which you will present to your classmates. Your presentation should be informed by Unit 1.1 or other secondary sources that you can find.

c Share your magazine covers with your classmates and deliver your presentation in which you compare and contrast the ways political power is constructed on magazine covers for both male and female leaders.

d Create a wall display with your class's magazine covers, or an online collage or mood board. Alongside each cover, write a list of adjectives to describe the way the leaders look.

3.7 When you think of politics and politicians, you may think of elections and campaigns. In your studies of language, you will find that political campaigns provide a wealth of interesting texts for analysis, such as posters, signs, speeches, commercials and print advertisements. Texts 4.28–4.31 are four advertisements for political parties in the UK, taken from past decades. Study the advertisements and discuss your answers to this question: what techniques do these advertisements use in order to influence voters?

Text 4.28

Text 4.29

Text 4.30

Text 4.31

CONCEPT

Communication

Political parties are *communication* machines, as every message is carefully constructed and targets an audience for a specific effect. For this reason, campaign season is always an exciting time in the language and literature classroom.

AOE question

What are the different ways in which people are affected by texts?

Political campaigns affect voters in different ways, but their purpose is clear: they aim to convince voters to vote a certain way. Can an advertisement's effectiveness be measured by votes? Although that is not so easy to measure, political polls may go up or down for candidates after advertisements have appeared. Texts 4.28–4.31 may seem to be less relevant, and from a distant time and place. Can you find a more recent political advertisement that has affected you? Share it with your classmates and explain how this text might (or might not) convince you to vote a certain way.

3.8 Did you notice that all of the campaign ads (Texts 4.28–4.31) were negative? **Negative campaigning** has – for better or worse – become common practice in many election campaigns in the Anglophone world over the past decades. Here is a list of negative campaigning techniques. Can you find evidence of one or more of these in Texts 4.28–4.31?

a **Attack ad** – an attack ad points to the faults of an opponent's political platform, ideas or personality.

b **Argument ad hominem** – this argumentation fallacy describes an attack on a person rather than an attack on his or her ideas.

c **Name calling** – calling someone names is another form of negative advertising.

d **Contrast ad** – unlike attack ads, contrast ads include information about both candidates, highlighting the negative traits of one political party to reinforce the positive traits of the other.

e **False dichotomy** – closely related to contrast advertising is false dichotomy, the argumentation fallacy that presents only two choices in a debate, where in fact there are many.

f **Fearmongering** – politicians sometimes stir up fear in order to win votes, as they present themselves as the solution to a scary problem. This is also known as scaremongering.

TOK

As you study negative campaigning, you may wonder if there are any ethical rules that politicians are not willing to break. This raises the question: *How do we know what is right or wrong?* The simplest answer is probably the golden rule: treat others as you would like to be treated. In these negative campaigns (Activities 3.7–3.9), are politicians treating each other with respect? Or is the matter more complicated? If a candidate is truly corrupt, is it not the public's right to know? Does the opponent not have a duty to tell them?

Deontology is the study of duties and rule-based ethics. Can you, as a class, come up with a short list of rules for political campaigns, taking into consideration people's duties and rights?

CONCEPT

Culture

Negative campaigns and advertisements are characteristic of certain cultures. Some cultures take these techniques much further than others. How do Texts 4.28–4.31 compare to the election culture in your country? Are they more negative or less negative than what you are used to seeing? How have trends in negative advertising changed over the years in your country? Why is this?

Time and space

3.9 Attack advertising and negative campaigns have been around for decades. Here is a list of famous negative US presidential campaign advertisements that can easily be found through an online search.

a Get into small groups and assign each group a different advertisement from the list.

b Prepare a short presentation on your group's advertisement. In your presentation, show your classmates the video and analyse the kinds of techniques used by the political parties, using stills from the video. Furthermore, find out more about the political climate and context of the advertisement and comment on how this context adds meaning to the advertisement:

- 'Daisy Girl' by Lyndon B. Johnson's 1964 presidential campaign
- Walter Mondale TV ad: 'Roller Coaster' against Ronald Reagan
- 'Willy Horton' ad against Michael Dukakis
- 'Swift Boat Veterans for Truth' about John Kerry
- 'Historical Campaign Ad: Windsurfing (Bush–Cheney '04)' against John Kerry

- '3 a.m. White House Ringing Phone' by Hillary Clinton
- 'Big Bird – Obama for America' TV ad against Mitt Romney
- Hillary Clinton's attack ads on Donald Trump
- Trump's dark attack ad against Clinton on corruption.

AOE question

How can cultural contexts influence how texts are written and received?

Applying this question to the texts that you have seen so far in this unit, discuss how culture shapes the production and reception of texts. All of the negative campaigns from Activity 3.9 are from the USA. All of the print advertisements from Activities 3.7 and 3.8 are from the UK. Are these cultures similar or different in their political campaign practices? How are these cultures similar to or different from your country's culture with regard to campaign practices?

Intertextuality: connecting texts

3.10 After listening to each group's presentation of a different negative campaign and advertisement from Activity 3.9, go back and look for structural similarities between the advertisements that were listed there.

a Do they follow a pattern? What common methods do they use?

b As a group, write a bullet-pointed, 'how-to' list for creating a negative campaign.

c Share your group's list with those of other groups and discuss which structural techniques and sequences are most effective for this text type.

3.11 Do an online search for an attack ad called 'Hillary 1984 (Vote Different)', which went viral in 2008 during the Democratic primaries in the USA. Watch this advertisement and compare it to Apple Macintosh's '1984' advertisement, which can also be found through an online search. Read Unit 1.3 on advertisements and film techniques, which features the Apple Macintosh '1984' commercial.

a Take notes on the advertisements, using a table, in which you comment on various aspects of the videos.

b Get into pairs, choose an 'aspect' to focus on.

c Together, in pairs, write a few sentences of comparative analysis in which you:

- make a claim about the texts and your aspect
- refer to examples from the videos
- explain how these references support your claim.

d What phrases did you use to compare and contrast the texts? Read out your sentences to your classmates. As a class, make a list of useful phrases for comparing and contrasting texts. You will need this list for Activity 3.12.

Aspect	Apple Macintosh's '1984'	'Hillary 1984 (Vote Different)'
Purpose		
Audience		
Message		
Theme		
Tone		
Mood		
Symbolism		
Allusion		
Analogy		
Copy (text)		
Sound		

3.12 Text 4.32 is a passage from *Nineteen Eighty-Four*, by George Orwell. In this passage, the narrator describes a scene from a futuristic, **dystopian** world in which people are brainwashed by a totalitarian state and their leader Big Brother. Part of their brainwashing includes participation in the Two Minutes Hate, in which they watch video footage of the leader of the opposition party, Emmanuel Goldstein, shout obscenities and throw things violently at the screen. Discuss your answers to these questions. Use the useful phrases for comparison which you listed in Activity 3.11:

a How is the activity in this passage similar to or different from the '1984' Apple Macintosh commercial?

b Are there real hate rallies like the one depicted here? Can you compare or contrast this scene with something from real life?

c Do an online search for comparisons between the novel *Nineteen Eighty-Four* and the presidency of Donald Trump in the USA. Several websites have made connections between news stories and passages from the novel. Are these comparisons accurate and fair, or are they inaccurate and unfair? In groups, prepare an informed answer to this difficult question.

AOE question

What can diverse texts have in common?

Comparing a passage from *Nineteen Eighty-Four* to the language of a contemporary political rally may seem a far stretch. Nevertheless, truth can be stranger than fiction, and reality can be scarier than fantasy. Are you reading a literary work in class that has parallels to real-world politics? What are the points of similarity?

Text 4.32

Nineteen Eighty-Four

Extract

George Orwell 1949

In its second minute the Hate rose to a frenzy. People were leaping up and down in their places and shouting at the tops of their voices in an effort to drown the maddening bleating voice that came from the screen. The little sandy-haired woman had turned bright pink, and her mouth was opening and shutting like that of a landed fish. Even O'Brien's heavy face was flushed. He was sitting very straight in his chair, his powerful chest swelling and quivering as though he were standing up to the assault of a wave. The dark-haired girl behind Winston had begun crying out 'Swine! Swine! Swine!' and suddenly she picked up a heavy Newspeak dictionary and flung it at the screen. It struck Goldstein's nose and bounced off; the voice continued inexorably. In a lucid moment Winston found that he was shouting with the others and kicking his heel violently against the rung of his chair. The horrible thing about the Two Minutes Hate was not that one was obliged to act a part, but, on the contrary, that it was impossible to avoid joining in. Within thirty seconds any pretence was always unnecessary. A hideous ecstasy of fear and vindictiveness, a desire to kill, to torture, to smash faces in with a sledge-hammer, seemed to flow through the whole group of people like an electric current, turning one even against one's will into a grimacing, screaming lunatic. And yet the rage that one felt was an abstract, undirected emotion which could be switched from one object to another like the flame of a blowlamp.

Towards assessment

3.13 Text 4.33 is a campaign speech by Jack Layton, delivered in Québec, Canada in 2011. Imagine it were a text that appeared on your Paper 1 exam, with this guiding question:

In what ways does the speaker, Jack Layton, use language that is indicative of the text type, in order to achieve his purpose?

You can conduct this mock Paper 1 exam by following method a, b or c:

a You have 5 minutes to read the stimulus text, and 1 hour and 15 minutes to write an analysis of it. Answer the question with pen and paper. Ready, steady, go!

b On your own, study the defining features of speech writing from Unit 1.7. Try to find evidence of these features in Text 4.33. Revisit the assessment criteria for Paper 1 at either standard or higher level. At your own pace, write an analysis of Text 4.33, answering the exam question.

c As a class, study the defining features of speech writing from Unit 1.7. Try to find evidence of these features in Text 4.33.

- Revisit the assessment criteria for Paper 1 at either standard or higher level and discuss them.
- Review the elements of a good Paper 1 analysis and study a good sample response in Chapter 5.

TIP

You have to walk before you can run. Before you are ready to write a Paper 1 analysis under exam conditions, you should practise under easier circumstances and with more help. Activity 3.13 shows how you can prepare with more support systems (c) before taking the exam under exam conditions (a).

- As a class, collectively plan an analysis of Text 4.33. Create a mind map and outline for the essay.
- Agree on a thesis statement.
- Agree on five topic sentences and assign each topic sentence to a different group.
- As a group, write the paragraph for which you are responsible. Collate your paragraphs in an online document which you, your classmates and teacher can edit in real time.
- When you are satisfied with your analysis, display it for others in your school to read and learn from.

Text 4.33

Campaign speech

Abridged

Jack Layton 2011

Hello my fellow New Democrats! Thank you for this warm welcome. I am very happy to be here with so many friends and terrific candidates!

Something is happening in Québec right now, there is a wind of change. A wind that blows along the St-Lawrence River. From Côte-Nord to Montréal, where I was born, to Gaspésie, to Québec City, to Trois-Rivières. A wind of renewal coming from as far as James Bay, Abitibi-Témiscamingue and Outaouais. And blowing through Hudson, the city where I was raised. Wind from every corner in Québec, which will breathe new life into politics.

In this election, Canadians have said loud and clear. That too many families can't make ends meet. That too many seniors are living in poverty. That they have had enough of the same old debates. They deserve better. That is why we should dare to bring about change.

Change that is now necessary because Ottawa is running in circles. Because for too long, we have replaced scandals with different scandals, scandals that Quebecers could not tolerate anymore. Because some want to benefit from divisive politics. Because issues that matter to most Quebecers are yet to be settled. [. . .]

I am committed to do things differently in Ottawa. I am committed to get results in the first 100 days as your Prime Minister. Not in four years. Now. Because people need help now. That's my commitment to you. My friends, I am ready to be your Prime Minister, and I fully understand what this means.

A Prime Minister's job is to make sure the government works for those who have elected him, and not for big corporations. A Prime Minister's job is to bring people together. Build bridges between urban and rural areas and bring closer the different point of views which exist in this country. A Prime Minister must ensure Parliament represents the values you cherish. Values like: Tolerance, compassion, pride in our differences, respect for democracy, cooperation. Those values are shared by all Canadians. My friends, we will work together to bring those values back to Parliament. No matter which party you supported in the past, we can put the old debates aside and work together to achieve real change. [. . .]

It starts with a vote – your vote. And so, I'm calling on you – on May 2nd – to mark your ballot for change. Together, we can do this. We can show that: Here, our priority is job creation, the environment and world peace. Here, we dare to use words like "change," "hope," and "progress." Here, we dare to look beyond old politics and have the audacity to ask for something better. Here, we dare to look cynicism directly in the eye, and have faith that the best has yet to come. And especially because there is so much to do.

The time has come for someone to take on those responsibilities. We are ready to take on this challenge! It can't be done without you. Let's work together. Let's roll up our sleeves and start the work right now. Thank you!

3.14 In this activity you will use your analysis of Text 4.33 that you wrote for Activity 3.13.

a Compare your analysis of Text 4.33 with the sample analysis that has been provided here. How similar was your analysis to the approach taken by this student? How different were the aspects of the text that you focused on?

b Assess this sample analysis using the assessment criteria for Paper 1 at the beginning of this book. As a class, discuss your marks.

c Read the annotations to the sample Paper 1 script carefully. How could you improve your analysis by taking these points into consideration?

d After writing a Paper 1 analysis on Text 4.33 and comparing it to the sample analysis, save your work in your learner portfolio and reflect on your Paper 1 writing skills. What did you learn from this activity? What do you still need to work on? How are you going to develop these skills?

Paper 1 – Sample 1

Guiding question

In what ways does the speaker, Jack Layton, use language that is typical of the text type, in order to achieve his purpose?

Analysis

In 2011 Jack Layton delivered a speech to his fellow New Democrats in Québec, encouraging them to vote for him as the new Prime Minister of Canada. His use of language, especially his use of anaphora, tricolon and pronouns, is typical of speech writing and helps him achieve his purpose of getting people to vote for his New Democrats party.

Notice the thesis statement uses words from the guiding question. This is good practice.

Notice how the thesis statement answers the guiding question.

Political speeches are often full of anaphora, and Jack Layton's speech is no different. Anaphora is the repetition of a word or phrase at the beginning of a sentence. He uses anaphora to give his speech a sense of direction and pace, so that listeners are captured and eager to learn more about his campaign promises. Already in his introduction, Mr Layton speaks of a 'wind of change' (line 3). Then he elaborates on this change by starting three sentences with the word 'wind': 'A wind that blows along the St Lawrence River' (line 3), 'A wind of renewal coming from as far as James Bay' (line 5), and 'Wind from every corner of Québec'

After you refer to a stylistic device, be sure to explain it.

(line 7). The audience imagines both physical winds blowing across these landmarks, along with figurative winds of change of leadership in the country. Furthermore, he emphasises the importance of the task of running for 'Prime Minister', as he repeats these words at the beginning of nearly each sentence later in his speech: 'A Prime Minister's job is to make sure the government works' (line 23), 'A Prime Minister's job is to bring people together' (line 24), and 'A Prime Minister must ensure Parliament represents the values you cherish' (line 26). By starting each sentence with this title, he emphasises the respect he has for that position and the way he intends to use that position to change lives for Canadians. Listeners are more likely to associate him with the office of Prime Minister after he has repeated the title so often. In return, they are more likely to vote for him.

This paragraph includes two examples of anaphora, with detailed reference.

Any strong Paper 1 analysis should refer to target audience frequently.

Like many political speakers, Jack Layton knows how to use tricolon to show how much he has to offer the people of Canada. Tricolons are lists of three, which give audiences a sense of quantity. Throughout his speech he uses tricolon, particularly with regard to abstract values, with which no one could really disagree, such as 'Tolerance, compassion, pride in our differences, respect for democracy, cooperation' (line 28). Although this is not necessarily a list of three, they comprise a list of ideals that appeal to the listeners' sense of ethos. Towards the closing of his speech, he uses tricolon to list big challenges that he is willing to face as Prime Minister with the people of Canada, such as 'job creation, the environment and world peace' (line 36). If these tasks sound too daunting for his audience, he reassures them with another tricolon immediately thereafter: 'Here, we dare to use words like "change," "hope," and "progress"' (line 36). These values appeal to a progressive audience and they encourage them to be optimistic about Canada's future with Jack Layton as Primer Minister. This is also more likely to make listeners vote for him.

Avoid quoting something as an example when in fact it is not.

Even though this paragraph is about tricolon, it manages to include a reference to another rhetorical feature.

A good structure for the ending sentence of a paragraph is 'X makes the reader do/feel/think Y'.

Finally, Jack Layton uses pronouns, as every good speech should use them, to present himself as a leader and evoke a sense of belonging for all Canadians. He regularly switches from 'I' to 'you' and 'they' to 'we'. For example he begins by speaking about Canadians and what 'they' have said about poverty, which is why 'we should dare to bring about change' (line 11). This shifts the focus from other people out there to 'us' right here, closer by, as members of an inner circle, giving the audience a sense of belonging. Similarly, he begins line 19 with 'I am committed to do things differently in Ottawa' (line 19), which eventually shifts to the second-person pronoun with 'That's my commitment to you' (line 21). This makes their vote for him seem like a vote for themselves, as it takes the focus away from him and puts it onto the listeners. By putting the people before himself Jack Layton shows selfless leadership.

The stimulus text has many more examples of the second-person pronoun, but the student has made a selection of a selection for the sake of time. Rather than taking off points for what's missing, examiners mark what you have included. Pick your battles wisely.

Another good structure

All in all the stylistic features used by Jack Layton, such as anaphora, tricolon and use of pronouns, are typical of campaign speeches for candidates for Prime Minister. He uses these features to engage his audience, appeal to their sense of ethos, make them trust his leadership abilities and include them in his vision for a greater Canada.

In your conclusion, return to the author's purpose and answer the question again.

Paper 1 – Sample 1 – Examiner's marks and comments

Criterion A: Knowledge, understanding and interpretation: 4 out of 5 marks

The student has a good understanding of the speech. The analysis states clearly that the purpose of the speech is to win votes and include voters in his 'vision for a greater Canada'. Jack Layton's criticism of political scandals and his call for change are not found in this analysis. Nonetheless, the points that are made are well supported by many references and relevant quotations from the speech.

Criterion B: Analysis and evaluation: 5 out of 5 marks

The analysis focuses on three stylistic features of the speech: anaphora, tricolon and pronouns. Each paragraph evaluates the effects of these features on the audience. Words such as 'appeal', 'encourage' and 'associate' are excellent for establishing how the audience is affected by Layton's speech.

Criterion C: Coherence, focus and organisation: 5 out of 5 marks

The analysis returns to the main points at the beginning and ending of each paragraph, making it coherent and effective. It follows a clear structure and has a strong sense of organisation. This is due to its focus on the guiding question throughout the analysis.

Criterion D: Language: 5 out of 5 marks

This analysis is a good example of concise writing. No words are wasted and every sentence contributes to the analysis. The three terms – anaphora, tricolon and pronouns – are used accurately. Connectives such as 'all in all', 'for example' and 'finally' are also effective in establishing a clear register for the analysis.

3.15 While this unit has mostly focused on non-literary texts, you may see similar political themes in your literary works. You may want to practise writing a Paper 2 essay on *one* of the four questions listed here. You can find more guidance on how to write a Paper 2 essay in Chapter 6.

a In what ways do characters in two of your literary works demonstrate leadership qualities that inspire others?

b To what extent and for what reasons might two of your literary works be considered 'political'?

c In what ways do two works of fiction that you have read offer insight into the real-life history and struggles of a nation or people?

d In what ways and for what reasons are opposing political ideologies depicted in two of the literary works that you have read?

Higher level extension

3.16 After reading and studying Text 4.33, you may wonder why politicians speak the way they do. Is there a kind of school that teaches politicians to use the English language in a particular way? Read this extract from a text. Think of it as a puzzle. Can you solve the puzzle and figure out what the speaker means to say? Why has the speaker used these words to say these things?

> 'While freely conceding that the Soviet regime exhibits certain features which the humanitarian may be inclined to deplore, we must, I think, agree that a certain curtailment of the right to political opposition is an unavoidable concomitant of transitional periods, and that the rigors which the Russian people have been called upon to undergo have been amply justified in the sphere of concrete achievement.'

3.17 Did you manage to solve the puzzle? Perhaps it helps you to know that it was written in 1946, at a time when the Soviet leader Joseph Stalin was deporting political dissidents to Siberia, after both Allied Forces and the Soviet Union had defeated Nazism in Europe. It may have been spoken by a British politician, telling concerned citizens to ignore the Soviet Union's crimes, because they fought hard in the war. Who wrote the text? George Orwell wrote this as an example of the kind of language that was being used by politicians and academics after the Second World War.

Read Text 4.34. Several claims (a–e) have been highlighted from Orwell's essay. As a class, discuss:

- what you think Orwell means by each claim
- whether or not you agree or disagree with each claim, with your reasons
- if there is modern-day evidence to support each claim.

a In our time it is broadly true that political writing is bad writing.

b In our time, political speech and writing are largely the defence of the indefensible.

c But if thought corrupts language, language can also corrupt thought.

d The great enemy of clear language is insincerity.

e Languages have all deteriorated . . . as a result of dictatorship.

Text 4.34

Politics and the English Language

George Orwell 1946

In our time it is broadly true that political writing is bad writing. Where it is not true, it will generally be found that the writer is some kind of rebel, expressing his private opinions and not a 'party line'. Orthodoxy, of whatever colour, seems to demand a lifeless, imitative style. The political dialects to be found in pamphlets, leading articles, manifestos, White papers and the speeches of undersecretaries do, of course, vary from party to party, but they are all alike in that one almost never finds in them a fresh, vivid, homemade turn of speech. When one watches some tired hack on the platform mechanically repeating the familiar phrases – *bestial, atrocities, iron heel, bloodstained tyranny, free peoples of the world, stand shoulder to shoulder* – one often has a curious feeling that one is not watching a live human being but some kind of dummy: a feeling which suddenly becomes stronger at moments when the light catches the speaker's spectacles and turns them into blank discs which seem to have no eyes behind them. And this is not altogether fanciful. A speaker who uses that kind of phraseology has gone some distance toward turning himself into a machine. The appropriate noises are coming out of his larynx, but his brain is not involved, as it would be if he were choosing his words for himself. If the speech he is making is one that he is accustomed to make over and over again, he may be almost unconscious of what he is saying, as one is when one utters the responses in church. And this reduced state of consciousness, if not indispensable, is at any rate favourable to political conformity.

In our time, political speech and writing are largely the defence of the indefensible. Things like the continuance of British rule in India, the Russian purges and deportations, the dropping of the atom bombs on Japan, can indeed be defended, but only by arguments which are too brutal for most people to face, and which do not square with the professed aims of the political parties. Thus political language has to consist largely of euphemism, question-begging and sheer cloudy vagueness. Defenceless villages are bombarded from the air, the inhabitants driven out into the countryside, the cattle machine-gunned, the huts set on fire with incendiary bullets: this is called *pacification*. Millions of peasants are robbed of their farms and sent trudging along the roads with no more than they can carry: this is called *transfer of population* or *rectification of frontiers*. People are imprisoned for years without trial, or shot in the back of the neck or sent to die of scurvy in Arctic lumber camps: this is called *elimination of unreliable elements*. Such phraseology is needed if one wants to name things without calling up mental pictures of them. Consider for instance some comfortable English professor defending Russian totalitarianism. He cannot say outright, 'I believe in killing off your opponents when you can get good results by doing so'. Probably, therefore, he will say something like this:

'While freely conceding that the Soviet regime exhibits certain features which the humanitarian may be inclined to deplore, we must, I think, agree that a certain curtailment of the right to political opposition is an unavoidable concomitant of transitional periods, and that the rigours which the Russian people have been called upon to undergo have been amply justified in the sphere of concrete achievement.'

The inflated style itself is a kind of **euphemism**. A mass of Latin words falls upon the facts like soft snow, blurring the outline and covering up all the details. The great enemy of clear language is insincerity. When there is a gap between one's real and one's declared aims, one turns as it were instinctively to long words and exhausted idioms, like a cuttlefish spurting out ink. In our age there is no such thing as 'keeping out of politics'. All issues are political issues, and politics itself is a mass of lies, evasions, folly, hatred, and schizophrenia. When the general atmosphere is bad, language must suffer. I should expect to find – this is a guess which I have not sufficient knowledge to verify – that the German, Russian and Italian languages have all deteriorated in the last ten or fifteen years, as a result of dictatorship.

But if thought corrupts language, language can also corrupt thought. A bad usage can spread by tradition and imitation even among people who should and do know better. The debased language that I have been discussing is in some ways very convenient. Phrases like *a not unjustifiable assumption, leaves much to be desired, would serve no good purpose, a consideration which we should do well to bear in mind,* are a continuous temptation, a packet of aspirins always at one's elbow. Look back through this essay, and for certain you will find that I have again and again committed the very faults I am protesting against. By this morning's post I have received a pamphlet dealing with conditions in Germany. The author tells me that he 'felt impelled' to write it. I open it at random, and here is almost the first sentence I see: '[The Allies] have an opportunity not only of achieving a radical transformation of Germany's social and political structure in such a way as to avoid a nationalistic reaction in Germany itself, but at the same time of laying the foundations of a co-operative and unified Europe.' You see, he 'feels impelled' to write – feels, presumably, that he has something new to say – and yet his words, like cavalry horses answering the bugle, group themselves automatically into the familiar dreary pattern. This invasion of one's mind by ready-made phrases (*lay the foundations, achieve a radical transformation*) can only be prevented if one is constantly on guard against them, and every such phrase anaesthetises a portion of one's brain.

3.18 In your discussion from Activity 3.17 on Text 4.34, you may have referred to modern-day politicians and their use of language. Can you think of a modern-day politician who has used language in ways that George Orwell describes in his essay? Or has the language of politicians evolved since 1946?

a Research a modern-day, English-speaking politician and find examples of their use of language in speeches or social media postings.

b Think of a line of inquiry that would allow you to explore this politician's use of language in an HL essay. Find both primary and secondary sources which allow you to explore this line of inquiry.

c Read Chapter 7 about the HL essay, to find out what is expected of you. Study the sample in that chapter and the assessment criteria in the introduction to this coursebook.

d Write a thesis statement that answers your line of inquiry, shows the scope of the essay and makes a claim. Draw mind maps around this statement and plan an outline of your essay before writing it.

e Show your teacher one completed draft and ask for feedback which is informed by the assessment criteria.

f Submit your final draft to your teacher. This may or may not be the HL essay that you submit to the IB.

Extended essay

Activity 3.18 asks you to write an HL essay about the language of a particular politician. You may find such a wealth of material that you decide to write a Category 3 extended essay on the topic. The unique language of Donald Trump's tweets, for example, has been analysed by linguists in journals and articles, and you will find plenty of secondary sources to support a 4000-word essay. If you decide to explore this type of essay, be sure to focus on *one* politician, with frequent reference to actual language in primary sources.

Further reading

- *The Metaphors We Live By*, a book by George Lakoff and Mark Johnson, has been very influential in the world of linguistics. Its main thesis suggests that metaphors are everywhere in how people communicate with each other.
- *Get Me Roger Stone* is a documentary about the career of Roger Stone, a political strategist who changed American politics, resulting in the election of Donald Trump. He is known for his use of **dirty tricks**, which are unethical or illegal campaign practices intended to disrupt or sabotage other people's campaigns.
- *Politics and the English Language* by George Orwell can be found online in its full version. It is a timeless essay that gives you insight into the political climate of his times and may inform your understanding of politics and language in our present time.

REFLECT

This unit on language and politics has invited you to explore several text types, such as magazine covers, advertisements, commercials, speeches and essays. What have you added to your learner portfolio throughout this unit? Could you consider 'politics' a 'global issue' for your portfolio?

You may want to think of a more narrowly defined issue to explore in your portfolio, and study the language of politicians on this issue. As you do this, think of the politics that affect you. How do policies and politicians affect your life and future?

Paper 1: Guided textual analysis (SL/HL)

What is expected of you in your exam for the Paper 1: Guided textual analysis?
What kinds of skill should you develop during your language and literature course to prepare for this exam?
How can you develop these skills?

In this unit you will:

- learn about the requirements and expectations for the Paper 1 exam
- discuss the strengths and weaknesses of several samples of students' work
- develop writing skills for analysing unseen, non-literary texts in a coherent and appropriate way.

5

Paper 1

Word bank

textual analysis
author
text
reader
purpose
style
structure
audience
meaning
thesis statement

Learning objectives

- gain a better understanding of what is expected of you on the Paper 1 exam by engaging with stimulus texts, sample responses, the assessment criteria and marking notes
- develop your skills in textual analysis by annotating texts, drawing mind maps, applying the assessment criteria and writing your own Paper 1 analysis.

Standard and higher level students receive the same Paper 1 exam for English A: Language and Literature.

When you open your exam booklet, you will notice two non-literary texts, each accompanied by a guiding question.

- For standard level you will have 1 hour and 15 minutes to write an analysis on *one* of the two texts of your choice.
- For higher level you will have 2 hours and 15 minutes to write *two* analyses, one on each of the texts.

Both standard and higher level students are marked according to the same assessment criteria, which you can find in the introduction of this coursebook. For both standard and higher level students, the Paper 1 exam accounts for 35% of your final course grade.

How should you prepare for your Paper 1 exam? The answer is simple: you should practise analysing texts regularly throughout your language and literature course. You should practise writing under various conditions, receiving meaningful feedback on your work.

This chapter prepares you for the Paper 1 exam by offering strategies for unpacking the stimulus texts, organising your ideas and shaping your analysis. There are three examples of students' analyses, which show you the pitfalls to avoid and the models to emulate. By engaging with stimulus texts, the assessment criteria and marking notes, you will gain a better understanding of what is expected from you on your Paper 1 exam. By doing the activities, you will hone your skills in **textual analysis** and develop your appreciation of how meaning is constructed through language.

Getting started

5.1 Paper 1 is an exercise in textual analysis. What is textual analysis? What does it look like? Here is a definition which you may want to write out and place prominently in your classroom. You may wish to do the same with the stimulus text and the analysis of it.

Definition of textual analysis
Textual analysis is the process of ascertaining how *meaning* is constructed through *language*.

Stimulus text for analysis
Australian Airlines brings the Airbus A380 to Sydney.

Example of textual analysis
The use of alliteration in this newspaper headline, with the 'a' sound repeated in '<u>A</u>ustralian <u>A</u>irlines' (line 1) and '<u>A</u>irbus <u>A</u> three-<u>ei</u>ghty' (line 1) gives the reader the impression that the plane flies as smoothly as it sounds.

In textual analysis, there are three agents that shape meaning: the **author**, the **text** and the **reader**.

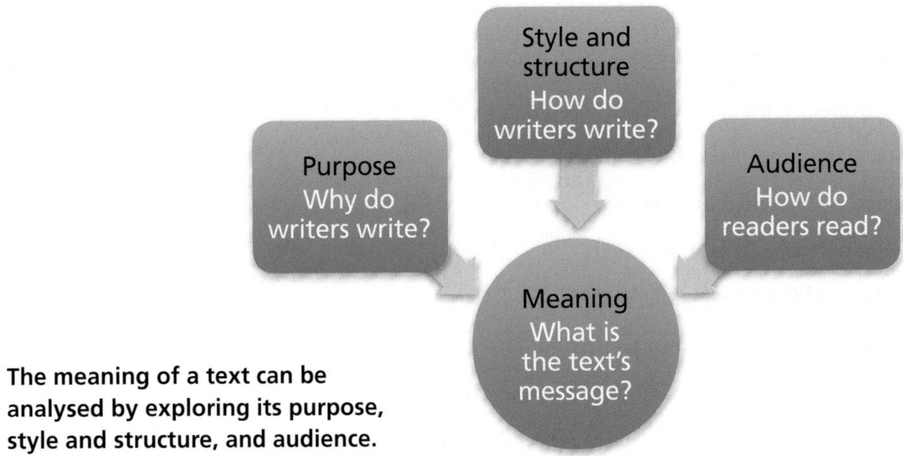

The meaning of a text can be analysed by exploring its purpose, style and structure, and audience.

The diagram helps you visualise this relationship.

You may not be aware of it, but textual analysis happens all around you. Have you read a movie review recently? Have you responded critically to a social media post? Have you ever tested and talked about a new product? All of these situations involve someone commenting critically on how meaning is being constructed.

Consider a broad definition of 'text' to include anything with meaning. Let's use the example of this basketball shoe, worn by Minnesota Lynx forward Maya Moore.

Purpose	Why did Nike create this shoe?	To boost sales, to honour Michael Jordan, to give a basketball player a little hope that they can fly like Jordan.
Style and structure	How did Nike construct this shoe?	With synthetic materials, a design, a few words ('Air Jordan') and a few images, one of which is the iconic silhouette of Michael Jordan flying through the air.
Audience	Who would buy this shoe?	Anyone who wants to play basketball, impress friends and dream of flying like Michael Jordan, including Maya Moore.
Meaning	What is the shoe's message?	Michael Jordan is one of basketball's greatest players. Wear Air Jordans and you can be great like him.

Consider this shoe, an 'Air Jordan' worn by Maya Moore, as a 'text' for analysis. What is its 'meaning'? See Activity 5.1.

a Get into pairs and choose a different item for analysis from this list.

b For the item that you have chosen, do an online search to find a suitable image and perhaps an explanation of the item.

c Draw a table like the one used for the Air Jordan example, with the different aspects of text analysis in the left column, relevant questions in the middle column and your short answers in the right–hand column.

d Present the image of the item to your classmates and report on your findings.

e How does this activity help you understand the nature of textual analysis? Discuss the value of this activity with your classmates and teacher.

Items for analysis

- a Alessi's Juicy Salif citrus squeezer, designed by Philippe Starck
- b the Great Wall of China
- c a Big Mac hamburger from McDonald's
- d an indigenous Australian didgeridoo
- e the last musical concert you attended
- f 'For the Love of God' by Damien Hirst
- g a 'Hard Rock Cafe' T-shirt from any city of choice
- h a red telephone box, traditionally found in the UK
- i the album cover of *Sgt. Pepper's Lonely Hearts Club Band* by The Beatles.

CONCEPT

Communication

Arguably, your language and literature course is really a course in *communication* arts and textual analysis. The word 'language' in the course title 'Language and Literature' refers to the styles, structures, forms and media used to construct meaning. This may be misread to refer only to grammar and vocabulary (which are also forms and structures) or to 'non-literary texts' (which are also part of the course). As you analyse texts, looking for meaning, ask yourself: what is being *communicated*? This is a good starting point.

5.2 In this activity you will focus on texts with words. It helps to start with smaller texts, before analysing longer ones. Here are six very short texts (a–f). In response to each text, write a very short piece of textual analysis – just one or two complete sentences. In your analysis comment on:

- the purpose of the text
- the reader's response
- the author's choice of style
- the meaning or message of the text.

You may wish to refer to one or more of the stylistic devices listed in this box. For text a, you may find it helpful to use the example from Activity 5.1 (about the Airbus A380) as a model for an analysis on a very short text.

parallelism	hypophora	imperative	euphemism	metaphor
repetition	alliteration	rhyme	ellipsis	use of pronouns

- a Clearance sale: everything must go!
- b Why join Miles and Smiles? Because we go the extra mile for you!
- c Good evening, Berlin! Are you ready to rock?
- d Lord, bless these gifts which we are about to receive.
- e Mr Brian Hull flying to Hong Kong: you are delaying the flight. Please proceed to Gate D12 immediately.
- f If you lift it up, put it down. If you spilt it, clean it up. If you used it up, replace it. If you're finished, flush it.

5.3 Share your answers from Activity 5.2 with your classmates. Do you notice any kinds of sentence structures that are particularly effective in analysing texts in general? Are they similar to some of the suggested sentence structures offered here? Rewrite one of your answers, using elements from these sentence structures.

a Through the use of . . . the author achieves her purpose of . . .

b Text X uses . . . in order to make the reader feel . . . .

c The author of Text X aims to . . . , which can be seen in line X and the use of . . . .

d The language of Text X has a . . . effect on the reader, through the author's use of . . . .

e The tone of the text is . . . which is established through the author's use of . . . .

Paper 1 – Specimen

5.4 You have considered an analysis about a shoe or a short sentence. But how should you approach a Paper 1 exam text? The 'See, Think, Wonder' approach, from Harvard Project Zero's 'visible thinking routines', is helpful for Paper 1 stimulus texts in general. Study Texts 5.1 and 5.2 as if they were in an SL/HL Paper 1. For each text, write a few words under each column in a table as shown here.

	What do you *see*? What concrete images stand out?	What does this make you *think* about? What abstract ideas or concepts come to mind?	What does this make you *wonder*? What questions do you have? What predictions can you make?
Text 5.1			
Text 5.2			

TIP

Text 5.1 is a very *visual* text. You can expect one or both of the texts on the exam to have visual elements. See Chapter 1 for advice on how to analyse visual texts such as cartoons, comic strips and magazine covers.

5 Paper 1

Text 5.1

Meaning = depressed people need to be heard, Audience = people who know depressed people, Purpose = raise awareness, Style = artwork, dialogue, symbolism

A comic about depression?!

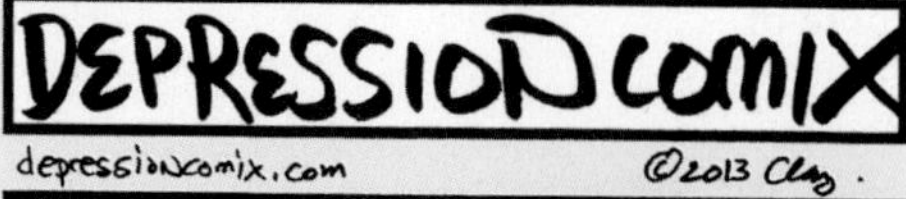

funny spelling, trendy

tone = perturbed rhetorical question

body language = stand-offish

apron = symbol for tidiness

gradient: light behind mother, dark behind daughter

eyebrows down

mask = symbol

eyebrows up!

reverse camera angle, behind mask reveals her angst

heart = symbol of love

smile is fake, simple drawing style, cartoony

DIALOGUE
SYMBOLISM
ARTWORK

slumped shoulders

contrast her clothing and hair to mother's

why so much blank space?

ellipsis = hesitant

bold font emphasises theme = depression

no speech bubble, words behind mother, too many words, accusations, clearly NOT listening to daughter

body language same as panel 1

mask returns, nothing accomplished

No! Mother made the mistake!

Guiding question

In what ways does the artist use the features of this text type to convey a message about depression?

Text 5.2

An Open Apology to All of My Weight Loss Clients

Abridged extract

Iris Higgins 2013

Dear Former Weight Loss Clients (you know who you are):

I'm sorry. [. . .]

I owe you an apology, my former client and now friend, who I helped to lose too much weight. Who I watched gain the weight back, plus some. Because that's what happens when you put someone on a 1,200 calorie diet. But I didn't know. If you're reading this, then I want you to know that you have always been beautiful. And that all these fad diets are crap meant to screw with your metabolism so that you have to keep buying into them. I think now that I was a really good weight loss consultant. Because I did exactly what the company wanted (but would never dare say). I helped you lose weight and then gain it back, so that you thought we were the solution and you were the failure. You became a repeat client and we kept you in the game. I guess I did my job really well.

And now I wonder, did I do more harm than good? When I left, you all wrote me cards and sent me flowers. I still have those cards, the ones that tell me how much I helped you, how much I cared. But I'm friends with some of you on Facebook now, and I look at your photos and you look happy. And beautiful. And not because you lost weight since I saw you last. But because I see YOU now. You. Not a client sitting in my chair, asking for my assistance in becoming what society wants. But you, a smart and lovely woman, who really doesn't need some random company telling her there's something wrong with her.

So I'm sorry because when you walked in to get your meal plan, I should have told you that you were beautiful. I should have asked you how you FELT. Were you happy? Did you feel physically fit? Were you able to play with your kids? There were so many of you who never needed to lose a pound, and some of you who could have gained some. And maybe sometimes I told you that. But not enough. Not emphatically. Because it was my job to let you believe that making the scale go down was your top priority. And I did my job well.

I am sorry because many of you walked in healthy and walked out with disordered eating, disordered body image, and the feeling that you were a "failure." None of you ever failed. Ever. I failed you. The weight loss company failed you. Our society is failing you.

Just eat food. Eat real food, be active, and live your life. Forget all the diet and weight loss nonsense. It's really just that. Nonsense.

And I can't stop it. But I can stop my part in it. I won't play the weight loss game anymore. I won't do it to my body, and I won't help you do it to yours. That's it. End game.

Guiding question

In what ways does the language of this text reflect its purpose?

5.5 Before you write your analysis of a stimulus text, you should take approximately 10 minutes to annotate the text, write an outline or draw a mind map to organise your ideas.

Why annotate the text? If you consider the assessment criteria, you will see that you are assessed on your ability to be perceptive and analytical. Annotating the text allows you to engage more with the text, making you really see and think about it. Annotating is a skill that requires practice. What does it mean to annotate a text? Here are several annotation strategies that you may want to practise:

- Use different-coloured highlighter pens to group your ideas.
- Ask questions of the text (who, what, when, where, why and how?), as if you could interview it or its author.
- Use a conceptual framework, such as the acronym MAPS (Meaning = Audience + Purpose + Style) and make notes on your application of these concepts in the margin.
- Underline or circle words that stand out.
- Draw lines and make links between words.
- Write 'this-means-that' notes in the margin, with arrows to key words and phrases.

Text 5.1 has been annotated for you by a student, as an example. Discuss the kinds of strategies that the student has used here. In a similar way, use appropriate strategies for annotating a copy of Text 5.2. Take 5 to 10 minutes to do this.

Then place your annotated copy of the text onto a large table for everyone in your class to see. Walk around the table to see what strategies other classmates used. What can you learn from their annotations?

5.6 Annotating texts is like casting a net to see what you catch. The next step is to understand what you have caught, sort through it and present it in a meaningful way. In other words, you need to make a plan for writing your analysis. Eventually, you may want to make an outline or mind map to record your ideas (Activity 5.7). Before you do so, however, you should formulate a thesis statement.

A thesis statement for a Paper 1 analysis should:

- answer the guiding question
- articulate the text's main message
- identify the main stylistic features that construct this message.

These points in your thesis statement do not have to be in this order. The first point may happen automatically by focusing on the second and third bullet points. The thesis statement comes at the end of the first paragraph of your analysis. Here is an example of a thesis statement in response to Text 5.1.

> *Thesis statement for Text 5.1*
>
> The artist uses the stylistic devices of comic strips, such as symbolism, artwork and dialogue, to effectively convey his message that readers should take depression seriously and listen to other people's problems.

Write a thesis statement that would help you write an analysis of Text 5.2. Look through your annotations of the text (from Activity 5.5) one more time before you do this.

TIP

How many stylistic features should you include in your thesis statement? Consider that each feature will form the basis of a body paragraph, that is, a main paragraph between the introductory and concluding paragraphs, which contains text relating to the thesis statement. Time constraints will determine how many and what kinds of features you can explore. It is recommended that you explore only *three* major features of a text.

Think in terms of 'major' and 'minor' features. The use of onomatopoeia, for example, is most likely a minor feature in a text. While it may play an important role in a text you are analysing, you may want to explore it in one sentence as part of a longer paragraph about diction or word choice. Major features include but are not limited to:

- symbolism
- narrative technique
- imagery
- figurative language
- diction
- syntax
- images.

Naturally, each text is different and the use of pronouns, for example, may require an entire paragraph.

AOE questions

Are you struggling to write a thesis statement? Besides the 'guiding question' which accompanies the stimulus text, you can find inspiration from one of the six AOE questions from the 'Readers, writers and texts' part of the course.

- How and why do people study language and literature?
- What are the different ways in which people are affected by texts?
- How can the 'meaning' of a text be constructed, negotiated, expressed and interpreted by readers and writers?
- How does the use of language vary among different types of text?
- How do the style and structure of a text affect its meaning?
- How can texts present challenges and offer insights?

5.7 Once you have a working thesis statement, try building a mind map around it. Here is a sample mind map, based on the thesis statement for Text 5.1. Create a similar mind map based on your thesis statement on Text 5.2.

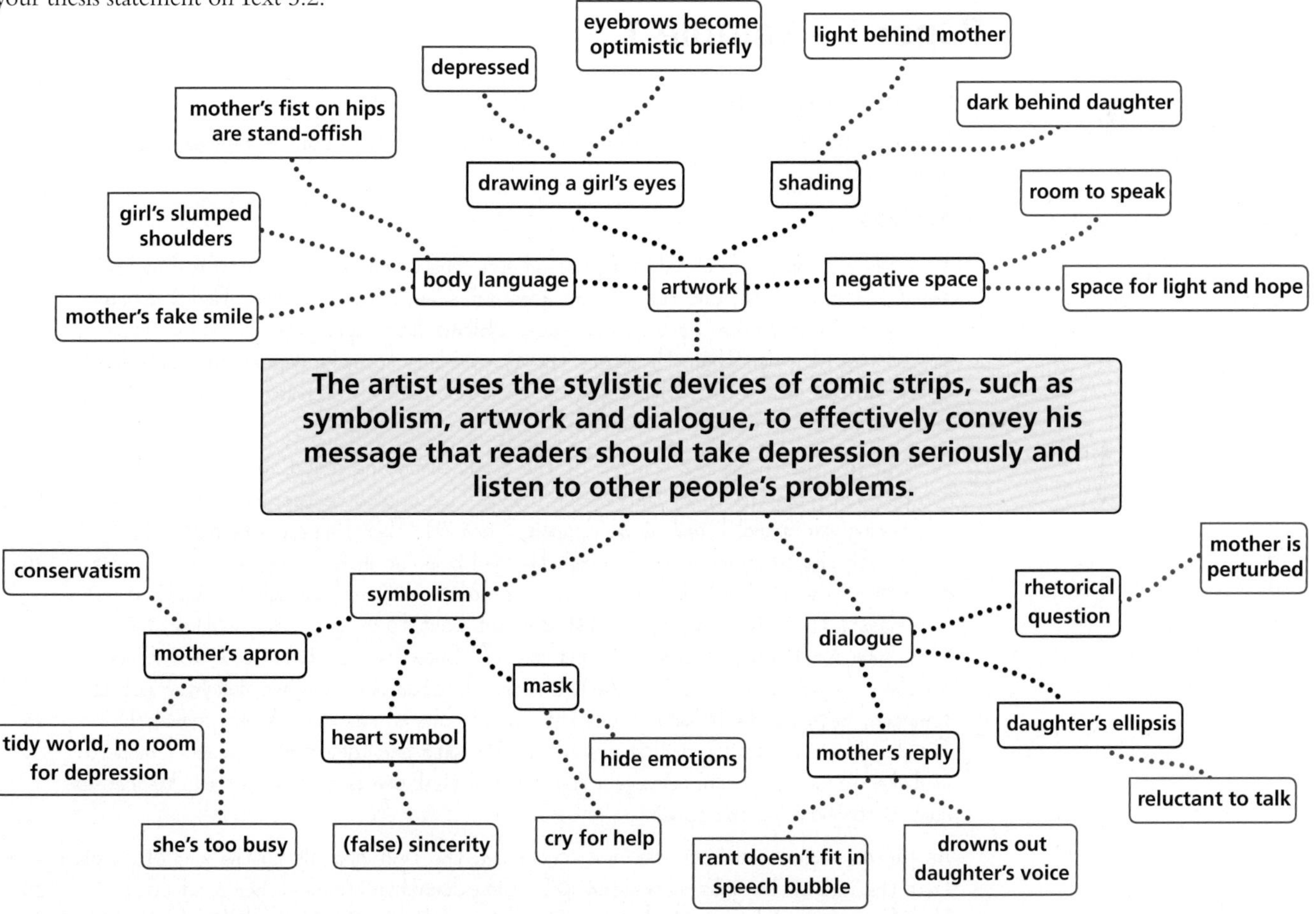

Creating mind maps around your thesis statement will save time and help you organise your ideas before you start writing your analysis.

Student sample responses

5.8 Here are two samples of Paper 1 analyses written by students. Sample 1 is poor and contains many errors that students commonly make on their Paper 1 analysis. Sample 2 is strong and may be helpful for use as a model analysis.

a Read both of these samples without looking at the assessment criteria for Paper 1.

b In groups, discuss the differences between the two samples by creating a list of *dos* and *don'ts* for Paper 1, using a table like the one shown here.

c Imagine that you had to teach other students what you should and should not do on your Paper 1 exam. Present your lists of *dos* and *don'ts* to your classmates. Collate everyone's ideas into one table.

The *dos* of a Paper 1 analysis	The *don'ts* of a Paper 1 analysis

Paper 1 – Sample 1

Guiding question

In what ways does the artist use the features of this text type to convey a message about depression?'

Analysis

Text 1 is a comic strip about a depressed girl. She would like to talk to her mother about her depression, but her mother does not seem willing to listen. Text 1 appeals to anyone who might be depressed or has problems with depression. It was written in 2013 by Clay Jonathan. He wrote this comic strip to make depressed people feel better about themselves. This essay will show how he uses techniques that are typical of comic strips to achieve his purpose.

First of all, the theme and content of the comic strip are about depression. This can be seen from the title, Depression Comix. It can also be seen from the words 'bothering you' (panel 1) and 'down' (panels 3 and 4). Then there is the piece of paper with the smile drawn on it, which the girl holds up in front of her face to hide her frown. This probably triggers the conversation between her and her mother. It suggests that she is depressed and does not want to show it. Her mother asks her: 'Why don't you just come out and say it?' Once she starts to talk about her problems (panel 3), her mother doesn't listen. Instead she tells her daughter not to complain, because she is 'young' and has 'practically no responsibilities' (panel 4). The daughter walks away and covers her mouth with her fake smile, saying 'I made a mistake' (panel 4). From her eyes, you can tell that she is still depressed. Depression runs throughout all the panels.

As far as audience and purpose are concerned, the text appeals to the kind of people that the author targets: depressed girls. Clay Jonathan has sketched a situation that they can relate to. Most likely, they have mothers who do not listen to their problems either. They can identify with the protagonist of this story and relate to her problems. The author wants them to feel comforted, knowing that they are not the only ones in this situation. He wants girls to know that they are not the only ones suffering from depression. They are not the only ones with mothers who do not listen. Perhaps the author went through this problem in life before and he wants to share his experience with others to comfort them. The author is successful in achieving his purposes, as the comic strip is very effective in its depiction of depression.

The tone and the mood of this text are dark and depressed. The author uses language to set the tone of the text. From opening line 'I can tell something is bothering you . . .' (panel 1) you sense that the tone is worrisome. The mother's body language, with her hands on her hips, indicates that a confrontation is about to happen, creating a confrontational mood. Then there are the dark colours that the author uses, which are all shades of black and white with a lot of grey, which makes you feel gloomy. The atmosphere is dark, like the blackness of the bold word 'down' (panel 3). It is also difficult to read the words behind the mother in panel 4, because they are so small and she is covering half of them. This may have been a mistake by the author, but you can still make out a few more 'dark' words, such as 'moping around' and 'ashamed' (panel 4).

Because this text is a comic strip, there is a lot of style in it, mostly artistic style. The artist uses a lot of shading, perhaps with the side of his lead pencil. The bottoms of the panels are darker than the tops of the panels, which is curious. Panel 3 has a lot of white space, suggesting there is hope for the main character. There is also a heart next to the mother's words in the second panel, suggesting that she really cares and might listen. But she doesn't. The cartoon style of the author is contrasted with the dark subject matter. With just a few lines, the artist can show the worried look on the mother's face in panel 1, her fake smile in panel 2 and her angry face in panel 3. The mother wears an apron, to suggest she is working hard in the house. The eyes of the main character are particularly drawn with care, to make her look sad and droopy. She wears a long-sleeved shirt under a short-sleeve shirt, which is typical of a depressed teenager. All in all, the artist uses style effectively to deliver his message about depression.

The structure of this comic strip helps the author explore the theme of depression too. It has four panels from top to bottom, with clearly defined frames around each panel. He uses speech bubbles, which are typical of the text type. The only exception to this is found in the last panel, where the words appear behind the mother. This suggests that she has so much to say that it does not fit into a speech bubble. The story begins with a problem or conflict. The rising action in panel 2 indicates that the problem might be solved. Panel 3 includes a lot of blank space, arguably the climax of the story. Panel 4 includes the falling action, as the problem is not resolved and the protagonist goes back to being depressed. This structure makes the reader feel depressed too.

To conclude, Depression Comix juxtaposes a dark theme, depression, with a light-hearted text type, the comic strip. The author, Clay Jonathan, achieves his purpose of comforting depressed teenage girls, by showing them an everyday example of what it is like to be depressed. He uses artistic style effectively to explore this theme and speak to his audience.

Paper 1 – Sample 2

Guiding question

In what ways does the artist use the features of this text type to convey a message about depression?'

Analysis

Text 1, a comic strip by Clay Jonathan written in 2013, explores the frustrations of depression. The comic strip is an interesting choice of text to explore this problem, as comics are not commonly associated with depression. Nevertheless, the artist uses the stylistic devices of comic strips, such as symbolism, artwork and dialogue, to effectively convey his message that readers should take depression seriously and listen to other people's problems.

Depression Comix uses symbolism to help the reader understand the nature of depression. The characters in this comic strip are defined by the symbols that they wear and use. The mother wears an apron, suggesting she is committed to working hard around the house. Her buttoned-up blouse and ironed collar indicate a level of reservation and conservatism, suggesting she likes a neat and tidy world, free from depression. The heart symbol in her speech in the second panel indicates that her words are sincere and heartfelt, though the reader learns quickly that they are not. Arguably, the most important symbol in all four panels is the daughter's mask: a simple card with an exaggerated, hand-drawn smile held in front of her mouth. It represents a feeble attempt to cover up her depression, which presumably is not appreciated in her house. It fails to cover her droopy eyes and long locks in front of her face, which also act as symbols of depression. The mask is lowered briefly (panels 2 and 3), when she thinks her mother cares, but it is quickly placed in front of her mouth again to conceal her depression. With this use of symbolism, Clay Jonathan seems to comment on the nature of depression, showing how depressed people cover up their emotions so as not to burden others, a strategy that only begets more depression.

The artist's style of drawing is effective in conveying his message that depressed people should be taken seriously. With a few simply drawn lines, Clay Jonathan knows how to portray and capture human emotions. The body language of the mother is standoffish in the first panel, created by her out-turned hands on her hips. The shading around the daughter's eyes and her small pupils under her heavily drawn eye lids reveal both her depression and suspicion of her mother's attempt to listen. Their footing and stance change in the second panel, an effect created by a very different camera angle. The reader is able to see behind the daughter's mask, revealing an upward movement in her eyebrows and opening of her mouth. This suggests an eagerness to talk and share her sorrow. The smile on the mother's face, with its cliché shape, projects a kind of false sincerity. The artist seems to be warning readers from using this kind of fake niceness with depressed people. The blank, negative space in the third panel functions as space for the girl to vent her frustrations and feel a sense of hope. The use of white in this panel is juxtaposed against the dark shades of grey that dominate the area around the girl in every other panel. Unfortunately, it dissipates as quickly as it arrives, as the greys cover the fourth panel. The mother's words cover any white space or sense of hope that was created previously. There is literally no room for the daughter's words, and so she is not heard and her feelings of depression are not taken seriously. Clay Jonathan uses shading, lines and camera angle to convey his message that depressed people need and deserve space to be heard.

Finally, the artist uses dialogue and speech bubbles in his comic strip to give the reader insight into the challenges of depression. The mother seems bothered by the daughter's mask and says 'I can tell something is bothering you . . .' (panel 1). The use of ellipsis suggests she is perturbed, together with the rhetorical question that follows, 'Why don't you just come out and say it?' (panel 1). The daughter seems surprised that she is allowed this opportunity to speak. The line 'It's okay?' (panel 2) makes the reader wonder how often she is given this chance to talk and if the mother is sincere when she says 'That's what I'm here for ♡' (panel 2). The use of ellipsis in the third panel further emphasises this notion that she is never given room to speak, as she starts reluctantly and is cut off abruptly '. . . well, I'm kind of down . . . and . . .'. The word 'down' (panel 3) in bold becomes the focus of the mother's retort 'Down? What do you have to feel down about? You have practically no responsibilities. You're young and you have your whole life ahead of you' (panel 4). This response fails to acknowledge the daughter's feelings. While the daughter struggles to express herself, the mother has a long statement ready, drowning out her daughter's voice. The artist emphasises how dominant the mother is, by having her words dominate the background of the final panel. They do not even fit into a speech bubble, the common convention for dialogue in comic strip writing. What's worse, the daughter feels responsible for the situation which her mother has created and almost apologises by stating 'I made a mistake' (panel 4), when in fact it is the mother who is mistaken. With this use of dialogue, the artist shows how depressed people need to be heard. One cannot listen to another person's concerns when they are voicing their own opinions, and not listening only makes depression worse.

To conclude, the comic strip 'Depression Comix' is Clay Jonathan's means of warning readers about the dangers of not listening to depressed people. Through his use of symbolism, drawing and dialogue he gives readers insight into the challenges of being depressed. Depressed people, he seems to say, need to be heard and taken seriously. Otherwise their depression will only get worse.

Paper 1 – Sample 1 – Examiner's marks and comments

Criterion A: Knowledge, understanding and interpretation: 2 out of 5 marks

The main premise of this analysis is vague and rather inaccurate, as it states that Clay Jonathan wrote the comic strip to 'make depressed people feel better about themselves'. The evidence provided does not support this argument. Other statements, such as 'Depression runs throughout all the panels', are very superficial. Conjecture, such as 'the author went through this problem in life before' or '[the words behind the mother] may have been a mistake by the author', is not necessary. The conclusion shows some insight, commenting on the text type and purpose, though it is too little too late. The very generic thesis statement, 'This essay will show how he uses techniques that are typical of comic strips', is not helpful either.

Criterion B: Analysis and evaluation: 2 out of 5 marks

Through a poor sense of organisation (see below) this criterion is affected as well. With the exception of the 'tone and mood' paragraph, it is difficult to see how the author's choices create meaning and have an effect on the reader. Although the analysis notices a lot of detail, it rarely evaluates the effectiveness of these details. The analysis summarises too much.

Criterion C: Coherence, focus and organisation: 2 out of 5 marks

This analysis, in a rather artificial way, has five body paragraphs: one on theme and content, another on audience and purpose, another on tone and mood, another on style and a final one on structure. This method is ineffective because it fails to show the relationship between these elements. The 'style' and 'structure' paragraphs read like shopping lists, as they do not explain why these elements matter. There is little coherence between paragraphs, as they could have appeared in any order.

Criterion D: Language: 3 out of 5 marks

The language of this analysis is adequate and generally accurate, varied and effective. Despite an absence of analytical terms, complex sentence structures and academic vocabulary, the student's message is communicated clearly.

5.9 Once your class has compiled a list of dos and don'ts for Paper 1 (from Activity 5.8), turn to the assessment criteria for Paper 1 in the introduction to this coursebook.

Beside each point on your lists, write the letters that correspond to the letters of the relevant assessment criteria (A–D).

- Does your class focus on a particular criterion?
- How was your intuitive understanding of 'good' and 'poor' textual analysis reflected in the criteria?

5.10 Assess Sample 1 using the assessment criteria. Write comments and give a mark for each criterion. Then compare your comments and marks with those of the examiner. How are they similar or different? What kinds of comments and marks would you give Sample 2? Compare your comments and marks for Sample 2 with those of a classmate.

5.11 Besides the assessment criteria, examiners use marking notes to mark students' scripts. As you can see from this example, these marking notes are lists of text-specific points to look for in both good and very good to excellent analyses.

a Study the notes carefully. What are the differences between 'good' and 'excellent'?

b What kinds of verbs are used to start each bullet point? Do these verbs coincide with the diagram in Activity 5.1 of this chapter, which shows how meaning is constructed?

c Does Sample 2 do everything mentioned under the 'good to excellent' analysis?

d Based on your understanding of these marking notes, would you change the marks that you gave Samples 1 and 2? Why would you do this?

e In groups, try writing your own marking notes for Text 5.2, using a copy of the template provided. Discuss the challenges that you face in doing this. What are the advantages of doing this exercise?

Paper 1 – Marking notes for Text 5.1

The marking notes (notes for examiners) are intended only as guidelines to assist marking. They are not offered as an exhaustive and fixed set of responses or approaches to which all answers must rigidly adhere. Good ideas and approaches not offered here will be acknowledged and rewarded as appropriate. Similarly, answers which do not include all the ideas or approaches suggested here will not be penalised so as to distort appreciation of individuality.

Guiding question

In what ways does the artist use the features of this text type to convey a message about depression?

A good analysis will:

- identify the target audience as people who are interested in depression
- understand that the message of the text is about the difficulties faced by people who suffer from depression
- explore the comic strip as a medium to engage the reader on the topic of depression
- analyse how the structure of the text, with four panels, comments on depression
- comment on the tone of the characters' words and the mood of the text.

A good to excellent analysis will:

- identify the audience as people who either suffer from depression or know people who have suffered
- understand that the message of the text is about the importance of listening to people who suffer from depression
- explore how the comic strip uses features such as speech bubbles, shades of grey and drawing style to engage the reader on the topic of depression
- analyse how the structure of the four panels of the comic strip tells a story in which the girl's hopes of being heard are built up and then crushed by her mother, only causing her more agony and a deeper sense of depression
- comment on how the tone of the characters' words reveals their frustrations with each other and how the mood of the text is therefore disheartening.

Paper 1 – Marking notes for Text 5.2

Guiding question

In what ways does the language of this text reflect its purpose?

A good analysis will:	*A good to excellent analysis will:*
• ...	• ...
• ...	• ...
• ...	• ...
• ...	• ...
• ...	• ...

5.12 What makes Sample 2 so much better than Sample 1? Besides the quality of the ideas, they are organised in a much more coherent way. How is Sample 2 organised? Four different highlighter pens have been used here to highlight the different purposes of the sentences in a sample paragraph from the student's analysis.

Type	Function
Point	Make a claim about how the author's purpose is achieved through language.
Evidence	Support the claim with examples and quotations that illustrate the author's use of language.
Evaluate	Analyse how this use of language constructs meaning and evaluate the effectiveness of the author's use of language.
Link	Link back to the thesis statement and the author's purpose

Depression Comix uses symbolism to help the reader understand the nature of depression. The characters in this comic strip are defined by the symbols that they wear and use. The mother wears an apron, suggesting she is committed to working hard around the house. Her buttoned-up blouse and ironed collar indicate a level of reservation and conservatism, suggesting she likes a neat and tidy world, free from depression. The heart symbol in her speech in the second panel indicates that her words are sincere and heartfelt, though the reader learns quickly that they are not. Arguably, the most important symbol in all four panels is the daughter's mask: a simple card with an exaggerated, hand-drawn smile held in front of her mouth. It represents a feeble attempt to cover up her depression, which presumably is not appreciated in her house. It fails to cover her droopy eyes and long locks in front of her face, which also act as symbols of depression. The mask is lowered briefly (panels 2 and 3), when she thinks her mother cares, but it is quickly placed in front of her mouth again to conceal her depression. With this use of symbolism, Clay Jonathan seems to comment on the nature of depression, showing how depressed people cover up their emotion so as not to burden others, a strategy that only begets more depression.

Look carefully at the structure of the third and fourth paragraph of this analysis. On a copy of the text, use highlighter pens to identify the patterns of sentences that give *points*, *evidence*, *evaluate* and *link* (PEEL).

5.13 The PEEL structure, as explained in the previous activity, gives you an idea of how paragraphs are organised in essays and commentaries. How should an entire essay or Paper 1 analysis be structured? While an essay can have as many body paragraphs as necessary, you should be conscious of the time constraints. You may find that you can only write three body paragraphs, an introduction and a conclusion effectively in the allotted time.

Use this plan to write an outline for a Paper 1 analysis of Text 5.2.

Paragraph	Type	Function
Introduction	Opening line	State why the topic matters.
	The basics	State the topic, author's name, year of publication and contextual information.
	Thesis statement	Articulate the message of the text and how it is constructed using several stylistic features.
Body paragraph 1	Point	Make a claim about how the author's purpose is achieved through language.
	Evidence	Support the claim with examples and quotations that illustrate the author's use of language.
	Evaluation	Analyse how language constructs meaning and evaluate the effectiveness of the language.
	(Repeat)	(Go back and forth between evidence and evaluation.)
	Link	Link back to the thesis statement and the author's purpose.
Body paragraphs 2 and 3	See previous	Repeat the PEEL structure for each paragraph.

Extended essay

You may find the PEEL method useful for organising presentations, TOK essays or your extended essay. Before you submit a draft of your extended essay, check to see if your paragraphs are coherent and easy to read. Using the PEEL method, together with elements from this Paper 1 outline, your essay will score better on both Criterion D (presentation) and Criterion C (critical thinking) for the extended essay.

Conclusion	To conclude	Restate the author's purpose.
	Key features	State how a few stylistic features were instrumental in achieving this purpose.
	Message	Repeat the text's main message and state why this is meaningful.

Over to you

5.14 So far in this unit you have explored two stimulus texts (Texts 5.1 and 5.2) as they would appear on a Paper 1 exam. You have read two examples of students' responses on Text 5.1, both poor and good. You have been asked to write your own thesis statement (Activity 5.6), mind map (Activity 5.7) and outline (5.13) on Text 5.2. You are now ready to write your own complete analysis of Text 5.2.

a Write an analysis of Text 5.2 individually, in your own time. Time yourself as you write it, even if you do not write under exam time constraints.

b Bring your analysis to class for a fellow student to assess, using the assessment criteria. Ask your teacher to assess your analysis, using the assessment criteria.

c Read Sample 3, which is a good example of a student's analysis of Text 5.2. Read it once and then, without looking at it again, ask yourself which ideas you could use to inspire your own analysis. Rewrite one paragraph or your complete analysis, keeping this sample in mind.

d When you have finished your analysis, discuss with your teacher how Sample 3 helped you rewrite your own essay.

Paper 1 – Sample 3

Guiding question

In what ways does the language of this text reflect its purpose?

Analysis

Text 5.2 is a letter of apology from a former weight loss consultant to her former clients. She wants to apologise to them in the form of an open letter, because she feels guilty for having misled them and does not want more women to be misled by diet companies in the future. Through the author's use of syntax, pronouns and verb tense, the letter of apology feels authentic and is effective in exposing the diet companies' practices.

First, the author's use of syntax makes the letter sound informal, very personal and heartfelt. Syntax, which is the use of punctuation, word order and sentence structures, can help establish the mood of a text. Iris Higgins uses many short and choppy sentences to make the letter sound like an improvised but well-intended speech from a friend to a friend. The use of parentheses in the opening address, for example, 'Dear Former Weight Loss Clients (you know who you are)' (line 1) makes readers believe that the author is confiding in them. The first sentence is short and punchy, 'I'm sorry' (line 2). She does not embellish her writing, but

Define the text type in the introduction.

'Through the use of . . .' is an excellent way to start any sentence in a Paper 1 analysis, including your thesis statement.

Good topic sentences are built around a stylistic feature.

Notice how often the verb 'make' is used in this paragraph. The sentence structure is 'X makes the reader feel Y'.

rather makes her statements clearly and directly. Furthermore, many sentences are not grammatically correct, in the way that people do not always speak in complete sentences when they speak from the heart. For example, she writes 'I owe you an apology, my former client and now friend, who I helped to lose too much weight. Who I watched gain the weight back, plus some' (line 3), which digresses with multiple clauses and uses several commas to make the letter sound like the spoken word. Furthermore, sentences start with 'And' and do not include subjects, such as 'But I'm friends with some of you on Facebook now, and I look at your photos and you look happy. And beautiful' (line 16). Not only does this style sound chatty and personal, but it is also strong and honest. It is because of this direct style that Iris Higgins's opinion about the diet companies seems true and strong. She claims that 'all these fad diets are crap meant to screw with your metabolism so that you have to keep buying into them' (line 7). Higgins's use of syntax contributes to her frank tone and is effective in exposing the evils of the dieting companies.

Be sure to use words like 'because' or phrases such as 'for this reason' in order to establish a relationship between style and meaning.

Notice the number of quotations in this paragraph. Be sure to offer ample illustrations of your points to score well on Criterion A.

Notice how the language of this last sentence mirrors the language of the thesis statement.

Secondly, Higgins's use of pronouns plays an important role in establishing rapport with the reader and criticising the diet companies. She goes back and forth between the first-person pronoun 'I' and the second-person pronoun 'you'. For example, she explains: 'I did exactly what the company wanted (but would never dare say). I helped you lose weight and then gain it back, so that you thought we were the solution and you were the failure. You became a repeat client and we kept you in the game' (line 9). She even capitalises the word 'YOU' (line 19) to stress the reader's sense of self. Higgins also includes herself as part of 'the company' by using 'we', but takes responsibilities for her actions by using 'I' when writing, 'I guess I did my job really well' (line 12). Her apology and criticisms of the diet companies are emphasised further through the use of pronouns in the third-to-last paragraph, where she states: 'None of you ever failed. Ever. I failed you. The weight loss company failed you. Our society is failing you' (lines 32–33). The final pronoun 'our' in 'our society' shows how the problems of self-image and obsession with weight loss are general and not only created by the dieting companies. Higgins's switch from the second person to the third person is also interesting in line 20, which reads 'But you, a smart and lovely woman, who really doesn't need some random company telling her there's something wrong with her'. This suggests that the reader is one of many women suffering from the diet companies' misleading information. The use of pronouns throughout this letter highlights how Higgins has changed her mind about dieting, and taken a stance that is more noble or ethical.

Return to the author's purpose frequently in your Paper 1 analysis.

Some verbs to consider using include: show, illustrate, suggest, imply or highlight.

Iris Higgins's use of verb tenses helps establish her relationship with her former clients and her criticism of the diet companies. There is a certain sense of urgency created by her letter in its use of the present continuous, such as 'If you're reading this' (line 6) or 'society is failing you' (line 33) and the present simple, such as 'And now I wonder' (line 14) or 'because I see YOU now' (line 18). The key phrase 'I am sorry' (line 30) is also, notably, in the present simple tense. All of this sense of urgency in the present tense is contrasted with the sense of shame in the past tense, which is used to describe the author's old self and role in the diet industry, such as 'it was my job to let you believe that making the scale go down was your top priority' (line 28). Lines like 'I did my job well' (line 29) are contrasted with the last lines of the letter 'But I can stop my part in it' (line 36), which shows a change in character. Her determination to change is emphasised even more as the author switches into the future tense: 'I won't play the weight loss game anymore. I won't do it to my body, and I won't help you do

While this essay focuses on seemingly basic stylistic features, such as pronouns and verb tenses, they are used very effectively. You do not have to impress examiners with your knowledge of specific devices, such as chiasmus or anadiplosis unless they are truly relevant.

it to yours' (line 36). This makes the letter end on a positive note and gives the reader an uplifting feeling that they, too, do not have to listen to diet companies anymore.

'What is the effect of language on the reader?' is a good question to answer after every illustration.

All in all, Iris Higgins aims to expose the sinister tricks of the dieting companies by confessing to her role in playing them. Whereas she once told her clients they were too fat and put them on 1200 calorie diets, she now stands by them in their efforts to feel happy in their bodies. She uses different verb tenses, pronouns and syntax to show the reader that she has, indeed, changed her ways and is opposed to the 'nonsense' (line 35) of the diet industry.

In your conclusion, return to the author's purpose, the major stylistic features in the text and the effect of these on the reader.

Paper 1 – Sample 3 – Examiner's marks and comments

Criterion A: Knowledge, understanding and interpretation: 5 out of 5 marks

The student goes out on a limb with some comments by making claims about how the friendly tone is established through syntax. But these claims are supported by relevant examples from the text. In fact, the analysis is full of well-integrated quotations from the letter. The thesis statement is very thorough, focusing on both the authenticity of the letter and its purpose of exposing the diet companies' practices. The student understands the position of the author in relation to the reader and the diet companies, as she makes reference to both parties frequently.

Criterion B: Analysis and evaluation: 5 out of 5 marks

The analysis is very perceptive and detailed in its exploration of the stylistic features and the effects of these on the reader. The subtleties of the text, such as a switch in verb tense, are deconstructed carefully.

Criterion C: Coherence, focus and organisation: 5 out of 5 marks

This analysis is effectively organised. Each body paragraph connects Higgins's use of language to Higgins's purpose, while commenting on the effects of this language on the reader. The use of linking words acts as signposts for the reader of this analysis, giving it a sense of direction. It retains focus on the criticism of the diet companies throughout.

Criterion D: Language: 5 out of 5 marks

The analysis uses a broad range of synonyms, terms and sentence structures, making it pleasant to read. The student's style is concise, which is effective in delivering a complicated message about diet companies and Higgins's past. It is nice to see terms such as 'syntax' defined accurately.

5.15 After working through the practice exercises in this chapter, you should now be ready to attempt a mock Paper 1 exam.

- Use Texts 5.3 and 5.4 to practise taking the Paper 1 exam under exam conditions. At standard level you have 1 hour and 15 minutes to write an analysis on one of these texts.
- At higher level you have 2 hours and 15 minutes to write two separate analyses, one on each text.
- All students have 5 minutes of silent reading time, in which you may not write on your exam script or text booklet.

Are you ready? Steady? Go!

Text 5.3

Guiding question

In what ways does this text capture the reader's imagination?

Text 5.4

First letter from Gandhi to Hitler

Mahatma Gandhi 1939

Herr Hitler
Berlin
Germany

Dear friend,

Friends have been urging me to write to you for the sake of humanity. But I have resisted their request, because of the feeling that any letter from me would be an impertinence. Something tells me that I must not calculate and that I must make my appeal for whatever it may be worth.

It is quite clear that you are today the one person in the world who can prevent a war which may reduce humanity to the savage state. Must you pay the price for an object however worthy it may appear to you to be? Will you listen to the appeal of one who has deliberately shunned the method of war not without considerable success? Any way I anticipate your forgiveness, if I have erred in writing to you.

I remain,

Your sincere friend

M.K. Gandhi

Guiding question

How does the context of this letter help shape its meaning?

REFLECT

This unit began by showing you that textual analysis is happening all around you, especially if you consider anything and everything as a text.

- How have the skills introduced in this chapter for analysing texts – such as 'meaning', 'audience', 'purpose' and 'style' – changed the way you look at texts you see around you?
- How have the skills for writing an analysis – such as mind mapping, annotating, writing thesis statements and PEEL paragraphs – changed your way of preparing and writing papers for school in general?
- What do you need to do to become better prepared for your Paper 1 exam for English A: Language and Literature?

Discuss your answers to these questions as a class.

Chapter 6

Paper 2: Comparative essay (SL/HL)

What is expected of you in your exam for the Paper 2: Comparative essay?
What kind of skills should you develop and what knowledge of your literary works should you acquire during your course?
How can you develop these skills and build this knowledge of your works?

In this chapter you will:

- learn about the requirements and expectations for the Paper 2 exam
- discuss the strengths and weaknesses of several samples of students' work
- develop your own skills for writing a comparative analysis of literary works.

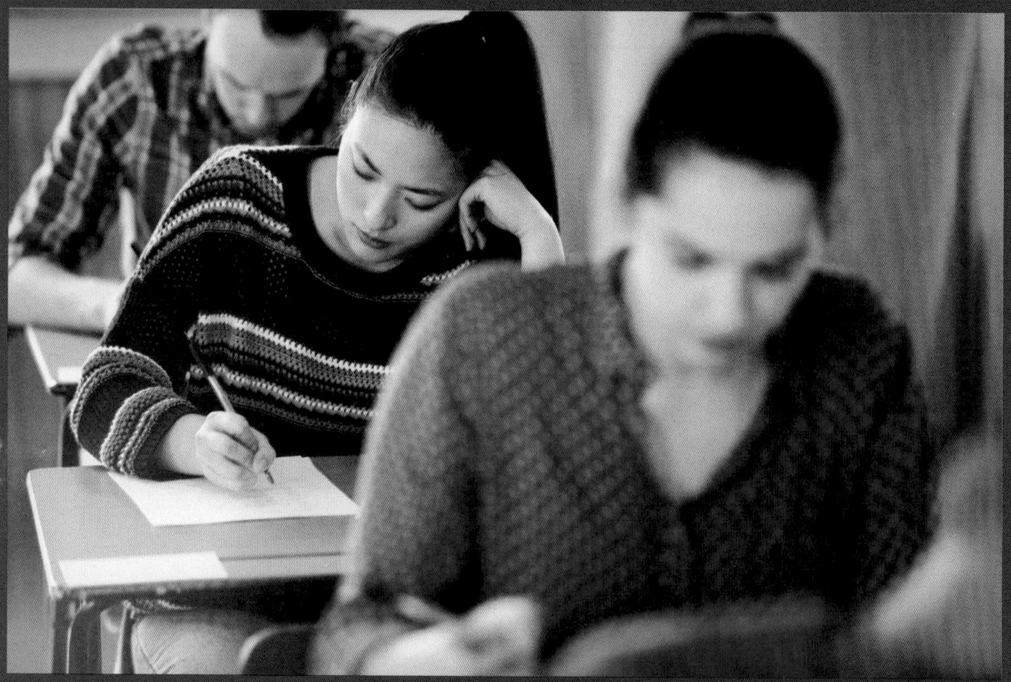

Learning objectives

- become familiar with the kind of questions that you can expect in your Paper 2 exam
- understand what is expected of you in the Paper 2 exam by engaging with examples of students' essays, the assessment criteria and marking notes
- develop the skills for writing an effective Paper 2 essay.

Word bank

context of composition
technique
context of interpretation
theme
thesis statement
frame narration
connective
point of view
motif
free indirect speech

Standard and higher level students receive the same Paper 2 exam for English A: Language and Literature. In fact, as the focus of Paper 2 is literature, it is the same Paper 2 that English A: Literature students receive.

When you open your Paper 2 exam booklet, you will see *four* essay questions, asking you to compare *two* of the literary works that you have read. You are not allowed to write about the literary work that you explored in your individual oral (Chapter 8) or have written about for your HL Essay (Chapter 7). At both standard and higher level, you have 1 hour and 45 minutes to write an essay in response to *one* question. Both standard and higher level students are marked according to the same criteria, which you can find in the introduction of this coursebook. For standard level students, the Paper 2 exam counts towards 35% of your final course grade. For higher level students, the Paper 2 exam counts towards 25% of your final course grade.

How do you prepare for your Paper 2 exam if the essay questions are unknown? In order to be prepared for any question, it is recommended that you practise writing essays, both in and out of class, about the literary works you are studying. You can practise writing responses to past exam questions, or to the 12 questions in this chapter. You will also find two good examples of students' responses to learn from.

Essay writing is a skill like any other; it requires practice. Writing about novels and plays requires careful study and classroom discussion, as you will need a thorough understanding of the literary works you are studying in class. While the Paper 2 comparative essay may be one of the more challenging components of your assessment, preparing for it will give you better insight into these literary works. It will also help you develop useful essay-writing skills which you can use in further education.

Getting started

6.1 Ask yourself these questions:

- Which literary works am I going to write about?
- What do I know about these works?
- What do they have in common?

As you read and discuss the literary works that your teacher assigns you, you should make the connections between these works visible for all of your classmates to see. How could you do this?

- Create a poster on a wall of your classroom which includes a hexagon diagram like the one here, which was created for an HL class. If you are taking the course at standard level, you can create a square diagram.
- Draw a line between each point on the diagram, connecting the literary works. On these lines place labels that describe the connections between the works. These labels can describe the writing styles, genres (text types) and themes that connect the works.
- Discuss your class's diagram periodically throughout your course, as you read and explore your literary works as a class.

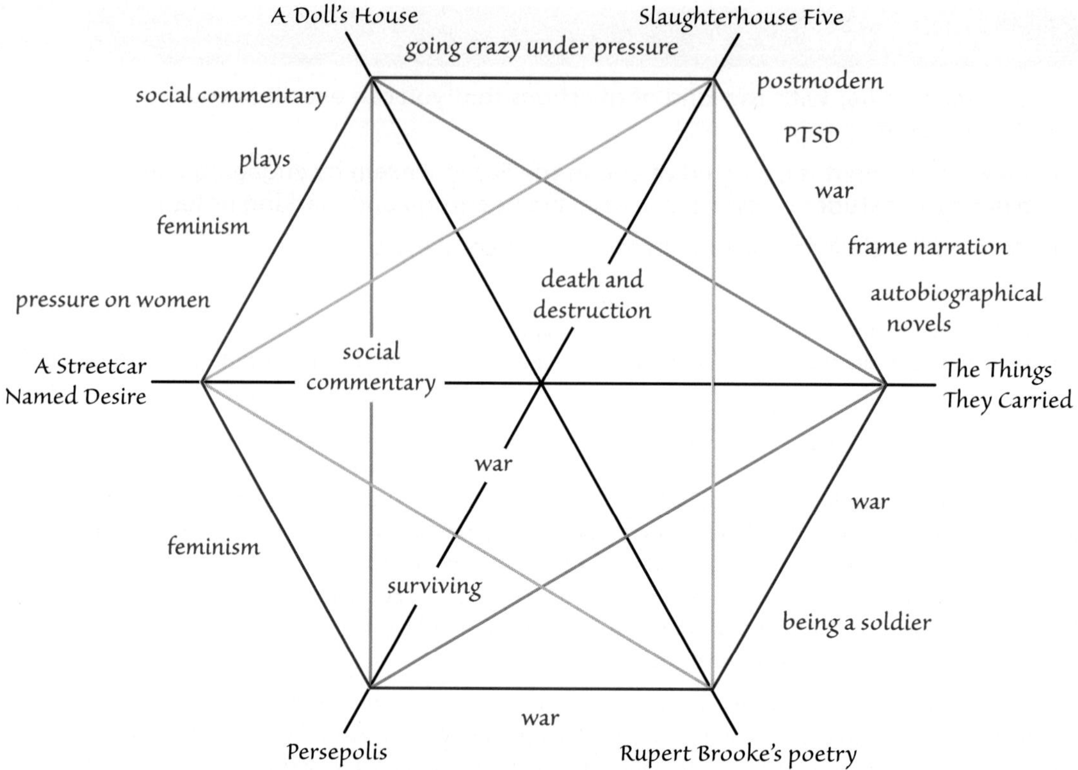

Specimen Paper 2 SL/HL papers

6.2 What kind of questions can you expect on your Paper 2 exam? Although they are unseen questions, you can, to some extent, predict the types of questions that will appear. Here are three specimen Paper 2 exams. Read the questions from each specimen paper and create several categories into which these questions can be placed according to their commonalities. What are the types of question you see reoccurring on each exam? Can you use this information to predict the kind of questions that will appear in the exam?

Paper 2 – Specimen 1

a Authors sometimes tell their stories in a non-linear fashion. Compare how and for what reasons the authors of at least two works that you have read have told their stories in a non-linear fashion.

b The meaning of a literary work can change over time. Compare how the meanings of two literary works that you have read have changed over time.

c 'Fight or flight' is a term used to describe human responses to adverse circumstances. Compare how the authors of two literary works that you have read have depicted such human responses to adverse circumstances.

d Authors often write fiction as a means of social commentary. Compare how the authors of two works that you have read have written works of social commentary.

Paper 2 – Specimen 2

a Literary works are received differently in different places and times. Compare how two literary works that you have read have been received differently by different audiences.

b In what ways and for what reasons do two literary works that you have read appeal to their audiences' eyes and ears? Compare and contrast the ways in which they appeal to the auditory and visual senses of their audiences.

c Literary works often depict a struggle between genders. Compare how two of the works that you have read depict a struggle between genders.

d Authors of literary works often write because they feel their stories need to be told. Compare the authors' reasons for writing two literary works that you have read.

Paper 2 – Specimen 3

a Pablo Picasso once said that 'Art is a lie that makes us realise the truth'. Compare how the authors of two literary works help their readers 'realise the truth'.

b One characteristic of a literary work is that it never stops speaking to audiences. Compare how two literary works have continued to speak to their audiences over time.

c Suspense is what keeps readers turning the pages of literary works. Compare and contrast the ways in which the authors of two literary works build suspense and capture the imagination of their readers.

d The struggle against injustice is a theme that speaks to readers. Compare the ways in which the authors of two literary works have depicted unjust worlds.

6.3 How did you organise the specimen questions into categories? While there may be many different ways of making sense of these questions, they can be broken down into four global categories.

a The **context of composition**: For what reasons do writers write? How do contextual factors, such as time and place, influence their writing?

b Style or **technique**: How do writers write? What choices do they make? What techniques do they use to convey their message?

c The **context of interpretation**: How do readers read literary works? How does the context of the reader determine the reception of a text?

d Topic or **theme**: What is the message of a work? What themes do the works explore? How do they comment on these themes?

AOE questions

Study the 18 AOE questions for your IB English A: Language and Literature course, which can be found in the introduction to this coursebook. How similar or different are they to or from these specimen Paper 2 questions? Can you identify elements from the four categories of question in Activity 6.3 (a–d) in the AOE questions from this course?

TIP

After reading the 12 exam-style essay questions, try writing your own essay question. Show it to your teacher and ask them for comments. If you can write good essay questions, you're in a good position to answer an unseen question yourself.

TIP

The four categories of questions, as described in Activity 6.3, correspond to the MAPS acronym for textual analysis that is introduced in Chapter 5: meaning (topic or theme) = audience's response (context of interpretation) + purpose of the author (context of composition and theme) + style of the text (or technique).

Return to the specimens for Paper 2 and write a corresponding category (a–d) beside each question. You can use a table like this one. There may be more than one letter which is applicable to each question. An example has been completed for you.

	Specimen 1	Specimen 2	Specimen 3
a Context of composition			
b Style or technique	Question 1 (non-linear narrative)		
c Context of interpretation			
d Topic or theme			

6.4 Take a look at the assessment criteria for Paper 2 which can be found in the introduction of this coursebook. In what ways are categories a–d assessed? What if you decide to write about a 'style or technique' question in your Paper 2 exam? Your question may give you an advantage on Criterion B in this case. A context or theme question may give you an advantage on Criterion A. Nevertheless, you will be assessed on all criteria.

Take, for example, Question 2 of Specimen Paper 1: 'The meaning of a literary work can change over time. Compare how the meanings of two literary works that you have read have changed over time.'

There is no mention of the authors' use of style or technique, yet you are assessed on your ability to analyse style and technique on Criterion B. While it is not advisable to change the question, be sure that your essay addresses all of the assessment criteria when answering the question.

Look carefully at the three specimens for Paper 2 and discuss how each question may be biased towards Criterion A or Criterion B.

TIP

There is one way to ensure that you will score well on your essay despite a question that is biased towards a particular criterion. Be sure that your answer addresses a 'why' (author's purpose), 'how' (author's style) or 'what' (meaning), even if these elements are not in the exam question.

6.5 In the first 5 minutes of your Paper 2 exam you will select one of the four essay questions, and this decision will affect the nature of your essay. Naturally, you will want to select a question that is appropriate for the literary works that you have read. What if there are no appropriate questions? You have no choice but to apply one of the questions to the literary works you have studied.

Selecting a question is a skill that you can practise. Make a table like the one shown here. Along the top of the columns, write the titles of the literary works you have studied in class. In the first column, write some of the key words from one of the three Paper 2 specimen papers provided after Activity 6.2. Discuss the opportunities and pitfalls of answering each question in relation to each work. You may also find that one of the questions is not possible, or too complex, to answer properly in 1 hour and 45 minutes; you may want to ignore it altogether.

Specimen 1 questions	*A Streetcar Named Desire*	*A Doll's House*	*The Things They Carried*	*Slaughterhouse Five*
1 Non-linear narration	Not applicable	Not applicable	Perfect. Flashbacks, frame narrator	Perfect. Time-tripping, flashbacks, Tralfamadore
2 Meaning changes over time	Impossible question	Impossible question	Impossible question	Impossible question
3 'Fight or flight'	Perfect. Blanche is running away, Stanley fights Blanche, Stella tolerates him	Difficult. Perhaps Nora is a fighter. Problem is not so black and white	Perfect. O'Brien tries to run to Canada, but then 'flees' to Vietnam	Difficult. Billy is not a fighter. He is not running away either
4 Social commentary	Yes. Clearly a commentary on marriage and gender roles	Yes. Commentary on traditional marriage and patriarchy	Yes. Criticism of war, senselessness of war	Yes. Criticism of war, senselessness of war

Note: *Persepolis* has already been used for an HL essay. Rupert Brooke has already been used for the individual oral.

6.6 A table like this one should help you to decide which question or questions are most appropriate for the works you are studying. The next step is to unpack the question. There are several strategies for doing this. You can:

- create a mind map around the question
- use highlighter pens and annotations
- ask questions about the question.

For this activity, a classmate or your teacher can pretend to be the question. You can ask them any question you want, to try to understand what the question 'means'. Imagine you are putting the question on trial in court. Here are some examples of the kind of questions that you could ask if you were to question the fourth question in the third specimen Paper 2. Ask similar questions of your classmate or teacher in this role-play activity, based on another question from the specimen papers.

Example question

'The struggle against injustice is a theme that speaks to readers. Compare the ways in which two authors of two literary works have depicted unjust worlds.'

- What do you mean by 'the struggle against injustice'?
- Why does this 'struggle' speak to readers?
- Who is struggling? The characters in these literary works?
- What is meant by 'unjust worlds'? Are they real places that readers know? Or are they fictional worlds created by the author?
- It's fine to compare the ways in which the authors depict these unjust worlds, but 'why' have they decided to depict these worlds?

6.7 After selecting a question (Activity 6.5) and questioning it (Activity 6.6), could you, in a very concise way, answer the question? If you are able to do this, you may have a **thesis statement** (these were discussed in Chapter 5 on Paper 1).

What does a thesis statement for Paper 2 look like? Here are two examples. What qualities do they share?

a *The Things They Carried* by Tim O'Brien and *Slaughterhouse Five* by Kurt Vonnegut both show how soldiers struggle to deal with war and its aftermath unsuccessfully. The authors both use a disjointed and non-linear narration to show readers how soldiers remember, experience and suffer from the horrors of war.

b *A Streetcar Named Desire* by Tennessee Williams and *A Doll's House* by Henrik Ibsen both use stage direction, music and symbolism in order to construct their social commentary and convey their feminist message.

6.8 Try writing your own thesis statement, based on a question from one of the Paper 2 specimen papers and two of the literary works that you have read in class. Be sure that your thesis statement:

- answers the question
- articulates the authors' purpose in writing
- refers to some stylistic features.

6.9 Once you have a thesis statement, try 'unpacking' it by creating a mind map around it, as shown in this example.

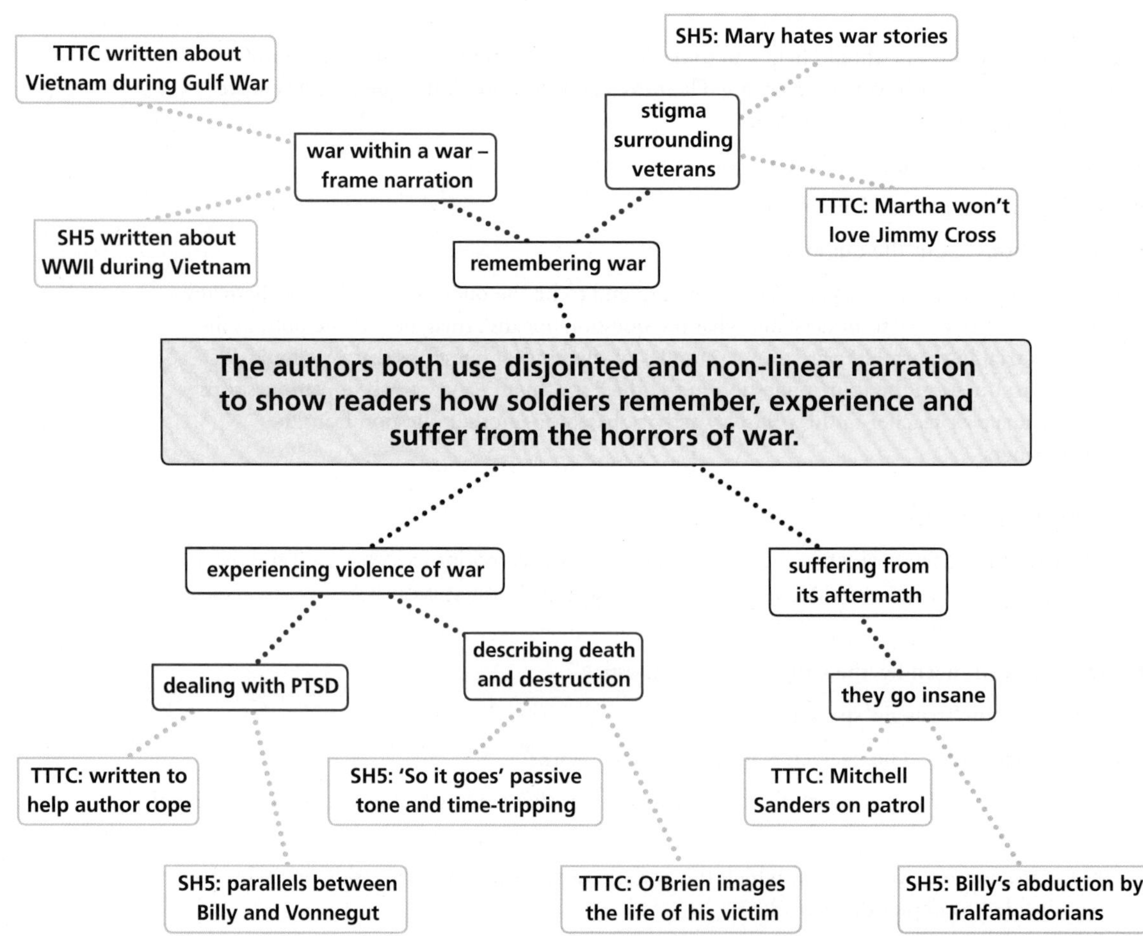

Student sample essays

6.10 Before you write your own Paper 2 essay, you may find it helpful to assess an essay written by another student. Divide the class into four groups and read this student's essay (Sample essay 1). Each group should focus on *one* criterion from the assessment criteria for Paper 2. Explore these questions in your group. Discuss your responses to these questions and find evidence from Sample essay 1 to support your answers:

- Group A: How much knowledge and understanding has the student shown of the works? To what extent does the student make use of knowledge and understanding of the works to draw conclusions about their similarities and differences in relation to the question?
- Group B: To what extent does the student analyse and evaluate how the choices of language, technique and style, and/or broader choices made by the writers, shape meaning? How effectively does the student use analysis and evaluation skills to compare and contrast both works?
- Group C: How well structured, balanced and focused is the presentation of ideas?
- Group D: How clear, varied and accurate is the language? How appropriate is the choice of register, style and terminology?

The question for Sample essay 1 is Question 1 in Specimen Paper 1, from Activity 6.2.

Paper 2 – Sample 1

Essay question

Authors sometimes tell their stories in a non-linear fashion. Compare how and for what reasons the authors of at least two works that you have read have told their stories in a non-linear fashion.

Comparative essay

Readers are often intrigued by war stories, because they want to know if people can persevere in adverse circumstances. *The Things They Carried* by Tim O'Brien and *Slaughterhouse Five* by Kurt Vonnegut both show how soldiers struggle to deal with war and its aftermath unsuccessfully. The authors both use a disjointed and non-linear narration to show readers how soldiers remember, experience and suffer from the horrors of war.

> You do not have to open with a sweeping generalisation. Rather, include a statement that is relevant to your thesis, like this one.

> Write a thesis statement that answers the question.

Both novels are written by authors who remember their experiences of one war in the context of another war, using non-linear narrative structures. In 1990, during the Gulf War in Kuwait, Tim O'Brien wrote the novel *The Things They Carried*, which is about the Vietnam War of the 1960s. O'Brien, who is a Vietnam veteran, writes as a soldier who is traumatised by the violence that he experienced, mixing 'truth-story' with 'happening-truth' to create a work that is neither truth nor fiction, neither memoir nor novel. For example, one chapter, called 'Love', is about how O'Brien meets with another veteran, Jimmy Cross, years after the war to drink coffee and gin and remember the atrocities for which they could not forgive themselves. His friend tells O'Brien about a woman he loved, Martha. But his love was unrequited, because Martha was scared to be with a veteran who had experienced such violence, and this left him heartbroken. There seems to be an inescapable stigma surrounding Vietnam

> Make your first body paragraph about both works.

veterans. This story within a story shows the reader how war never stops damaging the lives of its veterans, long after it is over.

Examiners are looking for connectives in a comparative essay. Use words such as 'similarly' or 'in contrast' frequently.

Through a similar use of **frame narration**, Kurt Vonnegut shows how the effects of the Second World War have haunted its veterans even after it ended. The novel, which is semi-autobiographical, was written at the height of the Vietnam War in 1969. Vonnegut begins *Slaughterhouse Five* with a dialogue between him and a fellow veteran O'Hare and his wife Mary. O'Hare's wife is angry with Vonnegut for writing a novel about the war, because she assumes that he will glorify war. Vonnegut promises her, though, that his novel will discourage young men from fighting in wars. He explains that it will be short and jumbled because there is nothing intelligent one can say about a massacre. Furthermore, he dedicates the novel to her, which is a clear sign to readers that he aims to uphold his promise to Mary. In the context of 1967, when this work was written, the protest movement against the Vietnam War was growing. This use of frame narration shows the reader how Vonnegut finds war senseless. This extra layer of narration is very similar to O'Brien's way of telling his stories in *The Things They Carried*, which the author uses for the same purpose of showing the adverse effects of war on its veterans and warning against the senselessness of the Gulf War. The non-linear, broken narration, which includes veterans remembering war, acts as a reminder to people of how the atrocities of war live on.

Return to the purpose of the authors towards the end of each paragraph.

The last sentence of each paragraph should return to the essay question and possibly use some of the key words from the essay question.

The disjointed and non-linear narrative is also used in both novels as a way of showing readers how soldiers experience and deal with extremely violent situations. In *The Things They Carried*, O'Brien remembers killing a young Vietnamese man, distancing himself from the violent action by describing the gruesome destruction of the young man's body without emotions. The victim's eye was shot through like a 'star', his body was 'oatmeal' and parts of his face were 'missing'. Instead of writing about his feelings of guilt and disgust, O'Brien uses imagery. Furthermore, he fantasises about the young Vietnamese man's youth, growing up at school, possibly being teased by others for his love of calculus. This flashback is contrasted with the description of a butterfly landing on the young man's nose. O'Brien's platoon mate rationalises that if O'Brien hadn't killed the boy, someone else would have. This use of dialogue, imagery and non-linear structure allows O'Brien to retell this violent act without facing his pain or showing remorse for killing the young man.

You do not need to include exact quotations in your essay, as you will not have the works with you in the exam room. This integrated approach of a few words, together with paraphrasing, is effective.

The main character of *Slaughterhouse Five*, Billy Pilgrim, uses similar though different devices for coping with post-traumatic stress disorder (PTSD). Billy Pilgrim, a fictional character, is, like Vonnegut himself, a Second World War veteran, prisoner of war (POW) and survivor of the bombing of Dresden. The novel ends with the protagonist climbing out of a mountain of dead bodies. The imagery is very gruesome and graphic. Every time Billy puts one dead body behind him, another appears on the horizon. In a sense, this is an analogy of war itself, as Vonnegut suggests that once one war finishes another one begins. 'So it goes', the narrator states throughout the novel after someone is killed, which is frequently. This passive phrase suggests that death and destruction are inevitable. The language makes the reader feel as helpless as the protagonist but willing to accept the atrocities for what they are. In a similar way O'Brien

For Criterion B, it is important to return to the effects of the language on the reader.

adopts a helpless tone throughout *The Things They Carried* by using phrases such as 'this is true' to suggest that the horrible events should be accepted for what they are. Just as O'Brien's mind wanders and scenes flash forward or backward every time there is a violent situation, so too does Billy's. Billy believes that he was abducted by aliens, the Tralfamadorians, who taught him to time travel, using 'the fourth dimension'. This allows him to look back at the horrors of war as just one time in his life and also to flash forward to other, better times. This device for coping with PTSD is more extreme than O'Brien's use of imagination and 'truth-story', though it serves the same function. The non-linear storylines of both works show their readers how veterans deal with PTSD.

This is good comparison of both works.

This essay paraphrases parts of the novels without overly summarising. See how this explanation of the 'fourth dimension' is made relevant to the essay question.

Finally, both works use non-linear structures to show readers how wars inflict mental damage on veterans. In *The Things They Carried*, several characters are depicted as mentally unstable. One story is about Mitchell Sanders, who went on patrol and eventually went crazy after hearing strange noises, like talking monkeys, cocktail parties and chanting. Even after he ordered the whole region to be burnt down by air strikes, he still heard the noises. Eventually Sanders admits to O'Brien that he had embellished parts of his story, which makes the reader question Sanders's sanity and reliability as a narrator.

In a similar way, Billy Pilgrim is insane and Vonnegut's story is nothing but fantasy. While Kurt Vonnegut claims that 'most' of his story about Billy is true, it would be impossible for anyone to have such knowledge of another man's thoughts and actions. What's more, Vonnegut's story about Billy's encounters with the Tralfamadorians, his sexual contact with a film star and his time travelling must be fantasy, despite Vonnegut's very matter-of-fact tone. There are hints that Billy is perceived as crazy by other characters, such as his optometry clients and his daughter, who finds him freezing in a house with a broken boiler. The reader, however, suspends all disbelief in Vonnegut's story, because it is based on the premise that nothing could be more absurd than surviving the firebombing of Dresden, which killed over 135 000 people in one night. In fact, Vonnegut himself survived the bombing, as is described in this fictional tale, as a prisoner in a meat locker. Vonnegut and O'Brien both earn a certain right to tell fantastical, non-linear stories that comment critically on war, because they both survived the horrors of war.

Notice how the second, fourth and sixth body paragraphs of this essay compare *Slaughterhouse Five* to *The Things They Carried*. It is useful to compare the second work in light of the first.

Any contextual information which is relevant to the question addresses Criterion A.

To conclude, both novels use a non-linear, disjointed narration to show the reader how veterans remember, experience and suffer from war. The novels are written in the context of one war about another war as a warning that war will always be horrific. Both Vonnegut and O'Brien mix fact and fiction as a means of making the senselessness of war sensible to readers.

It is impossible to be repetitive when using language from the exam question.

Try to end your essay with some words of wisdom. It is difficult, but you can discuss and prepare these ideas in class.

Paper 2 – Sample 1 – Examiner's marks and comments

Criterion A: Knowledge, understanding, interpretation and comparison: 8 out of 10 marks

The student is very knowledgeable about the two novels and shows a high degree of understanding. There are many references to the contexts in which the works were written, including biographical information on the authors. Interpretations of the novels are very insightful, as the student explores the authors' common purpose of commenting on the senseless violence of war. For the most part, these interpretations are relevant to the essay question, about the non-linear storylines. While the novels are compared throughout the essay, the student struggles, at times, to compare them in relation to the question.

Criterion B: Analysis and evaluation: 9 out of 10 marks

The essay question lends itself well to analysis and evaluation, as it asks for an exploration of non-linear narrative techniques. What is more, the literary works are very appropriate for this question, as they are written in a non-linear fashion. The student includes quite a few references to the works, commenting on a broad range of stylistic features, such as imagery, unreliable narrator, flashbacks, fantasy, tone, while maintaining focus on the non-linear nature of both texts and the effects of these on the reader.

Criterion C: Coherence, balance, focus and organisation: 5 out of 5 marks

This essay takes a very balanced approach, alternating its focus on each work and comparing them in passing. The essay has a strong sense of structure, which is due to the connective phrases and linking words.

Criterion D: Language: 5 out of 5 marks

The student's use of English is very academic and articulate. Very complex ideas are articulated effectively through the student's use of vocabulary and syntax. Literary terms are used accurately throughout the essay.

6.11 In Activity 6.10 you were asked to focus on one criterion and find evidence from Sample essay 1 to answer questions about your criterion. Now shuffle the groups in your class so that at each table there is at least one expert on each criterion.

In these new groups, discuss the marks that you would award to Sample essay 1 on all criteria. Read the level descriptors of the assessment criteria carefully in the introduction of this coursebook.

With reference to the level descriptors, would you describe this essay as 'poor' or 'good'? What are its strengths and weaknesses? How do you think it could be improved?

6.12 How is Sample essay 1 organised? Is there a structure that the student is following for constructing the essay? Use different coloured highlighter pens to identify sentences in the essay that have different functions.

6.13 Have you identified a pattern in the student's writing in Sample essay 1? Besides including an introduction and conclusion, the three pairs of body paragraphs follow a pattern, which can be described by the acronym PEACE ACT. See the explanation in the table. See if you can find evidence of this structure in body paragraphs 3–6 of Sample essay 1.

The table gives a summary of the structure that the student has used. You may find it helpful to use this structure to organise your own Paper 2 essay.

	Description	Example
Introduction		
Hook	A general statement that captures the attention of readers and makes them care about the topic.	Readers are often intrigued by war stories, because they want to know if people can persevere in adverse circumstances.
Basics	Include the names of the authors, the titles of their works and the main messages conveyed in them.	*The Things They Carried* by Tim O'Brien and *Slaughterhouse Five* by Kurt Vonnegut both show how soldiers struggle to deal with war and its aftermath.
Thesis	This is the key idea of your essay. It should come at the end of the introduction. It answers the essay question, makes a claim about the authors' purpose, and mentions several stylistic techniques that they use.	The authors both use a disjointed and non-linear narration to show readers how soldiers remember, experience and suffer from the horrors of war.
First body paragraph		
Point	Make a point about both authors' purpose in writing and comment on their shared use of style. This sentence is also called the 'topic sentence'.	Both novels are written by authors who remember their experiences of one war in the context of another war, using non-linear narrative structures.
Evidence	Give evidence from the work to support the first point. This can be a quotation or paraphrase. It should illustrate the author's style or technique.	For example, one chapter, called 'Love', is about how O'Brien meets with another veteran, Jimmy Cross, years after the war to drink coffee and gin and remember the atrocities for which they could not forgive themselves. His friend tells O'Brien about a woman he loved, Martha. But his love was unrequited, because Martha was scared to be with a veteran who had experienced such violence, and this left him heartbroken.
Analysis	Explain how this evidence supports the point that is made in the topic sentence. Establish a relationship between writer's style and writer's purpose. Describe the effects of the language on the reader.	There seems to be an inescapable stigma surrounding Vietnam veterans. This story within a story shows the reader how war never stops damaging the lives of its veterans, long after it is over.

TIP

The student who wrote this essay may seem to have had an unfair advantage. She has read two novels, both of which were about war and both of which included non-linear narration. She was lucky with the questions that appeared on the exam paper.

Her teacher gave her the opportunity to compare and contrast by selecting works that were similar. They were from the same genre (text type), which also gave her an advantage.

Return to your hexagon (HL) or square (SL) diagram of the literary works you are reading (Activity 6.1) and discuss the advantages that you may have when writing about pairs of literary works that you are studying.

Second body paragraph		
Compare	Compare how the second work is similar to, or different from, the first with regard to the point made in the first paragraph's topic sentence about style and purpose.	Through a similar use of *frame narration*, Kurt Vonnegut shows how the effects of the Second World War have haunted its veterans even after it ended.
Evidence	Offer evidence from the second work to compare use of style and technique.	Vonnegut begins *Slaughterhouse Five* with a dialogue between him and fellow veteran O'Hare and his wife Mary. O'Hare's wife is angry with Vonnegut for writing a novel about the war, because she assumes that he will glorify war.
Analysis	Explain how this second example has an effect on the reader and constructs the author's message.	This use of frame narration shows the reader how Vonnegut finds war senseless.
Compare	Compare, again, how the first and second work relate to the stylistic feature and main point of the topic sentence.	This extra layer of narration is very similar to O'Brien's way of telling his stories in *The Things They Carried*, which the author uses for the same purpose of showing the adverse effects of war on its veterans and warning against the senselessness of the Gulf War.
Tie back to thesis	Connect the ideas of the last two paragraphs to the thesis statement, commenting on the author's shared use of style and purpose.	The non-linear, broken narration, which includes veterans remembering war, acts as a reminder to people how the atrocities of war live on.
Third and fourth paragraph		
Follow the same PEACE ACT structure of the first two paragraphs		
Fifth and sixth paragraph		
More PEACE ACT		
Conclusion		
To conclude	Offer a clear signpost that the essay is coming to an end.	To conclude . . .

Reiterate	Use language from the essay question and/or thesis statement to reiterate the authors' purpose and use of language.	. . . both novels use a non-linear, disjointed narration to show the reader how veterans remember, experience and suffer from war. The novels are written in the context of one war about another war as a warning that war will always be horrific.
Wise words	Try to end with a generalisation that is not too sweeping and connects to the opening sentence of the essay.	Both Vonnegut and O'Brien mix fact and fiction as a means of making the senselessness of war sensible to readers.

TIP

The Paper 2 exam is a closed-book exam. You do not have to memorise quotes from your literary works in order to get good marks. Use a few quotations from your works if they are relevant to the question. You can paraphrase sections of the play or novel, though be careful not to *summarise* the story.

6.14 A well-written essay is coherent. A coherent essay is one that can be taken apart and easily put back together again, because its parts follow in a logical order. Here is another sample essay. This one, however, has been cut into several parts and scrambled up. The parts are still organised into five major sections (introduction, first and second paragraphs, third and fourth paragraphs, fifth and sixth paragraphs and conclusion). You may find the PEACE ACT model useful for putting the body paragraphs back together again.

The question for Sample essay 2 is Question 2 from the second Specimen Paper 2, from Activity 6.2.

Paper 2 – Sample 2

Essay question

In what ways and for what reasons do two literary works that you have read appeal to their audiences' eyes and ears? Compare and contrast the ways in which they appeal to the auditory and visual senses of their audiences.

Scrambled essay

Introduction

a These three techniques appeal to the visual and auditory senses of the audience and help convey the authors' message that women deserve equal respect to men.

b By nature, plays appeal to an audience's visual and auditory senses, as they are meant to be performed.

c The play *A Doll's House*, written by Henrik Ibsen in 1879, depicts the struggles of the protagonist, Nora, in a patriarchal Norway. *A Streetcar Named Desire*, written by Tennessee Williams in 1947, portrays a similar struggle, where the protagonist Blanche Dubois is pitted against Stanley Kowalski, a dominating man in a patriarchal New Orleans.

d Both works criticise the times and places in which they were written through a variety of techniques, such as symbolism, stage directions and music.

First and second body paragraphs

e The decorated Christmas tree helps establish a joyous mood with the audience, as it is a symbol that the original target audience, Norwegians in the 19th century, could relate to.

f In *A Streetcar Named Desire,* Tennessee Williams employs the symbol of the paper lantern with similar effectiveness.

g In both plays the authors have included symbolism, which adds depth to the plays and conveys their messages in both convincing and aesthetic ways.

h The symbol of a bare Christmas tree conveys a very effective message that this marriage is not all that it is made out to be and comments critically on gender roles in Norwegian homes in the 19th century.

i Like the Christmas tree in *A Doll's House*, the paper lantern in *A Streetcar Named Desire* is a sign that times are difficult for women in a male-dominated world.

j Mitch, one of Stanley's poker friends, is instructed by Blanche to place a paper lantern over a bare light bulb. Blanche hates bright lights because they reveal the reality from which she is trying to hide. The paper lantern helps distort reality and makes it more difficult for Mitch to tell her age.

k Perhaps the most effective symbol in *A Doll's House* is the Christmas tree, which depicts the transformation of Nora, the main character. In the beginning of the play, the tree is decorated, symbolising Nora's festive and happy mood. She is happy to be celebrating Christmas without worrying about money.

l In the second act, however, the tree is stripped of its decorations, symbolising Nora's distressed and disturbed mood after her conversation with her husband, Torvald Helmer. At this stage in the play, she feels like poisoning her own children, a mood which is captured by the tree that is stripped of its decorations.

m The paper lantern is also fragile and it tears easily. When Stanley tears down the lantern, the audience feels that a part of Blanche is torn. She is exposed for who she is: an emotionally unstable woman who is running away from her problems. The torn lantern is a symbol that signifies that the era of the Southern belle is over and that men like Stanley Kowalski are now in charge.

Third and fourth body paragraphs

n In *A Doll's House*, Ibsen states in the beginning that the stage includes 'bound books in shelves, polished furniture and firewood by the fireplace'. These stage directions indicate that the Helmers are rather bourgeois, upper middle-class people.

o Secondly, the stage directions in both plays help create an atmosphere that appeals to the audiences' eyes and ears, and set the stage for social criticism.

p Although Williams's set is significantly rougher than that of *A Doll's House*, the effect on the audience is quite similar: they show audiences how women are trapped by the order or disorder of the world that men have created.

q In contrast to *A Doll's House*, *A Streetcar Named Desire* is set in a rougher neighbourhood of New Orleans in the 1940s, which is bordering on poverty.

r As the play progresses, the audience feels all of the pressures which come along with this setting, where everything must be in its place, restricting one's freedoms. The nice home also acts as a false façade that covers their marital problems.

s As Williams describes in his stage directions: 'The buildings look grey, there is warmth in the atmosphere, the stairs are crooked.'

t The audience understands that New Orleans has departed from its decadent, aristocratic past and has become more working class. There is no more room for the refined manners of the old South and Blanche Dubois.

Fifth and sixth body paragraphs

u These words seem appropriate for Blanche, who tries to keep up appearances with her cheap dresses and paper lanterns.

v The Varsouviana Polka is a motif that runs through the play, as Blanche hears it every time she thinks of her dead husband. The Varsouviana Polka is like a carousel tune, which was playing when Blanche's husband committed suicide. Because it plays throughout, the audience understands that Blanche cannot escape his death. The audience feels her shame and guilt as she feels responsible for driving him to suicide after discovering his homosexuality.

w In fact she is dancing to save her life, and, in the context of 19th century Norway, the audience would have realised this. Ibsen included this music as a social criticism of his times, where women were driven to hysteria by the men in power.

x Finally, in both plays, music plays an important role in establishing the atmosphere and conveying the authors' message of social criticism.

y Just as 'Paper Moon' and the Varsouviana Polka make the audience of *A Street Car Named Desire* pity Blanche, so too does the audience of *A Doll's House* pity Nora when they hear the dance of the Tarantella, as the music symbolises the pressures under which the women are suffering in these respective patriarchies.

z In a similar way, Williams employs music in *A Streetcar Named Desire* as a means of expressing his social criticism of his times.

aa In *A Doll's House* the audience sees and hears Nora dance to the Tarantella, which adds to the tension of the play. The audience of the time would have known the dance and the myth of tarantism. The song is named after the tarantula spider, whose bite would make victims dance wildly. In actuality many women in the 19th century suffered from hysteria, because they were under so much pressure from men. Women were encouraged to dance this dance until exhaustion, as a kind of 'cure' for hysteria. The dance, however, is meant to be danced in pairs. Since Torvald shuts himself in his office, Nora must dance it alone. She begs him to watch her dance wildly, so that he is distracted and cannot read the blackmail letter from Krogstad, which would ruin her life and expose her secret.

bb 'Paper Moon' is another song motif that the audience hears in the play. Its lyrics are sung by Blanche as she lies in the bathtub: 'It's only a paper moon, sailing over a cardboard sea. But it wouldn't be make-believe, if you believed in me.'

Conclusion

cc Both audiences can see how the pressures on women in a male-dominated world are hard to bear and, as a result, they are more open to the ideals of feminism.

dd To conclude, both playwrights, Henrik Ibsen and Tennessee Williams, employ visual and auditory techniques, such as symbolism, stage directions and music, to create an atmosphere and convey a message that comments critically on society.

ee Both playwrights depict how times are changing in their respective societies.

TIP

When you have written a practice essay on two literary works and an essay question, chop it up into multiple parts for a classmate to put back together again, as has been done in the example from Activity 6.14. If your classmate is successful in putting your essay back together, then you will have written a coherent essay.

Paper 2 – Sample 2 – Examiner's marks and comments

Criterion A: Knowledge, understanding, interpretation and comparison: 7 out of 10 marks

The essay shows good knowledge and understanding of the works. Interpretations frequently draw on similarities and differences between the works. Comments on the authors' purposes of challenging patriarchal societies show the student's level of understanding. Unfortunately, real comparison between the works is rather superficial and not always in relation to the question.

Criterion B: Analysis and evaluation: 7 out of 10 marks

Sentences such as 'Ibsen included this music as a social criticism of his times, where women were driven to hysteria by the men in power' are very good in analysing the literary works. While techniques such as music, stage directions and symbolism are explored in some depth, they are not always compared across literary works. Furthermore, the term 'stage directions' is interpreted in a narrow sense, as the student's comments focus only on the set and props and not on the speech directions for the actors.

Criterion C: Coherence, balance, focus and organisation: 5 out of 5 marks

This essay alternates between works very effectively, with two body paragraphs on music, two body paragraphs on stage directions and two body paragraphs on symbolism. There are multiple linking words, which act as signposts for the reader of this essay.

Criterion D: Language: 5 out of 5 marks

The language of this essay is very concise. Grammar, vocabulary and register are all very effective and accurate, expressing complex ideas in a way that is easy to read.

6.15 How did you know in which order to place the scrambled sections of Sample 2? You may have been looking for **connectives** or linking words. Work in small groups and draw a table like this one here. Go back through the essay and find words that can fit into each category.

Words that compare	Words that contrast	Words that point to previous ideas
Words that illustrate	**Words that explain**	**Words that list and order**

6.16 Did you find examples of all these connectives in Sample essay 2? As you practise writing your own Paper 2 essays, make sure you use connectives to make the structure of your essay clear. Here is a list of connectives for comparing and contrasting that you may find useful in your essay writing. Try writing a few sentences that compare two of the works that you are reading in class, using some of these connectives.

- alternatively
- also
- but
- even though
- in contrast
- just as . . . so too . . .
- nevertheless
- similarly
- too
- while
- although
- both
- despite
- however
- in fact
- like
- one the one hand . . . on the other . . .
- though
- whereas
- yet.

Answers to Activity 6.14 on the 'scrambled essay'

Introduction		Body 1	
1	B	5	G
2	C	6	K
3	D	7	E
4	A	8	L
		9	H

Body 2		Body 3	
10	F	14	O
11	J	15	N
12	M	16	R
13	I		

Body 4		Body 5	
17	Q	21	X
18	S	22	AA
19	T	23	W
20	P		

Body 6		Conclusion	
24	Z	29	DD
25	V	30	EE
26	BB	31	CC
27	U		
28	Y		

6.17 As well as using connectives, organising your ideas and writing effective thesis statements, what else should you do to prepare for your Paper 2 exam? You will need to acquire a thorough understanding of the works that you are reading and an ability to analyse the authors' use of language in relation to an (unseen) essay question. This is a long process which requires plenty of practice.

a Read Sample essay 3 and assess it according to the assessment criteria, which can be found in the introduction to this coursebook.

b Share your marks with your classmates. Discuss any differences of opinion, and the reasons for these.

c Compare your marks and comments with the examiner's marks and comments.

d Discuss how you think the student acquired this level of understanding of these two literary works. How do you think they prepared for this challenging exam?

The question for Paper 2 Sample essay 3 is Question 4 from the third Specimen Paper 2, from Activity 6.2.

Paper 2 – Sample 3

Essay question

The struggle against injustice is a theme that speaks to readers. Compare the ways in which two authors of two literary works have depicted unjust worlds.

Comparative essay

Readers are often captured by stories that depict some kind of injustice. Much as people would like to live in a just world, we know that reality is different. People suffer unnecessarily from injustice all around the world all the time. *Disgrace* by J.M. Coetzee and *The Tempest* by William Shakespeare both explore the theme of injustice and depict characters struggling to find justice. Although The Tempest is a play written in the early days of colonialism and *Disgrace* is a novel written in a post-colonial, post-apartheid South Africa,

Try to avoid such sweeping generalisations.

> It's fine to break up a thesis statement into two sentences. This last sentence of the thesis statement and the introduction is effective in addressing the essay question and the authors' purpose.

the works explore the theme of injustice through **point of view**, symbolism and **motif**. The authors show the importance of reconciliation and love as means of overcoming injustices.

> You can paraphrase and summarise the work if your illustration is relevant to the question. Write as if the examiner has read the literary works.

> Avoid ambiguous qualifiers.

In both *Disgrace* and *The Tempest*, the protagonists, David Lurie and Prospero, are powerful people who have become victims of some form of injustice. David Lurie, a white professor in South Africa, was fired from his university after having sex with a student. After he has 'fallen from grace' he moves to his daughter's farm, where he becomes the victim of a violent attack which leaves him physically scarred. The men who burn him also rape his daughter. Even though David and his daughter, Lucy, eventually learn the identity of the men, it seems impossible for them to be brought to justice because pressing charges could bring even more violence. Coetzee's novel is told from third-person point of view though it uses **free indirect speech** throughout the novel, telling readers his thoughts through a limited but omniscient narrator. This makes the reader somewhat sympathetic to David, despite the fact that he is a perpetrator of injustice as well. While he refuses to say 'sorry' to the university, he eventually comes to accept that his new existence, in a post-colonial, post-apartheid South Africa, means living modestly and working at an animal shelter.

> You can prepare for your Paper 2 essay by learning a set of adjectives that describe the characters, setting or mood of the works.

> Contrasting literary works is as important as comparing them, if your ideas are relevant to the essay question.

In a somewhat similar but also very different way, the protagonist in *The Tempest*, Prospero, is both a victim of one injustice and the perpetrator of another. Prospero and his daughter Miranda are stranded on an island after being usurped and banished by his brother, Antonio. Even though they seem to be the victim of power-hungry people, they too are guilty of stealing the power away from their island's rightful owner, Caliban. Through dramatic asides and dialogue, the audience learns that Caliban feels bitter about being enslaved by Prospero and Miranda. Nevertheless, the audience does not sympathise with him, because he is crass and savage in his ways. The perspective of the play favours Prospero, who seems to have a God-given, colonial right to bark orders at his servants Caliban and Ariel. Unlike David Lurie, Prospero does not end up a lowly outcast. Instead he returns to his dukedom as the rightful heir, because his brother sees the error of his ways and Prospero forgives him. While reconciliation is the answer to injustices of the past in both literary works, *The Tempest* suggests that some leaders are above apologising.

> Effective topic sentences include the stylistic feature which the paragraph aims to explore.

Both *The Tempest* and *Disgrace* use symbolism to explore the theme of injustice and comment on the nature of power in their worlds. In *Disgrace*, dogs appear throughout the novel, representing servitude and low status. There are dogs on Lucy's farm, which Petrus, her black farmhand, helps look after initially. In fact Petrus introduces himself to David as 'the dog-man', which suggests that he has a low status on the farm as well. Once the dogs are killed by the intruders, Petrus is relieved of his duties and acts more like an owner of the farm. He knows and protects the attackers, and he threatens to let them attack again, if he is not given land rights. Lucy agrees to marry Petrus for protection and her father is forced to accept there will be no justice. In fact, David Lurie becomes the new 'dog-man', as he volunteers at the animal shelter, putting dogs to sleep and disposing of their corpses. The symbol of the dog in *Disgrace* is Coetzee's way of commenting on how the injustices of apartheid are starting to reverse, as white people concede power to black people. Dogs also symbolise David's transition from detesting animals to loving them.

Symbols in *The Tempest* are used to a different end, as they point towards the coloniser's rightful power to inflict injustice on others. Prospero's books symbolise his power, which lies in his knowledge of magic. While his love for books, knowledge and magic are what cost him his dukedom before the start of the play, books also symbolise his power to regain his dukedom. After Prospero's brother, Antonio, and his shipwrecked crew come to Prospero's island, Caliban naively thinks he can guide Antonio to Prospero's books, steal them and regain control of the island. However, Prospero's use of magic and command of Ariel, his fairy servant, allow him to see and know all that happens on his island, and so he sets a trap for his enemies and regains his control over his dukedom. While Prospero and David Lurie are both powerful men of knowledge, they end up in very different places. The symbol of the dog in *Disgrace* is very different from the symbol of Prospero's books in *The Tempest*. Coetzee employs the symbolism of dogs in *Disgrace* to show how knowledge does not lead to an inherent right to rule. While the injustice that Prospero inflicts on Caliban seems rightful in the colonial context of this play, the injustice that David Lurie inflicts on young women does not go unchecked in post-apartheid South Africa.

Such sentences are very effective for Criterion A.

Both *The Tempest* and *Disgrace* explore the theme of injustice and they comment on the nature of power through the motifs of sex and love. In both works men attempt to exert power over women through sex. David Lurie, a middle-aged man, sleeps with a young prostitute frequently and takes advantage of his student, Melanie. David struggles to see the parallels between his daughter's rape and his own sexual prowess on the university campus. Nevertheless, something gradually changes in him as he works at the animal shelter. He develops a relationship with Bev Shaw, who is his age and unattractive. He sees a kind of nobility in loving her, just as he sees nobility in taking care of the dogs. Sex, for David, changes from being a means of exerting power over women to a means of loving someone. If there is any justice for Lucy's rape, it is that her father has stopped being a sexual predator. Through this motif of sex, Coetzee seems to comment on power relations in South Africa, suggesting that the injustices of apartheid can only be reconciled if the white ruling-class is willing to change their ways and accept the changes that come their way.

If it is not realistic to write this much in 1 hour and 45 minutes, you may want to alter your plan and focus on only two out of the three stylistic features from your thesis statement. Be sure to return to your thesis statement and edit the third feature out.

Such insights into literary works can be prepared before the exam through in-depth discussions and analysis.

Sex and love are motifs that can be found in *The Tempest* as well. Caliban tries to exert his power over Prospero by attempting to rape his daughter, Miranda. He regrets that his attempt was not successful, as he would have happily populated the island with little Calibans, as he says. Because Caliban behaves so savagely, Prospero feels entitled to take the island from him. He tries, in vain, to teach Caliban to be more civilised, but Caliban is a bad servant and not loyal to his master. In this colonial context, the audience senses that Caliban deserves any injustice that Prospero inflicts on him. In contrast, the injustice that Antonio inflicted on his brother requires reconciliation. When Prospero discovers that his daughter has fallen in love with his enemy's son, Ferdinand, it is easier to forgive his brother of any wrongdoing. The play ends with a moralistic soliloquy in which forgiveness is presented as the remedy for injustice. Similarly, David Lurie comes to realise this and drives to Melanie's parents' house to ask them for forgiveness for what he has done to their daughter. It is only through his love for dogs, Bev Shaw and his daughter, Lucy, that he realises that this step is necessary to right his wrongs and give Melanie's parents some sense of justice. When this novel was written in 1999, only a few years after the Truth and Reconciliation Commission, showing remorse and asking for forgiveness were easily identifiable themes for South Africans. In both literary works, love is depicted as a solution for solving injustice.

This is effective use of relevant, contextual knowledge.

In conclusion, the readers of *The Tempest* and *Disgrace* are taken on journeys to two very different worlds where characters struggle to overcome the injustices inflicted on them. Despite the one work being written hundreds of years after the other, and despite their different literary formats, both works employ point of view, symbolism and motif to show audiences that love and reconciliation are the solutions for overcoming injustice.

It is possible to write successfully about two different types of literary works, such as plays and novels. However, it can be *easier* to write about two works of the same text type.

Paper 2 – Sample 3 – Examiner's marks and comments

Criterion A: Knowledge, understanding, interpretation and comparison: 10 out of 10 marks

This essay shows excellent understanding of the novel and the play in relation to the essay question. The examples from the works are relevant to the question about injustice. Furthermore, the essay constantly compares and contrasts the works, pointing to key differences between Prospero and David Lurie with respect to the question about injustice.

Criterion B: Analysis and evaluation: 10 out of 10 marks

The essay is rather detailed about the use of literary features, such as free-indirect speech, motifs and soliloquys. The student evaluates the importance of these features in commenting on the themes of justice, colonialism and power. Even though the works are two different literary forms (a play and a novel), the student is still able to make meaningful comparison of how the authors construct meaning in similar and different ways. This is possible because the student focuses on overarching technologies such as point of view, symbols and motifs, and form-specific examples of these, such as dramatic asides and omniscient narration.

Criterion C: Coherence, balance, focus and organisation: 5 out of 5 marks

The essay develops the idea that reconciliation and love are needed to overcome the injustices caused by colonialism. It is coherent, because it gives examples from the works to support this claim. It is focused, because it explains the relevance of these examples in relation to the essay question. It is organised and balanced, as the paragraphs alternate between works and use connectives to compare and contrast them.

Criterion D: Language: 5 out of 5 marks

The essay is very well written, using a range of vocabulary, literary terms and sentence structures. Complex ideas are expressed effectively through the use of concise and accurate language.

CONCEPT

Culture

Have you noticed how all three of the students' essays have referred to the *culture*, time and place in which they were written and received? Culture and context are important in Paper 2, even though the terms themselves do not appear in the assessment criteria. As you practise writing essays, be sure to include comments about how culture is connected to the author's purpose or message.

Extended essay

You can write your extended essay on literary works that you have explored in class. Your essay should present a unique, creative and individual approach to these works, which was not developed under teacher guidance or group discussion. You may consider writing an extended essay about one or more literary works in English (Category 1) or comparing a work written in English with a work in translation (Category 2). The PEACE ACT model may prove useful for your extended essay if you are comparing and contrasting works – an approach which is highly recommended.

Over to you

6.18 You may need to write several practice Paper 2 essays before you feel confident in sitting your exam. Here are several ways to build up your essay writing and exam skills:

a Try writing an essay collaboratively as a class in an online document which you can all edit in real time. Brainstorm on a question as a class. Make mind maps and outlines. Assign small groups different paragraphs. Ask your teacher if they can edit some of the worst sentences of the essay in front of you and your classmates, so as to learn from the experience.

b Try writing a Paper 2 essay on one literary work only. Remove the comparative element to make the essay shorter and easier. You do not have to write under time constraint. The assessment criteria may be difficult to apply, but discuss your essay with your teacher to get feedback on your writing style and approach.

c Try writing a Paper 2 essay on a question of your choice from the three specimen papers in this coursebook or from a previous exam paper. Take time to research and write your essay, comparing both works. You may want to use text-editing software. Submit it to your teacher and ask what changes need to be made in order to earn more marks on the criteria. Make the necessary changes and resubmit your essay.

d Try writing a Paper 2 essay under exam conditions, in 1 hour and 45 minutes by hand on an unseen question. Remember the activities that were done in this chapter to prepare you, finding connections across literary works, unpacking the question, writing thesis statements, organising ideas and using connectives.

REFLECT

What did you learn from the activities and the sample essays in this chapter? Could you learn to write essays like those written by the students? Could you write essays that are better than these? What do you need to do in order to write an excellent Paper 2 comparative essay under exam conditions?

HL essay

At higher level, what is expected of you in your HL essay?
What skills will you need to develop in order to write this essay effectively and coherently?
How can you develop these skills throughout your studies and on your own as coursework?

In this chapter you will:

- learn about the requirements and expectations for the HL essay
- discuss the strengths and weaknesses of samples of students' work
- develop your own essay-writing skills.

Learning objectives

- understand what is expected for your HL essay by writing lines of inquiry, reading sample essays and applying the assessment criteria
- develop your own essay-writing skills
- be able to draft your own HL essay.

For English A: Language and Literature at higher level you are asked to write an essay of 1200–1500 words about a text and a line of **inquiry** of your own choice. This text may be one of the six literary texts that you are studying in class, either in English or in translation. If you write about a literary work, then you may not write about that work on your Paper 2 exam or discuss it in your individual oral. Instead of writing about a literary text, you may base your essay on a non-literary text or series of non-literary texts, one of which has been studied in class and all of which are taken from the same text type and the same producer, such as advertisements from the same advertising campaign.

A line of inquiry is a research question which acts as a guiding question for your research, pointing you towards **secondary sources**. The HL essay is an opportunity to explore a topic *and* text in a way that is original and creative, rather like a short extended essay. You may write your HL essay both inside and outside the classroom context, using text-editing software. You can discuss your line of inquiry with your teacher and discuss a complete draft with them, though your teacher may not annotate or edit your work. You can ask your teacher to mark your essay using the assessment criteria (reproduced in the introduction to this book), but keep in mind that your essay will be externally assessed by an IB examiner for 20% of your final mark.

In this unit you will read both good and poor examples of students' responses. These are to help you practise applying the assessment criteria and have a better understanding of the examiner's expectations. This chapter includes skill-building activities on essay writing that build on those you've learnt in Chapters 5 and 6.

Word bank

inquiry
secondary source
primary source
preliminary research
thesis statement
citation
bibliography
semantic field
synonym

TIP

Write more than one HL essay and submit the best one. Learn as much as possible from your first attempt by asking your teacher for feedback. Make sure that any further attempts at the HL essay are about texts that you have *not* written about previously.

Getting started

7.1 Here are several examples of good lines of inquiry. What do they have in common? Discuss the merits of these questions as a class and list some of the characteristics of good lines of inquiry:

a Through which linguistic devices and for what reasons does Nelson Mandela explore the theme of identity in his inaugural speech?

b To what degree are the communication techniques of Lance Armstrong inadequate in expressing remorse in his interview with Oprah Winfrey?

c How does the representation of reckless youth in Diesel's 'Stupid' campaign serve the purpose of selling fashion apparel?

d To what extent does Marjane Satrapi's graphic novel and memoir *Persepolis* promote intercultural understanding or divide cultures and people?

e In what ways and for what reasons does Carol Ann Duffy explore perspective in her collection of poetry *The World's Wife*?

7.2 These are examples of poor lines of inquiry. Using your list of good characteristics from the previous activity, discuss how each line of inquiry could be improved. You may need to research the topics and texts to be able to give an informed answer.

a Why is the British version of *The Office* so much better than the American version?

b To what extent has George Orwell's novel *Nineteen Eighty-Four* come true?

c Why was the Marlboro Man so successful in selling cigarettes?

d How loyal to the novel is the TV series *The Handmaid's Tale*? (see tip)

e How is Harry Potter a typically British schoolboy?

f In what ways was Jawaharlal Nehru successful in his fight for Indian independence?

TIP

Question 7.2d asks about the filming of a novel. This can lead to either a good or bad essay, depending on your focus. Examiners want to see you engage with a text. A film is a text. A novel is also a text. If you write your essay about a literary from your course, you are expected to analyse its use of language and not the cinematography of a *filmed* version of it.

If you want to analyse film as a non-literary text, try analysing the visual language of a TV show, series, documentary, commercial, music video, recorded speech or interview. If you want to analyse film as a literary text, be sure that the ***screenplay*** (the script for the film) is used as one of your school's two literary works of free choice.

7.3 After studying good lines of inquiry (Activity 7.1) and improving other students' lines of inquiry (Activity 7.2), you will now have a clearer idea of what makes a good question.

A good line of inquiry:

- offers an opportunity to analyse the language of a **primary source**
- requires an answer that is informed by secondary sources
- is answerable within the 1200–1500 word limit
- leads to an *argument* and not a *description*
- explores both the author's purpose and the reader's response
- explores one of the seven concepts from the language and literature course.

a Think about a text that you would like to explore. You may want to go back to a source text that interested you in Chapters 1–4 of this coursebook.

b Write your own line of inquiry, based on your text, on a sticky note.

c Place your sticky note on a board for all of your classmates to read.

d Ask your teacher to read aloud each line of inquiry from your class. As a class, discuss the opportunities and pitfalls for each line of inquiry. When your line of inquiry is discussed, take notes in a table like this one here.

Opportunities created by my question	Challenges presented by my question

TIP

Remember, if you write your HL essay about a literary work, you may not write about that work for your Paper 2 exam or discuss it in your individual oral. If you write your essay about a non-literary text, you will have an extra literary text available to use for your Paper 2 or individual oral exams, giving yourself one extra possibility in those forms of assessment.

CONCEPTS

Notice that the good lines of inquiry in Activity 7.1 each include one of the seven concepts from the language and literature course. Think of concepts as cornerstones for good lines of inquiry. Remember the seven concepts are:

- transformation
- representation
- communication
- creativity.
- identity
- creativity
- culture

Include one of these in the line of inquiry that you write for Activity 7.3 and the HL essay which you eventually submit.

7.4 In a famous speech to the United Nations in 2003 on the absence of weapons of mass destruction in Iraq, the US Secretary of Defense Donald Rumsfeld said:

> Reports that say that something hasn't happened are always interesting to me, because as we know, there are known knowns; there are things we know we know. We also know there are known unknowns; that is to say we know there are some things we do not know. But there are also unknown unknowns – the ones we don't know we don't know. And if one looks throughout the history of our country and other free countries, it is the latter category that tend to be the difficult ones.

While this may seem somewhat ridiculous, it is actually rather perceptive. It is useful for understanding the nature of research. Before you start your HL essay, try completing the first two columns of a Know, Want, Learn (KWL) table. This table shows how Rumsfeld's statement corresponds to this learning tool.

What I Know already	What I Want to find out	What I have Learnt
Known knowns	Known unknowns	Unknown unknowns
Point of departure for research	Target of research	What I discover (accidentally) through research

Research skills

One of the five approaches to learning includes research skills. As you prepare your HL essay, think about how you will develop your research skills. What kinds of skills are we talking about? Study the *Persepolis* mind map in Activity 7.11 and talk to your teacher about how you intend to develop some of these skills.

7.5 Do some **preliminary research** on your line of inquiry. This may include a discussion with your school's librarian or an online search. For each source that you come across, give short answers to these questions. After answering these questions, go back and fill in the final column (What I have Learnt) in the table from Activity 7.4.

a How relevant is this secondary source to my line of inquiry?

b What is the purpose of this secondary source? For whom is it written?

c How much authority and credibility does this source have?

d Does it change the way I see my line of inquiry? Would it be better to change my line of inquiry?

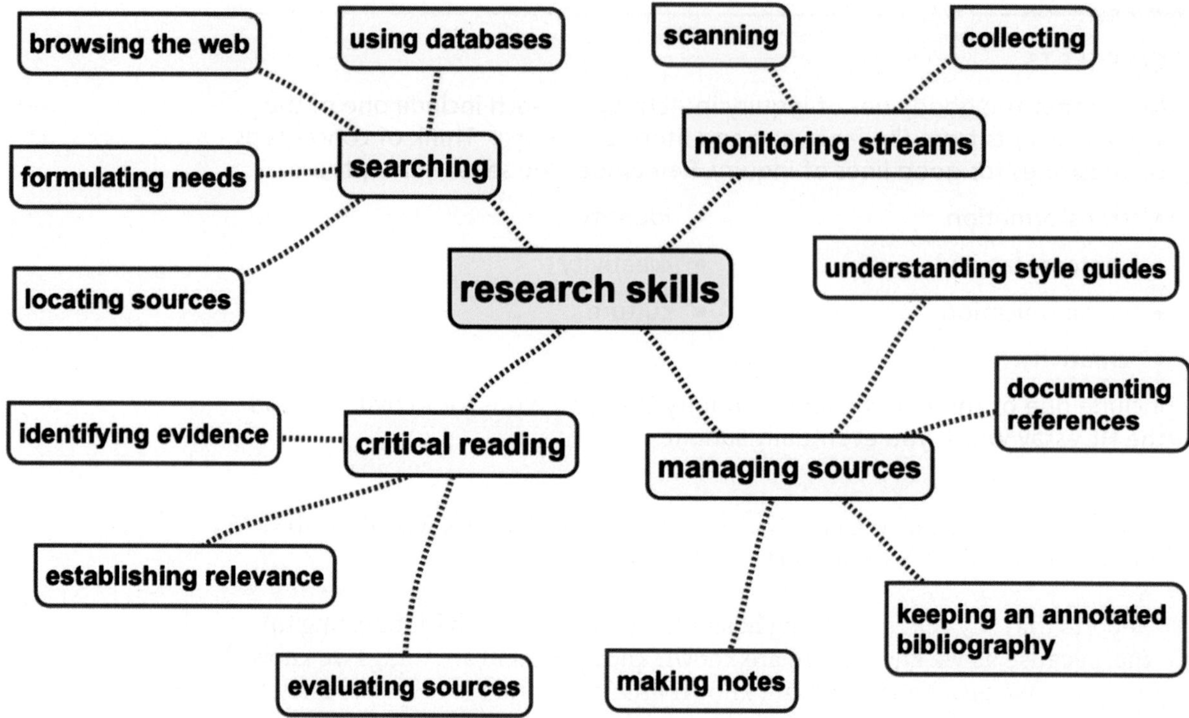

Be mindful of these research skills as you prepare your HL essay or extended essay. These skills are also very relevant for the extended essay.

Sample essays

7.6 You are about to read Sample 1, a good HL essay.

a Read the essay carefully.

b Write down three things that this essay does well which you can learn from. Write each item on a separate sticky note.

c Give your sticky notes to your teacher.

d On a board write four big columns, A–D, each corresponding to a different criterion for the HL essay.

e Look at the assessment criteria for the HL essay, which can be found in the introduction of this coursebook. Ask your teacher to read out each sticky note that you and your classmates wrote. After each sticky note is read aloud, decide as a class if the note belongs under Criterion A, B, C or D. Place the sticky note under the corresponding column.

f On which criteria do you need to focus? Were there any points that did not fall under any of the criteria? What are the key points you should remember in order to write a good HL essay?

AOE question

How can cultural contexts influence how texts are written and received?

You may notice that this question is answered in this first sample HL essay. Does this essay answer any other of the 18 AOE questions from the language and literature curriculum? As you begin to formulate your line of inquiry, ask yourself which AOE questions you will answer *implicitly* and which you will answer *explicitly*. Review all 18 AOE questions in the introduction of this coursebook. There are six questions for each of the three areas of exploration:

- Readers, writers and texts
- Time and space
- Intertextuality: connecting texts.

HL Essay – Sample 1

Line of inquiry

To what extent does Marjane Satrapi's *Persepolis* promote intercultural understanding or divide cultures and people?

Essay

In 2014, the American Librarian Association's Office for Intellectual Freedom placed the graphic novel *Persepolis* on their top ten 'challenged books' for that year (American Librarians Association Office of Intellectual Freedom, 2018). Seven years earlier, upon a screening of the film *Persepolis* at the Cannes Film Festival, Iran sent an angry letter to the French embassy in Tehran to protest against the film (Gulf News, 2007). The graphic novel and memoir by Marjane Satrapi has been widely discussed and taught since it came out in 2003. Interestingly it has been criticised in both the United States and the Middle East. This raises the line of inquiry: to what extent does Marjane Satrapi's *Persepolis* promote intercultural understanding or divide cultures and people? Through an analysis of the author's artistic style, narrative technique and use of symbolism, readers can see why the graphic novel promotes more intercultural understanding than divisiveness.

This essay opens with two secondary sources, which is not required. It is a good idea to start with a real-world problem or situation and build your essay around this.

Include your line of inquiry in your introduction, flagging it with the words 'line of inquiry'.

This thesis statement presents an argument. Writing an argumentative essay will increase your level of analysis (Criterion B) and reduce description.

For the most part, critics of *Persepolis* find the graphic novel too anti-Islamic. To understand this criticism and confusion, readers need to study the symbol of the veil in the graphic novel. From the opening pages it is clear that the veil, for Satrapi, symbolises the oppression of women and children (Figure 1). The first frames suggest that the veil is more about conformity than religion. In the splash at the bottom of the first page a teacher hands out veils to the girls at her school, only for the girls to behave absurdly with them, using them to jump rope, play horse or pretend to torture each other, saying 'Execution in the name of freedom' (Satrapi, 2003, page 3). It is from this point that the reader realises that *Persepolis* is not just a memoir about growing up, but it is about growing up during the Islamic revolution in Iran in the 1980s and the unhealthy effects of religious fundamentalism on young people coming of age. This is where critics easily confuse their interpretation of the veil as a symbol of religion with Satrapi's veil as a symbol of blind faith in a corrupt regime. In this sense, claiming that Satrapi is anti-Muslim misses the point of the

If you are going to write an analysis of a visual text, include screenshots to illustrate your ideas.

Check your essay to avoid long, run-on sentences like these.

It would be good to read a quotation from a critic to support this claim.

Figure 1, taken from *Persepolis*, page 3.

graphic novel entirely. In fact she uses the veil to warn people against the fundamentalists who have hijacked this Islamic symbol for their fascist purposes. Sharing her message with young people is more likely to encourage tolerance and spread awareness about the dangers of fundamentalism than turn them against Islam.

In the United States, parents of schoolchildren have also tried to ban Satrapi's graphic novel for opposite reasons: they fear it is too Islamic and anti-American. One father in Illinois 'questioned why a book about Muslims was assigned on September 11' (Williams, 2015). Here too, readers have missed the point of the graphic novel, which was written with the intent to give the West a window into the troubled history of Iran. As Marjane Satrapi explains in her introduction: 'This old and great civilization [Iran] has been discussed mostly in connection with fundamentalism, fanaticism and terrorism. As an Iranian who has lived more than half my life in Iran, I know that this image is far from the truth. This is why writing *Persepolis* was so important to me. I believe that an entire nation should not be judged by the wrongdoings of a few extremists' (Satrapi, 2003, page 2). For this reason, her memoir is broken down into episodes from her life, which involve real people who have tried to fight the hardships of totalitarianism from within the country, unsuccessfully. Her mother and father are capitalists and secularists, who fight for democracy.

It is good to include a quotation from a reader or critic.

It is good if you can find a secondary source that quotes the author of a text, commenting on the purpose of her text.

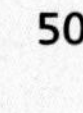

They host parties with intellectuals, they protest in the streets and they look out for family and friends. The plot, which culminates at the end of Part I, is about her parents losing their fight, despite their efforts, against religious extremism and an oppressive government, as they send their daughter, Marjane, to a boarding school in Austria for her own safety. Figure 2 shows Marjane's mother crying and falling into her father's arms. It captures the conflict they feel as parents who want the best for their only child but cannot provide it without sending her far away. Parents who try to ban *Persepolis* from American school libraries fail to see how its message is about the fight for freedom from persecution, an ideal which should inherently appeal to Americans, as their ancestors made sacrifices to migrate to the New World. Reading this graphic novel should help build common ground among readers and sympathy for anyone who has had to immigrate.

Central to this essay is the reader's response to the literary work. This is characteristic of textual analysis and the HL essay.

Figure 2, taken from *Persepolis*, page 153.

Another criticism of Marjane Satrapi's graphic novel is that it is too graphic in its depiction of violence. This is one of several reasons that the Chicago Public Schools (CPS) tried to ban Satrapi's graphic novel from school libraries (Berlatsky, 2013). There are certainly scenes of torture, in which a friend of the family is, in a rather clinical way, dismembered. This scene, like every page of the graphic novel, has been drawn in black and white, with no shades of grey. Her style of drawing is simplistic, abstract and cartoonesque, which is a curious choice for depicting ideas as complicated as torture and totalitarianism. In fact her style is the opposite of graphic, as it makes horrific images palatable for young readers. For example, when young Marjane is told how dissidents were tortured with an iron (page 51), she includes drawings of herself as a girl looking towards her mother's ironing board, wondering how it could be used as a torturing device. Young readers can identify with Marjane as a character, as they can only wonder about prisons and torture. If the purpose of Marjane Satrapi is to warn about the evils of totalitarianism, then these drawings and her drawing style make this message accessible to a wider audience, including young individuals. Denying young readers access to Satrapi's graphic novel is not going to protect them but deny them the opportunity to learn from the horrors of history. The banning of this graphic

Remember that textual analysis is also about the author's choices. This essay addresses a central feature of Marjane Satrapi's graphic novel. As you write your essay, ask yourself which choices the author of the text has made.

TIP

Notice how this essay on *Persepolis* includes images from the original work. Quotations from a primary source are essential in your HL essay. Depending on the type of text that you are exploring, it may be appropriate to include screenshots, stills, illustrations, transcriptions, diagrams or excerpts. Any text that you place in the essay should be included in the word count. Any words in visual texts, like the examples from *Persepolis*, are not included in the word count.

novel in Iran further acts as a denial of their violent history, which stifles any hopes of accountability and democracy in this country. Drawing her drawings in such a way could not confront the people of Iran with their history in a way that is more black and white than this, figuratively speaking.

Finally, Iranian critics of *Persepolis* claim that Satrapi's graphic novel incites revolutionary ideas. Rebellion is certainly a motif that runs throughout the novel as Marjane questions authority throughout her teenage years. She skips school and speaks out against her teacher's conformist activities of chest beating and slogan chanting. In each scene that shows action and dialogue, there is an older, wiser Satrapi providing narrative in voice-over boxes. The tone of this voice is often informative, like the voice-over of a documentary on the history of Iran, but also cheeky, as she reflects on the trials of growing up and becoming an individual. Figure 3 offers a good example of the multiple functions of the voice-over, which is clearly not there to instigate protest, but to inform readers about the history of her country and reflect on her life. In an interview with Golnaz Esfandiari she says: 'I did *Persepolis* not as a political act, but because I had enough of all the nonsense that was being said about my country, and I thought I would tell my story as a part of the truth about my country' (Esfandiari, 2010). Her story strikes a chord with readers and viewers who can identify with her as a victim of oppression and a survivor of war. As she described to CBS in 2007: 'Poor Muslims saw the humanity in the story, its personal point of view. They understood I'm not judging. I'm asking questions' (Ramsey, 2007). If *Persepolis* is criticised for inciting revolution, it is done so by those who fear critical thinking and the inherent truths of Marjane Satrapi's personal story.

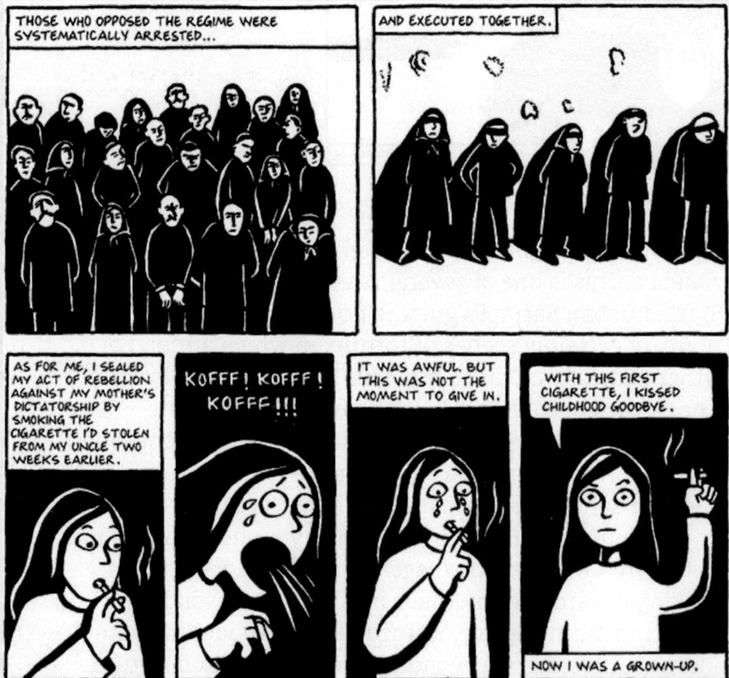

Figure 3, taken from *Persepolis*, page 117.

All in all, the graphic novel and memoir *Persepolis* by Marjane Satrapi has done more to build bridges across cultures than to divide people. Criticisms from readers in the United States in particular seem out of place, as Satrapi's story aims to promote religious tolerance and freedom of expression. Concerns that it is anti-Islamic are understandable, especially in light of Satrapi's use of the symbol of the veil to comment on oppression in a theocracy. Nevertheless, she seems to tell her story for the sake of telling her story, hoping that readers can come to their own conclusions and be more enlightened and informed about the history of a troubled nation.

This is an anticlimax. It was claimed earlier that the author wrote her graphic novel to promote intercultural awareness.

Works cited

While bibliographies are not required by the IB, the specific line of inquiry for this particular essay would be impossible to answer adequately without reference to secondary sources.

American Librarians Association Office of Intellectual Freedom. 'Top Ten Most Challenged Books Lists.' *American Librarians Association Office of Intellectual Freedom*, 9 April 2018, www.ala.org/advocacy/bbooks/frequentlychallengedbooks/top10.

Berlatsky, Noah. 'Sex, Violence, and Radical Islam: Why "Persepolis" Belongs in Public Schools.' *The Atlantic*, Atlantic Media Company, 19 March 2013, www.theatlantic.com/national/archive/2013/03/sex-violence-and-radical-islam-why-persepolis-belongs-in-public-schools/274152/.

Esfandiari, Golnaz. 'Interview: Marjane Satrapi - Esfandiari in "FP".' *Pressroom*, Radio Free Europe / Radio Liberty, 16 July 2010, pressroom.rferl.org/a/Press_Release_Golnaz_interviews_Marjane_Satrapi/2095797.html.

Gulf News. 'Iran Protests Cannes Screening of Movie.' *GulfNews*, Gulfnews, 21 May 2007.

Ramsey, Nancy. '"Persepolis" Creator Won't Return To Iran.' *CBS News*, CBS Interactive, 28 December 2007, www.cbsnews.com/news/persepolis-creator-wont-return-to-iran/.

Satrapi, Marjane. *Persepolis.* Pantheon, 2004.

Williams, Maren. 'Case Study: *Persepolis*.' *Comic Book Legal Defense Fund*, 2015, cbldf.org/banned-challenged-comics/case-study-persepolis/.

HL Essay – Sample 1 – Examiner's marks and comments

Criterion A: Knowledge, understanding and interpretation: 4 out of 5 marks

The line of inquiry invites binary and reductive thinking, as it questions whether Satrapi's graphic novel promotes intercultural thinking or divides people. It continues to explain how some readers 'miss the point', based on an analysis of the graphic novel *Persepolis*. The student's analysis seems to be superior or 'correct' for inherent reasons. Despite the student's biases, the 'wrong' readings are explored and unpacked through secondary sources, which adds validity to the student's interpretations. The inclusion of frames and pages from the primary source also helps reference the student's arguments effectively.

TIP

Examiners like to read poems, extracts, advertisements or other short texts that appear as appendices, if they are essential to understanding your essay. If you are writing analytically about an online commercial or short video, supply the examiner with a URL so that they can find the primary source online through a search.

Criterion B: Analysis and evaluation: 4 out of 5 marks

For the most part, the student analyses Satrapi's use of the features of the graphic novel effectively, exploring the style of drawing, narration and plot. The role that these elements play in answering the question, however, seem to take a back seat to the secondary sources and the student's opinions. For example, the student claims that the 'dismembered body' is not very graphic and is even 'cartoonesque'. These kinds of value judgement are to be taken at face value without detailed analysis or evaluation. Stylistic devices could have been featured more prominently in this essay at the topic-sentence level.

Criterion C: Coherence, focus and organisation: 5 out of 5 marks

The essay is well structured, exploring a different perspective on the graphic novel in each paragraph. The final sentences of each paragraph are especially good in adding coherence to the essay, as they return to the line of inquiry.

Criterion D: Language: 5 out of 5 marks

The student's use of English is very effective in constructing a persuasive argument. Thanks to the student's command of language, this essay is able to demonstrate evidence of analytical thinking.

7.7 Here is another sample of an HL essay (Sample HL essay 2). On a copy of this essay, annotate the student's work using a (red) pen. You should remember to:

- circle inappropriate vocabulary
- point to incoherent ideas
- ask questions in the margin
- make suggestions for rewording
- insert missing ideas
- underline key sentences
- identify the useful phrases
- give general feedback.

Ask your teacher to do the same. Compare your annotations with your teacher's feedback after this activity.

TIP

Keep in mind that your teacher will *not* be able to annotate your essay or a draft of it, if it will be submitted to the IB. By studying your teacher's annotations of other essays, however, you can learn from other students' mistakes.

HL Essay – Sample 2

Line of inquiry

To what degree are the communication techniques of Lance Armstrong inadequate in expressing remorse in his interview with Oprah Winfrey?

Essay

In a 2013 interview with Oprah Winfrey, Lance Armstrong confessed to using performance-enhancing drugs throughout his cycling career. This sent total shock around the world because he had denied allegations so vigorously in the years before. Millions of viewers expected Armstrong to show sorrow, remorse and regret in the interview. The interview, however, could not have been more disappointing for them. This raises the question: to what degree are the communication techniques of Lance Armstrong inadequate in expressing remorse in his interview with Oprah Winfrey? Through a careful study of Armstrong's use of diction, body language, fillers and verb tense, one can understand why his confession was not appreciated by viewers.

Five years after the interview, Lance Armstrong gave another interview on the podcast Freakonomics, in which he was asked what he had thought of the Oprah interview at the time. He was surprised that people had been so critical of his interview. He claimed that while the interview was never going to be easy, he was happy with his performance and was 'high fiving' Oprah after the show. He said it was impossible to please fans anyways. This kind of attitude is what got him into trouble with fans in 2013. No one felt he was being sincere with his apologies. Why was this?

First of all, it is clear throughout the interview from Lance's body language that he is a competitive person. After he gets through Oprah's simple yes/no questions that ask him to tell the truth about his lies, he begins to claim that his doping scheme was not as widespread or complicated as East Germany's schemes in the 1980s. Oprah warns him that fans will not be happy with an 'everyone was doing it' line of argument, but this is exactly what he does. He talks about a culture of doping and a generation of cyclists who were doing the same as he was doing. He defines 'cheating' as a means which gives someone an unfair advantage. In the context of the Tour de France, where everyone was doing it, he does not feel that 'cheating' is the most appropriate word. Furthermore, he is almost boastful about the fact that he passed each drug test, as a sign that he was smarter than the system. He sits with a wide crossed leg, which makes him look quite powerful as he says these things. His body language throughout the interview shows power and not regret, as if he is still in a battle to win. In fact he smirks between questions, almost to suggest that he is proud that he got away with it for so long.

Secondly, he uses fillers throughout the interview which make his confession much worse. Fillers are sounds like 'uhm' or 'like' which allow him to think aloud. Every time he is given an opportunity to express regret, he is reluctant to do so. Instead he takes more time than necessary to say words like 'sorry'. His answers are always hedged, saying things like 'that depends . . .'. Some things are black and white, like telling the truth and lying, and he almost seems to be making up lies on the show because he seems to be making everything up as he goes. When asked if he regretted suing Emma O'Reilly, who made public accusations against him, his first response

LEARNER PROFILE

Knowledgeable

An IB learner is *knowledgeable*. Compare the level of knowledge that is exemplified in Sample HL essay 1 compared to Sample HL essay 2. What does knowledge look like?

Sample HL essay 1 is clearly researched, and the student knows more about how the text has been received by readers.

Many of the interpretations in Sample HL essay 2, however, seem to come from the student's own responses, which are not always supported with evidence.

Read Criterion A carefully. How will you demonstrate knowledge and understanding in your HL essay?

is 'uh, well, honestly, I sued so many people so yeah I can't say sorry to everyone'. These answers are unconvincing to say the least. The fillers are particularly worrisome.

It is also clear from the interview that the interview was scripted to some extent, though he goes off script regularly. Oprah asks about how fame is like a magnifying glass, blowing up both his good and bad qualities, such as being a 'humanitarian' or a 'jerk'. He says that Oprah took the words out of his mouth, which cannot be true. Oprah seems to set him up for emotional moments, in which he should be able to show regret or remorse, but his choice of words is very curious. He continuously refers to his 'flaws' or imperfections, which make his mistakes seem minor. He adds that everyone is 'flawed', which seems to rationalise his choices. He claims that his 'ruthless desire to win' made him lie. He constantly blames other factors for his lying, dodging responsibility. For example, when asked if he was a 'bully', he says a clear 'yes', as Oprah had told him to say before, but then he adds that suffering from cancer made him a fierce competitor, which in turn made him into a 'bully'. Oprah, fortunately, shoots down this line of logic, and states that he had been accused of bullying people and taking EPO before his battle with testicular cancer. This is why his use of diction is very suspicious throughout the interview.

Finally, Lance Armstrong uses verbs in a curious way throughout the interview. When he speaks in the first person there are examples of 'meta-talk' in which he tells himself why he is doing what he is doing: 'I am here to say I'm sorry' or 'we promised "no holds barred" in this interview and that's what I'm doing'. He also speaks about himself in the third person on several occasions, which is rather strange and devious because it distances himself from his crimes. When he is asked to comment on other people, he declares that he does not want to use names. So he begins by saying 'There are people in this story and there are good people and bad people', which is an atrocious way to answer a question about his relations with Doctor Ferrari, the notorious 'doping doctor'. He also speaks about the scandals surrounding him as a thing or separate entity that he did not create. He claims 'I didn't know it was going to be this big', referring to the scandal that he created by lying about EPO. Oprah is visibly shocked when he goes off script on such moments and asks him to repeat what he has said and explain why he has used such language, warning him about how viewers will respond. He often does the things he tells himself not to do. For example he says: 'I'm not going to split hairs here', but then he goes on to elaborate how one form of cheating is different from another, which is different from another.

In the end, the interview does more harm to Lance Armstrong than good. After hearing him speak for an hour, it becomes clear to the audience that he has psychological problems, such as megalomania or sociopathy. He does not belong on a show like this making confessions to the whole world, which he will later come to regret. It sounds like he regrets getting caught more than he regrets using drugs. He is very cynical about the cycling sport and shows his hate toward the agencies that penalised him. His use of body language, fillers, diction and verb tense all show a complete lack of remorse about his active role in misleading cyclist fans around the world. He should not be allowed to ride in any bike races after this.

7.8 If you were to mark this Sample HL essay 2, using the assessment criteria, what mark would you award it? Mark the essay as if you were the examiner, applying the four criteria for the HL essay.

Work in small groups and try to agree on the marks your group will award this script. Record each group's marks into a table like this one, leaving a column available for the examiner's marks (do not look ahead).

	Group 1	Group 2	Group 3	Examiner
Criterion A				
Criterion B				
Criterion C				
Criterion D				

7.9 Here are the examiner's marks and comments for Sample HL essay 2, the HL essay on Lance Armstrong. Compare these marks to the ones that you and your class gave in Activity 7.8. Were your marks similar or different? Do the comments echo some of the ideas from your annotations of the essay in Activity 7.7?

HL Essay – Sample 2 – Examiner's marks and comments

Criterion A: Understanding and interpretation: 3 out of 5 marks

The student's response to the Lance Armstrong interview demonstrates an understanding of it. Some of the student's sentences, however, suggest he has not researched the wider context of the interview, such as '[Armstrong] should not be allowed to ride in any bike races after this', which shows a level of ignorance. The essay shows a satisfactory interpretation of the implications of the interview, focusing on how fans are rightfully critical of Mr Armstrong's performance. References to the text are generally relevant and mostly support the candidate's ideas. Some claims, such as the claim that the interview was 'scripted', need to be supported with evidence from both the primary source and secondary sources.

Criterion B: Analysis and evaluation: 3 out of 5 marks

The response demonstrates a generally appropriate analysis of Lance Armstrong's use of language, such as fillers and body language. Some paragraphs, particularly the one on diction and verb tenses, do not directly connect the effects of Armstrong's speech to his words and behaviour. There are occasional insights into how and why Armstrong was criticised after the interview, but these are not always clear and focused. The essay seems short and could have identified more textual features and their effects on the audience.

Criterion C: Focus and organisation: 2 out of 5 marks

Some organisation is apparent, though there is little focus. It is not clear what the purpose is of the second paragraph, and it possibly could have been integrated into the introduction. Although the text has a very good line of inquiry and **thesis statement** to answer it, the essay is not always coherent. For example the paragraph on diction does not mention the word diction until the final sentence of the paragraph. The system of quoting is not clear or accurate, as the quotations should have been accompanied with the corresponding time in the interview. A bibliography with the URL of the primary source would have been appropriate. The final body paragraph ends with an illustration and not a summative point, which is not good essay-writing practice. The conclusion introduces a new idea, namely Armstrong's disdain for the Anti-Doping Agency (ADA) – though this is not articulated clearly – and this too is poor essay-writing practice.

Criterion D: Language: 2 out of 5 marks

The candidate's language is sometimes clear and carefully chosen. There are words such as 'totally' and 'millions' which are inappropriate and inaccurate. The question 'Why was this?' at the end of the second paragraph is not the appropriate register. For the most part grammar is accurate, although errors and inconsistencies are apparent.

7.10 These examples of examiner's comments and marks will help you to understand what examiners are looking for in an HL essay. Return to Unit 1.12 on poetry which includes an example of a student's essay on a Seamus Heaney poem, 'Blackberry-Picking'.

a What does this essay have in common with the 'good' example essay (Sample HL essay 1) from this chapter? What do they do differently? Would they both score well in their own ways?

b Try assessing the essay from Unit 1.12 on the Seamus Heaney poem using the assessment criteria for the HL essay, which can be found in the introduction to this book.

TIP

Do you need to have secondary sources? The short answer is 'no'. Sample HL essay 1 uses secondary sources to argue its interpretation of *Persepolis* effectively. Sample HL essay 2, however, could have used a few secondary sources to back up its claims. In Sample HL essay 2, many in-text references are made to sources that have no **citations**. There is no **bibliography** or works-cited section to support the claims that are made. The essay in Unit 1.12 on 'Blackberry-Picking' does very well without any secondary sources. So the long answer is 'it depends on the nature of your work'.

Over to you

7.11 Before you write your essay, you need to have the language to do this. It helps to create **semantic fields** for yourself. These are clusters of words that revolve around a common topic or topics. Sample HL essay 1 uses an appropriate range of vocabulary and **synonyms**, which prevents the essay from sounding repetitive. The mind map shows you how the student prepared their vocabulary before writing their essay on *Persepolis*.

Create a similar mind map based on the text that you are writing about. Return to your line of inquiry from Activity 7.3 and think about the kind of vocabulary that you will need to write your essay.

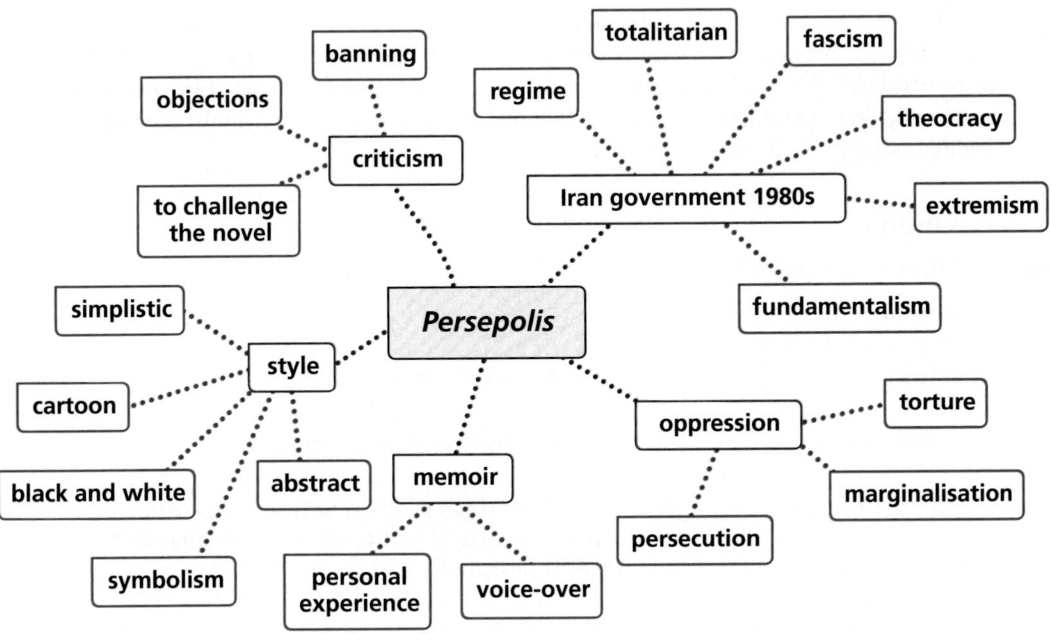

7.12 After thinking about the vocabulary that you will use to analyse and explore your text, return to your line of inquiry from Activity 7.3 and your preliminary research from Activity 7.4. What is going to be the thesis statement of your essay? A thesis statement for an HL essay will come at the end of your introduction and should:

- answer your line of inquiry
- mention the stylistic features that will be explored
- articulate the author's purpose and the reader's response.

Here are several examples to help you write your own thesis statement. Notice how the statements mirror the lines of inquiry, answering them and using some of the same vocabulary. Write your own thesis statement that answers your own line of inquiry.

Line of inquiry	Thesis statement
Through which linguistic devices and for what reasons does Nelson Mandela explore the theme of identity in his inaugural speech?	Through the use of metaphor, imagery and allusion, Nelson Mandela explores the notion of the 'rainbow state' as the new identity of South Africa in his inaugural address.
How does the representation of reckless youth in Diesel's 'Stupid' campaign serve the purpose of selling fashion apparel?	By depicting reckless behaviour, using double entendre and questioning the status quo, Diesel's 'Stupid' campaign aims to build brand loyalty and engage in participatory marketing.
In what ways and for what reasons does Carol Ann Duffy explore perspective in her collection of poetry *The World's Wife*?	Carol Ann Duffy uses perspective, allusion and plot twist in *The World's Wife* in order to make readers think differently about the position of women in the world.

TOK

You have learnt several essay-writing techniques in this and the previous chapters, which may also be helpful when writing your TOK essay. Exploring prescribed titles can be like exploring a line of inquiry. For these, you will also need:

- a thesis statement to answer your title
- mind maps to brainstorm ideas about relevant topics
- evidence from 'real-world situations' to support any points that you make.

Making an outline, as is done in Activity 7.13, is also a good idea. You may want to discuss your TOK essay with your teacher in order to develop your essay-writing skills further.

7.13 Now that you have a line of inquiry, some research, text-specific vocabulary and a thesis statement, you are ready to write an outline for your essay. Here is the outline which was used to prepare Sample HL essay 1 on *Persepolis*. It relies on the PEEL method (Point, Evidence, Evaluation, Link) which was introduced in Chapter 5. You may find it helpful to use a similar method for outlining your own HL essay.

Outline

HL essay on *Persepolis*.

Introduction

Hook	Show how *Persepolis* has received criticism.
Relevance	Ask why it has received criticism.
Line of inquiry	'To what extent does Marjan Satrapi's *Persepolis* promote intercultural understanding or divide cultures and people?'
Thesis statement	Through an analysis of the author's artistic style, narrative technique and use of symbolism, readers can see why the graphic novel promotes more intercultural understanding than divisiveness.

1st body paragraph

Point/topic sentence	*Persepolis* is perceived as anti-Muslim, because of its use of the veil as a symbol.
Evidence	Show the silly behaviour of children with the veil (page 3).
Evaluation	Show how the veil is not used as criticism of Islam, but a criticism of the fascist regime in Iran.
Link back to the inquiry	Explain how Satrapi's intention – to show how oppressive regimes hijack religious symbols – aims to give others insight into the history of Iran.

2nd body paragraph

Point/topic sentence	*Persepolis* has been banned because it's pro-Islam and anti-American.
Evidence	Provide a quote from an American critic and a quote from Satrapi on why she wrote it. Show Marjane's mother fainting (page 153).
Evaluation	Explain that the plot is about escaping persecution, which should appeal to Americans.
Link back to the inquiry	Make a connection to the thesis, so that the story builds understanding across cultures.

3rd body paragraph

Point/topic sentence	*Persepolis* is criticised for being too graphic and violent.
Evidence	Show how the dismembered body, in typical black/white style, is not graphic at all. It's rather clinical.
Evaluation	Explain how this style of drawing makes complicated issues accessible for a wider, younger audience.
Link back to the inquiry	The drawing style helps promote a kind of reckoning with the past.

4th body paragraph

Point/topic sentence	*Persepolis* is banned in Iran for inciting revolutionary ideas.
Evidence	Show Marjane's rebellious behaviour.
Evaluation	Explain how the voice-over is like a memoir, not a manual for overthrowing the regime.
Link back to the inquiry	Return to the idea of intercultural understanding. It's just her personal story.

Conclusion

To conclude	Criticisms are out of place.
Reiterate the evidence	Return to the veil as a symbol, the importance of the voice-over and the effect of the plot line on the reader.
Author's aims	Satrapi aims to give insight into the history of Iran and build bridges across cultures.

7.14 Are you ready to write your own essay on your own topic and text? Have you already discussed your idea with your teacher? Follow these steps:

a Return to your line of inquiry, your thesis statement and your outline. Does everything seem to be in place?

b Start drafting each paragraph, one at a time, using the PEEL method or another method that works for you. You may want to write the introduction and the conclusion after you have written your body paragraphs.

c Write a complete draft and ask your teacher for holistic written or oral feedback, based on the criteria for the HL essay. Again, your teacher may not annotate or edit your work.

d Take your teacher's feedback into consideration, as you rewrite your essay.

e Throughout your course, write several essays. Keep these on file. Before the final submission of your final essay, reread all of them and decide which one is the best. You may wish to edit an older essay, before submitting it to the IB, as long as your teacher has only given feedback on one version.

7.15 Sample HL essay 2 on Lance Armstrong had a lot of potential. If you were to write an outline of this essay, you would see that it lacked coherence and is not well organised. Can you do a better job?

a Do an online search for Lance Armstrong's confessional interview with Oprah Winfrey in 2013.

b After watching this interview, discuss the thesis statement of Sample HL essay 2 and its main arguments. Do you agree or disagree with the student's arguments?

c If you are not happy with the student's line of inquiry, think of a better one. Discuss your line of inquiry with your teacher.

d Do some research which will help you answer your line of inquiry. Try to find secondary sources from other critics who have made interpretations of his interview. Keep track of these secondary sources in an annotated bibliography. This is a system of keeping track of sources, where you write notes beside each source that you have studied about its value to your essay. You do not have to submit this annotated bibliography with your essay.

e Create a mind map and write a clear and well-structured outline for an improved essay on the Lance Armstrong interview. Discuss your outline with a classmate or your teacher.

f Write your own essay on the Lance Armstrong interview with Oprah Winfrey. Be sure to answer your line of inquiry.

g Compare your essay to the essays of your classmates. How unique are your arguments? What other points have your classmates addressed?

h Mark a classmate's essay, using the assessment criteria for the HL essay.

i Add this trial HL essay to your learner portfolio. Return to it before you write your actual essay.

Extended essay

You must not write your extended essay about the same literary work that you have analysed in your HL essay. This is called 'double dipping' (that is a real IB term) and it is not allowed!

You may, however, write your extended essay about a different literary work by the same author that you have studied in class.

TIP

Activity 7.15 invites you to write an essay on a topic and text that your entire class is exploring. This is a useful exercise, where you can compare your work to that of your classmates. But this approach may not allow you to express your own ideas. For this reason, you may not want to submit this essay to the IB. Alternatively, you may want to work on other well-known confessional speeches, for example:

- Tiger Woods
- Bill Clinton
- Richard Nixon.

You could compare and contrast two speeches to ensure originality. In brief, you should create situations where you can discuss your topic and texts with others without plagiarising their work or both working on a single essay. Academic honesty is about your own integrity.

REFLECT

In Chapters 5–7 you have learnt about the three forms of written assessment for your external exam: Paper 1, Paper 2 and the HL essay. Consider these questions:

- In what ways are these forms of assessment similar or different?
- How different or similar are the assessment criteria for these forms of assessment?
- Which skills do you need to develop to be successful in all three forms of assessment?
- How will you develop these skills?

Individual oral (SL/HL)

How do you develop your understanding of 'global issues' through the learner portfolio?
What kinds of text must you find to explore a global issue in your individual oral?
What is expected of you during this form of internal assessment?
How can you come to the oral prepared, with an effective outline and two appropriate texts?
How will you be marked?

In this unit you will:

- learn about the requirements for preparing and conducting the individual oral in your school with your teacher
- read a sample individual oral and assess it according to the assessment criteria
- develop your own individual oral and the outline that you will use for it.

Learning objectives

- understand the expectations for the individual oral at higher and standard level, by studying and marking a sample oral
- develop your own speaking skills by engaging in activities that help you prepare your own individual oral.

Word bank

global issue
curate
thesis statement
antithesis
diction
volta
sonnet
alliteration
subsequent questions

For your English A: Language and Literature internal assessment at higher and standard level, you will conduct an individual oral. In this assessment you will speak for at least 10 minutes and then converse for up to 5 minutes with your teacher about *two* texts and a global issue from your learner portfolio. Your individual oral should address this prompt:

Examine the ways in which the global issue of your choice is presented through the content and form of one of the literary works and one of the non-literary texts you have studied.

Global issue

Global issues are significant, transnational and relevant to everyday contexts.

For each global issue in your learner portfolio, you can **curate** texts, conduct research, document relevant activities and make notes. The topics in the units of Chapters 2–4 are examples of global issues. Before the individual oral, you can talk to your teacher about the global issue that you intend to prepare. Everyone in your class can do an individual oral on a different global issue.

AOE question

How do texts engage with local and global issues?

This question, from the area of exploration 'time and space' in this course, is arguably the main question for the individual oral. Does this mean that your presentation should be full of background contextual information on the texts? Look carefully at the assessment criteria for the individual oral. Your individual oral is an exercise in textual analysis. Your knowledge, understanding and interpretation of the texts are being assessed, *not* their contexts.

Extract from a literary work

To prepare your individual oral on your global issue of choice, you will be required to find an extract up to 40 lines long from *one* of the literary works that you have read in class. This may be:

- a passage from a novel, play or short story
- a poem or an extract from a poem
- song lyrics or an extract from song lyrics
- a passage from prose, non-fiction.

You do not have to include two shorter poems to meet the 40-line requirement. Short poems can be very dense, meaningful and ideal for the individual oral.

Remember that once you select an extract from a particular literary work for your individual oral, you may no longer use this work for your Paper 2 or HL essay. Be sure to bring a clean copy of this extract to the individual oral.

For the sake of simplicity, the word 'text' will be used in this unit to discuss the extract being analysed from the literary work.

Non-literary text

You will also need to bring a clean copy of a non-literary text that is up to 40 lines long or a visual text that fits onto one page. This text should be taken from a 'body of work' and have a 'sense of authorship'. For example, a photograph should be taken from a series of photographs by the same photographer, or an advertisement should be taken from an advertising campaign. You may discuss your choice of text with your teacher before the exam. You need to inform your teacher about your choice of texts (both literary and non-literary) at least a week before the exam.

> **TIP**
> Select your literary work first. Then define your global issue. Then find a non-literary text that goes well with this issue. This procedure is the easiest because you only have six works to choose from at HL and four at SL. The number and nature of literary works will determine which global issues you can explore.

Outline

You must also prepare and bring to the exam an outline which consists of ten bullet-pointed notes on one page. You should not use these points as a script, and you should avoid giving a rehearsed response. They should serve as prompts or signposts to help you structure your analysis.

Conducting the IO

You should come to the individual oral exam with a clean, non-annotated copy of the texts (or extracts) and your outline. Your teacher will record your individual oral.

You will begin by giving a 10-minute analysis of the texts. You should analyse your texts as a means of exploring the global issue that you have selected. Be sure to give both texts equal attention meaning that you need to explore each text for 5 minutes. In this time, be sure to comment on the 'sense of authorship' of each text and the 'body of work' from which it was taken.

After 10 minutes, your teacher will have a 5-minute discussion with you about your global issue and the texts.

Assessing the IO

Your teacher will give you marks, applying the assessment criteria for the individual oral (you can find these in the introduction to this book), which are the same for standard and higher level students. The audio recording of the individual oral may be sent to the IB for moderation, meaning that an IB moderator may listen to your recording and adjust your teacher's marks accordingly.

At standard level your individual oral counts for 30% of your final grade. At higher level your individual oral counts for 20% of your final grade.

> **TIP**
> It is a good idea to practise by doing 'mock' individual orals. Try doing these under exam conditions. The literary extract and non-literary texts you use for your practice orals should be different from those you will use in your actual exam. You cannot pick which oral counts for your final grade. Your real oral exam is the one that counts.

Getting started

8.1 Look at this list of global issues. What do they have in common? What are the key characteristics of a global issue? Discuss these characteristics as a class:

- fair trade
- immigration
- corruption
- work-related stress
- screen addiction
- parenthood
- censorship
- feminism
- racism
- poverty
- nationalism
- inequality
- class difference
- fundamentalism

TIP

The word 'issue' has two meanings: 'topic' or 'problem'. Topics such as 'coming of age' or 'sportsmanship' do not include a problem, though they may lend themselves to an excellent individual oral. Problems such as 'poverty' or 'censorship' may also lend themselves to a good individual oral. Either way, be sure that your **thesis statement** leads to a 'persuasive interpretation' (Criterion A) of the texts that you are analysing.

8.2 Read Texts 8.1 and 8.2. You can find out more about them through an online search. Using your list of key characteristics for a global issue from Activity 8.1, think about the possible global issues that could be explored through these texts. You do not have to compare the *stylistic* features of the texts. Instead, you should ask yourself what the texts are about.

Text 8.1

Rupert Brooke was already well known as a poet when the First World War broke out in 1914. His poetry encouraged young men to enlist and fight in the war. He died of sepsis in 1915 in Greece, on his way to Gallipoli with the British Mediterranean Expeditionary Force.

The Soldier

Rupert Brooke 1914

If I should die, think only this of me:
That there's some corner of a foreign field
That is for ever England. There shall be
In that rich earth a richer dust concealed;
A dust whom England bore, shaped, made aware,
Gave, once, her flowers to love, her ways to roam,
A body of England's, breathing English air,
Washed by the rivers, blest by suns of home.

And think, this heart, all evil shed away,
A pulse in the eternal mind, no less
Gives somewhere back the thoughts by England given;
Her sights and sounds; dreams happy as her day;
And laughter, learnt of friends; and gentleness,
In hearts at peace, under an English heaven.

Text 8.2

In the Event of Moon Disaster

William Safire 1969

Fate has ordained that the men who went to the moon to explore in peace will stay on the moon to rest in peace.

These brave men, Neil Armstrong and Edwin Aldrin, know that there is no hope for their recovery. But they also know that there is hope for mankind in their sacrifice.

These two men are laying down their lives in mankind's most noble goal: the search for truth and understanding.

They will be mourned by their families and friends; they will be mourned by their nation; they will be mourned by the people of the world; they will be mourned by a Mother Earth that dared send two of her sons into the unknown.

In their exploration, they stirred the people of the world to feel as one; in their sacrifice, they bind more tightly the brotherhood of man.

In ancient days, men looked at stars and saw their heroes in the constellations. In modern times, we do much the same, but our heroes are epic men of flesh and blood.

Others will follow and surely find their way home. Man's search will not be denied. But these men were the first, and they will remain the foremost in our hearts.

For every human being who looks up at the moon in the nights to come will know that there is some corner of another world that is forever mankind.

Text 8.2 is a speech written for US President Nixon to read in case Neil Armstrong and Edwin Aldrin did not return safely from the Apollo 11 mission to the moon in 1969.

8.3 What do Texts 8.1 and 8.2 have in common? What global issue do they explore? Select one global issue that you discussed as a class in Activity 8.1. Imagine that you were going to do your individual oral on these texts. How would you prepare it?

See the diagram for a visual organiser of the individual oral. Then try answering these questions and write your answers on a board for your classmates and teacher to see:

a What is your global issue?

b What will you argue? What will be your thesis statement?

c Which stylistic features or devices from the first text are relevant to your global issue?

d Which stylistic features from the second text are relevant to your global issue?

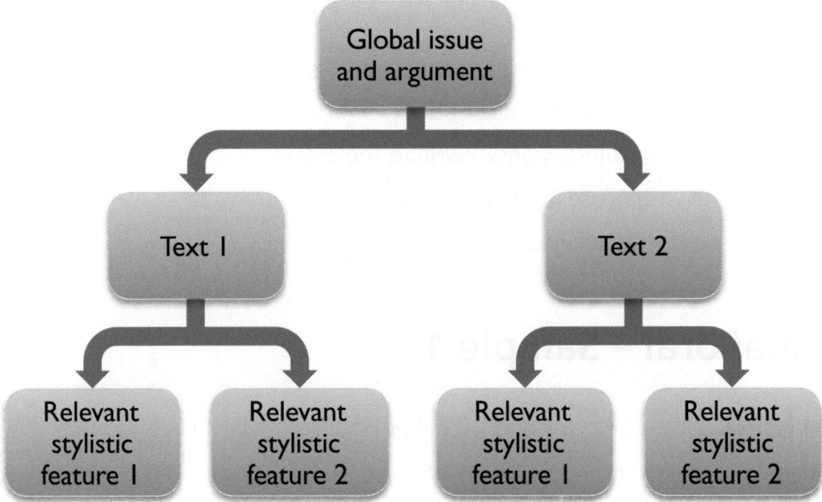

It may help to think of your individual oral as hanging from a central global issue. The stylistic features that you focus on in your oral should act as supporting evidence for your argument on your global issue.

8.4 Before the individual oral, you need to prepare a one-page outline of ten bullet points to take with you into the exam.

a Imagine you were going to give an individual oral on Texts 8.1 and 8.2. What would you put into your outline that you would bring into the exam? Take some time, possibly outside class, to write this outline. Use text-editing software if you prefer. This outline can be rough and it does not have to include complete sentences. It only needs to be useful for you during an oral exam.

b Bring your outline to class and display everyone's outlines together on a large table or wall. Compare everyone's strategies for preparing this individual oral on Texts 8.1 and 8.2.

c As a class, compile a list of note-making strategies. Note that this is a different skill from note-*taking*. Note-*making* may include mind maps, graphic organisers, tables or arrows that help you make sense of the texts in relation to the global issue.

Sample individual oral

8.5 Read this transcript of a student's individual oral exam and the outline that accompanies it. As you read, compile a list of 'things I hadn't expected'. These may be things you hadn't expected about the individual oral exam itself, or the student's comments on the texts. Compare your list with those of your classmates and discuss any similarities or differences.

TIP

Remember MAPS from Chapter 5? Meaning = Audience + Purpose + Style. On a copy of this individual oral, highlight, using four different colours, where you see evidence of these four elements:

- 'meaning' – points that are relevant to the global issue and argument being explored
- 'audience' – how the texts were received
- 'purpose' – the authors' intentions in writing these texts
- 'style' – how the writers use language to a certain end.

Do you notice a pattern in this student's individual oral?

Individual oral – Sample 1

Global issue

Patriotism

Transcript

It is always good to start with the 'why'. But be careful. You only have 10 minutes to analyse two texts. So be concise.

Student: Can I start? OK. I'd like to start my individual oral by introducing my global issue, which is patriotism. And I'd like to talk a little bit about why I chose this issue. I think it started in class, when we were focusing on war. As you know, we read a few novels about war and a collection of poetry from the First World War. Out of all the poetry we read, I really liked the poem 'The Soldier' by Rupert Brooke for a couple of reasons: first of all, I liked his style and structure, which I'll talk about more later. But I think what I liked most about him as a poet and person was his willingness, as a young man – not much older than me – to face death for his country. I have a lot of respect for that, probably because I live in a very peaceful world. And the kind of peace and freedom that I enjoy today is largely due to people like Rupert Brooke, who were willing to die for their country.

More background information than this is not necessary.

Signposts like these help give the individual oral a sense of organisation.

My global issue is patriotism. And besides talking about 'The Soldier', I'm going to talk about a speech called 'In the Event of Moon Disaster', which was written by William Safire in 1969. William, or Bill, Safire was Richard Nixon's speechwriter. In 1969 he had to write a speech for the President, which would have been read if the astronauts, Edwin Aldrin and Neil Armstrong, had died on their mission to the moon. Of course, as we all know, the astronauts returned home safely and this speech was never read on TV. Nevertheless, it's an interesting text and it ties in to my global issue of patriotism. As I'll explain, it shows how these men were willing to die for a greater cause.

An individual oral can have a thesis statement too.

So, my thesis statement and argument for my individual oral will be that people need patriots and heroes who are willing to die for their country and the greater good of humanity. And both Bill Safire and Rupert Brooke know how to remind readers of this importance for human sacrifice. They achieve it through their use of language, including the use of **antithesis** and **diction**.

I'll start by analysing Brooke's poem 'The Soldier', which was published in 1914, when the Great War broke out. The poem's purpose is to encourage young men to go and fight in the war. And it makes a lot of use of antithesis, which is the act of contrasting one idea with another. Actually, the whole poem contrasts life and death. The first part is about death, which is seen immediately in the famous first line: 'If I should die, think only this of me'. And the second part, after the **volta** in line 9, is all about life. It includes words like 'heart', 'pulse' and 'laughter' for example. I think Brooke juxtaposes death and life, in that order, to show how the soldier continues to live on – even after he's dead – in the hearts and minds of the English people. In line 11, for example, he says that after he's dead he 'Gives somewhere back the thoughts by England given'. So, by contrasting 'gives' with 'given' it's his way of saying that his death is like paying gratitude to England for his happy youth.

If you are going to refer to a stylistic feature, define it as well.

This is more an example of juxtaposition than antithesis.

This, on the other hand, is actually an example of antithesis.

A similar use of antithesis is found in line 4, where he uses the words 'rich' and 'richer'. When speaking about his dead body in its grave, he says 'In that rich earth a richer dust concealed'. He's using antithesis here again to reassure readers that his death is not in vain. His body is 'richer' because, as he explains in lines 5 to 8, his body was shaped by England. And England gave him 'flowers to love' and 'ways to roam'. In fact he says quite literally that his body belongs to England in line 7, when he says he is 'A body of England's'. All of this explains what he means earlier in the poem when he says, quite poetically: 'If I should die, think only this of me: / That there's some corner of a foreign field / That is for ever England.' I can imagine how those words were received by young men all around England in 1914. And this is how the poem encouraged them to go and fight in the Great War. It was like he was telling them that they would be remembered as heroes for dying abroad.

While words such as 'like' may sound colloquial, it is also important for you to express your ideas fluently. This example of 'like' is actually appropriate for this context. Practise speaking in a formal register more often in preparation for your exam.

Besides using antithesis, the poem also uses diction to incite patriotism and heroism. Diction, I should define, is the poet's choice of words and Brooke has chosen his words very carefully in this **sonnet**. For example, rather than using the word 'grave' he refers to a 'corner of a foreign field' in line 2. And this is a curious choice of words, because you would think of a hero's grave as a big tomb or monument and not a small, insignificant 'corner'. This kind of humble modesty is seen again in line 5, when he refers to his body as 'dust'. This word relates to the natural world and it sounds really pure. There are more words like it in the first stanza, such as 'earth', 'flowers', 'air', 'rivers' and 'suns'. All these references to nature are contrasted with the abstract nouns in the second stanza, such as 'thoughts', 'dreams', 'gentleness', 'peace' and 'heaven'. This transition from concrete things in the natural word to abstract ideas is really important for the meaning of the poem. I think it's Brooke's way of telling soldiers that they'll be remembered long after they're dead. It's like saying that their seemingly insignificant bodies, which are buried in that dirt far away from home, are actually significant. They are, in a way, the price that England has to pay for 'hearts at peace, under an English heaven'.

Even though this student has elected not to focus on the sonnet structure of the poem in this individual oral, it is good to include the literary term.

So, to finish my analysis of 'The Soldier', I'd like to say that Rupert Brooke uses antithesis and diction quite effectively to incite patriotism among his readers. It's also probably why so many English people know this poem and hear it on Armistice Day.

To move on to the Bill Safire speech: I'm going to explore its use of antithesis and diction as well. And I'm going to show how he uses these things to make

TIP

Notice that the student clearly states their thesis statement and argument at the end of their introduction. This will help them on Criterion A when they are asked to draw conclusions from the texts in relation to the global issue. For this reason it is important to integrate the global issue into your thesis statement. Notice how the word 'patriot' appears in this student's thesis statement. This is good practice.

It helps your analysis to work with interesting texts. This speech is very well chosen because it is rich in meaning.

This is a good way of integrating quotations into a claim or argument.

not only Americans but also all the people of the world feel proud of these two astronauts: Buzz Aldrin and Neil Armstrong. It's an interesting speech because it was never actually read out loud. As I'll show in my analysis of this speech, Safire's goal was to show how their deaths – if they had died – would not have been in vain. In fact he wanted to show how their sacrifice would have been meaningful for the advancement of the whole world, and the 'brotherhood of man', and not just for one country.

It's good to have a few examples of one single point of analysis.

Like I said before, antithesis is a way of contrasting ideas, and Safire's speech is full of it. Almost every line of his speech uses parallel structures to contrast ideas, often using similar words. And he uses antithesis to advance his idea that the death of the astronauts should make the world feel more united. The opening line is a good case in point. It reads: 'Fate has ordained that the men who went to the moon to explore in peace will stay on the moon to rest in peace.' Besides contrasting their exploration with their deaths, his emphasis is clearly on 'peace' here. So I think Safire repeats this word to suggest that peace was actually the purpose of their mission and that their deaths will help bring peace to the world.

TIP

You may be surprised that the student does not talk about other literary features such as iambic pentameter, rhyming scheme, enjambment or **alliteration**, all of which are relevant to this poem. They decided to focus on just diction and antithesis. With a little less than 5 minutes to talk about each text, you have to select your key points carefully. This student has chosen wisely.

This interpretation is supported by another use of antithesis in lines 11 and 12: 'In their exploration, they stirred the people of the world to feel as one; in their sacrifice, they bind more tightly the brotherhood of man.' I think that's a very important line in the speech because it shows how the death of these astronauts brings people together in hope, wonder and sorrow. The idea that Buzz Aldrin and Neil Armstrong belong to everyone, not just America, is developed a few lines before this in lines 8–10, where antithesis is used again: 'They will be mourned by their families and friends; they will be mourned by their nation; they will be mourned by the people of the world; they will be mourned by a Mother Earth that dared send two of her sons into the unknown.' So by contrasting 'family' and 'nation' with 'the people of the world' and 'Mother Earth', Safire broadens the purpose of the speech. And he implies that the astronauts died for everyone's sake.

It is not necessary to quote more source text than this.

Looking at the time, I should probably say just a few words about the diction and then conclude. First of all, the word that is most prevalent throughout the whole speech is 'man' or 'mankind', and it also serves the purpose of unifying readers and listeners. It appears in line 4, when he says that the astronauts 'know that there is hope for mankind in their sacrifice'. It also appears in line 16, 'Man's search will not be denied', suggesting that people will go on to explore space even after Aldrin and Armstrong are dead. And it appears in the final line, which is an allusion to the poem I analysed earlier: 'For every human being who looks up at the moon in the nights to come will know that there is some corner of another world that is forever mankind.' Besides the loneliness of space that's expressed in the phrase 'corner of another world', the phrase that stands out most here is 'forever mankind'. Many listeners who know Brooke's poem would hear that the word 'mankind' has replaced the word 'England'. And this

The student has identified a structure which the texts have in common. While the individual oral is not a comparative analysis, it is advisable to make connections between texts and the global issue.

TIP

Do you have to explore the same stylistic devices for each text? This student explores the use of diction and antithesis in both texts, but you do not have to follow this strategy. Remember that Criterion B asks you to use your knowledge and understanding of each of the texts to analyse and evaluate the ways in which authors' choices present the global issue.

replacement is pretty significant, I think. It implies that we've moved away from a time of fighting wars for the glory of a nation, and it implies that we've started exploring space as a united world for peace instead.

This leads me to the conclusion of my talk. I'd like to argue that both texts are all about bringing people together. I've analysed how they both use diction and antithesis to achieve this purpose. And I've shown how they both explore the global issue of patriotism and dying for one's country or dying for a greater cause. I think people need heroes, not just as role models or for spiritual guidance. But I think that it takes the sacrifice of a hero to remind people what they have in common and what values are worth fighting for.

Teacher: OK, thanks for that. I found it particularly interesting that the two texts shared a line. Or that one text, as it were, stole a line from the other.

Student: Yeah, that's why I selected the speech in the first place, actually.

Teacher: I want to return to a few things that you said earlier.

Student: Sure.

Teacher: You said that you chose the poem and the speech in order to comment on the issue of patriotism. But I sensed that during your presentation of the speech, you talked more about dying for 'mankind' or world peace than dying for a country or nation. Do you think that the speech is patriotic?

Student: Yes, I do. I think that it is very patriotic, actually. I looked up the definition of patriotism before researching this oral presentation and I noticed that it has a pretty broad definition. It's not to be confused with nationalism. Patriotism is all about unifying people, usually of one homeland but it doesn't have to be. It's about getting people to rally around one purpose or one cause or shared system of values. So I thought the speech was pretty appropriate for my issue.

Teacher: OK, that makes sense.

Student: And there's another thing. And I didn't really have much time to talk about the context of the speech, but keep in mind that the American President would have read it on TV in 1969 during the Cold War. And there was a real 'Space Race' between the Americans and the Soviets. So it would have been seen as a real loss for America in this race if the astronauts had died. But Bill Safire's speech would have made it seem like a loss for humanity instead.

Teacher: Right, that is a good point. I hadn't thought of that. Context is important to these texts. Do you want to talk about the context of the texts any more? Is there any other way that context adds meaning to them?

Student: Well, not really. But I suppose it's worth noting that Rupert Brooke was already a pretty famous poet in his time. And so his poem 'The Soldier' was the last of five poems that were widely read, and he was pretty influential in convincing young men that war was a noble cause.

Teacher: You said earlier that the poem made you appreciate the peaceful world you live in even more. Can you see, in this poem, where you gain that appreciation?

Student: Well, I suppose it's just on reflecting on the poem that I came to that appreciation. But if I were to put my finger on a single place in the poem, I'd say the second stanza is really about peace. It's about a soldier who has died or is dying and the thoughts and memories that that soldier would have of England, possibly from before the war. I'll read out the last three lines, which is about that: 'Her sights and sounds; dreams happy as her day; / And laughter, learnt

Start the conclusion with the global issue.

The purpose of your teacher's subsequent questions is to help you elaborate on any ideas that you mentioned and give you an opportunity to include ideas that you missed.

TIP

The student uses some *meta-language*, meaning they talk about what they are going to talk about. The student says: 'Looking at the time, I should probably say just a few words about the diction and then conclude.' Although this may sound strange, it acts as a signpost for the teacher and makes the presentation coherent.

The student takes the lead here, which is rewarding. He raises a very good point about the meaning of the text in context.

TIP

During the 5-minute discussion with your teacher, they will ask you '**subsequent questions**'. These should be open-ended and full of possibilities, giving you opportunity to expand on what you have already mentioned. Use this moment to squeeze in what you did not have time to mention before.

of friends; and gentleness, / In hearts at peace, under an English heaven.' It's very tranquil and peaceful, possibly because of all the alliteration in 'sight' with 'sound', 'dream' with 'day' and 'hearts' with 'heaven'.

Teacher: Yes it is rather melodious, I suppose.

Student: And maybe that's why it makes me appreciate peace. It sounds peaceful.

Teacher: Aha, I can see you took a course in language and literature. Is there anything else you'd like to add, before we finish?

Student: No, not really. I just want to say that I really enjoyed working with these two texts. I almost wanted to compare and contrast them because they are so similar yet different. I like how the one clearly inspired the other. And I can just imagine Bill Safire reading 'The Soldier' in the White House with Nixon worrying about Armstrong and Aldrin in the background. But that's it. I'm happy I could connect the text to the global issue, patriotism.

Teacher: Yes, well done on that. We'll call it good then, OK? All right.

LEARNER PROFILE

Communicator

An IB learner is a *communicator*. What does that mean for you, in your individual oral? In the 5-minute discussion between you and your teacher, make sure you offer complete answers to your teacher's questions. If you receive a 'yes' or 'no' question, do not simply reply with a 'yes' or 'no' or short answer, but elaborate on what you know and show how this knowledge is relevant to the global issue. Do not be afraid to show initiative during the discussion.

Individual oral – Sample 1 – Outline

The IB suggests ten bullet-pointed notes for the outline. This outline has seven main points, which is a different but acceptable format. Just ensure that your outline is legible and useful for you. Use one side of the paper only. The points are prompts and should not lead to a rehearsed response.

Introduction

Global issue: Patriotism. Why I picked 'The Soldier': I like WWI poetry and Rupert Brooke. He died for peace and freedom. Why I picked 'In the Event of Moon Disaster': it's interesting because of its context.

Thesis statement: Humanity needs heroes who are willing to die for their country and a greater cause. Safire and Brooke remind readers of the importance of sacrifice in their texts through their use of antithesis and diction.

'The Soldier'

Antithesis & patriotism.

It's good to include the IO's main illustrations in the outline.

Example 1: Compare death 'If I should die, think only this of me' (stanza 1) to life 'heart', 'pulse' and 'laughter' (stanza 2) → The soldier lives on even after death in the hearts and minds of the English people.

Example 2: 'gives somewhere back the thoughts by England given' (11) → he pays gratitude to England with his life.

Example 3: 'In that rich earth a richer dust concealed' (4) → shows how he was shaped by England.

Link back to patriotism. How does this motivate young men to go to war?

Diction & patriotism.

Example 1: 'corner of a foreign field' (2) and 'dust' (5) → humble modesty.

Example 2: Compare 'earth', 'flowers', 'air', 'rivers' and 'suns' (stanza 1) to 'thoughts', 'dreams', 'gentleness', 'peace' and 'heaven' (stanza 2) → shift from concrete, tangible nature to abstract, intangible ideas means the soldier will be remembered.

In the Event of Moon Disaster

This is good use of headings.

Antithesis & patriotism for all the people of the world.

Example 1: 'Fate has ordained that the men who went to the moon to explore in peace will stay on the moon to rest in peace' (1–2) → explore/die and the purpose = peace on earth.

Example 2: 'In their exploration, they stirred the people of the world to feel as one; in their sacrifice, they bind more tightly the brotherhood of man' (11–12) → their death brings people together.

Example 3: 'They will be mourned by their families and friends; they will be mourned by their nation; they will be mourned by the people of the world; they will be mourned by a Mother Earth that dared send two of her sons into the unknown' (8–10) → astronauts die for everyone's sake.

Diction & patriotism for all the people of the world.

Example 1: 'Man' and 'mankind' (16, 4) → unifying listeners.

Example 2: 'For every human being who looks up at the moon in the nights to come will know that there is some corner of another world that is forever mankind' → allusion to Brooke, world unity is more important that one nation or war between nations.

Conclusion

Authors use diction and antithesis to unite people (patriotism). People need heroes. Heroes die for their cause.

8.6 Activity 8.4 asked you to prepare an outline on Texts 8.1 and 8.2 as if you were going to give an individual oral on these texts. Compare the student's outline to your own. Discuss your answer to these questions as a class:

a How was the student's outline different from your own?

b How helpful was this outline to the student who gave this individual oral?

c How can you use text-editing software to make your outline an effective tool for preparing your individual oral?

d What can you do to ensure that your notes do not lead to a scripted or rehearsed individual oral?

8.7 Did the student's individual oral go the way you thought it would go?

a How would you have organised it differently?

b What different issue and ideas would you have explored?

c In what ways would your individual oral have been different?

8.8 On a copy of the student's individual oral, highlight some of the sentence structures, phrases and vocabulary that you might find useful for analysing literary and non-literary texts. In your learner portfolio, make a list of useful phrases and sentences that you could use during your own individual oral on any texts.

TIP

What if your individual oral exam sounds scripted, memorised or rehearsed? This is not a good situation. Your teacher may ask you to do a new individual oral on entirely different texts, which means it's 'back to the drawing board'. Make sure that your notes are like stepping stones that help you go from text to text, from device to device, from example to example, referring back to the global issue frequently and effectively, without sounding rehearsed.

8.9 How well do you know the assessment criteria for the individual oral? Here is a list of skills a–k that the student did well.

For each skill, decide which of the criteria (A, B, C or D) it relates to.

Then check the IO assessment criteria in the introduction of this coursebook and find out if your answers are correct:

a using relevant quotations from the source texts

b including signposts

c commenting on the contexts in which the texts were written and received

d using words like antithesis correctly

e connecting ideas back to the main argument frequently

f offering insightful comments on the effects of the language on the reader

g sounding persuasive

h speaking without sounding repetitive

i offering insight into the author's purpose

j sounding logical

k reading between the lines.

8.10 Now that you have a better understanding of the assessment criteria, go back and read the transcript of the sample individual oral and mark it according to the assessment criteria. In small groups, discuss the marks that you would give it and try to come to an agreement within each group. As a class, take an inventory of every group's marks and discuss where you see any disagreement. Then compare your marks to the examiner's marks. Do you agree or disagree with the marks the examiner has awarded the student?

Individual oral – Sample 1 – Examiner's marks and comments

Criterion A: Knowledge, understanding and interpretation – 8 out of 10

There is good understanding of the texts, though it would have been good to hear more about how 'The Soldier' fits into Rupert Brooke's poetry as a whole. The interpretations of this poem are almost entirely focused on the global issue of patriotism. With regard to the speech, however, the candidate's interpretations are less relevant to the global issue of patriotism. He does well by giving a broad definition of patriotism in the discussion, but the relevance of this text to that issue is still questionable. He refers to both texts frequently to support his claims.

Criterion B: Analysis and evaluation – 8 out of 10

Analysis and evaluation of the texts are relevant and at times insightful. Antithesis and diction are interesting stylistic features to focus on, and they gave the student sufficient opportunity to touch on other features in passing. Although the comparison of the first and second stanza of 'The Soldier' is not an example of antithesis, it gives insight into the author's intention and the connection to the issue of patriotism. Unpacking the phrase 'corner of a foreign field' is very effective to this end as well. Similarly, unpacking the phrase 'distant world that is forever mankind' is done effectively.

Criterion C: Focus and organisation – 9 out of 10

The analysis is both focused and organised. In particular, the candidate returns to the issue of patriotism and self-sacrifice frequently. Simple phrases such as 'for example' and 'in line number . . .' give the presentation a clear sense of direction and purpose. The signposts, such as 'I should define' or 'to move on to the Bill Safire speech', also help the individual oral along. There is evidence of a plan and a method. There is evidence of Point, Evidence, Evaluation, Link (PEEL).

Criterion D: Language – 9 out of 10

The candidate uses language effectively and appropriately. Vocabulary and syntax are varied and free from errors. Some literary terms, such as 'volta' and 'sonnet' were only used in passing, though they were used accurately. Other literary terms, such as 'antithesis', were over-applied. Overall the candidate's register is academic and analytical.

Over to you

8.11 Building on the experience and understanding that you have gained from this unit so far, prepare an individual oral on Texts 8.3 and 8.4, following these steps:

a Decide on an appropriate global issue to which you can connect these texts effectively.

b Carry out some research on this issue and the two texts. Find out more about the contexts in which the texts were written and received.

c Articulate an argument and a thesis statement in a proposal to your teacher. Briefly discuss the appropriateness of your global issue, thesis statement and argument with your teacher.

d Make an outline, and practise doing your oral a few times in front of a mirror before recording yourself doing the individual oral for 10 minutes.

e Share your recording with your teacher and ask them to privately listen to everyone's recording from your class. Ask your teacher to create a list of good and bad practice that they heard in the recordings. This list should be anonymous and shared with everyone in the class.

f As a class, discuss the challenges and opportunities that were created by this activity.

g If possible, your teacher may be able to play a recording of a very good performance on these two texts from a previous student. Discuss this recording.

TIP

While it is helpful to do mock individual orals on works that you have studied in class, it is also a good idea to practise with texts that you have not studied. This gives you the opportunity to transfer the skills and concepts that you have developed in class to new texts. It will also ensure that everyone's actual individual oral exam, on works from the course, remains unique and original.

Text 8.3

Little Red Cap

Carol Ann Duffy 1999

At childhood's end, the houses petered out
into playing fields, the factory allotments
kept, like mistresses, by kneeling married men,
the silent railway line, the hermit's caravan,
till you came at last to the edge of the woods.
It was there that I first clapped eyes on the wolf.

He stood in a clearing, reading his verse out loud
in his wolfy drawl, a paperback in his hairy paw,
red wine staining his bearded jaw. What big ears
he had! What big eyes he had! What teeth!
In the interval, I made quite sure he spotted me,
sweet sixteen, never been, babe, waif, and bought me a drink,

my first. You might ask why. Here's why. Poetry.
The wolf, I knew, would lead me deep into the woods,
away from home, to a dark tangled thorny place
lit by the eyes of owls. I crawled in his wake,
my stockings ripped to shreds, scraps of red from my blazer
snagged on twig and branch, murder clues. I lost both shoes

but got there, wolf's lair, better beware. Lesson one that night,
breath of the wolf in my ear, was the love poem.
I clung till dawn to his thrashing fur, for
what little girl doesn't dearly love a wolf?
Then I slid from between his hairy matted paws
and went in search of a living bird – white dove –
which flew, straight, from my hands to his open mouth.
One bite, dead. How nice, breakfast in bed, he said,
licking his chops. As soon as he slept, I crept to the back
of the lair, where a whole wall was crimson, gold, aglow with books.
Words, words were truly alive on the tongue, in the head,
warm, beating, frantic, winged; music and blood.

But then I was young – and it took ten years
in the woods to tell that a mushroom
stoppers the mouth of a buried corpse, that birds
are the uttered thoughts of trees, that a greying wolf
howls the same old song at the moon, year in, year out,
season after season, same rhyme, same reason. I took an axe
to a willow to see how it wept. I took an axe

to a salmon to see how it leapt. I took an axe to the wolf
as he slept, one chop, scrotum to throat, and saw
the glistening, virgin white of my grandmother's bones.
I filled his cold belly with stones. I stitched him up.
Out of the forest I come, with my flowers, singing, all alone.

Carol Ann Duffy's anthology of poems *The World's Wife* takes memorable characters, stories and myths and presents them in a new – often funny – way, so that readers become more conscious of the ways in which gender roles are constructed in fairy tales and literature. 'Little Red Cap' is a good example of this.

TIP

While it may be tempting to compare and contrast your texts in the individual oral, you are not assessed on your ability to do this. Instead, focus on each text (in relation to the global issue) for 5 minutes. During the discussion, you may find that comparing texts increases your level of analysis, which could have a positive effect on your marks.

Text 8.4

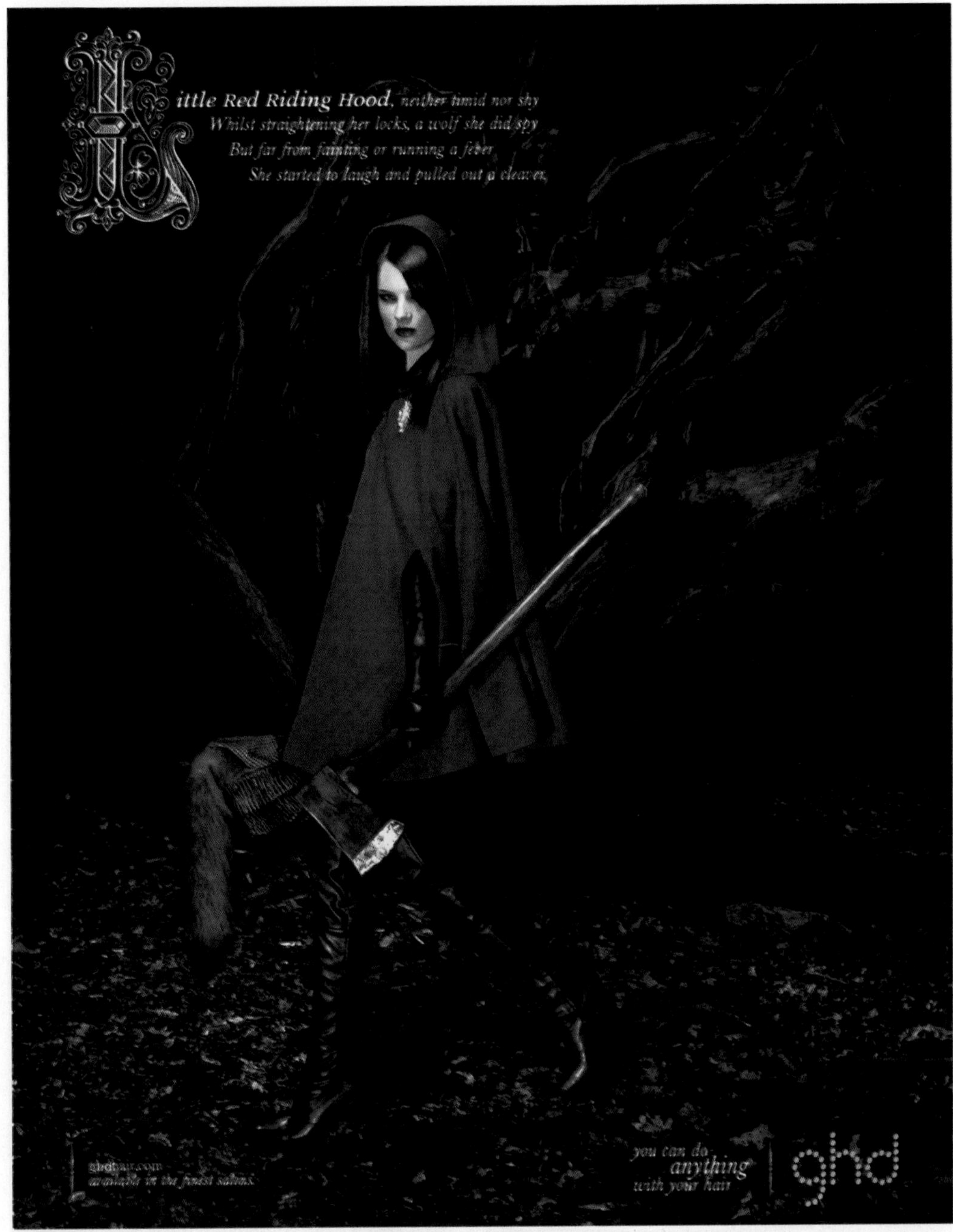

CONCEPT

Representation, perspective

Are you stuck for a global issue, as you study these two texts on Little Red Riding Hood? Looking at the key concepts from this course may help you find something meaningful. Hint: explore the *representation* of men and girls in the texts. How do these texts rely on *perspective* to communicate their message? How is this message universal or global? How is this an issue or a problem?

8.12 Think about the literary works that you have read at higher or standard level.

a On which works do you think you will want to write your Paper 2 and, where applicable, your HL essay?

b Which works does that leave you for your individual oral?

c For each of the works that you consider for the individual oral, make a list of global issues that you could explore. You may not have explored these issues in class yet.

d For each issue, think about non-literary texts that could be used for a presentation on this topic.

e Write a proposal which you can discuss with your teacher, answering these questions:

- What is your global issue? Why did you select this?
- What texts will you explore? Why did you select these?
- What will you argue? What will be your thesis statement?
- On which stylistic features or devices will you focus in the first text? How are these features relevant to the global issue?
- On which stylistic features or devices will you focus in the second text? How are these features relevant to the global issue?

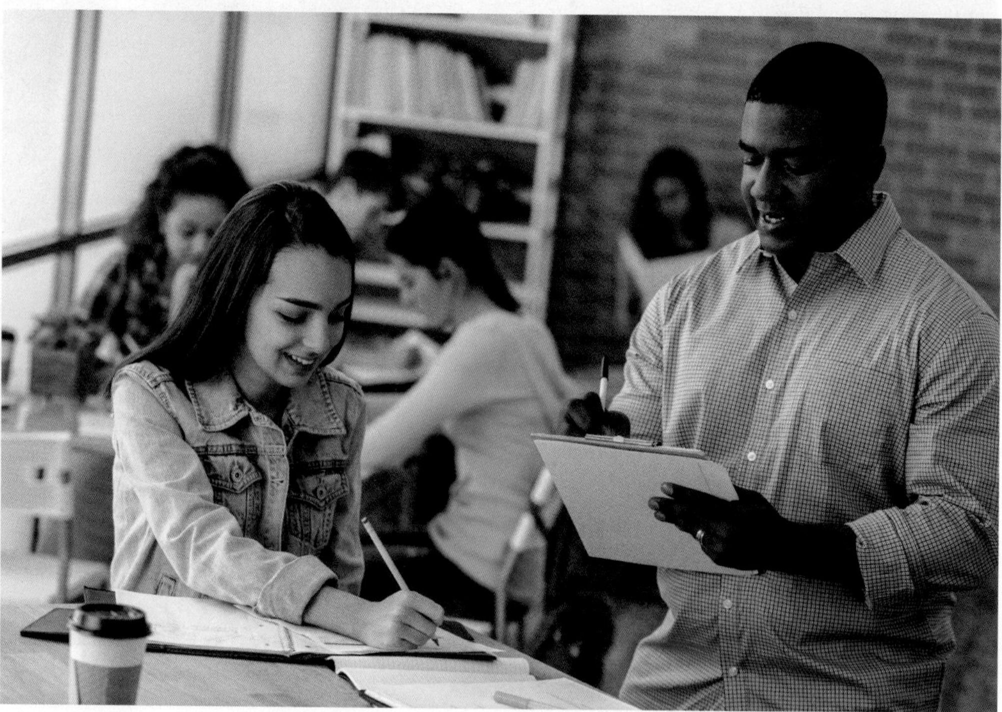

You can discuss your proposal for the individual oral with your teacher in advance of the exam. You must tell your teacher which texts you will use for your individual oral a week before your exam.

8.13 Before you do your final individual oral exam, make sure that you have prepared by taking these steps, most of which have been explored in this unit:

a Listen to other students' individual orals and find out how they scored according to the assessment criteria.

b Do a mock individual oral on Texts 8.1 and 8.2, Texts 8.3 and 8.4, or other texts of your choice. Be sure that you receive meaningful, constructive feedback on your mock exams, based on the assessment criteria. In this way you can learn from your mistakes and become familiar with the assessment criteria.

c Discuss the literary works that you have studied in class with your teacher and classmates, identifying some of the key features from each text.

d Select (a passage from) a literary work that you intend to use for an exploration of a global issue. Select (an extract from) a non-literary text that also allows you to explore this global issue.

e Write a proposal (Activity 8.12) and discuss it with your teacher.

f Turn your proposal into an outline, which you can use in your exam. Type up your outline, using text-editing software, and prepare clean (not annotated) copies of your two texts.

g Practise doing your individual oral alone a few times, to gain confidence and familiarity with the texts and your arguments.

h Arrange a time with your teacher to conduct the official individual oral.

REFLECT

In this chapter you have:

- read a transcription from an individual oral
- applied the assessment criteria
- practised outlining or note-making
- prepared an individual oral on two texts that were unrelated to your coursework (Texts 8.3 and 8.4).

Consider these issues:

- What more do you need to do in order to feel confident before taking the individual oral exam?
- Which preparation strategies did you find particularly useful in this chapter and how can you develop your skills further?
- Discuss further strategies with your teacher and classmates.
- Reflect on what you have learnt from this chapter.

Glossary

Note: the numbers in brackets refer to the units in which the key terms appear.

act – a collection of scenes in a play or piece of drama (1.11)

advertising techniques – the tools used by advertisers to capture their audiences (1.2)

advertorial – an advertisement that gives information about a product or service in the form of an editorial or journalistic article (1.2)

African American Vernacular English (AAVE) – a variety of English, also sometimes called Ebonics (3.1)

airbrushing –the process of concealing particular features of a person in a photograph through digital retouching (2.3)

alienation – in fiction, the way in which a character becomes isolated by other characters or by their setting (1.10)

allegory – a story that reveals a hidden truth, moral or political message (1.3)

alliteration – the repetition of a sound at the beginning of adjacent words (1.7, 1.12, 8)

allusion – a reference to something without mentioning it explicitly (1.7, 2.3, 3.2, 4.1, 4.2)

ambient advertising – advertisements that make use of their physical surroundings in order to construct meaning (1.2, 4.1)

amplification – a rhetorical device where the speaker or writer embellishes the sentence by adding more information to it, to increase its worth and understandability (1.7)

anadiplosis – a form of repetition in which the last word of one clause or sentence is repeated as the first word of the next sentence (1.7)

anaphora – the repetition of a word or phrase at the beginning of successive clauses (1.7, 2.1, 2.3)

anchoring – a term used in semantics to refer to the way in which an otherwise ambiguous form is given meaning by the presence of another form, such as a caption, illustration or commentary (1.1)

anecdote – a short, personal story, sometimes revealing a truth about human nature (1.9, 2.3, 3.3)

antagonist – in fiction, the character who prevents the protagonist from achieving his or her purpose (1.10, 4.2)

anti-advertising – an advertising campaign that seems to break the rules of advertising (2.3)

antithesis – in rhetoric, the contrasting of one idea with another opposite idea (1.7, 8)

apartheid – a former policy of racial segregation in South Africa (3.1)

appeal – in rhetoric, a mode of persuasion (1.7)

appeal to authority – an argumentation fallacy that suggests people in a position of power are always right because of their position (3.3, 4.1)

appeal to fear – an argumentation fallacy in which a person tries to create support for an idea by increasing fear towards an alternative (4.1)

appeal to probability – an argumentation fallacy in which one makes an assumption or a prediction by referring to what is likely to be the case (2.1)

argument – in rhetoric, a line of reasoning aimed at demonstrating a truth or falsehood (1.7)

argument ad hominem – an argumentation fallacy which attacks the speaker's character instead of the speaker's arguments (4.3)

argumentation fallacy – the use of invalid or faulty reasoning when constructing an argument (2.1, 4.1)

assertion – in rhetoric, a strong declaration or forceful conviction based on belief (4.1)

association – the establishment of a connection between a person, place, thing or idea and another person, place, thing or idea (1.2, 2.1)

assonance – the repetition of the same sound between syllables of nearby words, caused by the repetition of vowels (1.12)

atmosphere – in literature, the feeling or mood that a writer creates by describing a setting, objects or characters (1.10, 4.1)

attack ad – in political campaigns, an advertisement that is designed to attack an opposing candidate or political party (4.3)

audience – in textual analysis, the reader and the role of the reader in constructing meaning from a text (5)

author – the writer or creator of a text (5)

awareness campaign – in advertising, a collection of commercials or advertisements that aims to spread awareness of a public problem (2.2, 2.3)

bandwagon effect – in advertising, an appeal to a psychological phenomenon in which people do something because other people are doing it too (1.2)

banner – an image-based advertisement that appears across a website or web page (1.2)

Bechdel test – a measure of the representation of women in film or fiction, in which at least two women talk to each other about something other than a man (2.2)

bias – an inclination or prejudice towards one person or group in an unfair way (1.4)

bibliography – a list of sources to which an essay or academic paper refers (7)

billboard – a large outdoor board for displaying advertisements (1.2)

biographical criticism – a form of literary criticism which uses a writer's biography in order to show a relationship between the author and his or her works (4.2)

blank verse – in poetry, verses with regular metrical feet, usually iambic pentameter, but without rhyme (1.12)

blog post – a piece of writing that is published on a blog (1.9)

body language – the way people communicate using facial expressions and body movements (1.1, 1.11)

cacophony – a harsh discordant mixture of sounds (4.1)

caesura – in poetry, a pause that is created by natural speech or punctuation rather than metre (1.12)

camera angle – the angle at which a camera films its subject or a photograph is taken in relation to its subject (1.3, 1.5)

camera shot – the amount of space in relation to its subject, which is seen in a frame of film (1.3, 2.2)

capitalisation – the inclusion of capital letters in a word (2.3)

caption – a title or explanation that accompanies an image (1.1, 1.4)

caricature – a picture, description or imitation of a person which exaggerates that person's features or character traits (1.4, 1.5)

cartoon – a single-panel drawing which often uses humour and satire to construct a message (1.5)

cartoonification – the process of turning an object or person into a cartoon by drawing them in a stylised or abstract way (1.5)

catharsis – the process of releasing – and being relieved from – strong or repressed emotions (1.11)

celebrity endorsement – a form of advertising that involves a famous person in order to promote a product (1.2)

censorship – the suppression of information or freedom of speech (4.1)

character – in fiction, a person, animal or figure created by an author through language (1.10, 1.11)

characterisation – in fiction, aspects of a character that bring that character to life in the mind of the reader (1.10, 1.11)

chiasmus – a rhetorical device in which words, grammatical constructions or ideas are repeated in reverse order (1.7)

cinematography – the art of photography and camerawork in film-making (1.3)

citation – a quotation from, or reference to, a book, paper or author (7)

civil rights – the rights of citizens to political and social freedom and equality (3.1)

click bait – headlines or articles on web pages intended to attract attention and encourage visitors to click on a link to another web page (1.8)

climax – in fiction, the point in the plot in which the conflict reaches its highest point (1.10)

colloquialism – vernacular language, typical of a social group or region, which is both informal and figurative in use (3.1)

colonial discourse – a way of using language that establishes a relationship between colonial powers and colonised people (3.2)

colonialism – a policy or practice of acquiring full or partial political control over another country (3.2)

comic – a periodical containing a series of multiple panels (1.5)

commercial – a TV or radio advertisement (1.2)

composition – the placement or arrangement of visual elements in a text or, in visual art, the arrangement of visual elements in a work of art in relation to the subject of the art (1.1, 4.1)

condescension – a way of 'talking down' to someone in a patronising way (2.1)

conflict – in fiction, a kind of struggle: (a) between a character and society, (b) between a character and the natural world, (c) between characters, or (d) within a character (1.10, 4.2)

connective – a word or phrase that links clauses and sentences (6)

connotation – the feelings that a word can invoke in a person (2.1)

consonance – the repetition of the same sound between syllables of nearby words, caused by the repetition of consonants (1.12)

context – in textual analysis, the time, place and people that influence the way a text is interpreted (1.8)

context of composition – the factors which influence the way in which an author creates a text, such as time, place or movement (6)

context of interpretation – the factors which influence the way in which a reader makes sense of a text, including time and place (6)

contrast ad – a political advertisement which includes information about opposing candidates, highlighting the negative traits of one political party to reinforce the positive traits of the other (4.3)

copy – the body of written text in an advertisement, usually explaining the benefits of the product or service (1.2)

costumes – in drama, the clothing worn by the performers (1.11)

counterstereotype – in advertising, the inclusion of people who challenge social constructs or stereotypes (2.2)

couplet – in poetry, two verses that belong together and often rhyme (1.12)

cultural appropriation – the inclusion of artefacts, symbols or ideas from one culture into another, without consideration for the culture of origin (3.2)

cultural bias – the process of giving one culture preference over another (3.2)

cultural sensitivity – an awareness of and respect for cultural differences between people (3.2)

culture jamming – the practice of criticising and subverting advertising or consumerism in the mass media (2.2)

curate – to select, organise and look after a collection of objects (8)

dadvertising – advertising which targets fathers, usually in a caring role (2.2)

degradation – the process of degrading someone or something (2.3)

denotation – the literal or primary meaning of a word (2.1)

denouement – in fiction, the point in the plot in which the conflict of a story is resolved and there is room for reflection (1.10)

deontology – the study of the nature of duty and obligation (4.3)

diacope – the repetition of a word or phrase with one or two intervening words (1.7)

dialect – a variety of language which is specific to a region or social group (3.1)

dialogue – in fiction, the language spoken between characters (1.11)

diction – an author's choice of words (1.10, 8)

diegetic sound – any sound that originates from the people or things within the world being filmed, on screen or off screen (1.3)

digital retouching – the use of software to alter a photograph (2.3)

direct speech – the inclusion of a person or character's speech, using his or her words and quotation marks (1.10)

dirty tricks – in political campaigns, unethical practices or pranks used to disrupt or sabotage an opposing party's campaign (4.3)

discrimination – an unjust or prejudicial treatment of people based on sex, race, age or other grounds (2.1)

disinformation – information which is intended to mislead, such as propaganda or biased reporting (1.8, 4.1)

dolly – the vehicle on which a camera is placed in order to track its subject while moving (1.3)

drama – in literature, plays that are written for theatre, TV, radio or film (1.11)

dramatic aside – in drama, an instance when a character speaks briefly and directly to the audience without being heard by the other characters on the stage (1.11)

dysphemism – the opposite of a euphemism, a word or expression to make something sound more unpleasant than is usually acceptable (1.8)

dystopia – an unpleasant, bad or totalitarian place, the opposite of utopia (1.3, 4.3)

ears – the upper corners of a newspaper or magazine's front page which contain teasers (1.1)

ellipsis – the omission of words from a sentence which can be understood from contextual clues, sometimes indicated by a set of dots, '. . .' (3.3)

emanata – symbols and icons used in comic strips to represent emotion or activity (1.5)

emancipation – the process of being set free from legal, social or political restrictions (3.1)

empire – an extensive group of states or countries ruled over by a single state (3.2)

English sonnet – a type of sonnet that consists of three quatrains and a couplet, with a rhyming scheme of abab cdcd efef gg (1.12)

Englishes – the multiple forms of the English language which are understood and spoken (3.1)

enjambment – in poetry, the continuation of a sentence across lines or verses without pause (1.12, 3.2, 3.3)

entrance – in drama, the act of coming on stage or entering a scene (1.11)

enumeration – a rhetorical device which mentions or numbers items one by one (2.3)

ephemeral – lasting for only a short period of time (1.6)

ethnic diversity – characteristic of a group of people from different backgrounds, cultures, religions or race (3.1)

ethnography – the scientific description of peoples and cultures with their customs, traditions and habits (3.2)

ethos – in rhetoric, an appeal to the audience's sense of ethics or principles (1.7, 4.2)

euphemism – a word or expression that is used to make an unpleasant or embarrassing idea or thing sound more agreeable or acceptable (1.8, 4.1, 4.3)

exit – in drama, the act of leaving the stage or scene (1.11)

exposition – in fiction, the first part of the plot in which the characters, setting and conflict are introduced to the reader (1.10)

expression – a turn of phrase or idiom which does not have a literal meaning (2.2)

facetious – treating a serious matter with flippant or inappropriate humour (3.2)

facial expression – the way one uses one's face to communicate an idea or emotion (2.1)

facts – in news reporting, the events or things which are known to be true (1.8)

fake news – fabricated news stories which are intended to influence and mislead a target audience (1.8)

falling action – in fiction, the point in the plot in which the conflict of a story becomes resolved (1.10)

false dichotomy – a situation in which two alternative points are presented as the only options, when other options are also available (4.1, 4.3)

fearmongering – the action of deliberately arousing public fear or alarm about a particular issue (3.3, 4.3)

feature article – a newspaper or magazine article that deals in depth with a particular topic (1.8)

feminism – the advocacy of women's rights based on arguments that relate to gender equality (2.1)

feminist literary criticism – the art or practice of commenting critically on literary works by focusing on their representation of women and their advocacy for gender equality (2.1)

figurative speech – the use of words or phrases which are not intended to be taken literally (1.7)

foil – in fiction, a character whose traits are contrasted with those of another character, usually the protagonist (1.10)

formalism – a school of literary criticism and literary theory that analyses texts by exploring style, structure and purpose, without taking into account any outside influences (4.2)

frame narration – a literary technique that involves a story within a story (6)

free indirect speech – a narrative technique that uses the third person but allows the reader to read a character's thoughts and feelings (2.1, 6)

free verse – poetry that does not rhyme or have a regular rhythm (1.12)

freeze-frame – in drama or film, the act of stopping the action in order to point to a particular moment (1.11)

front page – the first page of a printed newspaper (1.8)

gaze – the direction of a facial expression (1.1)

gender bias – inclination or bias towards a particular gender (2.2)

gender equality – the state in which access to rights and opportunities is equal for men and women (2.1)

gender stereotyping – a process of narrowly defining social expectations for how men and women are expected to behave, dress and act (2.1)

glittering generalities – words that appeal to highly valued concepts or beliefs (1.8, 4.1)

global issue – in the language and literature course, a topic that is significant for many people in different countries across the world (8)

graffiti – writing or drawings on surfaces in public spaces without permission (1.6)

graphic art – two-dimensional, visual art, typically involving design, photography and typography (4.2)

graphic novel – a novel in comic-strip format (1.5)

guerrilla advertising – the placement of low-cost, unconventional advertisements or stickers in public spaces without permission (1.2)

guerrilla art – street art which incorporates its physical surroundings in order to construct meaning (1.6)

gutter – the space between the panels in a comic strip (1.5)

hashtag – a symbol, #, which acts as a way of organising, connecting and accessing information on social media platforms (2.3)

hate speech – language that expresses hatred of a group, directed at attributes such as race, religion, ethnicity, gender, disability or sexual orientation (3.3)

headline – the heading that leads a news story in a newspaper (1.1, 1.2, 1.8)

hegemony – dominance of one social group over another (3.2)

hindsight bias – the inclination, after an event, to see the event as predictable, despite there being no prior evidence (4.1)

human-interest story – in journalism, a feature article that explores a person or people in an emotional way, presenting their challenges and achievements so as to gain sympathy from the reader (1.8)

hyperbole – an exaggeration or statement which is not meant to be taken literally (3.3)

hypermasculinity – an exaggeration of stereotypical male behaviour, including an emphasis on strength and aggression (2.2)

hypophora – a figure of speech in which the speaker raises a question and then answers it immediately (1.7, 3.3)

iambic pentameter – a verse of poetry which contains five metrical feet, each consisting of one unstressed syllable followed by a stressed syllable (4.1)

icon – a term used in semiotics to refer to images that resemble the things that they represent (1.1, 1.6)

idiolect – the speech habits that are particular to an individual (3.1)

illustration – a visual text that adds meaning to written text (1.1)

imagery – language that appeals to the physical senses, such as sight, sound, smell, touch or taste (1.12, 3.3)

imperative – in grammar, a form of verb used to direct or give commands (2.1)

inflection – in speech, a change in pitch or loudness of the voice (1.11)

inquiry – the act of asking for information or showing curiosity (7)

internal rhyme – in poetry, the rhyming of words within a line of verse (1.12)

intonation – the rise and fall of the voice in speaking (1.11)

irony – saying one thing but meaning the opposite (1.4, 4.2)

labelling – describing someone or something in a word or short phrase (1.4)

language framing – in the social sciences, the use of language to create a perception of how individuals and groups should behave (4.3)

lighting – in drama, the craft of using light on objects or characters to a particular effect (1.11)

limited narrator – in fiction, a storyteller who only knows the thoughts and feelings of one character (1.10)

limited-omniscient narrator – in fiction, a storyteller who knows everything and all events but selects to tell them from one character's perspective (1.10)

lines – in drama, the words assigned to a particular character by a playwright (1.11)

linguistic determinism – the notion that human thought is determined by the language people use (2.2)

literary theory – the study of the methods used for analysing texts (2.1, 4.2)

loaded word – a word that is charged with emotion (1.8)

logo – a mark or emblem that is used to promote public identification and recognition (1.1, 1.2)

logos – in rhetoric, an appeal to the audience's sense of logic (1.7, 4.2)

male chauvinism – the belief that men are superior to women in terms of ability and intelligence (2.2)

manga – a style of Japanese comic books and graphic novels (3.2)

manifesto – a type of text used to declare policy or aims, especially from a political candidate or organisation (4.2)

manliness – the traditional quality for men of being strong and brave (2.2)

marketing – the process of promoting products or services, including market research and advertising (1.2)

Marxist literary criticism – a way of analysing literature which explores the representation of characters and the intention of an author in relation to social class, progressive values and the rise of the proletariat (4.2)

masculinity – possessing the qualities that are associated with being a man (2.2)

meaning – in literature, the values and ideas that are constructed by the author and understood by the reader (5)

memoir – a historical account of biographical information written from personal knowledge (1.5, 3.1)

metaphor – a figure of speech in which a non-literal comparison is made between objects or actions, without using words such as 'as' or 'like' (1.7, 1.12, 3.3, 4.3)

metonymy – a reference to a thing or idea by using one of its attributes, such as 'suit' for 'business person' (2.3)

metre – in poetry, the basic rhythmic structure in a verse (1.12)

metric foot – in poetry, the unit of measuring metre which groups stressed and unstressed syllables (1.12)

mise en scène – the arrangement of scenery, props and characters on a stage or set of a film (1.3)

misogyny – dislike of or prejudice against women (2.1)

monologue – a long speech by a character in a play or film (1.11)

montage – the technique of selecting, editing and piecing together separate sections of film to form a continuous whole (1.3)

mood – in textual analysis, the emotional connotations that surround the language of a text (4.1)

motif – a recurring element that has symbolic significance in a story (6)

mural – a painting on a wall, usually done with permission from the wall's owner (1.6, 4.1)

music – vocal or instrumental sounds combined in such a way as to produce beauty of form, harmony and expression of emotion (1.11)

name calling – an argumentation fallacy in which emotionally loaded terms are used to describe someone (4.1, 4.3)

narrative technique – in fiction, the ways in which a story is told, using point of view, speech and tense (1.10)

narrator – in fiction, the person or thing that tells the story (1.10, 3.1)

negative campaigning – in politics, a campaign that criticises an opposition party instead of promoting one's own party (4.3)

negative space – the space surrounding the subject(s) of an image (1.1, 1.5)

negativity bias – a tendency to give more weight to negative thoughts, emotions or social interactions than positive ones (3.3)

news satire – a type of satire which aims to imitate the conventions of news storytelling for humorous effect (1.8)

newsworthiness – the value of a news story, often described in terms of relevance to the target audience, its degree of negativity and extraordinariness (1.8, 3.3)

noble savage – a representation of a primitive person in an idealised, romanticised way (3.2)

non-diegetic sound – any sound, such as a voice-over or music, whose source is not present in the world being filmed (1.3)

objectification – the process of turning something or someone into an object (2.3)

offstage – in theatre, a reference to the action that does not happen on the stage and is not visible to the audience (1.11)

omniscient narrator – in fiction, a storyteller who seems to know everything about every character and event in the story (1.10)

onomatopoeia – the formation of a word from a sound that is associated with the thing that is named, such as 'woof' (4.1)

opinion column – a type of article in a periodical, which clearly expresses the writer's opinion (1.9)

othering – the process of treating people as though they are intrinsically different from and alien to oneself (3.2)

pan – to film from a camera that rotates on its axis (1.3)

panel – the individual frame which captures a moment from a sequence of events in a comic strip (1.5)

paralanguage – non-lexical ways of communicating by speech, including intonation, pitch, speed of speaking, hesitation noises, gesture and facial expressions (1.7)

parallelism – the repetition and aligning of components of a sentence so that they follow a similar construction or pattern (1.7, 2.3)

parody – an imitation of the style of a particular writer with deliberate exaggeration for humorous effect (2.1, 2.2)

passive voice – a narrative technique in which the subject of a sentence undergoes the action of the verb, such as 'the house was built' (passive voice) instead of 'he built the house' (active voice) (1.8)

pastiche – a text that imitates the style of another text or author (2.2)

pathos – in rhetoric, an appeal to the audience's sense of emotion (1.7, 4.2)

patriarchy – a system in which men hold the power and women are largely excluded from it (2.2)

patronising – treating someone with a false kindness, expressing a sense of superiority (3.2)

performance – in drama, the enactment of a playscript (1.11)

persona – a role or character that is adopted by an author or actor (1.7, 3.1)

personification – a form of figurative language in which human qualities are given to non-human things, events or ideas (3.3)

photograph – a picture made by using a camera (1.8)

playscript – a written version of a play or other dramatic composition (1.11)

playwright – the author of a playscript (1.11)

plot – the events of a story, presented in a sequence (1.10)

plot twist – an unexpected turn of events in a story (1.10)

point of view – the perspective from which a story is told, such as the first-, second- or third-person point of view (6)

political bias – a prejudice towards a particular political party or set of political ideas (1.8)

politically correct – avoiding language or actions that could potentially offend others (3.2)

polysyndeton – the repetition of coordinating conjunctions, such as 'and' or 'or' (1.7, 2.3)

positive discrimination – the process of awarding a strategic advantage to someone who is traditionally disadvantaged (3.1)

post-colonial reading – in textual analysis, a focus on the effects of colonialism and imperialism (3.2)

prejudice – preconceived opinion that is not based on reason or actual experience (2.1)

preliminary research – informal research which is aimed at designing the scope and method of research (7)

primary source – in textual analysis, a text that serves as the basis for analysis (2.1, 7)

problem and benefit – an advertising technique that presents the reader with a problem and a solution to this problem which involves the advertiser's product or service (1.2)

product placement – the practice of placing products or services in a feature film or TV programme (1.2)

progressive – the characteristic of advancing social change (2.2)

pronoun – a noun that refers to a person, such as 'I', 'you', 'they' or 'she' (2.1, 3.3)

propaganda – information, which is usually biased or misleading, used to promote a cause (3.3, 4.1)

props – the objects that are included in a play or filmed performance (1.11)

prose fiction – fiction writing without any metrical or rhyming structure (1.10)

prosody – in poetry, the patterns of rhythm and sound (1.12)

protagonist – in fiction, the character who moves the story forward (1.10, 4.2)

protest sign – a sign held by an individual, usually at a demonstration, expressing objection to something (4.2)

public opinion – views and opinions that are prevalent among the general public (1.4)

public service announcement – an advertisement which is disseminated, often without charge, for the purpose of raising awareness about a social issue (1.2, 1.3)

pun – a joke exploiting the different possible meanings of a word (4.2)

punchline – the last part of a joke, which is intended to reveal the humour of the joke (1.5)

purpose – in textual analysis, the intention of the author or the reason why a writer writes (5)

purpose-driven content marketing – a way for a brand to connect with its audience by supporting a cause (2.3)

quotation – a verbatim retelling of what a person has said (1.8)

racial bias – a tendency to show preference for one race over another (3.1)

racial profiling – the use of race or ethnicity as a grounds for suspecting someone of having committed an offence (3.1)

racism – the act of discriminating against someone, based on a belief that one's own race is superior to another's (3.1)

rape myth – a prejudicial, stereotypical or false belief about sexual assault and rape (2.3)

reader – in textual analysis, the person who interprets a text (5)

reader-response criticism – a school of literary theory that focuses on the reader's experience of a literary work, as opposed to an objective, formalist analysis of the text (4.2)

readership – the people who read a periodical such as a newspaper, magazine or book (1.8, 2.2)

referendum – a general vote by the electorate on a single political issue (4.3)

repetition – writing or speaking the same words multiple times (1.7)

reported speech – a speaker's words reported in subordinate clauses, using a reporting verb, such as 'he said that he would leave' (reported speech) instead of 'he said, "I will leave"' (direct speech) (1.8, 1.10)

reporting – giving a spoken or written account of what one has seen, heard or investigated (1.8)

representation – in media studies, the way in which someone or something is portrayed (2.1)

rhetorical device – a recognised technique or way of using words for conveying a particular meaning (1.7)

rhetorical question – a question which is asked to make a point rather than to receive an answer (3.3)

rhyming scheme – in poetry, the pattern of rhyme that comes at the end of each verse (1.12)

rhythm – in poetry, the sound created by a pattern of stressed and unstressed syllables (1.12)

riddle – a question or statement which presents a puzzle for someone to solve (2.1)

rising action – in fiction, the point in the plot in which the conflict heightens (1.10)

role model – a person looked to by others as an example to be imitated (2.2)

role reversal – in advertising, the inclusion of a person in a position where a person of an opposite sex, gender or age is expected (2.2, 2.3)

rule of thirds – a guideline for composing visual texts which suggests that, if it were divided into nine equal parts, the subject should appear where the grid lines of these parts intersect (1.1)

sarcasm – the use of irony to mock or express contempt (4.2)

satire – the use of humour, irony, exaggeration or ridicule to expose and criticise people's stupidity (1.5)

scansion – in poetry, the process of marking the stresses in a poem and discerning its use of metre (1.12)

scene – in drama, a unit of action, often a part of an act (1.11)

secondary source – in textual analysis, a text that informs an opinion about a primary source or text (2.1, 7)

self-esteem – confidence in one's own worth or abilities (2.3)

self-image – the way one perceives oneself (2.3)

semantic field – a set of words that are thematically related to each other (7)

sensationalism – the presentation of a story or idea in such a way as to provoke excitement, often at the expense of accuracy (3.3)

set – in drama, the backdrop or arrangement of objects to represent the place where a story takes place (1.11)

setting – the place or surroundings where a story takes place (1.10)

sex in advertising – the inclusion of sex in advertising in order to sell a product or service (2.3)

sexism – prejudice, stereotyping or discrimination based on gender differences (2.1)

shockvertising – advertising that is shocking and explicit (2.3)

signature – in advertising, the placement of the advertiser's logo and name (1.2)

signified – a term used in semiotics to describe the meaning that is created by any kind of form (1.1)

signifier – a term used in semiotics to describe any form that takes meaning, such as a word, sign, symbol or even colour (1.1)

signpost – in writing, a connective word that tells the reader where the text is going, such as 'next' (1.9)

simile – a figure of speech involving the comparison of one thing with another thing of a different kind (1.12)

situational irony – when the opposite happens from what is expected in a particular situation (1.4, 1.6, 3.3)

slogan – a short, memorable phrase used in an advertising or political campaign (1.2, 4.2)

social commentary – a message that criticises society and the ways in which that society is organised (1.6)

social construct – an idea that has been created and accepted by the people of a society, often related to social class, gender, race or age (2.2)

socialisation – the process of learning to behave in a way that is acceptable in society (2.2)

soliloquy – in drama, a speech given by a character to himself or herself, so that the audience but no other characters can hear the character's thoughts (1.11)

sonnet – a poem of 14 lines, with a formal rhyming scheme, often containing ten syllables per line (4.1, 8)

sound – in drama and film, the music, speech and noises that are heard by the viewers either produced within the world of fiction (diegetic sound) or superimposed on the world of fiction (non-diegetic sound) (1.11)

source – the person or text that is referenced as the starting point of information (1.8)

speech bubble – a bubble drawn above a character in a comic strip or cartoon to indicate the character's speech (1.5, 3.3)

speech directions – in drama, the instructions given in the playscript by the playwright to the actors on how to deliver the lines (1.11)

sponsored link – a paid advertisement in the form of a hypertext link on a website that shows up on search results (1.2)

spoof – the humorous imitation of a text in which its features are exaggerated (2.2, 2.3)

spoof ad – a fictional advertisement for a non-existent product, which makes fun of an actual advertisement for a real product (1.2)

stage – in theatre, the floor or platform on which actors perform (1.11)

stage directions – in drama, the instructions given in the playscript by the playwright to the director on how to stage the play (1.11)

staging – in drama, the process of selecting, designing, adapting to or modifying the performance space for a play or film (1.11)

stanza – in poetry, a collection of lines or verses, distinguished by a line break between the previous or next stanza (1.12)

stencil – a thin sheet of cardboard, plastic or metal with a cut-out design, allowing an artist to paint the same profile multiple times (1.6)

stereotype – a widely held but oversimplified image or idea of a particular person or thing (3.1)

still – a frozen frame of a moving image or film (1.3)

stock image – a professionally created photograph or image which is available for purchase on a royalty-free basis (3.3)

street art – artwork that appears in public spaces, usually without permission (1.6)

structure – in textual analysis, the way in which the coherence of a text is constructed (5)

style – in textual analysis, the way in which a writer writes (5)

subheading – a secondary heading or opening line, intended to expand on a headline or summarise a text (1.8)

subsequent questions – the kinds of questions that teachers ask students after students have presented their ideas in an oral presentation (8)

subvertising – a portmanteau of 'subvert' and 'advertising'; a practice of making spoofs or parodies of corporate and political advertising (1.2, 2.2)

suffrage – the right to vote in an election (2.1)

surrealism – an artistic and literary movement which includes unnatural, fantastical or irrational depictions of the world (2.3)

syllable – a unit of pronunciation having one vowel sound (1.12)

symbol – a mark or sign that is understood to represent an idea, object or relationship (1.1, 1.5, 1.6)

symbolism – the use of symbols to represent ideas (1.4, 4.2)

symmetry – in a visual text, the mirroring or correspondence of visual features (1.5)

synonym – a word that has a similar meaning to another word (7)

syntax – the selection and arrangement of words and phrases to create meaning (2.2)

taboo – a social custom, behaviour or practice that is considered inappropriate or forbidden by a group of people (2.3)

tagline – a catchphrase or slogan, especially used in advertising (1.2)

target audience – the group of people that a writer or speaker has in mind as a readership or audience (1.7)

tautology – saying the same thing twice, but using different words (1.9)

teasers – in newspapers or magazines, the short text boxes on the front page that encourage the reader to read full versions of these articles inside the newspaper or magazine (1.1, 3.3)

technique – in textual analysis, the skills, devices or style of the author (6)

tension – in literature, the feeling of an unresolved problem or unfulfilled events (1.10)

testimonial – in advertising, the featuring of a happy customer and a quotation about the benefits of a company's product or service (1.2)

text – in textual analysis, anything that has been constructed to convey meaning (5)

textual analysis – the study of texts in order to ascertain meaning (5)

theatre – the place in which dramatic performances are given (1.11)

theme – in literature, the main idea of the author (6)

thesis statement – the sentence or sentences that come at the end of a text's introduction, which serve the purpose of outlining the scope of the text and capturing the text's main idea or message (5, 6, 7, 8)

thinspiration – something that acts as an inspiration for dieting or anorexic behaviour (2.3)

thought bubble – a bubble drawn above a character in a comic strip or cartoon to indicate what a character is thinking (1.5)

tone – the general attitude created by a text (2.1)

topical – current or relevant to current events (1.4, 1.9)

tricolon – a list of three parallel clauses, phrases or words without interruption (1.7)

trompe l'oeil – a two-dimensional style of art that creates an illusion of three dimensions when viewed from a particular perspective (1.6)

truncated sentence – a sentence that misses words out (2.3)

unreliable narrator – in fiction, a story-teller whose reliability may be questioned by the reader (1.10)

verse – in poetry, a line of writing (1.12)

visual narrative – the storyline that is suggested through an image (1.1, 1.2)

voice – the quality that makes an author's style unique (1.9)

voice-over – spoken narration which is included as non-diegetic sound in film (1.3, 3.2) or in a separate box in a comic frame (1.5)

volta – in poetry, a turning point of argument or thought (1.12, 8)

warmongering – the encouragement of advocacy of going to war with other countries or groups (4.1)

weasel word – a word that intentionally creates ambiguity (1.8, 3.3)

xenophobia – a fear or dislike of people who are foreign (3.1)

zoom – a camera shot that moves from a long shot to close-up shot (zoom in) or vice versa (zoom out) (1.3)

Index

'1984' Apple Super Bowl commercial (Ridley Scott) 15–16

acts and scenes, in stage plays 75
Adichie, Chimamanda Ngozi 54
advertisements
  attack ads 246
  and beauty 126–30, 137–8
  colonialism 172
  contrast ads 246
  conventions of 9–13
  gender stereotyping 92, 94–6, 100–1, 113–15, 117–21
  political campaigns 244–5
  and race 145, 157–8
  and sex 130–1
  spoof advertising 116
  use of association 93
  visual images 5, 6
advertising techniques 12
affirmative action 154
African American Vernacular English (AAVE) 145–7
airbrushing 126
alienation 63
Allegory of the Cave (Plato) 16
alliteration 35, 80, 81
allusion 36, 37, 133, 141, 230
ambient advertising 10, 213
American Civil War 148
amplification (rhetorical device) 35
anadiplosis (rhetorical device) 35
anapests 82
anaphora 34, 99, 141
anchoring, of meaning 5
anecdotes 54, 56, 141, 203
antagonist 63, 224
anti-advertising 128
anti-climax 309
antithesis (rhetorical device) 34, 36, 37
apartheid 150
appeal (rhetoric) 35
appeal to authority 203, 208
appeal to fear 208
appeal to probability 93
Apple Macintosh '1984' commercial 15–16, 248
argument ad hominem 246
argumentation fallacy 93
Aristotle 67
Armstrong, Lance, interview with Oprah Winfrey 311–14, 318
art, criteria for 31
assertion (propaganda technique) 208
association
  in advertising 12
  and gender stereotypes 93
assonance 81
atmosphere, in fiction 63
awareness campaigns 128

bandwagon effect 12
Banksy 30–3, 211
banners, advertising 10
Beah, Ishmael, *A Long Way Gone* 215–16
Bechdel test 118
Benetton advertisement 157–8
bias
  in newspapers 45, 194
  in political cartoons 19
bibliographies 309
billboards 10, 192
biographical criticism 227
Black Boy (Richard Wright) 160–1
Black Power salute 148–9
Blackberry-Picking (Seamus Heaney) 84–7
blank verse 81
blogs 52–7
body language 7–8, 68
Booker, Christopher 59
Boroditsky, Lera 241, 242
Brathwaite, Edward Kamau, 'Wings of a Dove' 177
Brexit referendum 43–4, 192
Bright Star (John Keats) 80–1
British Empire 163
Broetry (Brian McGackin) 117
Brooke, Rupert, 'The Soldier' 323
Bush, George W., State of the Union Address 208–9

caesura 80, 81
Calvin and Hobbes (comic strip) 26, 28–9
camera angle 16, 27
camera shot 16
captions 5, 22
caricature 22
Carlin, George 210
cartoonification 28–9
cartoons
  colonialism 176
  comics 24–9
  immigration 186
  manga version of *The Tempest* 170–1
  political 19–23, 232–4
catharsis 67
celebrity endorsement 12
censorship 219
characterisation 62, 64, 68
characters
  in fiction 62, 63
  in playscripts 68
Chast, Roz 59
Chekhov, Anton 5
Chiarella, Tom, 'What is a Man?' 111–13
chiasmus 35
Chopin, Kate, *The Story of an Hour* 60–1
cinematography 14, 17
classics 15, 84
click bait 49
climax, in fiction 62, 64
Collins, Billy, *Introduction to Poetry* 78–9
colloquialisms 147
colonial discourse 165
colonialism 163–84
comics 24–9, 170–1
commercials 14–18
communication
  street art 32
  through symbols and logos 3
composition, of images 4
condescension 96
conflict, in literature 62, 63, 224
connectives (linking words) 294–5
Conrad, Joseph, *Heart of Darkness* 165–6
consonance 81
context
  of composition 281
  of interpretation 281
  in news articles 47, 48
copy, advertising 12

counterstereotype 120
couplet 81
Covey, Stephen 45
cultural appropriation 163
cultural contexts 40, 76, 299, 305
cultural sensitivity 163
culture jamming 116

dactyls 82
deconstruction, of images 2–5
democracy 235
denouement 63, 64
deontology 246
diacope (rhetorical device) 34
dialects 145
dialogue 73, 75
diegetic and non-diegetic sound (film) 16
digital retouching 126–8
dimeters 83
direct speech 64
disinformation 49
Doll's House, The (Henrik Ibsen) 68–71
domestic violence 133–4
'double dipping' 318
drama 67
Duffy, Carol Ann
  The Diet 136–7
  'Little Red Cap' 334
Dunbar, Paul Laurence 148
  Speakin' At De Cou't-House 146–7
dysphemism 45

ears (magazine covers) 7
eating disorders 129
ellipsis 193
emanata (comics) 27
emigrants 185
emoticons 3
English sonnet 80, 81
enjambment 81, 189
entrance, in stage plays 75
enumeration 141
ephemeral art 30
essay writing skills
  comparative essay 279–99
  for higher level 301–19
ethics, use of photographs 192
ethnic diversity 157
ethnography 184
ethos (rhetoric) 35, 236
euphemisms 45, 210, 255
examples, in blog posts 54, 56

exposition, in fiction 62, 64
expressions, linguistic 109

facts, in news articles 47, 48
fake news 49
falling action, in fiction 63, 64
false dichotomies 246
false dichotomies (propaganda technique) 208
fearmongering 192, 246
features articles 51
feminism 91, 97–107
feminist literary criticism 104–7
fiction, prose 58–66
figurative speech 36, 37
films 14–18
foil 63
font types 7
formalism 225
Francis, H. E., *Sitting* 223–4
free indirect speech 106
free verse 81
Freeman, Hadley 53–6
front page (newspaper) 43

Gandhi, Mahatma 227–9
gender bias 110
gender stereotyping 91–6
Gilman, Charlotte Perkins, *Females* 102
glittering generalities (propaganda technique) 45, 208
global issues 321, 323, 325
graffiti 30–3
graphic novels 24–9, 170–1, 211–12
Grass is Singing, The (Doris Lessing) 104–7
Great Gatsby, The (Scott Fitzgerald) 49–50
guerrilla art 32
gutter (comics) 27

hashtag (#) 141
hate speech 192
headlines and subheadings 46, 48
Heaney, Seamus, *Blackberry-Picking* 84–7
Heart of Darkness (Joseph Conrad) 165–6
hegemony 167
Hemingway, Ernest 58
'How movies teach manhood' (Colin Stokes) 118–19
human-interest stories 51
hyperbole 193
hypermasculinity 117–18

hypophora (rhetorical device) 36, 37, 203

iambs 82
Ibsen, Henrik, *The Doll's House* 68–71
icons 3, 32
identity
  and gender 54–5, 106, 111–13
  and race 146–7
  and self-image 129
idiolect 145
illustrations 5
imagery, in poetry 80, 189
images, deconstruction of 2–5
immigrants 185
immigration 185–204
individual orals 101–4, 135, 320–7
inflection, of voice 68
internal rhyme 81
interpunctuation 73
intertextuality 100, 116, 132
Introduction to Poetry (Billy Collins) 78–9
irony 22, 32

job descriptions 110

Kallaugher, Kevin 23
Keats, John, *Bright Star* 80–1
Kennedy, Robert, Statement on the assassination of Martin Luther King (1968) 39–40
King, Martin Luther, 'I have a dream' 152–4
Kipling, Rudyard, 'The White Man's Burden' 174–5

language, and gender 92
language framing 242
Layton, Jack, Campaign speech 249–51
Lazarus, Emma, 'The New Colossus' 190–1
Lessing, Doris, *The Grass is Singing* 104–7
letter-writing 158–9
lines of inquiry 301–3, 315
linguistic determinism 109
literary texts 58–66, 223–7
literary theory 104, 224–5
Little Red Riding Hood 334–5
loaded words 45
logos (rhetoric) 35, 236
logos (visual design) 3

magazine covers 6–8, 242–3
male chauvinism 114
Mandela, Nelson
  'An ideal for which I am prepared to die' (1964) 150–1
  Inaugural Speech, Pretoria (1994) 151–2
manga version of *The Tempest* 170–1
manliness 108
MAPS (acronym) 264, 326
marketing material 10
Marxist literary criticism 224
masculinity 108–9
McGackin, Brian, *Broetry* 117
'Me too' movement 140
meta-language 329
metaphor 35, 189, 241
metonymy 133
metre, in poetry 80, 81, 82–3
Miller, J. Howard 97–8
mind maps 265, 284, 314–15
mise en scène (film) 16
misogyny 92
monologue 75
montage (film) 16
moon landing (1969) 324
murals 213

name calling (propaganda technique) 208, 246
narrative technique 62, 64
Nazi propaganda film 193
negative campaigning 246
negative space 4, 27
negativity bias 194
'New Colossus, The' (Emma Lazarus) 190–1
news satire 49
newspapers
  articles 43–51
  and immigration 193–4
Newsweek (magazine) 6
newsworthiness 46, 48–9, 194
Nineteen Eighty-Four (George Orwell) 248–9
Nixon, Richard 324
'noble savage' 165
novels 58–66

Obama, Barack, speech (2008) 36–7
objectification 132
offstage action, in stage plays 73, 75
opinion 56
  in blog posts 54
Orwell, George
  Nineteen Eighty-Four 16, 248–9
  Politics and the English Language 254–5
'othering' 165
Owen, Wilfred, 'Dulce et Decorum Est' 217–19

palindrome 55
panels (comics) 27
paralanguage 34
parallelism (rhetorical device) 36, 37, 141
parody 97, 116
pastiche 116
pathos (rhetoric) 35, 236
patriarchy 118
patronising tone 165
PEACE ACT structure 65
PEEL structure 272, 316
pentameters 83
Persepolis (Marjane Satrapi) 24–5, 28, 305–10, 315–17
personas 41, 158–9
personification 189
perspective 6, 17, 44, 209
photographs
  analysis of 7, 209–10
  concrete images 29
  ethical use of 192
  news articles 48
  political use of 192, 195
Picasso, Pablo 58
Plato, *Allegory of the Cave* 16
playscripts 67–76
playwrights 67
plot, in fiction
  plot twists 61
  seven basic plot types 59
poetry
  definitions 77
  key features 80–1
  metre 82–3
  poetic language 78
political bias (newspapers) 43
political campaigns 244–6, 249–51
political cartoons 19–23, 232–4
political correctness 173
politicians, language use 240, 254–6
politics, and language 240–56
polysyndeton (rhetorical device) 36, 37, 141
positive discrimination 154
post-colonialism 172–3
posters
  feminism 97
  political campaigns 244–5
  political protest 221–3
  war 97, 207
Powell, Enoch, Birmingham Speech 201–3
preliminary research 303
primary sources 106, 302
print advertising 11–12
problem and benefit (advertising technique) 12
pronouns, effect of 96, 189
propaganda 192–3, 207–8
prose fiction 58–66
prosody 81
protagonist 63, 224
protest, political 221–39
protest signs 230
public opinion 19
public service announcements 14
punchline (comics) 27
puns 230
purpose-driven content marketing 128

quotations
  in news articles 46, 48
  from primary source 308

racism 144–62
rape myths 133–4
reader-response criticism 224
readership 43, 113
repetition (rhetorical device) 36, 37
reported speech 51, 64
representation
  and cartoons 29
  and gender 8, 93
  and race 162
  in theatre direction 76
research skills 304
rhetorical devices 34–8
rhetorical questions 193
rhyming scheme 80, 81
rising action, in fiction 62, 64
role models, in film 119

role reversal 119–20, 132
rule of thirds 4
Rumsfeld, Donald 303

Sacco, Joe, *Palestine* 211–12
Safire, William, In the Event of Moon Disaster (speech) 324
Said, Edward 165
Satrapi, Marjane, *Persepolis* 24–5, 28, 305–10, 315–17
scansion 82
scenes, in stage plays 75
Scott, Ridley, '1984' Apple Super Bowl commercial 15–16
Scott Fitzgerald, F., *The Great Gatsby* 49–50
secondary sources 106, 301
semantic fields 314
sensationalism 193
setting, in fiction 62, 63
sex, and advertising 130–1
sexism 92
sexual assault 133–4
Shakespeare, William, *The Tempest* 167–71
Shelley, Percy Bysshe, 'Men of England' 225–6
Shire, Warsan, 'Home' 187–9, 197–8
'shockvertising' 128
short stories 58–66
signatures, advertising 12
signifiers/ signified 2–3, 5
situational irony 22, 32, 186
slogans
  in advertising 12
  protest signs 231
social commentary, and street art 32
social constructs 110
socialisation 109
sonnet 80, 81
sound and music, in stage plays 75
sources, for news articles 46, 48
Soyinka, Wole, 'Telephone Conversation' 203–4
Speakin' At De Cou't-House (Paul Laurence Dunbar) 146–7
speech bubblies (comics) 27
speech directions, in stage plays 73, 75
speeches 34–42, 208–9, 236
spondees 82
sponsored links 10
spoofs 116, 128, 132
stage directions 75
staging 73, 75
stanzas 80, 81
Statue of Liberty 191
stencil art 32
stills, in film or videos 14
Stokes, Colin, 'How movies teach manhood' 118–19
stories 58–66
street art 30–3, 211
Streetcar Named Desire, A (Tennessee Williams) 72–5
style or technique 281
'subvertising' 116
suffrage movement *see* women's suffrage movement
surrealism 135
Syfes, Judy, *Why I Want a Wife* 98–9
syllables and metric feet, in poetry 80, 81
symbols 3, 22, 27, 32, 230
synonyms 314
syntax 113

taboos 131
taglines 12
target audience 41
tautology 55
teasers (magazine covers) 7, 193
Tempest, The (William Shakespeare) 167–71
testimonials, in advertising 12
tetrameters 83
textual analysis
  definition 258
  skills for 259–77
Thatcher, Margaret 242–4
theatre 67
themes 281
thesis statements 264–5, 284, 315, 323
Thibodeau, Paul H. 241, 242
tips, in blog posts 54, 56
tone 98
topical material 54, 56
transformations, of texts 170
transformative texts 38, 79
Tremearne, Captain A. J. N., *The Niger and the West Sudan* 164
tricolon (rhetorical device) 35, 36, 37
trimeters 83
trochees 82
trompe l'oeil 32
truncated sentences 127

UKIP (UK Independence Party) 192–3
unreliable narrator 64
Uys, Jamie, *The Gods Must be Crazy* (film, 1980) 182–4

verses, in poetry 80, 81
visual narrative 5, 12
visual texts 2–8
vocabulary, gendered 110
voice, in blog posts 54, 56
voice-over 182
volta, in poetry 80, 81

Wainaina, Binyavanga, 'How to write about Africa' 177–81
Walker, Alice, *The Flowers* 62–3
war
  advertisements 213
  cartoons 212
  euphemisms 210
  and language 206
  literary texts 215–20
  propaganda 207–8
  speeches 208–9
  street art 211, 213
'We the People' (poster, 2017) 196–7
weasel words (propaganda technique) 45, 193
'What is a Man?' (Tom Chiarella) 111–13
Why I Want a Wife (Judy Syfes) 98–9
Williams, Tennessee, *A Streetcar Named Desire* 72–5
Winfrey, Oprah
  Golden Globes Award speech 138–41
  interview with Lance Armstrong 311–14, 318
Wise, Tim 162
Woman's Weekly (magazine) 93–5
women's suffrage movement 101–4
Wright, Richard, *Black Boy* 160–1

xenophobia 144

Yousafzai, Malala, speech to the United Nations 236–9

Acknowledgements

The authors and publishers acknowledge the following sources of copyright material and are grateful for the permissions granted. While every effort has been made, it has not always been possible to identify the sources of all the material used, or to trace all copyright holders. If any omissions are brought to our notice, we will be happy to include the appropriate acknowledgements on reprinting.

Text 1.1 Biscuit Eight LLC/GI; Text 1.2 Fine Art Images/Heritage Images/GI; Text 1.3 Joby Sessions/MacLife Magazine/GI; Text 1.4 Robynmac/GI; Text 1.5 Katyakatya/GI; Text 1.6 Stockcam/GI; Text 1.7 Bortonia/GI; Texts 1.8, 1.9, 1.10, 1.10, 2.3, 2.6, 2.14, 2.22, 2.24, 2.28, 3.1, 3.7, 3.14, 4.25, 4.26, 4.31, 4.32 and 8.4 Images courtesy of The Advertising Archives; Text 1.12 Newsweek cover © November 23 2009, Newsweek. All rights reserved, used under license. Cover photo reproduced with the permission of Brian Adams; Text 1.13 The Age (Melbourne) magazine cover reproduced by permission of Fairfax Syndication; Text 1.14 Romolo Tacani/GI; Text 1.16 Designed by Jeski Social Camapign © www.jeski.world; Text 1.17 Image Courtesy of Keep America Beautiful, Inc; Text 1.18 Tata Motors 2010; Text 1.19 World History Archive/Alamy Stock Photo; Text 1.20 by Dave Granlund courtesy of Cagle Cartoons; Text 1.21 Pictorial Press Ltd/Alamy Stock Photo; Text 1.22 reproduced with the permission of Kevin Kallaugher; Text 1.23 and Chapter 7 excerpts from *Persepolis: The Story of A Childhood* by Marjane Satrapi, translation © 2003 by L'Association, Paris, France. Used by permission of Pantheon Books, an imprint of the Knopf Doubleday Publishing Group, a division of Penguin Random House LLC and Penguin Random House UK, All rights reserved; Text 1.24 and related figures *Calvin and Hobbes* © 1986 Watterson. Reprinted with permission of Andrews McMeel Universal; Text 1.25 Peter Macdiarmid/GI; Text 1.26 Matt Cardy/GI; Text 1.27 Graham C99 via Flickr.com; Text 1.30 reproduced with the permission of The Independent; Text 1.31 reproduced with the permission of Solo Syndication; Text 1.32 reproduced with the permission of MirrorPix and London News Pictures; Text 1.33 © 2016 New York Post. All rights reserved. Used under license; Text 1.34 'Boris Johnson and Michael Gove prepare 'dream team' to lead government' by Michael Wilkinson, reproduced with the permission of Telegraph Media Group Limited; Text 1.36 Roz Chast/The New Yorker Collection/The Cartoon Bank; Text 1.37 'Identity is the issue of our age: so why can't we talk more honestly about trans women?' by Hadley Freeman, reproduced with the permission of Guardian News & Media Limited; Text 1.38 Roz Chast/The New Yorker Collection/The Cartoon Bank; Text 1.40 'The Flowers' from *In Love & Trouble: Stories of Black Women* by Alice Walker © 1973, renewed 2001 by Alice Walker. Reprinted by permission of Houghton Mifflin Harcourt Publishing Company and Joy Harris Literary Agency. All rights reserved; Text 1.42 Extract from *A Streetcar Named Desire* by Tennessee Williams, © Tennessee Williams 1947. Reproduced by permission of New Directions Publishing Corp & Sheil Land Associates Ltd working in conjunction with Georges Borchardt Inc; Text 1.43 Billy Collins, 'Introduction to Poetry' from *The Apple That Astonished Paris* © 1988, 1996 by Billy Collins. Reprinted with the permission of The Permissions Company, Inc., on behalf of the University of Arkansas Press, www.uapress.com; Text 1.45 'Blackberry-Picking' from *Opened Ground: Selected Poems 1966-1996* by Seamus Heaney © 1998 by Seamus Heaney. Reprinted by permission of Farrar, Straus and Giroux and Faber and Faber Ltd; Text 2.1 Ivory Soap (BH0851), JWT. Competitive Advertisements Collection, David M. Rubenstein Rare Books & Manuscripts Library, Duke University; Text 2.2 'Works' Page from *Woman's Weekly* (UK edition), Volume 1 number 1 from November 4, 1911 reproduced with the permission of TI Media; Text 2.4 John Parrot/Stocktrek Images/GI; Text 2.5 Abridged extract from 'Why I Want A Wife' by Judy Syfers, Ms. Magazine, 1971 © Judy Brady (Syfers); Text 2.7 PJF Military Collection/Alamy Stock Photo; Text 2.9 'America When Feminized' by Lauren Younker, Courtesy of the Tennessee State Library & Archives; Text 2.10 *The Grass Is Singing* by Doris Lessing © 1950 by Doris Lessing, renewed © 1978 by Doris Lessing. Reprinted by permission of HarperCollins Publishers USA and HarperCollins Publishers UK; Text 2.12 from *Results at the Top: Using Gender Intelligence to Create Breakthrough Growth* by Barbara Annis and

Richard Nesbitt, Wiley, 2017; Text 2.13 'What is a Man?' by Tom Chiarella for Esquire 2015, reproduced with the permission of author; Text 2.16 poem from *Broetry* by Brian McGackin 2011, reproduced with the permission of Quirk Books; Text 2.17 thanks to Kookai France; Text 2.18 © Oregon Center for Nursing 2002; Texts 2.22, 2.23 courtesy of Adbusters.org; Text 2.21 'You are not a sketch' for Star Models 2013 by Edson Rosa; Text 2.25 by permission of Salvation Army South Africa; Text 2.26 by permission of Make Your Move! Missoula; Text 2.27 'The Diet' by Carol Ann Duffy 2002, reproduced with permission of Pan Macmillan via PLSclear; Text 2.29 speech by Oprah Winfrey; Text 3.3 The History Collection/Alamy Stock Photo; Text 3.4 reproduced with the permission of Nelson Mandela Foundation; Text 3.6 Excerpt from speech by Dr Martin Luther King, Jr. Reprinted by arrangement with The Heirs to the Estate of Martin Luther King Jr., c/o Writers House as agent for the proprietor New York, NY. © 1963 Dr. Martin Luther King, Jr. © renewed 1991 Coretta Scott King; Text 3.9 pp23-4 from *Black Boy* by Richard Wright, Copyright 1937, 1942, 1944, 1945 by Richard Wright, renewed © 1973 by Ellen Wright, reprinted by permission of HarperCollins Publishers and Random House UK; Text 3.10 *The Niger and West Sudan* by Captain A.J.N. Tremearne 1910 © British Library Board (010097.h.16.); Text 3.13 pages from *The Tempest* by Richard Appignanesi and Paul Duffield in the Manga Shakespeare series published by and used with permission of SelfMadeHero; Text 3.18 'Wings of a dove' by Edward Kamau Brathwaite, reproduced with permission of Oxford University Press via PLSclear; Text 3.19 'How to write about Africa' by Binyavanga Wainaina in Granta, used by permission of The Wylie Agency (UK) Limited; Text 3.20 script excerpt written by Jamie Uys and film still from 'The Gods Must Be Crazy' © 1980 Twentieth Century Fox, All rights reserved; Text 3.21 by David Horsey, courtesy of Tribune Content Agency; Text 3.22 Jason Patterson/The New Yorker Collection/The Cartoon Bank; Text 3.24 'Home' © 2011 by Warsan Shire; Text 3.26 Jack Taylor/GI; Text 3.27 Bundesarchiv, Film Collection, B-58854 © Transit Film GmbH; Text 3.28 reproduced with the permission of Solo Syndication; Text 3.29 Eric Baradat/GI; Text 3.30 'Greater than fear', 'Defend dignity' and 'Protect each other' artworks from *We The People* by Shepard Fairey, reproduced with the permission of Amplifier; Text 4.1 Historica Graphica Collection/Heritage Images/GI; Text 4.2 Photo12/GI; Text 4.3 John Parrot/Stocktrek Images/GI; Text 4.4 Universal History Archive/GI; Text 4.6 Cesar Gorriz Rey/GI; Text 4.7 David Silverman/GI; Text 4.8 p100 (cropped) from *Palestine* by Joe Sacco, © Joe Sacco, courtesy of Fantagraphics Books; Text 4.9 by permission of Walker Zurich www.walker.ag; Text 4.10 Education Images/GI; Text 4.11 Excerpt from 'A Long Way Gone' by Ishmael Beah, reproduced with the permission of Farrar, Straus and Giroux and HarperCollins Publishers Ltd., © (2007) Ishmael Beah; Text 4.13 Granger/Shutterstock; Text 4.14 'Make Love, Not War' poster by Weisser, 1967 (litho), American School, (20th century)/Private Collection/Prismatic Pictures/Bridgeman Images; Text 4.15 'Free South Africa' by Keith Haring 1985 © Keith Haring Foundation; Text 4.16 'Power to the People' by Shepard Fairey Courtesy of Shepard Fairey/obeygiant.com; Text 4.20 Edward Crawford/GI; Text 4.21 by Mark Hurwitt 2011, reproduced with the permission of author; Text 4.22 Malala Yousafzai's speech to the United Nations 2013, reproduced with permission of Curtis Brown Group Ltd; Text 4.24a and 4.24b Thibodeau PH, Boroditsky L (2011) *Metaphors We Think With: The Role of Metaphor in Reasoning.* PLoS ONE 6(2): e16782. https://doi.org/10.1371/journal.pone.0016782 © 2011 Thibodeau, Boroditsky; Text 4.25 and Text 4.26 © Guardian News & Media Ltd 2019; Text 4.27 © Guardian News & Media Ltd 2018; Text 4.28 © The Economist Group Limited, London (2013); Text 4.29, 4.30 The Conservative Party Archive/GI; Text 4.33 Excerpt from *Nineteen Eighty-Four* by George Orwell © 1949 by Houghton Mifflin Harcourt Publishing Company, renewed 1977 by Sonia Brownell Orwell. Reprinted by permission of Houghton Mifflin Harcourt Publishing Company, A.M. Heath & Co. Ltd., and Penguin Random House. All rights reserved; Text 4.35 'Politics and the English Language' by George Orwell (© George Orwell, 1946) reproduced with the permission of Houghton Mifflin Harcourt Publishing Company, A.M. Heath & Co. Ltd and Penguin Random House; Text 5.1 'Depression Comix' by Clay Jonathan, 2013, © Clay Jonathan; Text 5.2 The article 'An Open Apology to All of my Weight Loss Clients' by Iris Higgins, published in The Huffington Post, 16/08/2013, © Iris Higgins; Text 5.3 Movie Poster Image Art/GI; Text 8.3 'Little Red-Cap' from *The World's Wife* by Carol Ann Duffy. © 1999 by Carol Ann Duffy. Reprinted by permission of Farrar, Straus and Giroux & PLS Clear.

Acknowledgements

Additional images, in order of appearance

Cover: Sean Gladwell/Getty Images *Inside:* **Chapter 1:** Thanawat Thiasiriphet/GI; nami64 via DeviantArt; John Dickson/GI; Ray Tang/Anadolu Agency/GI; Jeff Spicer/GI; Michael Loccisano/GI; Paramount/GI; Everett Collection Inc./Alamy Stock Photo; Brendan Smialowski/GI; Johnny Eggitt/GI; **Chapter 2:** Maskot/GI; David Levenson/GI; Philippa Griffith-Jones/Alamy Stock Photo; Lucasfilm/Bad Robot/Walt Disney Studios/Kobal/Shutterstock; The India Today Group/GI; Dpa picture alliance/Alamy Stock Photo; Paul Drinkwater/NBCUniversal/GI; **Chapter 3:** Photography taken by Mario Gutiérrez/GI; Ullstein bild/GI; API/Gamma-Rapho/GI; Media24/Gallo Images/GI; Agence France Presse/GI; Bettmann/GI; Ilya S. Savenok/GI; Ollie Millington/GI; Touchstone/Kobal/Shutterstock; Donald Cooper/Shutterstock; Panoramic Images/GI; Moviestore collection Ltd/Alamy Stock Photo; John Owens/GI; Varun Dahotre/GI; Aubrey Hart/Evening Standard/GI; **Chapter 4:** Fayek Tasneem Khan/Getty Images; Brooks Kraft LLC/GI; Kevin Winter/GI; Stephen Lovekin/GI; Fotosearch/GI; Leemage/GI; Dinodia Photos/GI; Luiz Rampelotto/GI; **Chapter 5:** smolaw11/GI; Cal Sport Media/Alamy Stock Photo; **Chapter 6:** CaiaiImages/GI; **Chapter 7:** PeopleImages/GI; **Chapter 8:** Commercial Eye/GI; Culture Club/GI;Hulton Archive/GI; Colin McPherson/GI; Steve Debenport/GI.

GI= Getty Images

About the author

Brad Philpot has a passion for language, literature and learning. He has experience teaching English as a first and second language, in primary and secondary schools in the Netherlands and Turkey. Since 2010 he has worked as a consultant, textbook author, workshop leader and examiner. Through Philpot Education he has organised professional development opportunities for thousands of teachers around the world on a broad range of topics.